The Social Ecology of Border Landscapes

THE ANTHEM SERIES ON INTERNATIONAL ENVIRONMENTAL POLICY AND AGREEMENTS

The **Anthem Series on International Environmental Policy and Agreements** seeks to consolidate research on global environmental governance, providing a prescriptive policy-making agenda based on sound analysis and empirical insights. A planetary vision of environmental governance has been growing over the past several decades and is often operationalized through international environmental agreements. Even though such treaties are often nonbinding and have marginal punitive power against violators, they are gaining credibility in international relations. This series focuses on evidence-based research that helps strength the "system" of multinational environmental decision making and governance.

The Social Ecology of Border Landscapes

Edited by
Anna Grichting and Michele Zebich-Knos

ANTHEM PRESS

Anthem Press
An imprint of Wimbledon Publishing Company
www.anthempress.com

This edition first published in UK and USA 2019
by ANTHEM PRESS
75–76 Blackfriars Road, London SE1 8HA, UK
or PO Box 9779, London SW19 7ZG, UK
and
244 Madison Ave #116, New York, NY 10016, USA

First published in the UK and USA by Anthem Press 2017

British Library Cataloguing-in-Publication Data
A catalogue record for this book is available from the British Library.

ISBN-13: 978-1-78527-135-9 (Pbk)
ISBN-10: 1-78527-135-0 (Pbk)

This title is also available as an e-book.

CONTENTS

List of Illustrations   vii

Preface   ix

List of Contributors   xi

Introduction   Social Ecologies and Borderlands   1
                      Anna Grichting

Part I. FRAMES: MAPPING SOCIAL ECOLOGIES IN BORDER TERRITORIES

Chapter One   On the Agency of Borderlands   19
                      Emmanuel Brunet-Jailly

Chapter Two   Social Ecology and Transboundary Conservation:
                      (Re)connecting Nature and People in Borderlands   37
                      Kevan Zunckel

Chapter Three   Social Ecologies and Structural Violence:
                      Boundary-Making as Nature-Making in a Gated Globe   53
                      Hilary Cunningham and Stephen Bede Scharper

Part II. BRIDGES: RESILIENCE, RESTORATION AND RECLAMATION

Chapter Four   Borders as Zones of Experiential Learning: The Case of the
                      Balkans Peace Park Project   71
                      Todd Walters and Saleem H. Ali

Chapter Five   Social Ecologies in Borderlands: Crane Habitat Restoration
                      and Sustainable Agriculture Project in the Democratic
                      People's Republic of Korea   89
                      Hall Healy, George Archibald and Arthur H. Westing

Chapter Six   Socio-ecological Transformations in Riparian Zones:
                      The Production of Spaces of Exclusion and the
                      Uneven Development of Resilience in the Sonoran
                      Borderlands   107
                      Lily A. House-Peters

Chapter Seven   From No-Man's Land to Every-Man's Land:
                     Socio-ecological Approaches to Reclaiming Shared
                     Spaces in Border Landscapes, with Examples from
                     Germany and Cyprus   131
                     Anna Grichting

**Part III. CORRIDORS: CATALYSTS AND COLLABORATION
            IN CONFINED SPACES**

Chapter Eight   Ensuring Hope in Militarized Landscapes: The Case of
                     Lebanon   153
                     Rabih Shibli

Chapter Nine   Domesticating and Enlarging One's Territory: Day-to-Day
                     Politics in a Confined Space—The Shu'fat Refugee Camp in
                     East Jerusalem   169
                     Sylvaine Bulle

Chapter Ten   Urban Alternatives and Collaborative Economics in
                     Belfast's Contested Space   181
                     Brendan Murtagh

**Part IV. PORTALS: DIALOGUE, EXCEPTION AND
           RETERRITORIALIZATION**

Chapter Eleven   Australia Day: A Social Ecology Dialogue across Aboriginal
                     and White Cultures   197
                     Carol Birrell and Stuart B. Hill

Chapter Twelve   Re-legislating the Soil: Enclosures and Exception at the
                     Amazon Frontiers   209
                     Paulo Tavares

Chapter Thirteen   Mediterranean Edges: Reterritorializing Natural and
                     Social Ecologies   231
                     Verena Andermatt Conley

Conclusion   Making Sense of Social Ecology, Borders and
                     the Environment   243
                     Michele Zebich-Knos

Index   255

ILLUSTRATIONS

Figures

2.1 The global distribution of transboundary protected areas (TBPAs)   40

2.2 An illustration of the evolving paradigms within the conservation fraternity over the past 50 years   45

2.3 The relationship between ecosystem goods and services emanating from healthy, functioning ecosystems and human well-being   47

4.1 Thethi National Park, Albania   77

4.2 Lake Plav, Montenegro   78

5.1 Crane Habitat Restoration and Sustainable Agriculture Project Area—Anbyon, DPRK   95

5.2 Photo of Red-crowned and White-naped Cranes in Korea's Demilitarized Zone   99

6.1 Map of the binational San Pedro River watershed   108

6.2 Map depicting *ejido* property boundaries and private property boundaries in the Mexican portion   110

6.3 Groundwater concessions for the Mexican San Pedro   112

6.4 Privatization and sale of riparian land and water rights to Minera María   119

7.1 Structural representation of topology of the Rhizome   133

7.2 The Skulpturenpark Berlin Zentrum   139

7.3 Cyprus GreenLineScapes Laboratory   140

7.4 The Home for Cooperation in the Buffer Zone of Nicosia   142

7.5 (a) Flatro Bastion in Nicosia and (b) Flatro Bastion in Nicosia on Google Earth   143

7.6 From military buffer to laboratory of ecological planning and human reconciliation   145

8.1 Schematic drawing of the cover page of students' workbook, representing the theme of remodeling harshscapes   154

8.2 Convoy of United Nations Interim Force in Lebanon (UNIFIL) patrolling in southern Lebanon   156

8.3 An example of vacant structures funded by the Lebanese government to develop areas under Israeli occupation in southern Lebanon   157

8.4 Terraced hilly terrain showing shrubs, olive trees and the tobacco plantation in Marwaheen village   158

8.5 AUB students working hand in hand with local farmers in the rehabilitation of Marwaheen pond   159

8.6   A "greenhouse" atop a corrugated metal roof improvised to secure
      natural lighting and ventilation necessary for plants' growth   162
8.7   High walls, barbed wires, metal fences and plastic sheets create a physical
      and visual buffer for the Women's Vocational Training Center (WVTC)   163
8.8   Three-dimensional model of the Urban Agriculture Center   164
9.1   Israeli security wall surrounding Shu'fat camp   171
9.2   Garden inside the camp, opposite the settlement of Pisgat Zeev   174
9.3   Extension and improvements in the camp   176
10.1 Religious distribution and neighborhoods within Belfast   186
12.1 The great enclosure: Lines of the state of emergency enforced over the
      Peruvian Amazon in 2009   210
12.2 Life-zoning cartography: *Mapa Ecológico del Peru*   215
12.3 and 12.4   Life-zoning diagram. Leslie R. Holdridge's ecology
                of Peru's territory   216
12.5 and 12.6   Land taxonomy. (a) Cover from *Mapa Ecológico del Peru* showing
                Leslie Holdridge's diagram (1995) and (b) extracts from the
                descriptive guide accompanying the life-zoning map of Peru   217
12.7 Resource terrain. Excerpt from the guide to the *Mapa Ecológico del Peru* 219
12.8 and 12.9   Ecology coded by law. Map of Peru's land-use potential   220
12.10, 12.11, 12.12   Political-legal enclosures   222
13.1 Imposing the space of the colonizer   236
13.2 Reappropriating the colonized space   239
C.1   Esperanza Base, Argentina's research station on the Antarctic Peninsula 251

Tables

2.1   A record of data reflecting the extent and growth of transboundary
      conservation efforts across the globe   39
2.2   The recommended stages and steps necessary to take a TBC initiative
      from concept to implementation   43
5.1   Anbyon, DPRK experimental plots: Crop yields from organic versus
      chemical fertilizers   97
5.2   Anbyon, DPRK experimental plots: Actual 2011 yields from organic
      versus chemical fertilizers   98
10.1 Residential segregation and mixing in Northern Ireland, 2001–11   184
10.2 Interface structures in Belfast   185
10.3 SRRP performance indicators   191

PREFACE

The idea for this book came out of the 2011 Conference on Environmental Diplomacy and Security in International Relations organized by the Institute for Environmental Diplomacy and Security (IEDS) at the University of Vermont (USA). Burlington, Vermont, is a small city nestled in the Vermont heartland and is also home to the founder of social ecology, Murray Bookchin. At the time, the university was also home to professor and IEDS director Saleem Ali, author of the highly acclaimed book *Peace Parks: Conservation and Conflict Resolution*. Without his encouragement and support, *The Social Ecology of Border Landscapes* would surely not have materialized. I should add that these inspirational events, institutions and scholarship took place within very idyllic local surroundings. Vermont borders Quebec, Canada, and, in Burlington, I found French-Canadian influences everywhere, from the food (poutine) to the bilingual, English-French language signs at the airport.

While certainly different from my current living arrangement near the Pacific Ocean in Southern California, the area and the conference sparked my interest in creating a book about borders and their relation to both the built and natural environments, but it was Anna Grichting's actions that turned this idea into reality. Selection for our conceptual framework was obvious—we would approach the topic from a social ecology perspective to illustrate that scholars and practitioners must never lose sight of the human drivers that shape borders, whether they abut a peace park, desert, fence or refugee camp. The book would be multidisciplinary and incorporate my perspective as a political scientist with Anna's expertise in architecture and planning. Naturally, it would include scholars and practitioners whose background and knowledge base are different from our own. It would also challenge readers to think out of the box—which is why we felt compelled to include a cognitive-border case (Chapter 11) devoid of physical frontiers, but able to increase awareness that psychological barriers often result from conflict and serve as coping mechanisms.

One of my favorite natural environments in Southern California is the Tijuana Estuary National Wildlife Refuge and Tijuana Slough, a salt marsh plain with tidal channels that extends south from San Diego to the Mexican border. This area covers 2,800 acres and is home to more than 370 bird species. While not the most scenic spot in California, for me as a political scientist and scholar of global policy, this area represents the notion that nature knows no borders. The impact of Mexico and its ongoing brush with border poverty is something that the estuary must deal with on a daily basis. It is especially problematic when hard rains wash sewage and trash from settlements on the bluffs down Tijuana's steep canyons on the Mexican side of the border and flow nearly unabated into the estuary and marshlands. While the marshlands happen to be on US territory, they are—first and foremost—marshlands within the area's natural ecosystem. The cities of San Diego to the north and Tijuana to the south sandwich the marshland between two urban environments and reinforce its "in-between" status.

Not only is the Tijuana Estuary a sage scrub ecotone—or transitional area between two ecosystems—from a biodiversity standpoint, but it also represents a useful example of cross-border cooperation to manage the impact of Mexico's pollution on US marshlands and coastal areas. Sewage contamination is an old issue and cross-border management began in 1934 when the United States and Mexico asked the International Boundary Commission to prepare a report on Tijuana's sewage problem. Today the South Bay International Wastewater Treatment Plant (SBIWTP), built in 1990 just two miles west of the San Ysidro port of entry on the US side, is a joint effort in which both countries share operation and maintenance. Initial costs were also a shared effort; Mexico and the United States contributed USD $16.8 million and $239.4 million, respectively, according to the U.S. Fish and Wildlife Service.

The pollution problem does not stop at the marshlands, but extends onto San Diego's beaches, especially Imperial Beach, where signs warn beachgoers about contamination on a regular basis. I wonder if the signs were there when my husband resided near Imperial Beach many years ago, and on one occasion walked his dog along the border only to have him (the dog) run carefree into Mexico. He returned after a quick whistle, for those were the days before the United States further securitized the area with an extended fence.

Cross-border pollution is a chronic problem as more people in search of employment opportunities cram into Tijuana's *colonias* (slums), which often lack adequate sewage and solid waste disposal systems. This border example is one to which I hold personal attachment, but, more important for the reader, it represents the border-management theme of "muddling through" and a shared relevance with many of the chapters in this book.

Michele Zebich-Knos
Los Angeles, CA (USA)
2017

CONTRIBUTORS

Saleem H. Ali is Blue and Gold Distinguished Professor of Energy and the Environment at the University of Delaware. He previously held the chair in sustainable resources development at the University of Queensland's Sustainable Minerals Institute in Brisbane, Australia. In addition he holds an adjunct professorship of environmental planning at the University of Vermont's Rubenstein School of Natural Resources (USA). His research focuses on environmental conflicts in the extractive industries and how ecological cooperation can promote peace in international relations. He is the author of three sole-authored books including *Treasures of the Earth: Need, Greed and a Sustainable Future* (2010), and *Environmental Diplomacy* (with Lawrence Susskind, 2014) and more than 100 peer-reviewed publications. He serves on the board of governors of the nonprofit environmental organization LEAD-Pakistan. Professor Ali received his doctorate in environmental planning from MIT, a master's degree in environmental studies from Yale University and a bachelor's degree in chemistry from Tufts University. Professor Ali can be followed on Twitter @saleem_ali.

George Archibald is one of the two cofounders of the International Crane Foundation (ICF) headquartered in Baraboo, Wisconsin. He received his undergraduate degree from Dalhousie University in Halifax, Nova Scotia, and completed his PhD at Cornell University. Along with Ronald Sauey, a colleague from Cornell, Archibald established the ICF in the spring of 1973, as the world center for the study and preservation of cranes. ICF's mission is met through a creative combination of field research, help to local people living near the cranes, public education, habitat protection and captive propagation and reintroduction. Today, ICF has 50 employees and supports conservation projects in 45 nations. For 27 years, Archibald served as the president of ICF. He continues to be employed full time by ICF and works on programs of his choosing in Bhutan, China, India, Ethiopia, North Korea, South Korea and Russia. Archibald has used the charisma of cranes to help unite people from diverse cultures and countries to work together to preserve habitat necessary for the survival of both cranes and people. In 2016, he published his memoirs: *My Life With Cranes, A Collection of Stories.*

Carol Birrell is an artist, writer and academic who explores the interaction between an Indigenous and Western sense of place. She currently teaches social ecology at the University of Western Sydney and before this taught Aboriginal education at Wollongong University. Her land-based arts practice for the past 12 years, called ecopoiesis, draws together movement, painting, photography, environmental sculpture and poetry, along with Indigenous understandings, as a base for ecological writing and exploring ecological identity. Carol has strong long-term collaborative relationships with several Australian

Aboriginal communities such as Yuin (south coast NSW) and Worrorra (west Kimberley) and researches the role of Aboriginal Elders in contemporary Australia. At present, she is writing a book on the life and teachings of distinguished Yuin Senior Lawman and Elder Max Dulumunmun Harrison. Recent published articles include "In the Belly of the Whale," which tells the story of cultural revitalization through a whale dreaming ceremony not enacted on Australian soil for at least 100 years; "Slipping Beneath the Kimberley Skin," a probing journey with an Aboriginal Elder into some of the most remote country on this planet; and "Crocodile as Teacher," which reexamines the critical crocodile experience of environmental philosopher Val Plumwood through the lens of Aboriginal understandings of country.

Emmanuel Brunet-Jailly, LLB (Aix-en-Provence), MA (Paris I—Sorbonne, and Virginia Polytechnic and State University), PhD (University of Western Ontario) is Jean Monnet Chair in European Urban and Border Policy and a professor in the School of Public Administration at the University of Victoria, British Columbia, Canada. Brunet-Jailly is also the editor of the *Journal of Borderland Studies*. His key research areas are comparative urban governance and the governance of cross-border regions, with a specific focus on comparative decentralization, horizontal and vertical governance, and the theorization of cross-border regions. His research work has appeared or is forthcoming in nine books and edited scholarly journals and in more than 50 articles and book chapters.

Sylvaine Bulle is an associate professor of sociology and a member of the Laboratoire Théorie du Politique (Université de Paris 8). Her fields of research include the sociology of conflicts and public problems, and pragmatist sociology. Bulle has conducted numerous surveys and research programs in Israel and Palestine concerning intercommunity violence, transformations of the state and neoliberalism. Her latest research focuses on political violence and radical protests, and her recent publications include "A Conflict of Spaces or of Recognition? Co-presence in Divided Jerusalem" and "L'État nous quitte. Question sociale, question urbaine et culturelle en Israël" ("The State Is Leaving Us: Social, Urban and Cultural Questions in Israel").

Verena Andermatt Conley teaches comparative literature and Romance languages and literature at Harvard University. Conley's research focuses on ecology and technology, and her major book publications include *Ecopolitics: The Environment in French Poststructuralist Thought* (1997) and *Spatial Ecologies: Urban Sites, State and World Space in French Culture* (2012). She is interested in the Mediterranean basin and teaches courses on the relation between Europe and North Africa. She is currently a fellow at Dumbarton Oaks, where she works on a project titled *From Colony to Ecology: Theory and Practice of Le Jardin d'Essai* (Algiers).

Hilary Cunningham is an associate professor of anthropology at the University of Toronto. Her research explores boundary-making as a multifaceted encounter with "nature" and focuses on "gated ecologies," that is, those nature-borderscapes in which human and nonhuman marginalization (and destruction) unfold as a contingent, interconnected reality.

Anna Grichting is a Swiss architect, urbanist and musician and holds a doctorate of design degree from Harvard University. She is currently assistant professor at the University of Qatar, and a fellow at the Institute for Environmental Diplomacy and Security, University of Vermont. She has lectured worldwide and taught theory and design studios at the Universities of Geneva and Harvard, as well as holding a position with the Aga Khan Award for Architecture. Her teaching and research focuses on blue and green networks, landscape and ecological urbanism, public art and public space, food urbanism and water-sensitive urban design. Her work on borders focuses on areas of conflict and their transformation as biological and cultural landscapes of memory. It began with a design project for the landscapes of the Berlin Wall, and she is working on a digital and dynamic atlas of ecological cooperation and is directing the GreenLineScapes Laboratory on the Buffer Zone of Cyprus. She is currently on the advisory board of the Korea DMZ Council, a board member of the Friends of Humanity Foundation in Switzerland and a fellow at the Institute for Environmental Diplomacy and Security, University of Vermont.

Hall Healy is a director and past chairman of the Board of the International Crane Foundation, a nongovernmental organization dedicated to preserving the 15 species of cranes and their habitats, and enhancing the lives of people residing near them, on five continents. He is a professional environmental facilitator, conducting training, facilitation and planning projects in the United States, Russia, China and Korea. Healy earned a BA degree in political science from Colgate University and an MBA from the University of Chicago. He has written two publications: "Environmental Management" for the American Management Association's (AMA) *Manufacturers Handbook* and *Packaging and Solid Waste*, coauthored; he has written numerous papers on conservation of natural resources in the Demilitarized Zone (DMZ) in Korea and on planning issues. He is past president of the DMZ Forum, an NGO dedicated to preserving species and habitats of Korea's DMZ; a past director of the board of trustees of the Illinois Chapter of The Nature Conservancy; and is on the governing board of the Chicago Zoological Society. He also is a member of the International Union for Conservation of Nature (IUCN) Task Force of Transboundary Protected Areas (TBPA) Committee, and of the IUCN Crane Specialist Group.

Stuart B. Hill is Emeritus Professor and foundation chair of social ecology in the School of Education at the University of Western Sydney, Australia. Prior to 1966, he was at McGill University (Montreal, Canada), where he taught and established Ecological Agriculture Projects, Canada's leading resources center for sustainable agriculture. Hill has published more than 350 papers and reports, and his latest books include *Ecological Pioneers: A Social History of Australian Ecological Thought and Action* (with Martin Mulligan, 2002), *Learning for Sustainable Living: Psychology of Ecological Transformation* (with Werner Sattman-Frese, 2008) and *Social Ecology: Applying Ecological Understanding to Our Lives and Our Planet* (with David Wright and Catherine Camden-Pratt, 2011). Hill was a member of more than 30 regional, national and international boards and committees, and was on the editorial board of five international refereed journals. Hill has worked in agricultural and development projects in the West Indies, West Africa, Indonesia, the Philippines, China and the Seychelles, as well as the United Kingdom, Canada, New Zealand and Australia.

Lily A. House-Peters is an assistant professor of sustainability science at California State University, Long Beach, USA, and also serves as the university's resilience commitment coordinator in the Office of Sustainability and Planning. House-Peters earned a PhD from the School of Geography and Development at the University of Arizona and is a broadly trained human-environment geographer interested in qualitative and quantitative approaches to water resources research and the human dimensions of environmental change. Her research interests draw into conversation current debates on natural resource conservation policy, drought and climate change adaptation strategies in dryland environments, and the translation of resilience and adaptive capacity into specific water resource governance logics.

Brendan Murtagh is a reader in the School of Planning, Architecture and Civil Engineering at the Queen's University Belfast. He has researched and written widely on urban regeneration, conflict and community participation, and his recent books include: *The Politics of Territory* (2002); *Authentic Dialogue* (with Murray, 2004); *Segregation, Violence and the City* (with Shirlow, 2006); and *Understanding the Social Economy* (with Bridge and O'Neill, 2013). He has held a number of recent research grants on urban regeneration from the UK-based Economic and Social Research Council (ESRC), the Joseph Rowntree Foundation and the Leverhulme Trust.

Stephen Scharper is an associate professor with the School of Environment at the University of Toronto. He is coeditor of *The Natural City: Re-envisioning the Built Environment* (2012) and author of *For Earth's Sake: Toward a Compassionate Ecology* (2013).

Rabih Shibli is the director of the Center for Civic Engagement and Community Service at the American University of Beirut (AUB) and an affiliated faculty member in the Department of Landscape Architecture. In September 2006, he founded and directed Beit Bil Jnoub, a nonprofit civil organization that was heavily involved in the reconstruction process in the aftermath of the "July War." Shibli has supervised the design and implementation of community-based projects that tackle pressing challenges facing local and refugee communities in Lebanon. His research focuses on community-based design as a tool to upgrade underserved areas and to alleviate tensions in contested landscapes. Shibli holds a bachelor's degree in architecture and a master's degree in urban design.

Paulo Tavares (Quito/London) is an architect and urbanist from Brazil and is currently a visiting professor at Princeton University. He teaches architecture at the Universidad Católica de Ecuador—Facultad de Arquitectura, Diseño y Arte, Quito, Ecuador, and has previously held teaching posts at the Centre for Research Architecture, Goldsmiths, and at the Visual Lab of the MA in Contemporary Art Theory, also at Goldsmiths, UK. His writings have appeared in many publications worldwide and his work has been exhibited in various venues including Centre for Contemporary Arts (CCA), Glasgow, Haus der Kulturen der Welt, Berlin, Portikus, Frankfurt and the Taipei Biennial 2012.

Todd Walters is the executive director of International Peace Park Expeditions, which applies experiential learning to environmental peace building through teaching accredited academic expeditions and fellowships. Walters has adapted Peace and Conflict

Impact Assessment methodology to transboundary protected areas and has produced short documentary films in the "Transcending Boundaries" series that portray multiple stakeholder perspectives concerning environmental peace building in transboundary protected areas. Walters is the first fellow at the Policy Center for Environment and Peace at Conservation International, a member of the Transboundary Conservation Specialist Group at the International Union for the Conservation of Nature, and a fellow at the Institute for Environmental Diplomacy and Security. Walters is a National Outdoor Leadership School certified adventure guide, has led expeditions in dozens of countries around the globe and has published a number of chapters and articles on environmental peace building.

Arthur H. Westing holds a BA degree in botany from Columbia University, and MF and PhD degrees from Yale University. A forest ecologist, Westing has been a research forester with the U.S. Forest Service, taught forestry, ecology and conservation, and served as dean of natural science at Hampshire College. He was twice a research fellow at Harvard University and a senior researcher at the Stockholm International Peace Research Institute (SIPRI) as well as at the Peace Research Institute Oslo (PRIO). For eight years, he directed the United Nations Environment Programme (UNEP) project on "Peace, Security, and Environment." Westing is the author of numerous publications in that subject area. He has also been on the faculty of the European Peace University (EPU), a member of the International Union for Conservation of Nature (IUCN) World Commission on Protected Areas, vice president of the International Society of Naturalists; and he has served on the board of the Korean DMZ Forum and on the DMZ Commission of the International Crane Foundation. He has been a consultant in environmental security since 1990 to the World Bank, UNEP, United Nations Educational, Scientific and Cultural Organization (UNESCO), the International Organization for Migration (IOM), the Government of Eritrea and other national and international agencies.

Michele Zebich-Knos is Professor Emeritus of political science and international affairs, and was founding director of the Master of Science in International Policy Management Program at Kennesaw State University/University System of Georgia (Atlanta, Georgia). She served on the external advisory board of The Institute for Environmental Diplomacy and Security (IEDS), University of Vermont, and is currently a research fellow at IEDS. She is author of numerous publications on environmental policy, including the chapter "Conflict Avoidance and Environmental Protection: The Antarctic Paradigm," which appears in *Peace Parks: Conservation and Conflict Resolution*. Her research on Antarctic tourism and global regulation appears as a chapter in *Diplomacy on Ice: Energy and the Environment in the Arctic and Antarctic*. Her current research interest includes security and environmental policy in the Arctic and appears, with coauthor Rebecca Pincus, in the 2016 volume of *Polar Geography*.

Kevan Zunckel is an ecologist and environmental scientist with an MSc in Environmental Science from the University of Cape Town and 30 years of experience. He is cochair of the IUCN WCPA Transboundary Conservation Specialist Group and was part of the team who compiled the recently published IUCN Best Practice Protected Area Guidelines Series No. 23: *Transboundary Conservation: A Systematic and Integrated Approach*. Closely following this was the endorsement of the Transfrontier Conservation Guidelines for the Southern African Development Community, which he authored in collaboration with practitioners from the region. He is also the Africa representative for the International Conservation Connectivity Network, which has strong parallels with transboundary conservation.

Introduction

SOCIAL ECOLOGIES AND BORDERLANDS

Anna Grichting

There is something infinitely healing in the repeated refrains of nature—the assurance that dawn comes after night, and spring after the winter.

—Rachel Carson, *The Sense of Wonder*[1]

Even in the most stressed border areas, humans can find solace and comfort in what nature offers us. While we, as scholars, methodically define and conceptualize our thoughts and research in dispassionate ways, those caught in the thick of conflict/post-conflict border spaces often abandon such pretentions to savor nature and grasp the small pleasures that make life bearable. Healing power manifests itself in the form of gardens for Palestinian refugees in the Shu'fat Refugee Camp along the Israeli wall, or in swatches of land along the former Iron Curtain that gave way to the Pan European Green Belt open for everyone to enjoy. When nature is in short supply, especially in compact refugee camps like Shu'fat, local residents find other ways to add meaning to their lives. The "Palace," or Shu'fat marriage hall, enriches camp life and also serves as a multipurpose location for shows and other ceremonies. And, when encountering not a physical border, but a cognitive one, allegories, replete with birds and waterways, sustain hope and comfort as they blend into Australia's Aboriginal storytelling.

In my travels and research along conflict borders, the most telling was that visionary and practical plans for the future transformation of these liminal spaces were seeded and imagined by nature lovers, environmental nongovernmental organizations (NGOs) and passionate planners. Through direct interaction with nature and ecosystems, and with the intention of softening these hard borders, projects and visions such as the German Green Belt, the Korean DMZ Peace Park, the Cyprus GreenLine Scapes Laboratory and the Balkans Peace Park Initiative were born. It is the intent of this book to show how ecologically based, mutualistic social structures can overcome borders and barriers, and create resilient spaces and communities.

Increased securitization of borders since 9/11 has amplified interest in finding ways to soften borders and to avoid the kind of discrimination, marginalization and other negative consequences that come from inscribing hard divisions between peoples, ecologies and societies. This volume brings to this debate the theoretical frames of social ecology—i.e., nature and society—and presents environmental mitigation strategies in the form of conservation corridors, peace parks and other activities that enhance exchanges and constructive interaction leading to conflict resolution. The social ecological perspective is proposed in terms of how it can suggest opportunities for solutions that would otherwise not be apparent, and to generate innovative approaches for softening hardened or conflicted borders.

Border Landscapes: Charting New Territories

Social ecology addresses the complex and interrelated relationship between nature and society and offers a perspective on how environmental issues are embedded in a social context. Border landscapes are loosely defined as interstitial spaces between territories or societies, in conflict or in competition, with fixed or moving boundaries. Social ecology as a critical social theory was originally founded by Murray Bookchin and emphasizes the complexity of relationships between people and nature and the importance of establishing more mutualistic social structures that take account of these relationships. It is within this context that the contributors to this book believe peace can thrive.

Other proponents of a social-ecological approach such as Samantha Stone-Jovicich and Fabinyi, Evans and Foale observe that the world systems approach, with its stress on capitalism and the political economy of global–local interconnections, has become an incomplete means for understanding change within the environment. Using a less idealistic approach to social ecology than that of Bookchin, these scholars urge us to consider the important role of space and its bio-geophysical characteristics that spur both ecological and social change.[2] This attention to locally defined spaces—be it along the Israeli wall, the former Berlin Wall or the Korean Demilitarized Zone (DMZ)—yields important human–environmental interactions and consequences that form the basis for a social ecological interpretation of environmental adaptation and change. Much like Stephen Wheeler, who uses social ecology as a new frame for the challenges of climate change, this volume approaches borders with a socio-ecological lens in order to uncover new visions or interpretations for positive transformation of margins, edges or interstices, especially where they are the result or source of conflict and separation.[3]

Social ecology as a framework has expanded to include social-ecological systems (SES), which emerged from critical social and resilience theories as a means of addressing the adaptive and complex structures and processes of the social and natural world.[4] A social-ecological system consists of a bio-geophysical unit, and its associated social actors and institutions, which regularly interact in a resilient, sustained manner, and that are defined by Singh and colleagues as having "several spatial, temporal, and organizational scales, which may be hierarchically linked."[5] Singh and colleagues define a social-ecological system as a "set of critical resources (natural, socioeconomic, and cultural) whose flow and use is regulated by a combination of ecological and social systems; and a perpetually dynamic, complex system with continuous adaptation."[6] The social-ecological system thus becomes our unit of analysis, and each case study in this book represents a different SES.

Throughout its chapters, this book examines examples of conflict related to the concept of border environments in a comprehensive and multidisciplinary manner that facilitates new approaches to constructing, managing and preserving our environment. This book holds useful implications for resolution of political conflicts and environmental management of ecosystems and aims to provide those involved in peace processes, whether practitioner or scholar, with concrete cases of how attention to the border landscape and its human–nature interaction can foster peace. It also provides those involved in the study or practice of border ecosystem planning and management with a more robust, integrative approach that encourages in-depth analysis of human–nature interactions during the policy-making process. Let nature enhance negotiations and become a tool, which can result in mutual benefit to humans and flora/fauna alike.

From theoretical and conceptual presentations on border environments, to case studies and concrete projects and initiatives, this book explores how social agency (i.e., social action) can activate ecological processes and systems, to create new sustainable landscapes across tangible and intangible territorial rifts. When we speak of tangible rifts, we mean the physical manifestations of the border. Intangible rifts are psychological (cognitive), social and political impediments, and are not clearly visible or comprehensible and can be more difficult to transcend.

It is known and accepted that the psychosocial barriers are often more difficult to overcome than the physical barriers, and this resistance may come as much from our political structure as from our social conditioning or personal fears. Stuart Hill, biologist and founding chair in social ecology at the University of West Sydney, Australia, uses the term "psychological woundedness" to mean the response to psychosocial barriers and suggests that this needs to be addressed before significant ecological change is possible. Anthropologist Sarah Green couches this woundedness in terms of marginality where indifference reigns among outsiders who often do not understand marginalized peoples and their lack of political or economic clout.[7] Such sensitivity to others demonstrated by Hill and Green guides us to the essence of what the reader will learn from this book, namely, that while political forces impose rules and regulations on border landscapes, they may simply overlook or find it difficult to stop micro-creations, or small gestures such as planting a communal garden, that help people cope with difficult living conditions. The creation of borders, after all, is nothing more than the provision of identity and differentiation to spatial practices, which can produce or reinforce conflict.

Fluidity of Borders, Society and the Environment

Ecology stresses interactive relationships between organisms and their environment, and borders are a very real part of that environment. In recent years, scholars have expanded their reference to border studies by adopting the term "critical border studies" to reflect a fluid interpretation of what constitutes a border. In this volume, borders are defined broadly to include territorial interfaces, marginal spaces (physical, sociological and psychological) and human consciousness. The traditional state-centric and geographically fixed "line in the sand" no longer characterizes borders. Rather, scholars such as Nick Vaughan-Williams assert that there are a myriad of borders, which split along ethnic, religious, racial, class, cultural, generational and national lines.[8] Kolossov and Scott also reaffirm the shift from traditional and geographically fixed state borders to include greater "socio-spatial and geographical scales" and recognize that the study of borders now encompasses numerous disciplines from political science and sociology to the arts, architecture and media.[9] Geographer Victor Konrad suggests that today's borders not only reflect an increased "security primacy," but must also absorb the environmental consequences of such security policies that create chokepoint border crossings and hardened barriers that inhibit previous patterns of dispersed border passages.[10] A particularly notable example cited by Konrad is the US–Mexico border in the Sonoran Desert ecosystem that will be discussed by Cunningham and Scharper, and House-Peters in Chapters 3 and 6, respectively.

Territorial or physical aspects of borders, and their implications for social interaction, still generate many of the issues discussed in this book. However, these issues are now framed within a broader border context that accommodates the rich variety of borders, including those that exist within the cognitive space of our minds and/or human consciousness. In the twenty-first-century world, borders are now moving targets and subject to change as circumstances warrant; rejecting this shift would do great disservice to the overall understanding of how people create and manage the space in which they live. While biologists refer to this space as a species' home range, human beings possess more than physical space, and can exhibit complex psychological components that represent cognitive borders against past or current injustices experienced at the hand of other dominant parties. This concept becomes obvious when reading Chapter 11 about Australia's Aboriginal culture and the cognitive or psychological border creation that takes place among its Indigenous population.

In this examination of borders, we have selected border landscape as the most precise concept within which to investigate the complexity of borders through multiple angles and different scales.[11] We include not only state and political borders, but also more natural/ecological and social/psychological/cultural boundaries, which open pathways for charting new territories that go beyond the political and territorial. A similar approach has been put forward by Suvendrini Perera, who argues that the spatial and conceptual complexity of the border as a space is not static, but fluid and shifting.[12] The challenge remains how to manage a border that may at times be invisible, as Brunet-Jailly asserts in Chapter 1. He maintains that typical border security functions in the United States, for example, have now moved deep into US territory away from the actual frontier between the United States, Canada and Mexico, and may not even be perceived as a border.

Border Ecologies and Edge Effects

Borders are interfaces between systems, territories and communities. They are also edges and as such, can also be viewed and analyzed through their positive qualities from an ecological point of view. In the past, border scholarship has focused on economic, cultural, social and political aspects of boundaries and boundary making. Less explored are the complex relations between borders and nature, which Cunningham describes as distinctive geophysical processes and ecological systems. She posits that nature, like the politicized borders we see in our contemporary world, is also a result of complex phenomena, which include human influence and interactions.[13] To ignore the underlying factors behind human actions within an ecosystem is a mistake that deserves correction. Thus, the "so what?" question that we apply before judging any scholarship is relevant to this book precisely because one human action, such as building a fence, begets other consequences within that existing ecosystem. In the case of the Korean DMZ, the security zone results in improved species conservation, while the opposite might be true in another border region. The edge effect can indeed yield unexpected consequences.

From its origins in biology and ecology, the edge effect now holds a place in the study of borders. Edge effect is a concept that describes the influences two bordering communities have on one another in a transitional area, or ecotone. Cunningham notes that "An ecotone is an area where two different plant communities meet to create a distinctive interface between two ecosystems [...] An ecotone usually retains some of the characteristics of each community, but will often also contain species not found separately in either of the overlapping systems."[14] From a biological perspective, species of plants native to one border plant community, for example, may grow more abundantly in an ecotone, which, for a variety of reasons, provides "friendly" spaces for some species, but not for others. In keeping with the edge effect, South Korea's industrialization and overall development and North Korea's deforestation contributed to the DMZ ecotone as the only place in both countries in which certain native species survive.[15] Likewise, a human border ecotone also develops unique traits. For example, construction of the Israeli wall resulted in adaptive changes within Palestinian border communities along the wall that more distant Palestinian communities may not feel compelled to manifest.

Cunningham writes of a world that may be going green, but is also creating what she labels as "gated ecologies." This relates to certain forms of border fencing aimed at restricting large, economically displaced populations and other security barriers, which Cunningham views as often simply "laid over natural environments without proper understanding of, or an interest in, the ecosystems they criss-cross, subdivide and disrupt."[16] House-Peters's chapter on the San Pedro River that crosses the US–Mexico border illustrates this gated community concept in a very obvious manner. From a social ecological perspective, positive human, cultural and political interaction with nature is as important as wilderness preservation in developing an environmentally sustainable approach to contemporary problems.

This process emphasizes what humans do in a border environment, but as the readers progress through the chapters of this book, they will notice that this process is not a one-way street. Rather, as the Belfast and Berlin Wall examples illustrate, sometimes it is about what the environment does for humans. Ignored interstitial spaces arise to become natural habitats of merit, beauty and delight for nearby human residents as well as experimental ecological communities. In the case of the DMZ, an entire swatch of land between North and South Korea, still heavily mined and foreboding, is now recognized worldwide for its thriving ecosystem. (While some animals succumb, mines apparently do not create an ecological disturbance to endanger animal populations.) Certainly this is a ray of hope for all to appreciate as the DMZ remains an antagonistic symbol for humans, but is a "friendly ecotone" for Korea's flora and fauna.

An Integrative Conceptual Framework

This book interprets border behavior through the lens of a social ecological framework in which the social context plays a pivotal role, while political and spatial elements take on essential explanatory functions within the framework. The contributors view these three contexts—social, political and spatial—as complementary and symbiotic, and whose purpose it is to clarify the complex nature of border relationships, especially those resulting from conflict and disputes. Much of this book explains how conflict, often resulting from local, regional or global political and policy decisions, influences the way in which people deal with physical and cognitive (psychological) borders to create their own space, or environment of adaptation, conservation and daily survival.

However, this book also presents positive outcomes resulting from political decisions. While political decisions can lead to conflict, we would be remiss to ignore the cooperative results that arise, for example, from the attempt to create a peace park along formerly war-torn Balkan borders, or by the nonprofit International Crane Foundation to preserve the Red-crowned Crane just beyond Korea's DMZ. Konrad aptly observes that the subsequent stages of any border spatial reordering toward security primacy, be it along the US–Canadian border, the Israeli–Palestinian divide or elsewhere, is capable of encouraging a distinct borderlands community culture that can result in empowerment of stakeholders and "more balanced approaches at the intersection of two nations."[17] This raises hope for more humanized and effective security that inhabitants would welcome in places like the Shu'fat Refugee Camp along the Israeli wall (see Chapter 9.)

We believe that examining the relationship between humans and nature can help us explain how physical and cognitive borders evolve and take on unique spatial characteristics as a result of conflict. Many of the chapters in this volume emphasize "space" and how people create their own spatial environment along borders as a coping mechanism. In its broadest definition, spatial ecology examines spatial patterns (patterns of place) and their connection to biota (including humans) and the environment. Spatial ecology's emphasis, according to biologists Ian Billick and Mary Price, is on how "the spatial location of a [physical] point affects its properties via ecological exchanges with neighboring points."[18] Scholars traditionally associate spatial ecology with the fields of biology, ecology and geography, but the term also reaches into discussions surrounding architecture, landscape ecology and the philosophy of space.[19]

The notion of space in relation to borders now includes both tangible/physical and intangible/cognitive aspects—and not simply physical points in space.[20] Tangible space at a border crossing is easily understood if we see a wall or border fence in its midst. Yet, intangible border space mainly exists within our own minds, as Katherine Morrissey's work illustrates. She refers to such spaces as "mental territories" or mental boundaries, which people create around their perceived sense of space.[21] Morrissey's approach, for example, reinforces the centrality Aboriginal coping mechanisms and behaviors that manifest as an intangible border between Australia's white and Aboriginal populations.

On a given spatial scale, local, regional or global, we can distinguish two different approaches: the field of landscape ecology and the field of metapopulation ecology. According to Moilanen and Nieminen, landscape ecology examines systems that are relatively well connected and possess a great deal of suitable habitat while metapopulation ecology deals with "interactions between spatially distinct [separate] local populations" in a highly fragmented, and often small habitat.[22] The metapopulation concept is a useful one for us to consider since it emphasizes fragmented and less well-suited environments such as the Palestinian examples in Chapters 8 and 9. Border landscapes often display such metapopulation characteristics especially when one national group is forced to reside within a small-boundaried space, while others are not. However, confinement in a small-boundaried space does not imply that spatial interactions outside the space do not occur. In fact, we often observe the "flow of phenomena across space."[23] For our purpose in this book, we see this flow move within (and between) both physical and cognitive spaces, which is how several of the contributors apply spatial ecology in their own research. The notion of flow expressed in Chapter 13, for example, illustrates Verena Andermatt Conley's near-poetic portrayal of Mediterranean—and more specifically Algerian—space within the *Jardin d'Essai.*

Adaptation, conservation and survival amid the chaos of conflict translate into a myriad of tangible accommodations that are familiar to architects and artists trained in design and able to visualize how humans physically shape the natural environment in order to create a less hostile living space. It is the architect/urban planner, for example, who proposes the design of a border garden along the Israeli–Palestinian divide in Jerusalem in order to make a more fluid and harmonious division separating the two peoples.[24] Such physical dimensions may sow future seeds for the adoption of a broader tool called a peace park or transboundary protected area. For example, the architectural group SAYA/Design for Change proposed a peace park between Syria and Israel in the Golan Heights, which SAYA cofounder Yehuda Greenfield-Gilat outlined in his 2009 United States Institute of Peace report.[25]

Conversely, the policy maker may have a border-peace objective for that space, but cannot implement the policy without the help of architects or planners. Such cooperation holds the potential for decreasing conflict, but we must recognize that experts in their respective fields do not always speak the same methodological language that others easily understand. This is why we chose the social context as a common ground with which to build an analytical framework for better understanding border issues. As applied in this book's chapters, the reader will uncover how "the political" decision translates into the spatial reality for those most closely affected by the decision. In some cases, it is the local Palestinian population that creates coping responses to the Israeli-built wall (Shu'fat Refugee Camp)—and in others, it is the natural environment (Balkans Peace Park, Redcrowned crane habitat) that sparks humans into conservation action.

Since spatial/environmental and political creations ultimately fall within the relationship between humans and nature (i.e., social ecology), we place both spatial ecology and political ecology under the greater "umbrella" of social ecology. Political ecology is an increasingly used term that has been transformed over the years into its own "politics-focused" conceptual framework to explain human-made (anthropogenic) environmental degradation. It bears the markings, as Tim Forsyth posits in his analysis of Piers Blaikie's writings on political ecology, of a global political economy that can lead to both social marginalization and environmental degradation.[26] Political ecology has evolved to include not only global, but also national and locally relevant political factors and actions of political institutions that are responsible for causing environmental degradation as well as improvement. Brunet-Jailly suggests that borderlands, and the border landscapes that are formed within them, result in continual interactions between "the actions of people (agency)" and are constantly under the influence and control of existing power structures.[27] This politicized atmosphere is especially salient in Chapter 12, where Paulo Tavares makes an argument for linking Peru's Amazonian environmental degradation to both national-political and global-economic forces. Political ecology thus seeks to realign multilevel linkages between the environment and political forces especially as they pertain to conflict and "hierarchies of power."[28]

Blending political, social and spatial ecologies into one comprehensive framework plucks readers from their disciplinary comfort zone and transports them into the myriad of border landscape cases within this book. Thus, the architect's spatial orientation melds with the political scientist or public policy scholar's penchant for political interpretation, while social factors familiar to sociologists add a comprehensive dimension to the other two. The result is one framework, with one interpretive social context as anchor.

Border landscapes encompass not only the physical divide between nation-states, such as the Demilitarized Zone separating North and South Korea, but also divisions that result from cognitive barriers constructed as a coping mechanism. As mentioned earlier, this latter type is the focus of Birrell and Hill's chapter in which demarcation between Aboriginal and white Australians takes on a psychological dimension by Australian Aborigines in order to assuage racial injustice. One might call these coping mechanisms a limited and/or indirect means for achieving conflict resolution. Like Birrell and Hill, Madsen's research on the Tohono O'odham from southern Arizona and northern Sonora, Mexico recognizes the spiritual aspects of native peoples toward their ancestral land and the confusion it causes when political powers clash with long-standing indigenous behaviors.[29] In other examples, such as the Balkans examination in Chapter 4, a clearly defined political process culminating in the creation of a peace park hit a temporary impasse because peace park organizers did not sufficiently address local inhabitants and politicians' sensibilities and concerns. Using this interpretive framework, contributors to this book recognize the need for an adaptable approach that encompasses both physical and psychological borders.

The political realities of a border space are not only the result of centralized policies and strategies, but are also influenced and created by the fragmented border populations on either side of the boundaries. Within the framework we have described in previous paragraphs, we are particularly interested in looking at the interactions between these border communities and their border landscape ecologies, and how they can manifest and influence positive, sustainable and peaceful developments.

Structure of this Volume

This volume is divided into four parts along different spatial and conceptual categories: frames, bridges, corridors and portals. Each part demonstrates how borders, both tangible and intangible, are not merely beholden to politics and power, but also represent human–nonhuman interactions, which seek to make life bearable and to conserve nature in areas of current or former conflict. Part I (Frames) provides a theoretical (Chapter 1) and practical (Chapters 2 and 3) framework that positions border environments in the subsequent chapters and cases. Chapter 1 begins with the basic notion that borders constantly evolve and that we must change with the times to recognize the nuances that accompany the modern border, for that border may extend well into a nation-state or even into the cognitive realm.

In Chapter 1, Brunet-Jailly also goes beyond territorialist or geopolitical policy traditions to focus on the agency of borders, that is, the activities of social, economic and political individuals, the processes of production and reproduction of borders and borderlands and the praxis of bordering and de-bordering. These borderlands total more than 10 million square kilometers around the world and often remain out of human and market reach.

Among these are newly established transboundary areas protected by international and local agreements—"borderless" borderlands for flora and fauna where native human activity is curtailed and regulated. Transboundary conservation in the form of peace parks (Chapter 2) encourages practical environmental solutions that foster conservation and assuage physical border conflicts through cooperative management practices, while the gated ecologies concept in Chapter 3 helps policy makers shape solutions to the social and ecological issues surrounding security fencing.

Part II (Bridges) examines contemporary liminal territories, from geographical border zones in the Balkans, Korea, between the United States and Mexico to the social margins reflective of Cyprus and a unified Germany. Part II also presents projects and initiatives that highlight socio-ecological practices of resilience, restoration and reclamation that bridge territorial rifts, which celebrate and conserve nature, as the Balkans Peace Park Initiative (Chapter 4) and the crane habitat restoration project (Chapter 5) illustrate.

The case studies and projects in Part II also attempt to mitigate possible or existing conflicts and rifts, with initiatives that straddle the border, that act on the edge or that mirror the other side. Dynamic bridges can be created through the flows of goods, peoples and ideas for collective ecological goals. In Chapter 4, Walters and Ali explore the impact of the recent Balkan war on the landscape, ecosystem and local communities through multiple perspectives of transboundary environmental and social issues, and through the bridges and rifts that link and separate the social communities on either side such as environmental, social, political, economic, cultural and security matters. In a post–Balkan war era, it is essential to recognize what spurs disagreement and which actors demonstrate resiliency and a willingness to allow large-scale, long-term planning for a peace park. The Balkans Peace Park Initiative may have commenced with an excess of idealism, but it quickly returned to the harsh reality that local sentiments hold sway in making a peace park work. Walters and Ali's chapter presents an honest assessment of lessons learned in the process and an admission that local sentiments must be understood and recognized before one can expect to see a well-functioning peace park.

In Chapter 5 Healy, Archibald and Westing build on the migratory routes of the sacred and legendary Red-crowned and White-naped Cranes across the Korean Demilitarized Zone (DMZ) to propose a non-confrontational way to interact and dialogue with North Korea. Situated along the DMZ in North Korea, the Anbyon project has several goals— increase food production for humans, encourage wild cranes to return and protect/ enhance biodiversity. The project also contributes to numerous Ramsar Strategic Plan Goals and to North Korea's top science goals of food security, energy security and health care. It is a model of conservation and sustainable agriculture that could be replicated throughout the Korean Peninsula.

House-Peters's Chapter 6 recognizes that border ecology is indeed affected by the transboundary nature of rivers and argues that private Mexican mining interests exert power over water interests that impact both sides of the San Pedro River watershed. The chapter also incorporates expropriation and communal land changes in Mexico and conservation in the United States as explanatory drivers to understand how the San Pedro River riparian space evolved to its current state. Conservation serves to pre-serve a natural flora-fauna habitat while often excluding human economic activity in the space—as is the case on the Arizona side of the border. The San Pedro River flows north from Mexico into Arizona and, in 2014, was subject to a toxic-tailings spill. The case represents the significance of a binational watershed and how tangible frontiers affect the environment. Ironically, binational negotiations in this case appear to be less conflictive than those within Mexico or the United States. House-Peters explains these riparian issues via political, institutional and environmental factors and the power strug-gle between Mexican authorities and local Sonoran communities. The latter have under-gone significant changes over the past 20 years and experienced a shift from communally held land and water to increased privatization of these resources. In her analysis of this riparian transboundary region, House-Peters questions the strength of resilience theory and of its ability to explain policies that promote the resilience of one set of actors, yet actively undermine the resilience of others.

In the San Pedro Riparian National Conservation Area (SPRNCA) along the Arizona side of the border, agrarian and grazing activities no longer occur while livestock graz-ing and agricultural production continue on the Mexican side. Such disparities reveal the uneven and possibly ineffective nature of transboundary border conservation whose management is to focus, at least theoretically, on what is "best" for the environment.

Part II of this book also investigates the interstitial spaces of borders—enclaves, buffer zones and Green Lines. It also examines projects and processes that activate social and ecological co-creation, create laboratories of biocultural diversity and engage in the criti-cal documenting of post-conflict social exchanges in landscapes of memory, while exam-ining common policies in confined territories. In Chapter 7, Grichting introduces the Military Buffer Zone in Cyprus as a shared social and ecological space for the Cypriot communities. With diverse spatial scales and multiple stakeholders—from the national and international actors to the local and communal participants and users—these physi-cal and conceptual shared spaces must rise beyond the polarized sphere of bicommunal-ism to embrace the mosaic of social and ethnic groups that produce the landscapes of Cyprus. Creating a shared space also involves a shared process, one that will co-create common spaces for the coexistence of multiple ecologies and social groups and that will include landscapes, memorial spaces, public infrastructures and institutions.

Part III (Corridors) examines spatial projects within the thick or interstitial space of borders, such as the militarized landscapes of Lebanon, Israel/Palestine and the Catholic–Protestant divide in Belfast, Northern Ireland. It also explores "laboratories of social and ecological co-creation," investigates biodiversity in interstitial no-man's lands, and docu-ments post-conflict social exchanges in confined territories such as refugee camps. Shibli and Bulle examine the border divide that derives largely from the Palestinian conflict and armed exchanges on Lebanon's southern border with Israel. Small manifestations such as the creation of a marriage hall that doubles as a youth center help make life bearable for inhabitants of border refugee camps like Shu'fat. In Chapter 9, Bulle calls this the domestication of the environment and emphasizes how the ecology of simple physical and social activity is closely managed by Israeli authorities.

Shibli's background is in landscape design and ecosystem management, and his approach to conflicted border environments reflects how humans can create or maintain their environment under duress. Like Bulle, he emphasizes the small things that residents can do to make their often-chaotic environment bearable. The irony of his Marwaheen village example along the Blue Line between Israel and Lebanon is that it lies closer to the Israeli settlement of Zaari't than it does to any Lebanese village. One way to add balance to this tense environment is the upgrade of its communal pond/reservoir to what Shibli calls a public-amenity landscape that also provides irrigation to villagers' plants. The communal pond/reservoir in Marwaheen along the Lebanese–Israeli border is a small creation, yet it represents something more, a reminder to its inhabitants that water is the source of life for both human and nonhumans as desertification and war take their toll. This communal pond/reservoir illustrates the positive impact of local empowerment to preserve and enhance sustainable rural agriculture in an arid border region.

Chapter 9 examines the small Shu'fat refugee camp, located in East Jerusalem along the border formed with the Palestinian Territories, and now enclaved due to the presence of the security wall built by the State of Israel. The chapter's analysis focuses on the practical actions, spatial and communicative resources that the confined inhabitants mobilized despite the closure. It looks at the relations of Shu'fat citizens to their environment, at the concept of proximity, describing these *regimes of engagement* in the vicinity, which review the limits between public and private space, domestic space and environment. Bulle's objectives are to design the political dimensions of *nearness* by linking these regimes of engagement to social ecology as a new political form.

Far from the exceptional and peripheral space of frontier borderlands between nation-states, Murtagh (Chapter 10) presents us with the everyday spaces in Belfast, Northern Ireland, occupied by two previously warring religious groups, Catholics and Protestants, who now demonstrate that the city can indeed be "jointly owned." He introduces the idea of liminal space between accepting dominant narratives of identity and the hauntings of violence that have to do with the memories of past conflict—an interstitial space of memory where communities can resist the erasure of these painful histories. Marginality draws attention to the spatial contradictions found in sites, but also provides openings for aesthetic engagement and embodied practices that involve material thinking, collaborative human action and location.

Last, Part IV (Portals) describes activism, dialogues and processes of reterritorialization, exploring critical entry points and nodes through anthropology and cultural studies of (de)colonization and indigenous communities. Birrell and Hill's examination of Aboriginal coping mechanisms that create intangible or cognitive walls between their society and that of white Australians is the practical application of what we mean by intangible borders. It illustrates a certain social ecological resilience conveyed through allegory and stories—and indeed, it is a departure from the standard policy analysis found in the other chapters. Yet, it conveys the intangible border concept in a way that cannot be done using traditional policy analysis. It also reinforces our acknowledgment that some groups do not readily adopt Western (Australian) thought processes even if they reside within Australia's territorial borders. This is important for policy makers to understand, and the same could be said for the Chapter 12 case that pertains to Peru's indigenous peoples who seek greater control and decision-making power on their land. Border walls are most often physical in nature, but this chapter reveals that they can be psychological as well. The contributors chose to convey their message in dialogue fashion, which is well-suited to Aboriginal thought processes and means of expression.

Tavares's chapter examines what happens when economic and political interests clash with local indigenous ways and traditional agricultural methods. The mechanism by which Peruvian indigenous groups conveyed their demands in this case was through political activism begun in 2009. Activism thus becomes the practical means to achieve their stated goal of opposition to the implementation of a new Forest Law that would alter the legal framework that governs Amazonian lands. This legal change could also potentially alter the ecological balance of the forest. Tavares terms this process a reterritorialization and explains the conflict from both social and ecological approaches. The implication is that, since the "conquerors" never left, indigenous groups have no choice but to continue the dialogue with the Peruvian government. When dialogue fails, then activist demonstrations begin as a means to continue the process. The chapter is not only a case study of the demonstrations, but also raises important theoretical issues on the relationship between political sovereignty and ecological balance.

Unlike the Peruvian struggle or Aboriginal adaptation to Western dominance, the Mediterranean example in Chapter 13 examines what happens after the colonizer leaves. In this case, Algeria inherited a park previously reserved for foreigners, but which is now transformed into its own peaceful space for those very people initially excluded from its confines. The Jardin d'Essai has defined physical borders and now represents an almost dream-laden, botanical garden of repose and relaxation. It was taken back by Algerians, or to use Conley's term, it was "reterritorialized." The Franco–Algerian conflict over independence is now in the past, and the park represents one of the positive outcomes of the brutal war. It was not destroyed as a reminder of French repression, but instead transformed into a common space in which all Algerians, who often live in tight quarters, have the opportunity to enjoy nature and open spaces. The park exemplifies the desire to save and cultivate a part of nature in which humans can seek refuge following the horrors of war or repression. It also leads us to find similar behavioral patterns following the fall of the Berlin Wall and the Balkans war. In all instances, there was a willingness to create or conserve nature, not only for the benefit of flora and fauna, but also for human well-being. Such places, parks or nature reserves thus become places of repose and healing.

What this book conveys from all of these cases is the idea that creation of natural spaces, whether located within an ongoing conflict (Israel–Palestine) or postwar space (Balkans), is a way for humans to detoxify and heal from the ravages of violence. Natural spaces, no matter how small, demonstrate the social drive to find beauty in nature and serve as a valuable tool for enabling a lasting peace. Perhaps all peace negotiations should incorporate the creation of such spaces into their agreements. One way to do this along physical borders is for the creation of peace parks, and the Korean DMZ would be a good starting point.[30] Reterritorialization of natural spaces and boundaries by Indigenous communities may also open us to new ways of delimitating and administering our territories in a more sustainable and inclusive way. The natural environment will surely benefit from such an approach.

NOTES

1 Rachel Carson, *The Sense of Wonder* (New York: HarperCollins, 1998), 38.
2 Samantha Stone-Jovicich, "Probing the Interfaces between the Social Sciences and Social-Ecological Resilience: Insights from Integrative and Hybrid Perspectives in the Social Sciences." *Ecology and Society* 20 (2015): 25. http://dx.doi.org/10.5751/ES-07347-200225; M. Fabinyi, L. Evans and S. J. Foale, "Social-Ecological Systems, Social Diversity, and Power: Insights from Anthropology and Political Ecology." *Ecology and Society* 19 (2014): 28. http://dx.doi.org/10.5751/ES-07029-190428.
3 Stephen M. Wheeler, *Climate Change and Social Ecology: A New Perspective on the Climate Challenge* (New York: Routledge, 2012), 6.
4 Murray Bookchin, *The Ecology of Freedom: The Emergence and Dissolution of Hierarchy* (Oakland, CA: AK Press, 2005), 85–7.
5 Simron Jit Singh, Helmut Haberl et al., eds., *Long-Term Socio-ecological Research Studies in Society: Nature Interactions across Spatial and Temporal Scales* (New York: Springer, 2013), 11.
6 Ibid.
7 Sarah F. Green, *Notes from the Balkans: Locating Marginality and Ambiguity on the Greek–Albanian Border* (Princeton, NJ: Princeton University Press, 2005), 1–16.
8 Nick Vaughan-Williams, *Border Politics: The Limits of Sovereign Power* (Edinburgh: Edinburgh University Press, 2009), 1–13.
9 Vladimir Kolossov and James Scott, "Selected Conceptual Issues in Border Studies." *Belgeo* (*Revue belge de géographie*) 1 (2013), accessed January 5, 2015, http://belgeo.revues.org/10532.
10 Victor Konrad, "Borders, Bordered Lands and Borderlands: Geographical States of Insecurity between Canada and the United States and the Impacts of Security Primacy," in *Border Regions: Borders, Fences and Walls: State of Insecurity?* edited by Elisabeth Vallet (Burlington, VT: Ashgate Publishing, 2014), 87 and 91.
11 Anna Grichting, *Boundaryscapes. Recasting the Green Line of Cyprus* (doctor of design diss., Harvard University, 2008; Anna Grichting, *The Green Line of Cyprus: Human Development and Reconciliation through Environmental Cooperation.* HPCR Harvard Program for Humanitarian Policy and Conflict Research, Harvard University, 2006.
12 Suvendrini Perera quoted in Chiara Brambilla, "Exploring the Critical Potential of the Borderscapes Concept." *Geopolitics* 20 (2015): 14–34.
13 Hillary Cunningham, "Permeabilities, Ecology and Geopolitical Boundaries," in *A Companion to Border Studies*, edited by Thomas M. Wilson and Hastings Donnan (Oxford: Wiley-Blackwell, 2012), 374.
14 Ibid., 382.
15 Hall Healy, "Korean Demilitarized Zone: Peace and Nature Park." *International Journal on World Peace* 24 (2007): 61–83.
16 Hilary Cunningham, "Gating Ecology in a Gated Globe: Environmental Aspects of 'Securing Our Borders,'" in *Borderlands: Ethnographic Approaches to Security, Power, and Identity*, edited by Hastings Donnan and Thomas M. Wilson (Lanham, MD: University Press of America, 2010), 137.

17 Konrad, "Borders, Bordered Lands and Borderlands," 99.
18 Ian Billick and Mary V. Price, "The Ecology of Place," in *The Ecology of Place*, edited by Ian Billick and Mary V. Price (Chicago: University of Chicago Press, 2010), 4.
19 David Lindenmayer and Richard Hobbs, ed. *Managing and Designing Landscapes for Conservation: Moving from Perspectives to Principles* (Malden, MA: Blackwell Publishing, 2007); Verena Andermatt Conley, *Spatial Ecologies: Urban Sites, State and World-Space in French Critical Theory* (Liverpool: Liverpool University Press, 2012), 2.
20 John Agnew, "Borders on the Mind: Re-framing Border Thinking." *Ethics and Global Politics* 1 (2008): 175–91.
21 Katherine G. Morrissey, *Mental Territories: Mapping the Inland Empire* (Ithaca, NY: Cornell University Press, 1997), 23.
22 Atte Moilanen and Marko Nieminen, "Simple Connectivity Measures in Spatial Ecology." *Ecology* 83 (2002): 1131–45.
23 Reuel Hanks, ed. *Encyclopedia of Geography Terms, Themes, and Concepts* (Santa Barbara, CA: ABC-CLIO, 2011), 318.
24 Michael Sorkin, *The Next Jerusalem: Sharing the Divided City* (New York: Monacelli Press, 2002).
25 Yehuda Greenfield-Gilat, *A Renewable Energy Peace Park in the Golan as a Framework to an Israeli–Syrian Agreement* (Washington, DC: USIP, 2009).
26 Tim Forsyth, "Political Ecology and the Epistemology of Social Justice." *Geoforum* 39 (2008): 756–64.
27 Emmanuel Brunet-Jailly, "Power, Politics and Governance of Borderlands—the Structure and Agency of Power," in *Theorizing Borders through Analyses of Power Relationships*, edited by Peter Gilles, Harlan Koff, Carmen Maganda and Christian Schulz (Brussels: P.I.E.–Peter Lang, 2013), 29.
28 W. Neil Adger, Tor A. Benjaminsen, Katrina Brown and Hanne Svarstad, "Advancing a Political Ecology of Global Environmental Discourses." *Development and Change* 32 (2001): 681–715.
29 Kenneth D. Madsen, "A Basis for Bordering: Land, Migration, and Inter-Tohono O'odham Distinction along the US–Mexico Line," in *Placing the Border in Everyday Life*, edited by Reece Jones and Corey Johnson (Surrey, England: Ashgate Publishing, 2014), 102.
30 See Hall Healy, "Korean Demilitarized Zone: Peace and Nature Park." *International Journal on World Peace* 24 (2007): 61–83.

BIBLIOGRAPHY

Adger, W. Neil, Tor A. Benjaminsen, Katrina Brown and Hanne Svarstad. "Advancing a Political Ecology of Global Environmental Discourses." *Development and Change* 32 (2001): 681–715.
Agnew, John. "Borders on the Mind: Re-framing Border Thinking." *Ethics and Global Politics* 1 (2008): 175–91.
Billick, Ian and Mary V. Price. "The Ecology of Place." In *The Ecology of Place*, edited by Ian Billick and Mary V. Price, 1–10. Chicago: University of Chicago Press, 2010.
Bookchin, Murray. *The Ecology of Freedom: The Emergence and Dissolution of Hierarchy.* Oakland, CA: AK Press, 2005.
Bookchin, Murray. "What Is Social Ecology?" In *Environmental Philosophy: From Animal Rights to Radical Ecology*, edited by M. E. Zimmerman. Englewood Cliffs, NJ: Prentice Hall, 1993.
Brambilla, Chiara. "Exploring the Critical Potential of the Borderscapes Concept." *Geopolitics* 20 (2015): 14–34.
Brunet-Jailly, Emmanuel. "Power, Politics and Governance of Borderlands—the Structure and Agency of Power." In *Theorizing Borders Through Analyses of Power Relationships*, edited by Peter Gilles, Harlan Koff, Carmen Maganda and Christian Schulz, 29–44. Brussels: P.I.E.–Peter Lang, 2013.

Carson, Rachel. *The Sense of Wonder*. New York: HarperCollins, 1998.

Conley, Verena Andermatt. *Spatial Ecologies: Urban Sites, State and World-Space in French Critical Theory*. Liverpool: Liverpool University Press, 2012.

Cunningham, Hilary. "Gating Ecology in a Gated Globe: Environmental Aspects of 'Securing Our Borders.'" In *Borderlands: Ethnographic Approaches to Security, Power, and Identity*, edited by Hastings Donnan and Thomas M. Wilson, 125–42. Lanham, MD: University Press of America, 2010.

Cunningham, Hilary. "Permeabilities, Ecology and Geopolitical Boundaries." In *A Companion to Border Studies*, edited by Thomas M. Wilson and, Hastings Donnan, 371–86. Oxford: Wiley-Blackwell, 2012.

Fabinyi, Michael, Louisa Evans and Simon J. Foale. "Social-Ecological Systems, Social Diversity, and Power: Insights from Anthropology and Political Ecology." *Ecology and Society* 19 (2014): 28. http://dx.doi.org/10.5751/ES-07029-190428.

Forsyth, Tim. "Political Ecology and the Epistemology of Social Justice." *Geoforum* 39 (2008): 756–64.

Green, Sarah F. *Notes from the Balkans: Locating Marginality and Ambiguity on the Greek–Albanian Border*. Princeton, NJ: Princeton University Press, 2005.

Greenfield-Gilat, Yehuda. *A Renewable Energy Peace Park in the Golan as a Framework to an Israeli–Syrian Agreement*. Washington, DC: USIP, 2009.

Grichting, Anna. *Boundaryscapes: Recasting the Green Line of Cyprus*. Doctor of design diss., Harvard University, 2008.

Grichting, Anna. *The Green Line of Cyprus: Human Development and Reconciliation through Environmental Cooperation*. Harvard Program for Humanitarian Policy and Conflict Research (HPCR), Harvard University, 2006.

Hanks, Reuel, ed. *Encyclopedia of Geography Terms, Themes, and Concepts*. Santa Barbara, CA: ABC-CLIO, 2011.

Healy. H. "Korean Demilitarized Zone: Peace and Nature Park." *International Journal on World Peace* 24 (2007): 61–83.

Hester, Randolph T. *Design for Ecological Democracy*. Cambridge: MIT Press, 2010.

Jorgensen, Anna. "The Social and Cultural Context of Ecological Plantings." In *The Dynamic Landscape: Design, Ecology, and Management of Naturalistic Urban Planning* edited by Nigel Dunnett and James Hitchmough, 416–58. London: Spon Press, 2004.

Khelm, Nancy. "Engaging Local Residents—Instigating Ecological Projects—Building Regenerative Systems." www.socialecologies.net.

Kolossov, Vladimir and James Scott. "Selected Conceptual Issues in Border Studies." *Belgeo* (*Revue belge de géographie*) 1 (2013). Accessed January 5, 2015. http://belgeo.revues.org/10532.

Konrad, Victor. "Borders, Bordered Lands and Borderlands: Geographical States of Insecurity between Canada and the United States and the Impacts of Security Primacy." In *Border Regions: Borders, Fences and Walls: State of Insecurity?* edited by Elisabeth Vallet, 85–104. Burlington, VT: Ashgate Publishing, 2014.

Lindenmayer, David and Richard Hobbs, eds. *Managing and Designing Landscapes for Conservation: Moving from Perspectives to Principles*. Malden, MA: Blackwell Publishing, 2007.

Madsen, Kenneth D. "A Basis for Bordering: Land, Migration, and Inter-Tohono O'odham Distinction along the US–Mexico Line." In *Placing the Border in Everyday Life*, edited by Reece Jones and Corey Johnson, 93–116. Surrey, England: Ashgate Publishing, 2014.

Moilanen, Atte and Marko Nieminen. "Simple Connectivity Measures in Spatial Ecology." *Ecology* 83 (2002): 1131–45.

Morrissey, Katherine G. *Mental Territories: Mapping the Inland Empire*. Ithaca, NY: Cornell University Press, 1997.

Redman, C. L., J. M. Grove and L. H. Kuby. "Integrating Social Science into the Long-Term Ecological Research (LTER) Network: Social Dimensions of Ecological Change and Ecological Dimensions of Social Change." *Ecosystems* 7 (2004): 161–71.

Singh, Simron Jit, Helmut Haberl et al., eds. *Long-Term Socio-ecological Research Studies in Society: Nature Interactions across Spatial and Temporal Scales*. New York: Springer, 2013.

Sorkin, Michael. *The Next Jerusalem: Sharing the Divided City*. New York: Monacelli Press, 2002.

Stone-Jovicich, Samantha. "Probing the Interfaces between the Social Sciences and Social-Ecological Resilience: Insights from Integrative and Hybrid Perspectives in the Social Sciences." *Ecology and Society* 20 (2015): 25. http://dx.doi.org/10.5751/ES-07347-200225.

Transnational Institute of Social Ecology (TRISE). Accessed January 20, 2015. http://trise.org/mission.

Vaughan-Williams, Nick. *Border Politics: The Limits of Sovereign Power*. Edinburgh: Edinburgh University Press, 2009.

Wheeler, Stephen M. *Climate Change and Social Ecology: A New Perspective on the Climate Challenge*. New York: Routledge, 2012.

Wright, David, Catherine Camden-Pratt and Stuart Hill. *Social Ecology. Applying Ecological Understanding to Our Lives and Our Planet*. Gloucestershire: Hawthorn Press, 2011.

Part I

FRAMES: MAPPING SOCIAL ECOLOGIES IN BORDER TERRITORIES

Chapter One

ON THE AGENCY OF BORDERLANDS

Emmanuel Brunet-Jailly

In the 2004 movie *The Terminal*, an unsophisticated citizen of the fictitious country Krakozhia confronts the ambivalence of authority, the notion of in-betweenness and the true meaning of liminal space, after he lands in the United States only to learn that he is in border limbo due to political events out of his control. He is told by a border official, "You have no legal right to enter the U.S. and I have no right to detain you. It seems you have fallen through a small crack in the system. […] [U]ntil we get this sorted out, I have no choice but to allow you to enter the International Transit Lounge. I'm going to sign a release form that is going to make you a free man […] free to go anywhere you like within the confines of the International Transit Lounge."[1] This lighthearted example reads like a theater of the absurd, yet it occurs globally in more serious iterations as humans create and challenge international ordering principles that can subsequently impact both humans and nature. With specific reference to Chapter 5 of this volume, we should ask ourselves who actually thought the international ordering principle that resulted in the DMZ's creation would be beneficial to Korean wildlife.

Introduction: Borderlands, Limits and Liminalities

In *Nation and Narration*[2] Homi K. Bhabha criticizes "essentialist" readings of nationhood; these propagate a specific understanding of culture as a singular and possibly a historically homogeneous set of cultural traditions. In *The Location of Culture* he puts forward the idea that nations and their cultures are "narratives" that emerge out of discussions and confrontations with what he suggests are hybrids, in a process of production of a singular cultural identity. For Bourdieu, a similar cultural process emerges out of *distinction*—as the study of relations between social classes and status groups.[3] In the Weberian sense of *style of life* of differentiated collectivities, distinction is a cultural process where minute differences lead to fundamental individuation and the cultural production of class differences. Interestingly, Bhabha opposes ideas of hybridity and liminality and the "interrogatory, interstitial space"[4] to a retrograde historicism that dominates Western critical thinking. He writes: "The liminal figure of the nation-space would ensure that no political ideologies could claim transcendent or metaphysical authority for themselves. This is because the subject of cultural discourse—the agency of people—is split in the discursive ambivalences that emerge in the contest of narrative authority."[5] In other words, he suggests that our historical era needs to understand the "cultural in-betweenness"[6] of the post-orientalist and postcolonial world, where the agency of communities depends on translational and transnational processes of production of meaning.

Bhabha's powerful *essentialist* critique of the "liminal figure of nation-space"[7] also sheds light on our contemporary understanding of borders and boundaries, because humans have been marking territory for thousands of years, and because the meanings of borders and boundaries for societies have also evolved. Indeed, traditional foraging or nomadic societies already defended their occupation of areas they deemed necessary for survival when containing natural resources, water or plants. In this regard, what is modern is only the extremely precise state and international repertory and delineation of borders. The dominant view is that such precise borders, called boundaries, organize our international state system, where global positioning systems (GPS) draw boundaries thinner than the tip of a pen on paper.

Yet, competing meanings of what borders, borderlands or frontiers and boundaries are also suggest various functions. For instance, the frontier marks a *front* that is concerned by what is on the other side of a zone of transition, the frontier. Whereas the boundary bounds a territory, it is only concerned with what is within the bounded territory. Indeed, the boundary in international law is understood as the limit of sovereignty, that of the power of an authority over a people and a land. The borderland is the region bordering a bordered sovereign territory, whereas a border is often unclear.

So what is *modern* in the modern state system is the overwhelming idea that boundaries organize and delineate powers across the world, yet territorial integrity remains contentious in a contemporary world where sustainability questions have risen to challenge those strict ordering principles, and where, as Bookchin argues, a social ecology of our world "sheds light on human social problems and may lead to ecological dislocations."[8]

The primary argument of this chapter is that a social ecology of borders will help us understand more broadly the social ecology of territory, through two related propositions. First, for centuries, borders were territorial interfaces, marginal spaces of human consciousness, whereas the rather recent eighteenth century's *modern* international system imposed a territorial order, with rule of law and land surveyors, that organized bounded territories into a few colonial, sovereign and unalterable territorial units. Second, this international geopolitical system is now faced with serious challenges of self-determination and agency, for instance. Our social ecology of borderlands points to borders that are also areas where human social and economic flows, like sea tides, challenge the order of this international system. Indeed, although uninhabited areas are receding, natural reserves are emerging as peace parks around the world thanks to the post–Second World War implementation of internationally recognized natural reserves (i.e., peace parks), which further illustrate the various forms and functions of borders. In line with Bhabha's *The Location of Culture*, a social ecology of borderlands points to spaces of cooperation and confrontation of social and economic relations, where natural reserves and peace parks exemplify the current postmodern liminality of borderlands in a world where borders take many other forms and functions—where they are international boundaries, walls, virtual borders, natural reserves and peace parks and other forms, in an increasingly territorially divided world.

Four sections organize this argument. The first section reviews and questions our territorialist and geopolitical traditions. The influence of information communication technologies, globalizing trends and market and migration flows are the focus of the second section. The third section concentrates on borders, power and politics. And the fourth section discusses the increase in the number of state borders and vacillation. The conclusion suggests that in our era of security, borderlands are increasingly complex and multifaceted, visible and invisible, yet also fashioned by local agency, as evidenced through the examples of peace parks and natural reserves.

Borders Beyond our Territorialist and Geopolitical Traditions

As far back as 10,000 years ago, when harvesting, and later planting seeds, became fundamental to survival, humans started marking territories. Hence, marking or fencing territory is nearly as old as cities. Borders, boundaries and frontiers, or borderlands, illustrate functions changing across history and location; indeed, our understanding of the functions of borders is primarily grounded in our cultural relationship to territory, which can change over time. For instance, during the Roman empire, borders or "limes" were not understood as boundary lines. They were transit zones. In the same vein, because it was private property law that delineated territorial ownership, the borders of the empire or of the public space (*ager publicus*) were generally assumed to be limitless. The borderlands of the Roman Empire were not clearly marked, but were vast expanses of land where various forms of allegiances to Rome contributed to peace along with the presence of Roman legions; borderlands thus were collections of zones and areas of contacts between different peoples. Similarly, in Europe during the Middle Ages, it was a system of alliances and allegiances, sometimes personal, that organized the loyalties to the kingdom. For instance, as shown by C. V. Wedgwood, at the end of the Thirty Years' War in 1648, the German empire emerged from a federation of 300 rather small kingdoms. Today, in a similar fashion, the European Union's "neighborhood policies" aim to organize a *circle of friends* around the immediate periphery of all EU member states.[9]

In the same vein, in nineteenth-century China, it was the natural attributes of the border that seemed to determine its functions. It was sparsely populated, the population was foreign, and waterways and mountains separated those areas from the site of the emperor. In these examples, borders are loosely defined borderlands and frontiers that belong to hybrid and liminal categories. They are not the precisely defined boundaries that have come to organize, at least legally, state relations since the Peace Treaty of Westphalia (1648), which is rather recent in the history of humanity.

Westphalia established the first legal recognition of land possession by rulers of the world. It also subsequently implemented the exclusive, sovereign right of those rulers to exercise violence on their people within their territorial possession. In 1770, the invention of the chronometer allowed the accurate measurement of longitude, and thus for a cartographic and topographic revolution. Accurate mapping of possessions became possible, as well as the physical delineation and demarcation of all territorial boundaries. Within a century, boundaries had become both a physical and a legal object in the Western world.

The expansion of maps and law, however, resulted from both the processes of continued colonization and repertory of worldly possessions in international treaties.

Of particular importance is the Treaty of Versailles, which was negotiated at the end of the First World War during the Paris Convention of 1919. It generalized and enshrined in law and in maps the worldly possessions for three empires (the British, French and United States). During the first part of the twentieth century, between the First and the Second World Wars, the world's leading countries created forums to discuss world affairs; the League of Nations was short lived because of the war, but was suc-ceeded by the United Nations at the end of the Second World War in 1945, which then undertook to end colonization, thus giving life (in particular since 1950) to US president Woodrow Wilson's 1919 idea of self-determination of people. Since the 1950s, nearly 150 new member states have joined the international community in the United Nations, hence expanding greatly the number of kilometers of territorial borders around the world as well.

Yet, in the contemporary literature on border studies, there is a growing realization that we need to develop an understanding of borders that goes beyond those *territorialist* or *geopolitical* intellectual traditions. Indeed, during the 1980s, because of the work of the United Nations Conventions on the Law of the Seas (UNCLOS), and more recently, because of the rise of land, sea and air boundary disputes, as well as the upsurge of terri-torial disputes involving ethnic, religious and cultural communities, border scholars have been suggesting that we need to focus on the agency of borders to understand bordering processes. These include social, ecological, economic and political individual activities and resulting processes of production and *re*production, of *Vanished Kingdoms* as described by Oxford historian Norman Davies.[10] They are also borderlands and frontiers, which include bordering and debordering praxis, economically, ecologically, politically and cul-turally embedded in the specifics of a time. These are understood to include processes and practices of human groups across borders and borderlands. They are "B/Ordering space" as Van Houtum contends.[11]

In the contemporary era of security, immigration and market flows are increasingly the target of states' surveillance in their search for intelligence and area security[12] and their collaboration for a better understanding and control of what Manuel Castells calls *spaces of flows*.[13] State border policies, when visible, increase border walls, as is clearly observable on the US–Mexico border, across the city of Jerusalem, and increasingly else-where, in Bangladesh, Bulgaria, Greece, India, Kuwait, Morocco, Saudi Arabia, South/ North Korea, Spain or Turkey, where states have built walls similar to the Roman Lines of the second century (the Hadrian and Antonine Walls) or the Great Wall of China built in the third century BCE.

State border policies, when invisible, increasingly develop capacities to observe as well as spy on individuals. This has recently been decried in *No Place to Hide*,[14] where Glen Greenwald describes the spying capacity of the US National Security Agency, and analyzed in *The Politics of Possibility*,[15] where Louise Amoore details the rationales for vir-tual borders where single individuals become state security threats. Invisible borders are everywhere, but they exist at the margins of society and of state powers. They disappear where technology and humans have not yet settled or have only settled temporarily, and where humans have been unable to expand the reach of technology. These borderlands are, in a way, at the margins of humanity, or celebrate humanity through peace and friendship and through the protection of nature.

Borders, Ecology and Peace Parks

Border areas that attempt to celebrate ecosystems may be found in the form of nature reserves. There are approximately 10 million square kilometers of nature reserves around the world. They are classified into six categories by the International Union for the Conservation of Nature (IUCN): strict nature reserve, wilderness park, national park, natural monument, species management areas, protected land or seascapes and protected areas with sustainable use of natural resources. Although on the defensive globally, when formally identified as such, natural reserves are expanding in number and size, as are protected areas.

They are, for instance, found in the creation of international peace parks, which are transnational conservation areas established and managed by two or more countries. They promote biodiversity, cooperation and regional development. Often, they emerge out of areas protected by international and local agreements: the Bialowieza Forest along the Polish–Belarus border; Prespa Park along the newly delineated border of Macedonia, Albania and Greece; or again, the Fraternity Bioregion that was established in 1976 between Honduras, Guatemala and Bolivia. Indeed, other parks may have successfully established borderless borderlands for fauna and animals, but native human activity is curtailed. This is the case of the 36 peace parks that bring together Botswana, Zambia, Namibia, Angola and Zimbabwe and extend across a region as large as Italy across southern-northern-eastern Africa.

The study of borderlands, and power and politics, thus allows us to examine these complex mechanisms that produce and reproduce territorially defined ecologies, cultures, economies and ultimately local and central states. As illustrated by these examples of border policies, in most imaginaries, borders and walls are hard territorial lines; they are institutions that result from bordering policies,[16] and, because they are about people, for most settled territories, they are predominantly about inclusion and exclusion,[17] and they are also woven into varied cultural, ecologic, economic and political fabrics. In Chapter 4 of this volume, Walters and Ali incorporate this woven blend in their Balkans Peace Park Project—a project that relies on the true intent of transboundary peace parks as a means for peace and reconciliation as well as ecosystem conservation. Nature reserves thus become new territorial frontiers for areas of land that are the outcome of the (sometimes difficult) interactions and intersections between the actions of people (agency) within the constraints and limits placed by contextual and structural factors (structure).

Spenceley and Schoon's work on African peace parks cogently uses a social-ecological system (SES) to explain how such complex interactions can be made to work. Good management remains at the heart of such nature–human boundaries and, as Spenceley and Schoon note, requires a "robust and dynamic ecological landscape"—one that inevitably connects with human populations in and around the park. In turn, this SES encourages an ecological resilience in which natural habitats and humans coexist without causing serious harm to each other.[18] Yet, change is not without disruption especially as local inhabitants, traditionally reliant on agriculture and hunting, are often compelled to join a service industry such as tourism in order to survive.

The first lesson of our social ecology of territories is that borders have not always been expressions of a *modernity*, that is, understood as a precise repertory of territorial possessions. For most of human history, borders were not boundaries, but frontiers. However, contemporary advances in information and communication technologies have contributed to our current understanding of possible bordering processes where technology globalizes and individualizes bordering. It potentially expands secured bordering processes everywhere—yet in parallel new frontiers appear around the world that bring peace and nature reserves where conflicts had previously brought human and ecological dislocations. The next section focuses on the fragmenting and asymmetric impact of the global economy on borderlands.

Borders, Ecology and Globalization

The global economy modifies the politics of state relations in the intergovernmental and international arenas.[19] How it does so is a matter of debate: Some argue it is hollowing out while others suggest that it is more a matter of functional reorganization or multilevel governance. At the same time, it is clear that new information and communication technologies affect states, free trade integrates the economies of Europe and North America, and free-trade regimes pressure governments to ease regulations and to open new markets[20] and, furthermore, seem to enhance subnational entities as economic players.[21]

The global economy, new technologies and free trade areas transform the relations of states and other government tiers with market forces and make governing much more complex. For Saskia Sassen, new legal regimes "un-bundle sovereignties" and "denationalise territories," which has "disturbing repercussions for distributive justice and equity."[22] Similarly, Brenner claims that state spaces are being recalibrated, which leads regional–central government relations to be redefined from vertical, coordinative and redistributive to horizontal, competitive and developmentalist.[23] Keating, focusing on multination states in Europe, finds that along with constitutional reforms, an asymmetry of rights develops which further differentiates local and regional constituencies in a process where federal and centralized states seem to progressively resemble each other.[24] Castells, focusing on the information communication revolution, suggests a fundamental transformation of the relationship between politics and market forces: "spaces of places" and "spaces of flows."[25]

One of the important impacts of migration around the world is its impact on biodiversity and the natural ecosystems of the regions of the world most affected by transition. Migration takes many different forms, which like sea tides affect their environment. All upset their environment, but in varied fashion, and linked to immigration forms, rural to rural, rural to urban, urban to rural. The literature points to the rural-to-rural forms being much rarer than both other forms today. In some regions, the rural-to-urban drive is such that, over the past 20 years, millions of people have moved to urban centers.[26] This is the case across many African and Asian countries, including the world's most populated countries—India and China. Reasons for these movements include population growth, climate change and civil unrest.

The literature comparing such transformations across international case studies suggests that processes of multilevel governance have emerged and transform the nature of states; governments and politics retreat from equalization as they build on increasingly salient economic, ecologic and social and political differences of places. Policies of decentralization and financial downloading progressively empower local and regional actors, and, as a result, ecologic, economic, social and political asymmetries develop, which in turn encourage processes of production and reproduction of such asymmetric spaces.[27] Segments of the scholarship studying the impact of the global economy on the political, social and economic and ecological fabric of regions increasingly focus on the sustainable social construction of economies and the politics of places. Yet, as Buscher suggests, one central challenge is at the crossroad of the global economy that is alienated from ecological and developmental realities, and, local-global chains of conservation policy actors in the public, private and community domains. In his own words, these, however, struggle with the important "contradiction-riddled capitalist development."[28] Indeed, as Buscher details, neoliberalism contributes both to a mode of political construct that negates politics but asserts consensus-driven functional views in peace parks policies, yet the devolution of governance to the local level reasserts local-global politics.

Indeed, these debates emphasize what local power and local politics are, as well as the articulation of the resulting policy processes from the local to the global scale.[29] This raises important questions regarding the state as a self-governing political entity and power in frontier regions: the second lesson of our social ecology of territory is that technological advancements and market globalization are assumed to be primarily responsible for the weakening of the international state system. Trade flows and migrations transform the politics of place leading states to cooperate, and challenge the national bounding nature of borders, yet also impose a neoliberal political economy on borderlands and frontiers, including that of frontier natural reserves and peace parks, which contribute to the internationalization of conservation practices and to peace in areas of border disputes and conflicts.[30]

Borders, Power and Politics

In the 1980s and 1990s, much of the literature on *local power* (and local politics discussed later in this chapter) underscored the role of local leadership in the processes of construction and reconstruction of local power. The debates opposed public choice and Marxist views with scholarship highlighting the agency of local power, and in particular the role of leadership in the building of local coalitions. The key to successful communities, it was suggested, was to be found in the amalgamation of diverse local choices into community ones, and the resulting coupling of agent choices linking the local to the global. For instance, Dahl suggested that it was the aggregation of individual claims into communitywide ones that allowed community leaders to successfully articulate those claims across intergovernmental systems.[31] Dahl argued for a pluralist view where local leaders both arbitrated and aggregated community claims in their many efforts to articulate the local and global. Bachrach and Baratz argued that sociological views of power mirrored social stratification; that elitist and pluralists failed to see that inaction and indecision were in actual fact the failure to develop local power, which in turn was about authority, or the ability to gain authority.[32] Stone suggested stable and open regimes were central to the construction of homogeneous policy platforms and interests.

These views were further tested successfully across international and comparative studies broaching European, Canadian and Australian cases.[33] Kantor and Savitch argued successfully that in the face of structural market and intergovernmental constraints, it was the capacity that local coalitions had to *steer* popular culture and popular control that allowed for the development of policies reflecting local and regional popular choice. These authors' views became prominent in the literature because they demonstrated that what they called steering variables, popular culture and popular control could be influenced by education and that popular control in particular was all about local politics and engagement.[34] In sum, the discussion (although focused on power) pointed toward the fundamental role of local politics in articulating local claims in the global world.[35] What was local politics, then?

In *Regime Politics: Governing Atlanta*, Stone and Sanders (1987) suggested that local politics was about problem solving: politics is not just about public management, but also about the reconciliation of differences. It is the search for technical solutions to agreed-upon problems or generally accepted problems; and politics results from place-based mediation of conflicts and the reconciliation of competing interests, the social distribution of resources.[36] In brief, politics is understood in relation to the ability to marshal sources of power while limiting the influence of opposing forces—where culture, market forces and superior government policies may be both constraining, but also turned into powerful resources when they aligned with local agendas. Hence, it was the ability to articulate local forces into the multiple systems of markets and government levels that became central to local communities. Thus, power and politics are tightly linked and interrelated in the transformation of claims across states, regions and borderland regions. The primary role of politics is to work on common interests and to reconcile differences so as to empower local cross-border communities. The emergence of consensual solutions and the management of disputes and conflicts lead to power and coproduction of policies to address co-identified problems in border regions.[37]

These processes are particularly visible in borderland regions where ecological/environmental, economic, social and political asymmetries either serve or come into conflict with the recent security agenda of states, for instance. The top-down analyses of institutional changes and functional downloading, however, do not debate as effectively how local power and politics are also being transformed by these changes that are assumed to be structural.[38]

However, borderland scholars focusing on the agency of borderlands have documented various trends in which borderlands disappear as a result of peace parks and natural reserves[39] and economic regions[40] or even *bend* as a result of these far-reaching activities.[41] These scholars also document bottom-up processes—agents resisting the newly implemented security agenda[42] for economic, cultural or political reasons. For instance, expanding on Kenichi Ohmae's argument that intense trading relations in Malaysia erase boundaries,[43] Xiangming Chen, in *As Borders Bend*, suggests that the economic density of economic regions spanning international boundaries make borders so porous that they are factually inexistent. Chen argues that in the Bohai and Yellow Seas region, China, South Korea and Japan decentralized policies and relaxed border policies, which resulted in bending borders to include the entire borderland region: "The Bohai/Yellow Sea Subregion is tied together through almost exclusively ocean boundaries across a larger number of more populous cities."[44] Similarly, in Mozambique's Limpopo National Park, thanks to ongoing consultations, the role of the 18 communities in the park (buffer) zone has become fundamental for the development of irrigation schemes.[45] Both in the Bohai and Yellow Seas region, and in the Limpopo National Park, which forms part of the Great Limpopo Transfrontier Park, or Peace Park, between Mozambique, South Africa and Zimbabwe, it is local entrepreneurs, or civic and business activists, that lead bottom-up processes where economic, environmental or political policies impact the nature of the borderlands and turn a boundary into a secured frontier. The boundary is porous yet secure: in Bohai, it is trade that transforms local–regional relations, and, in Limpopo, it is thanks to ongoing consultations that 1,370 households voluntarily relocated to allow for the implementation of a new security infrastructure (a 56-kilometer fence).

In sum, state institutions, but also natural reserves or protected areas, culture and market policies are important to borderland regions. Indeed, as a result of those structuring forces, borderland communities may have different clout; culture or market forces are structural in borderlands, but local social sustainable/ecological movements also have the ability to become powerful agents: the third lesson is that globalized forces may influence the local politics and political clout of borderland communities but these appear to be the liminal figures of nation-space where the local agency of people weaves, in a process of singular production, their local cultures and political clout. For instance, political views regarding such issues as urban planning, organization and transportation, social, economic or security services, including peace parks and protected areas, illustrate such movements, but so does the emergence of self-determination principles that often justify border disputes today, as discussed later.

Borders, State Increase and Vacillation

A social ecology of borderlands underscores the ongoing increase of states and borderland disputes, while disputes and conflicts illustrate the vacillation of the international system. This process is salient in some parts of the Western world; as celebrated Oxford historian Norman Davies suggests, the undoing of the United Kingdom may start during his lifetime with a successful Scottish referendum.[46] But, a further illustration of this wave, like the process of imposition of self-determination by communities to their state structure, is found in the demography of states worldwide.

In 1919, the League of Nations recognized 69 states. In 1945, the newly established United Nations counted 47 member states. In 2014, the United Nations had 198 member states, and currently 13 states have disputable claims while two have special non-member observer status—the Holy See (the Papacy) and the State of Palestine. The position of the State of Palestine has been progressing very slowly, but progressing nevertheless, toward recognition. The latest new member-state has resulted from the creation of a state in southern Sudan. There are also a number of other unclear situations such as Kosovo, Taiwan and other cases that are commonly thought to be countries (Puerto Rico, Bermuda, Greenland, Western Sahara, Scotland and Northern Ireland) that may join the United Nations either with established states or separately through seeking independence. In sum, state increase is a demographic fact.

Because the number of states has increased fourfold over the past 65 years, it is incontestable that alongside increasing state numbers, another phenomenon is taking place: the production and reproduction of borders. Clearly, there is a slow but progressive increase in borders, and a transformation of international relations, where local and regional political clout and identity claims, including self-determination and independence, have transformed the international community downside-up.

Border scholarship actually details the impact of local politics as a central explanation of bordering and re-bordering processes, where boundaries as clear lines of demarcation may unify and filter people. At times, these people have multiple identities and legitimacies, but at other times, boundaries actually cut through communities' singular culture, as well as homogeneous national identity. There are numerous cases of "new" states that have formed out of, for instance, Czechoslovakia (Czech Republic, Slovakia), Ethiopia (Eritrea), Indonesia (East Timor), the Soviet Union (Kazakhstan, Kyrgyzstan, Uzbekistan) and Sudan (South Sudan).

There are also numerous border disputes. The US Central Intelligence Agency, for instance, documents well over 120 boundary disputes along the around 250,000 kilometers of the world's 325 international land boundaries, and 430 maritime boundary disputes. Indeed, territorial disputes are salient, but maritime boundaries are rising because only 209 of them are regulated by international agreements. It is important to note here that the scholarship has argued that the value of territory and maritime seabed is fundamental to such disputes, and simultaneously is at the core of the resolution of boundary disputes and conflicts. Yet, there are two ways to understand value. When there are tangible territorial values, such as oil, gas or mining resources, these are often understood as leading to positive gains on both sides of the boundary. On the contrary, in cases of intangible values where neither side is likely to be able to demonstrate gains, disputes persist. All in all, more than two-thirds of tangible disputes are resolved, but only one in four intangible conflicts—such as ethnic, religious, cultural and nationalist disputes—is ever resolved.[47]

Hence, the study of local power and politics allows us to understand aspects of the current transformation of borders and borderlands, the bordering and debordering processes at stake around the world that may confuse us as they also lead to greatly increased activism in borderland regions and to fundamental transformation of states, including the downfall of states that are prominently liberal, democratic and well established.

Interestingly, peace parks and Transboundary Protected Areas (TBPAs) are not just simple conservation areas. They are not simply neutral, or only technical policies. As Rosaleen Duffy contends, they emerge as part of the rise of global regulation and global governance where nation-states are not the (only) centers of power,[48] but where complex networks of actors effectively link the local and the global. In this context, peace parks bring together academics and policy makers within a global governance framework that participates from *new* fluid, mutable and nonterritorial structures and relationships of policy making resulting from networks of governance that are themselves fluid and fundamentally deterritorialized in nature. They are deterritorialized in nature because, in the area of environmental global governance, much innovation in policy making results from transnational, multisector organizations working together and in this process displace the traditional role of states.

In some African countries, in particular southern ones, TBPAs as well as peace parks have been used as vehicles for peaceful cooperation.[49] Indeed, TBPAs and Parks for Peace have been a successful initiative of the International Union for Conservation of Nature (IUCN), an international organization set up in 1948 in the wake of the United Nations. Its headquarters are in Gland (near Geneva) Switzerland, and it has 45 offices around the world and about 1,000 staff members. It works on global environmental issues around the world thanks to 1,200 members, including 200 governments and 11,000 scientists from 160 countries that voluntarily contribute expertise in six international commissions. The IUCN has observer status at the UN General Assembly, and it started promoting peace parks and protected areas in the 1990s.

When the IUCN program was initiated, few such parks existed, but since 1993 when there were about 70 worldwide, their numbers have expanded greatly, to currently 169 in 113 countries. They are believed to bring great benefits to states, including protected watersheds and better cross-border control over illegal activities. This latter point directly affects the natural environment and includes illegal logging, fire, pests, poaching, pollution and smuggling. The promotion of peace also comes along with the promotion of tourism, the difficult process of international cooperation coupled with environmental and ecosystem protection and, last, the promotion of information exchange and research. Peace parks are fundamentally territorial, but TBPAs can also include oceans, and therefore do not exclude such possible locations surrounding Australia, New Zealand, Madagascar, the Philippines, Iceland, Cuba, Jamaica and Antarctica. The fourth lesson is suggested by our social ecology of territory and borders: a new *modernity* in borders studies emerges where borders are primarily frontiers and areas of hybridity. They are liminal territorial and maritime areas where humanity in the face of the global economy reinvents solutions to human and socio-ecological dislocations.

Conclusion: Borders, Here, There, Everywhere?

Acknowledging the modern history of states, city-states and empires, and their current unravelling worldwide, brings more questions to the fore regarding the nature of borders. Indeed, today, for authors such as Balibar, borders "vacillate" because they are no longer at the boundary line itself.[50] In the tradition of the modern state system as understood by Westphalia, borders are the boundary line. They mark the end of one sovereign state and the beginning of another. But they are also where obligations and currency may change. They are where tolls are paid. They are where customs agents examine and inspect traded goods. They are where trafficking takes place, and where legal and illegal immigration crosses over. Yet today, there is a search for a global normality of the citizen-subject that would be internalized by individuals, and would be a reference of collective and individual identity (language, ethnicity, religion). This *ideal* border is internalized; it is an invisible border that biometric technology implements onto each moving object or individual. Internal controls are prominent zones of transit where populations wait for entry or exit; these are the areas where individuals negotiate their (entry and exit) rights. The border is not on the boundary line and can literally be located anywhere, across borderlands or lands within a state. Trade and exchanges across borders have exceeded natural/cultural controls and have reached limits—whether it is a radioactive plume from Chernobyl, the AIDS virus, mad cow disease or even CNN's images. Such exchanges cannot be stopped at the border. Border walls themselves are being questioned while also increasingly becoming a central strategy of boundary maintenance.[51]

From the study of borders, power and politics and our focus on natural reserves and peace parks, we learn that the agency of power is about the complex mechanisms that produce and reproduce liminal territories. These are areas of hybridity where cultures, ecologies, economies and, ultimately, central and local states confront each other. As a result, we learn that borders are not only boundary lines. Boundaries are institutions and result from bordering policies, and for most settled territories, they are predominantly about inclusion and exclusion. Indeed, we learn from our social ecology of borders that contemporary borders remain woven into varied local and global cultural and ecological, economic and political fabrics, and are fundamentally about people and thus, with Bookchin, about human social problems; hence, their interesting and diverse appearances. Alongside multiple peaceful means of negotiating territorial borders are nature reserves and peace parks where local communities can learn or relearn how to negotiate the daily requirements of co-managing peace and ecological dislocations.

NOTES

1 *The Terminal*, Screenplay by Sacha Gervasi, available at http://screenplayexplorer.com/?tag=the-terminal-movie-script.
2 Homi K. Bhabha, "DissemiNation: Time, Narrative and the Margins of the Modern Nation," in *Nation and Narration*, ed. Homi K. Bhabha (New York: Routledge, 1990), 291–322; Homi K. Bhabha, *The Location of Culture* (New York: Routledge, 1994), 139–70.
3 Pierre Bourdieu, *Distinction: A Social Critique of the Judgement of Taste*, trans. Richard Rice (Cambridge, MA: Harvard University Press, 1979).
4 Bhabha, *The Location of Culture*, 3.
5 Ibid., 148.
6 Shaobo Xie, "Writing on Boundaries: Homi Bhabha's Recent Essays," *ARIEL-A Review of International English Literature*, 27 (1996): 155–66.
7 Bhabha, *The Location of Culture*, 148.
8 Murray Bookchin, "What Is Social Ecology?" in *Social Ecology and Communalism* (Oakland, CA: AK Press, 2006), 19–52.
9 Margot Wallstrom, "Taking the European Union Forwards: The Next 50 Years." Speech by vice president of the European Union responsible for institutional affairs and communication strategy (2007). Lecture in front of the Netherlands Society for International Affairs, The Hague. SP07-144En. www.eu-un.europa.eu/articles/fr/article_6961_fr.htm.

10 Norman Davies, *Vanished Kingdoms: The History of Half-Forgotten Europe* (London: Allen Lane, 2011).

11 Henk van Houtum, Olivier Kramsch and Wolfgang Zierhofer, *B/Ordering Space* (Aldershot: Ashgate Publishing, 2005).

12 Emmanuel Brunet-Jailly, *Borderlands* (Ottawa: University of Ottawa Press, 2007); Emmanuel Brunet-Jailly, "Foreword: Beyond the Border Action Plan, a Context," *Canada-United States Law Journal*, 37 (2010): 273–88.

13 Manuel Castells, *The Informational City: Information Technology, Economic Restructuring, and the Urban Regional Process* (Oxford: Blackwell, 1989).

14 Glenn Greenwald, *No Place to Hide: Edward Snowden, the NSA, and the U.S. Surveillance State* (Toronto: McClelland & Stewart, Division of Random House of Canada, 2014).

15 Louise Amoore, *The Politics of Possibility: Risk and Security Beyond Probability* (Durham, NC: Duke University Press, 2013).

16 David Newman and Ansi Paasi, "Fences and Neighbours in the Post Modern World: Boundary Narratives in Political Geography," *Progress in Human Geography*, 22 (1998): 186–207.

17 Oscar J. Martinez, *Mexican-Origin People in the United States* (Tucson: University of Arizona Press, 2001).

18 Anna Spenceley and Michael Schoon, "Peace Parks as Social Ecological Systems: Testing Environmental Resilience in Southern Africa," in *Peace Parks: Conservation and Conflict Resolution*, ed. Saleem H. Ali (Cambridge, MA: MIT Press, 2007), 83–104.

19 Ivo Duchacek, Daniel Latouche and Garth Stevenson, eds., *Perforated Sovereignties and International Relations: Trans-sovereign Contracts of Subnational Governments* (New York: Greenwood Press, 1988); Thomas Risse-Kappen, *Bringing Transnational Relations Back In: Non-state Actors, Domestic Structures, and International Relations* (Cambridge: Cambridge University Press, 1995); Douglas M. Brown and Earl H. Fry, eds., *States and Provinces in the International Economy* (Berkeley: Institute of Governmental Studies and University of California Press, 1998); and Richard Balme, *Les Politiques du Neo-Regionalisme* (Paris: Economica, 1998).

20 Robert O. Keohane and Helen V. Milner, *Internationalization and Domestic Politics* (Cambridge: Cambridge University Press, 1996).

21 Kenishi Ohmae, *The Borderless World: Power and Strategy in the Interlinked Economy* (New York: HarperCollins Publishers, 1999).

22 Saskia Sassen, *Losing Control? Sovereignty in the Age of Globalization* (New York: Columbia University Press, 1996).

23 Neil Brenner, *New State Spaces: Urban Governance and the Rescaling of Statehood* (Oxford: Oxford University Press, 2004).

24 Michael Keating, *Comparative Urban Politics: Power and the City in the United States, Canada, Britain and France* (Aldershot: Edward Elgar, 1991).

25 Manuel Castells, *The Informational City: Information Technology, Economic Restructuring and the Urban-Regional Process* (Oxford: Basil Blackwell, 1989).

26 Doug Saunders, *Arrival City: The Final Migration and Our Next World* (Toronto: Alfred Knopf, 2010).

27 Xiangming Chen, *As Border Bends: Transnational Spaces in the Pacific Rim* (Lanham, MD: Rowman and Littlefield, 2005).

28 Bram Buscher, *Transforming the Frontier: Peace Parks and the Politics of Conservation in Southern Asia* (Durham, NC: Duke University Press, 2013), conclusion.

29 Emmanuel Brunet-Jailly and John Martin, *Local Government in a Global World* (Toronto: University of Toronto Press, 2010); and Chen, *As Border Bends*.

30 Buscher, *Transforming the Frontier*.

31 Robert Dahl, "The Concept of Power," *Behavioral Science*, 2 (1957): 201–15, and Robert Dahl, *Who Governs* (New Haven, CT: Yale University Press, 1961).

32 Peter Bachrach, and Morton Baratz, "Two Faces of Power," *The American Political Science Review* 56 (1962): 950–62.

33 Hank V. Savitch and Paul Kantor, *Cities in the International Market Place* (Princeton, NJ: Princeton University Press, 2002); Emmanuel Brunet-Jailly and Paul Martin, *Local Government in a Global World* (Toronto: University of Toronto Press, 2010).

34 Ibid. Savitch and Kantor, *Cities in the International Market Place.*

35 Ibid. Brunet-Jailly and Martin, *Local Governments in a Global World.*

36 Clarence Stone and Heywood Sanders, *The Politics of Urban Development* (Lawrence: University Press of Kansas, 1987); Clarence Stone, *Regime Politics: Governing Atlanta* (Lawrence: University Press of Kansas, 1989).

37 Emmanuel Brunet-Jailly, "Globalization, Integration and Cross-Border Relations in the Metropolitan Area of Detroit (USA) and Windsor (Canada)," *International Journal of Economic Development*, 2 (2000): 379–401; Emmanuel Brunet-Jailly, "Cascadia in Comparative Perspective: Canada–US Relations and the Emergence of Cross-Border Regions." *Canadian Political Science Review*, 2 (2008): 104–24.

38 Emmanuel Brunet-Jailly, "A Review of Cross-Border Cooperation in North America," in *Cross-Border Cooperation Structures in Europe*, eds. Iva Pires and Luis Dominguez (Brussels: P.I.E.– Peter Lang, 2014), 49–66; Emmanuel Brunet-Jailly, "In the Increasingly Global Economy, Are Borderland Regions Public Management Instruments?" *International Journal of Public Sector Management*, 25 (2014): 483–91; Emmanuel Brunet-Jailly and Tony Payan, "A Canadian Perspective on European Cross Border Regions," *Policy Research Initiative Working Papers* Series (Ottawa: Government of Canada, Policy Research Initiative, 2006).

39 Gerardo Budowski, "Keynote Presentation: Transboundary Protected Areas as a Vehicle for Peaceful Co-operation," paper prepared for the Workshop on Transboundary Protected Areas in the Governance Stream of the 5th World Park Congress, Durban, South Africa, September 12–13, 2003.

40 Kenishi Ohmae, *The End of the Nation States* (New York: Simon and Schuster, 1999).

41 Xiangming Chen, *As Border Bends: Transnational Spaces in the Pacific Rim* (Lanham, MD: Rowman and Littlefield, 2005).

42 Emmanuel Brunet-Jailly, *Borderlands* (Ottawa: University of Ottawa Press, 2007).

43 Ohmae, *The Borderless World.*

44 Chen, *As Borders Bend*, 138.

45 Peace Park Foundation, "The Global Solution, *Limpopo National Park Issues 2013, Revenue Sharing Cheque to Park Communities, 09 June 2014*," accessed June 23, 2014, www.peaceparks.org/pro-gramme.php?pid=25&mid=1009.

46 Davies, *Vanished Kingdoms.*

47 Robert Mandel, "Roots of Modern Interstate Border Disputes," *Journal of Conflict Resolution*, 24 (1980) 427–54; Paul Huth, *Standing Your Ground: Territorial Disputes and International Conflicts* (Ann Arbor: University of Michigan Press, 1996); Douglas Woodwell, "Unwelcome Neighbours: Shared Ethnicity and International Conflict during the Cold War," *International Studies Quarterly*, 48 (2004): 197–223.

48 Rosaleen Duffy, "Peace Parks and Global Politics: The Paradoxes and Challenges of Global Governance," in *Peace Parks: Conservation and Conflict Resolution*, ed. Saleem H. Ali (Cambridge, MA: MIT Press, 2007), 56–57, 66; Center for International Politics, Manchester University, United Kingdom, 2009.

49 Budowski, "Keynote Presentation."

50 Etienne Balibar, Ernesto Laclau, Chantal Mouffe and Christine Jones, *Politics and the Other Scene* (London: Verso, 2002).

51 Beatriz Lecumberri, "Los muros, una strategia geopolitica que alimenta la violencia," *La Republica*, October 28, 2006; Peter Staniland, "Defeating Transnational Insurgencies: The Best Offence Is a Good Fence," *The Washington Quarterly* (Winter 2005–6): 31–34; Eylal Weizman, *A travers les murs–l'architecture d'une nouvelle guerre urbaine* (Paris: la fabrique editions, 2008).

BIBLIOGRAPHY

Amoore, Louise. *The Politics of Possibility: Risk and Security Beyond Probability*. Durham, NC: Duke University Press, 2013.

Bachrach, Peter and Morton Baratz. "Two Faces of Power." *The American Political Science Review* 56 (1962): 950–62.

Balibar, Etienne, Ernesto Laclau, Chantal Mouffe and Christine Jones. *Politics and the Other Scene*. London: Verso, 2002.

Balme, Richard. *Les Politiques du Neo-Regionalisme*. Paris: Economica, 1998.

Bhabha, Homi K. "DissemiNation: Time, Narrative and the Margins of the Modern Nation." In *Nation and Narration*. Edited by Homi K. Bhabha, 291–322. New York: Routledge, 1990.

Bhabha, Homi K. *The Location of Culture*. New York: Routledge, 1994, pp. 139–70.

Bookchin, Murray. *Social Ecology and Communalism*. Oakland, CA: AK Press, 2006.

Bourdieu, Pierre. *Distinction: A Social Critique of the Judgement of Taste*. Translated by Richard Rice. Cambridge, MA: Harvard University Press, 1979.

Brenner, Neil. *New State Spaces: Urban Governance and the Rescaling of Statehood*. Oxford: Oxford University Press, 2004.

Brown, Douglas M. and Earl H. Fry, eds. *States and Provinces in the International Economy*. Berkeley: Institute of Governmental Studies and University of California Press, 1998.

Brunet-Jailly, Emmanuel. *Border Disputes A Global Encyclopaedia*. Los Angeles, CA: ABC-CLIO, 2014.

Brunet-Jailly, Emmanuel. *Borderlands*. Ottawa: University of Ottawa Press, 2007.

Brunet-Jailly, Emmanuel. "Cascadia in Comparative Perspective: Canada–US Relations and the Emergence of Cross-Border Regions." *Canadian Political Science Review* 2 (2008): 104–24.

Brunet-Jailly, Emmanuel. "Foreword: Beyond the Border Action Plan, a Context." *Canada United States Law Journal* 37 (2010): 273–88.

Brunet-Jailly, Emmanuel. "Globalization, Integration and Cross-Border Relations in the Metropolitan Area of Detroit (USA) and Windsor (Canada)." *International Journal of Economic Development* 2 (2000): 379–401.

Brunet-Jailly, Emmanuel. "In the Increasingly Global Economy, Are Borderland Regions Public Management Instruments?" *International Journal of Public Sector Management* 25 (2013): 483–91.

Brunet-Jailly, Emmanuel. "A Review of Cross-Border Cooperation in North America." In *Cross-Border Cooperation Structures in Europe*. Edited by Luis Dominguez and Iva Pires, 49–66. Brussels: P.I.E–Peter Lang, 2014.

Brunet-Jailly, Emmanuel and Martin John. *Local Government in the Global World*. University of Toronto Press, 2010.

Brunet-Jailly, Emmanuel and Anthony Payan. "A Canadian Perspective on European Cross Border Regions." In *Policy Research Initiative Working Papers* Series. Ottawa: Government of Canada, Policy Research Initiative. 2006.

Budowski, Gerardo. "Keynote Presentation: Transboundary Protected Areas as a Vehicle for Peaceful Co-operation." Paper prepared for the Workshop on Transboundary Protected Areas in the Governance Stream of the 5th World Park Congress, Durban, South Africa, September 12–13, 2003.

Buscher, Bram. *Transforming the Frontier: Peace Parks and the Politics of Conservation in Southern Asia*. Durham, NC: Duke University Press, 2013.

Castells, Manuel. *The Informational City: Information Technology, Economic Restructuring and the Urban-Regional Process*. Oxford: Basil Blackwell, 1989.

Chen, Xiangming. *As Border Bends: Transnational Spaces in the Pacific Rim*. Lanham, MD: Rowman and Littlefield, 2005.

Dahl, Robert. "The Concept of Power." *Behavioral Science* 2 (1957): 201–15.

Dahl, Robert. *Who Governs*. New Haven, CT: Yale University Press, 1961.

Davies, Norman. *Vanished Kingdoms: The History of Half-Forgotten Europe*. London: Allen Lane, 2011.

Dinan, Desmond. *The Politics of Persuasion*. Lanham, MD: University Press of America/Rowman and Littlefield, 1988.

Duchacek, Ivo, Daniel Latouche and Garth Stevenson, eds. *Perforated Sovereignties and International Relations: Trans-sovereign Contracts of Subnational Governments*. New York: Greenwood Press, 1988.

Duffy, Rosaleen. "Peace Parks and Global Politics: The Paradoxes and Challenges of Global Governance." In *Peace Parks: Conservation and Conflict Resolution*. Edited by Saleem H. Ali, 55–68. Cambridge, MA: MIT Press, 2007.

Greenwald, Glenn. *No Place to Hide: Edward Snowden, the NSA, and the U.S. Surveillance State*. Toronto: McClelland & Stewart, Division of Random House of Canada, 2014.

Huth, Paul. *Standing Your Ground: Territorial Disputes and International Conflicts*. Ann Arbor: University of Michigan Press, 1996.

Kantor, Paul with Stephen David. *The Dependent City*. Glenview, IL: Scott, Foresman and Company, 1988.

Keating, Michael. *Comparative Urban Politics: Power and the City in the United States, Canada, Britain and France*. Aldershot: Edward Elgar, 1991.

Keohane, Robert O. and Helen V. Milner. *Internationalization and Domestic Politics*. Cambridge: Cambridge University Press, 1996.

Lecumberri, Beatriz. "Los muros, una strategia geopolitica que alimenta la violencia." *La Republica*. October 28, 2006.

Mandel, Robert. "Roots of Modern Interstate Border Disputes." *Journal of Conflict Resolution*, 24 (1980): 427–54.

Martinez, Oscar. *Mexican-Origin People in the United States*. Tuscon: The University of Arizona Press, 2001.

Mollenkopf, John Hull. *The Contested City*. Princeton, NJ: Princeton University Press, 1983.

Newman, David and Ansi Paasi. "Fences and Neighbours in the Post Modern World: Boundary Narratives in Political Geography." *Progress in Human Geography*, 22 (1998): 186–207.

Ohmae, Kenishi. *The Borderless World: Power and Strategy in the Interlinked Economy*. New York: HarperCollins Publishers, 1999.

Peace Park Foundation—The Global Solution. *Limpopo National Park Issues 2013, Revenue Sharing Cheque to Park Communities*, June 9, 2014. www.peaceparks.org/news.php?pid=1365&mid=1410 &lid=1009. Accessed June 23, 2014.

Peterson, Paul E. *City Limits*. Chicago: University of Chicago Press, 1981.

Risse-Kappen, Thomas. *Bringing Transnational Relations Back In: Non-state Actors, Domestic Structures, and International Relations*. Cambridge: Cambridge University Press, 1995.

Sassen, Saskia. *Losing Control? Sovereignty in the Age of Globalization*. New York: Columbia University Press, 1996.

Saunders, Doug. *Arrival City, the Final Migration and Our Next World*. Toronto: Alfred-Knopf Canada, 2010.

Savitch, H. V. and Paul Kantor. *Cities in the International Market Place*. Princeton, NJ: Princeton University Press, 2002.

Spenceley, Anna and Michael Schoon. "Peace Parks as Social Ecological Systems: Testing Environmental Resilience in Southern Africa." In *Peace Parks: Conservation and Conflict Resolution*. Edited by Saleem H. Ali, 83–104. Cambridge, MA: MIT Press, 2007.

Staniland, Peter. "Defeating Transnational Insurgencies: The Best Offence Is a Good Fence." *The Washington Quarterly* (Winter 2005–6): 21–40.

Stone, Clarence N. *Regime Politics: Governing Atlanta*. Lawrence: University Press of Kansas, 1989.

Stone, Clarence N. and Heywood T. Sanders, eds. *The Politics of Urban Development*. Lawrence: University Press of Kansas, 1987.

The New Testament. "Lines In the Ground." (John 8:6).

The Terminal. Screenplay by Sacha Gervasi, available at http://screenplayexplorer.com/?tag=the-terminal-movie-script.

Van Houtum, Henk, Olivier Kramsch and Wolfgang Zierhofer. *B/Ordering Space.* Aldershot: Ashgate Publishing, 2005.

Wallstrom, Margot. "Taking the European Union Forwards: The Next 50 Years." Speech by vice president of the European Union responsible for institutional affairs and communication strategy. Lecture in front of the Netherlands Society for International Affairs, The Hague. 2007. SP07-144En. www.eu-un.europa.eu/articles/fr/article_6961_fr.htm.

Weizman, Eylal. *A travers les murs–l'architecture d'une nouvelle guerre urbaine.* Paris: la fabrique editions, 2008.

Woodwell, Douglas. "Unwelcome Neighbours: Shard Ethnicity and International Conflict during the Cold War." *International Studies Quarterly*, 48 (2004): 197–223.

Xie, Shaobo. "Writing on Boundaries: Homi Bhabha's Recent Essays." *ARIEL-A Review of International English Literature*, 27 (1996): 155–66.

Chapter Two

SOCIAL ECOLOGY AND TRANSBOUNDARY CONSERVATION: (RE)CONNECTING NATURE AND PEOPLE IN BORDERLANDS

Kevan Zunckel

Introduction

Much has been done about mainstreaming the concept of social ecology into biodiversity conservation and protected area management, with conservation practitioners embracing the need to enhance the relevance of their discipline within broader social, political and economic realms. The most demonstrable example is evident in the 5th International Union for the Conservation of Nature (IUCN) World Parks Congress, held in Durban, South Africa in 2003, with the theme "Protected Areas: Benefits beyond Boundaries," as well as its key messages,[1] among which were the calls for:

- A new deal for protected areas, local communities and indigenous peoples.
- A need to apply new and innovative approaches for protected areas, linked to broader agendas.

As challenging as it may seem for conservation practitioners to integrate these approaches into their work, it remains simple where this work falls within national jurisdictions. However, where multinational processes are required, the levels of complexity increase substantially, as does the relevance for the application of social ecological principles and thinking. The recently published IUCN World Commission on Protected Areas (WCPA) Best Practice Protected Area Guidelines Series No. 23, titled *Transboundary Conservation: A Systematic and Integrated Approach*,[2] states that approximately one-third of all terrestrial high biodiversity sites straddle national land borders, and it is therefore essential that neighboring states collaborate in their efforts to secure and protect these areas. While this statement still reflects a bio-centric bias, the Guidelines build on and expand the theme of the 5th IUCN World Parks Congress. They therefore serve as the basis from which this chapter has been compiled.

This chapter provides the reader with an indication of how transboundary conservation (TBC) may be used as a tool to facilitate social ecological processes and vice versa. It provides background information to contextualize TBC at the global scale before describing the principles and processes inherent in TBC initiatives, that is, what is necessary to get them going and to keep them going. Thereafter it provides insight into the linkages between the concept and social ecology before ending with thoughts and observations on the notion that TBC may be used as a mechanism to promote peace in border regions.

The Rationale for and Definitions of Transboundary Conservation

The statement regarding the number of high biodiversity sites that straddle national land borders serves to illustrate the importance of TBC initiatives, but is the tip of the iceberg. Boundaries, whether national or subnational, are determined through political processes, be these peaceful or negotiation through conflict, and history will show that they inevitably serve to secure sovereignty over resources such as land and minerals. As such there are many examples throughout the world where boundaries reflect scant regard and/or respect for ecosystems and ecological processes. While this was already evident with the prevalence of tribes and tribal wars between first nation peoples, it is likely that their hunter-gatherer basis for life served to link their boundaries to nature. However, as colonialism increased its grip on the world and land and resource-hungry so-called first world nations encroached on indigenous peoples' land, so the establishment of new boundaries became increasingly disconnected from nature, ecosystems and their processes. The dominance of the pioneering spirit inherent within the colonizing nations epitomized this disregard for nature and exacerbated the implications of poorly positioned boundaries.

The paradigm that prevailed in apartheid South Africa, and possibly holds true for many countries around the world even today, that good fences or boundaries make good neighbors, has served to entrench a sense of sovereignty and tunnel vision between nations. It is recognized that certain political dynamics may draw nations closer together such as the European and African Unions, but the sense of sovereignty persists together with political, economic, legal and often cultural differences that are superimposed onto and divide ecosystems and ecological processes affecting terrestrial, freshwater and marine environments and their associated species. With this division often comes different land management and use regimes that conflict and exacerbate the implications of the division.

The concept of TBC recognizes these realities and is intended to facilitate cooperation between nations that share common natural features as reflected in its definition as per Vasilijević and colleagues[3]: "Transboundary conservation is a process of cooperation to achieve conservation goals across one or more international boundaries." Within this definition is the recognition that there are a number of possible configurations depending on the extent of the ecosystems and natural features that have been divided, and their proximity to the boundaries concerned. This has resulted in the derivation of three types of TBC areas and one special designation, Parks for Peace, also called peace parks. First, there are the simple *transboundary protected areas* or TBPAs defined as "a clearly defined geographical space that includes protected areas that are ecologically connected across one or more international boundaries and which involves some form of cooperation." Then there are the more complex *TBC land and/or seascapes* or TBCL/Ss defined as "ecologically connected areas that include both protected areas and multiple resource use areas across one or more international boundaries and which involves some form of cooperation." Last, there are the *transboundary migration conservation areas* or TBMCAs, which are defined as "wildlife habitats in two or more countries that are necessary to sustain populations of migratory species and involve some form of cooperation."[4]

Global Trends and Distributions

It is unfortunate that there are no up-to-date data on the extent to which TBC initiatives have been established across the globe, but the work that has been done to track implementation of the concept does show linear growth as illustrated in Table 2.1. It is important to note that these data do not include all the transboundary types as defined earlier and, instead, focus on the TBPA configuration. It is therefore likely that an up-to-date and complete data set will show a substantially different, but still encouraging picture.

What is also interesting from the work of Lysenko and colleagues[5] is the global distribution of the TBPAs as illustrated in Figure 2.1. Here gaps appear in geographical distribution of TBC initiatives that need to be filled, or may be filled if the data set included all configurations, as well as those at a subnational level, of which there are numerous examples such as the Southern Appalachian Ecoregion in North America and the Great Eastern Ranges in Australia.[6] It would also be extremely useful if the data set could capture information such as how the initiatives were established, the participants involved and the roles they played and whether it was a top-down or bottom-up process.

Table 2.1 A record of data reflecting the extent and growth of transboundary conservation effort across the globe.

Author	Scope	Results
Thorsell and Harrison (1990)	Border parks	**70**
Zbicz and Green (1997)	Transfrontier protected area complexes	**136** (comprising 488 protected areas)
Zbicz (2001)	Internationally adjoining protected areas	**169** (comprising 666 protected areas)
Besançon and Savy (2005)	Internationally adjoining protected areas and other transboundary conservation initiatives	**188** (comprising 818 protected areas)
Lysenko et al. (2007)	Transboundary protected areas	**227** (comprising 3,043 protected areas)

Source: Vasilijević et al., 2015.

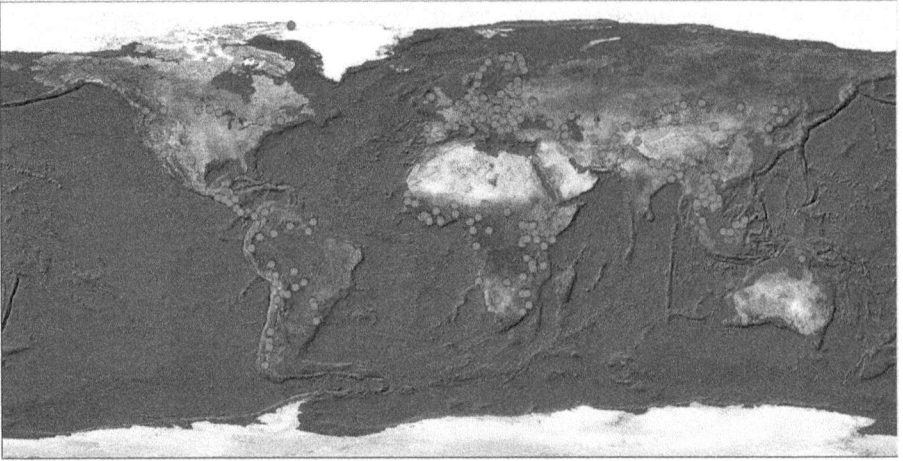

Figure 2.1 The global distribution of transboundary protected areas (TBPAs). *Source:* Lysenko et al., 2007.

The Principles and Processes to be Applied for Successful Transboundary Conservation Initiatives

Nature does very well without human interference, especially when this interference is driven at the rate and scale of that seen in what is being called the "great acceleration,"[7] that is, the period since the 1950s when industrialization and its related global impacts increased exponentially. The Demilitarized Zone, or DMZ, between the Democratic People's Republic of Korea (North) and the Republic of Korea (South), is a strip of land that is comprised of two-kilometer strips of no-man's land on either side of the boundary and in which there has been no human interference since 1953. In her book *Whispers of the DMZ*, Park (2013) documents nature's reclamation of this area, which was previously subjected to agriculture and related settlements.[8] Her book goes on to show how these self-restored natural features and ecosystems now present the two countries with an opportunity to establish a TBC area, possibly as a catalyst to peace and reunification.

While South Korea has been driving this process strongly for some time, its northern neighbors have not come to the table. These two extremes highlight the potential, but also the complex sociopolitical dynamics inherent in TBC processes and therefore the absolute necessity that they follow, and strongly reflect, social ecological principles on both sides of the DMZ. Perhaps the conservation of the Red-crowned Crane that Healy, Archibald and Westing highlight in Chapter 5 can serve as such a catalyst. Another avenue for the pursuit of "transboundary conservation diplomacy" could be the expansion of the Dorasan Peace Park, which is visible today by sparse signage on the South Korean side of the DMZ. While not a true peace park in the TBC sense of the term, Dorasan, as well as the reported briefing to international organization officials by South Korea at the January 2015 RAMSAR Convention Standing Committee meeting, could become catalysts for both North Korea and South Korea to create an ecological peace park. Creation of such a park has former South Korean president Park Geun-hye's support after she called for a World Peace Park along the DMZ during a joint session of the US Congress on May 8, 2014.[9]

Two excellent examples of where this has worked within the context of peace are the European Green Belt and the work being done by EcoPeace Middle East in the Jordan River Valley. While the latter has not yet succeeded in establishing a TBPA, its work across these troubled borders strongly reflects social ecological principles in that they are succeeding in reconnecting people divided across volatile political boundaries through their focus on a common dependence on a vital service that nature provides, namely, the provision of clean water.

The European Green Belt is a very large-scale TBC initiative. Stemming from the former east–west divide in Europe, the so-called Iron Curtain, it brings together 24 countries in a unique cooperative network aimed at creating an "ecological backbone" across Europe and supporting communities in their effort to cooperate and conserve nature across national boundaries.

Transboundary Conservation Principles: Building Trust, Confidence and Capacity

In order for people to engage constructively in TBC processes, they have to be willing to work outside of their geographic, institutional, social and cultural boundaries or silos. Such boundaries and silos provide safety and comfort, and it is necessary to draw people out of these familiar comfort zones and into places and dynamics that are hugely challenging, and at times intimidating and even confrontational. It is therefore essential that TBC processes are facilitated and managed in a way that allows for comfort zones to be challenged, but where the experience for the participants is ultimately one of positive growth within the context of cooperatively working toward a shared vision.

Inevitably, initiatives as complex and dynamic as these are driven by one or more champions who see the potential and the need for TBC and who take the first steps to pull the relevant participants together. Irrespective of the level at which a TBC initiative begins, that is, on the ground or from the top, it must embrace and be characterized by principles that work to create, maintain and strengthen bonds of trust between the participants. Some of the key principles that are essential to successful TBC work are listed and discussed briefly here.

Openness, honesty and transparency will help to work against the perception that conservation seeks to take land away from people and put up fences that will exclude them from access to the biodiversity, cultural heritage and other resources of the area in question. It is highly likely that these perceptions will persist and take some time to dispel, but this just serves to emphasize the need to make sure that all cards are on the table from the outset and are kept there at all times. Any break in confidence can set processes back and damage their credibility as well as that of those driving them. Such setbacks can prove costly in more ways than just financial.

Closely related to this is the need to avoid creating unrealistic expectations. This is particularly necessary where the champions are subjectively enthusiastic about their initiative and believe that they can deliver tangible benefits to all concerned. It is best to downplay any potential benefits and instead use the participant engagement processes to explore what these might be, and have the participants discover potential benefits themselves.

In terms of the participants who need to be engaged, it is essential that the processes be as inclusive as possible. In the early days of the transboundary negotiations between Mozambique, South Africa and Zimbabwe that led to the establishment of the Great Limpopo Transfrontier Park, the Peace Parks Foundation had produced a map of southern Africa depicting numerous potential TBC areas across the region without consultation with any of the countries affected. This was immediately perceived as a land-grabbing strategy and not well received—nor was the Peace Parks Foundation. Since then the Peace Parks Foundation has become a well-respected and highly effective catalyst for TBC in southern Africa, but this serves to illustrate the need for as much inclusiveness as possible from the outset. Many social ecologists and conservation managers now recognize the value of this inclusive strategy, which calls to mind Stuart Hill's writings that highlight the necessity for a sense of ownership in the process.

In order to accommodate the complex dynamics and large numbers and diversity of participants required to initiate, establish and manage TBC initiatives, the design of the process must include carefully crafted steps that work progressively but iteratively toward the ultimate goal. There must be a willingness to allow the process to return to previous steps where new information or perspectives indicate that amendments are required. This also speaks to the need for the process to be adaptable to receive this new information or new participants, or even to adjust its geographic scope.

What this highlights as well is the need for all participants, especially the champions, to be open to learn from each other. Participants come to these processes with different agendas, worldviews, perspectives, expectations and even fears, and when participants have the assurance that they can express themselves freely, they will gain confidence in the process as well as begin to drop their defenses and open themselves to learn from others. Such multi-stakeholder processes can be enriched by the application of this principle, which is particularly necessary where academic sciences come into contact with traditional knowledge systems. If participants know that they will all be treated equally, their willingness to contribute will be enhanced as will their capacity to learn from others.

An interesting perspective that illustrates this is the measure of poverty that is imposed on indigenous communities by the so-called first world. Why should a community who is subsisting happily off the land be considered poor? In fact, its members are probably happier than the first-world technocrats who are imposing this measure of well-being, and they are actually fully occupied in the implementation of their livelihood strategies. On a portion of land in South Africa known as the Wild Coast, the Xolobeni community is engaged in a battle against the South African government and an Australian mining company that wants to mine titanium from the dunes. Proponents of the mine are claiming that it will bring opportunities to the poor communities who live there, but the Xolobeni community claims that its land gives it all it needs and in fact, it has a rich existence.

As stated at the beginning of this section, these are some of the principles that need to be applied to TBC process, which implies that this list is not comprehensive. TBC champions will each bring their own styles and strengths to their processes, but they can use these principles as a checklist to ensure that their starting point at least has a solid foundation.

The Processes from Pre-feasibility, to Feasibility, to Implementation, to Evaluation

Application of these principles suggests that TBC processes need to be step-wise, iterative and adaptive, but just where these should start and what they should entail is discussed here. The IUCN WCPA Guidelines[10] provides a very detailed account of these processes that is based on work coming out of the protected area and conservation management literature.[11,12,13,14] Essentially, the steps put forward as global best practice provide for a cautious and objective approach designed to ensure that potential TBC initiatives are subjected to thorough pre-feasibility and feasibility testing before being taken into the implementation and development phases. This is to guarantee that initiatives are given the best chance of succeeding and for TBC champions to try to address the barriers to success, to enhance feasibility and retain credibility for the concept and its process. In this way, the champions and participants will develop an in-depth understanding and appreciation for the dynamics that are both within and beyond their control and/or influence, and tailor their processes accordingly.

It is acknowledged and understood that each TBC opportunity will present different permeations of natural, social, political and cultural dynamics and that these will dictate the best way by which to approach implementation. However, Table 2.2 captures the detailed thinking encapsulated in the IUCN WCPA Guidelines[15] and is presented here as

Table 2.2 The recommended stages and steps necessary to take a TBC initiative from concept to implementation.

WCPAs Framework	Context and Planning		Inputs and Processes	Outputs and Outcomes
Stages	**Diagnose**	**Design**	**Take Action**	**Evaluate**
Goals	**Determine the need for transboundary conservation**	**Match the process to the situation**	**Secure resources and implement actions**	**Learn and adapt**
Step 1	Identify if there is a compelling reason to act	Determine who should lead the effort	Assess the capacity to implement plans	Assess progress and outcomes
Step 2	Determine if there is a constituency for change	Mobilize and engage the right people	Develop an action plan	Determine if there is a need to continue
Step 3	Estimate the scope of the issue	Define the geographic extent	Secure financial sustainability	Adapt the management and action plans
Step 4	Estimate the capacity to work across boundaries	Negotiate a joint vision and develop management objectives	Implement the plans	Communicate progress

Source: Vasilijević et al., 2015.

a point of departure for those contemplating a TBC initiative, or for those who want to critically review an existing one.

With regards to the retrospective application of the Guidelines, the author was privy to an interesting situation regarding TBC work in and between the 12 member states that are part of the Southern African Development Community (SADC) in 2014. He was commissioned to compile the *TBC Best Practice Guidelines* for the SADC[16] and in the process tried to extract case studies reflecting application of best practice. This proved a difficult process as many of the SADC initiatives had preceded both these and the IUCN Guidelines and have been, and still are, strongly dependent on donor funding. One of these included a feasibility study that ironically concluded by recommending a donor conference.

What this illustrates is that the concept of TBC proves attractive to donors who are willing to invest large sums for medium-term projects. While this is hugely encouraging for those involved, it is unfortunately happening in the absence of objectively compiled long-term feasibility and business plans. The end result is that initiatives get going with great enthusiasm, but are unable to sustain themselves, especially where the participating countries lack the resources to integrate the initiatives into the appropriate institutions. This leads to the concept, and those involved driving it, losing credibility to the extent that it may have been better if nothing had been done in the first place.

This situation is not unique to southern Africa as is shown in the IUCN WCPA Guidelines. In preparation for the Section on "Assessing and securing financial sustainability," the IUCN WCPA's Transboundary Conservation Specialist Group was surveyed in relation to funding. The results from 53 initiatives from around the world showed that local, national and international NGOs are the second most important source of funding.[17] In addition, the survey revealed that one of the 10 most common obstacles or barriers to funding is the development of a donor-dependency culture that can severely compromise the long-term sustainability of any initiative.

However, while this paints a gloomy picture for TBC, this is simply because the conservation fraternity has been slow in coming to grips with the opportunities inherent within the concept. That is, when natural areas are maintained and ecosystems are enabled to function optimally, they produce and deliver a host of ecosystem goods and services that are of great direct and indirect value to people. A mountain of evidence shows that humanity's disregard for nature has dire consequences at the global scale to the extent that the earth has been pushed into the next geological time period, known as the Anthropocene.[18] This is a term used to describe the current geological period, starting from the eighteenth century when human activities began to impact global climate and ecosystems, as Brunet-Jailly discussed in Chapter 1 of this book.[19] This realization helps to highlight the value of nature, and it is up to TBC champions to embrace what may be termed as "Anthropocene thinking" and press the advantage home. Just exactly what this means is discussed further in the next section.

A Mechanism to Build Social Ecological Resilience

When a social ecological system is resilient, it has the capacity to absorb shocks, be these of human or natural causes, and to return to its original state.[20] Where this resilience has been compromised, it is likely that the same level of shocks will cause the system to move beyond the thresholds of its current desired state and into another that is less desirable, thus increasing the system's vulnerability to further shocks. This discussion serves to illustrate how the application of TBC processes can help to build the resilience of social ecological systems where these have been compromised by political boundaries.

The Evolution of Thinking within the Conservation Fraternity

First, it is appropriate to dwell briefly on the evolution that has taken place within the thinking of mainstream conservation, recognizing that not all conservationists are in accord with this. One may begin with the question as to why all the effort and focus on threatened species and ecosystems have not found traction with society in general, especially decision makers, as is evident by the negative trends related to the loss of biodiversity and ecosystem functionality globally.[21] The answer is likely to be that the conservation fraternity has failed to approach these challenges from the perspective of social ecological systems. In realization of this failing, the conservation fraternity has evolved from a position of excluding people with a focus on species, wilderness and protected areas, to a position where "people and nature" is the focus and environmental change, resilience, adaptability and socioecological systems dominate the discourse, as illustrated in Figure 2.2.[22]

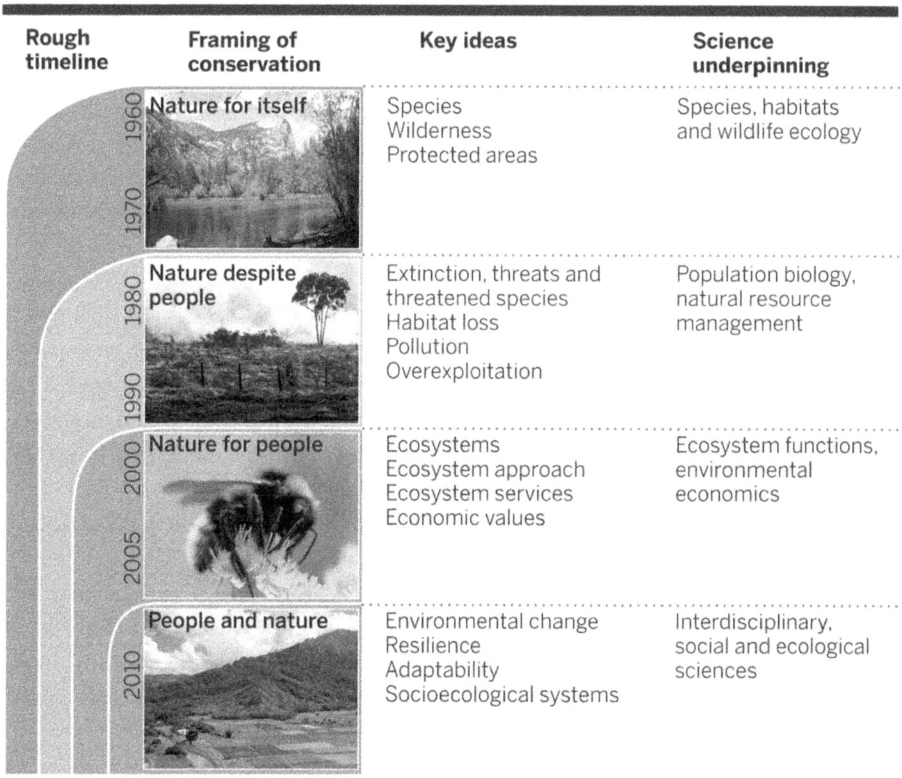

Rough timeline	Framing of conservation	Key ideas	Science underpinning
1960 / 1970	Nature for itself	Species Wilderness Protected areas	Species, habitats and wildlife ecology
1980 / 1990	Nature despite people	Extinction, threats and threatened species Habitat loss Pollution Overexploitation	Population biology, natural resource management
2000 / 2005	Nature for people	Ecosystems Ecosystem approach Ecosystem services Economic values	Ecosystem functions, environmental economics
2010	People and nature	Environmental change Resilience Adaptability Socioecological systems	Interdisciplinary, social and ecological sciences

Figure 2.2 An illustration of the evolving paradigms within the conservation fraternity over the past 50 years.
Source: Mace, 2014.

Importantly none of these paradigms has eclipsed the others, and therefore a complex "multiple framing" exists today, which often results in opposing schools of thought working against each other and adding to the complex dynamics of the social ecology around conservation, and especially TBC.

As one views the two more recent paradigms put forward by Mace[23] within the context of social ecological systems thinking, that is, "nature for people" and "people and nature," one may argue that little distinguishes them from each other, with the subtle shift in realigning the two and recognizing the need for a reconnection. However, the importance of the two paradigms is that they speak strongly to the opportunities that an ecosystem goods and services approach to understanding the full value of potential TBC initiatives brings to the discussion. As already discussed in a preceding section, poor financial viability characterizes many TBC initiatives around the world, and therefore it is essential that alternative approaches are found to turn this around.

Nature's Value to Society

At the risk of being too simple, it may be hypothesized that where TBC initiatives bring fragmented ecosystems together under an effective cooperative governance model, the capacity of these ecosystems to produce and deliver goods and services will be enhanced and therefore, so will their value to the beneficiaries. Since the Millennium Ecosystem Assessment (MEA)[24] succeeded in popularizing the concept and provided the definition that ecosystem services are simply the benefits people obtain from nature, it would appear that this hypothesis is not risky and that there is strength in its simplicity.

The MEA has provided to TBC champions a tool they can use together with their stakeholders to develop an understanding of the full suite of ecosystem goods and services that may be produced and delivered from a potential TBC initiative, who the beneficiaries of these services are or might be, the way in which the benefit is realized and the magnitude or relevance of the benefits. In this way, it is also possible for TBC champions to challenge their own way of thinking about an ecosystem and its associated species. While it may be the case that a certain species or suite of species are endangered and efforts to secure their persistence are not finding traction, by focusing instead on the ecosystem that hosts these species and the value of the ecosystem to people, it may be possible to obtain the necessary traction to secure the ecosystem and simply use the persistence of the endangered species as a measure of ecosystem functionality and thus enhance its capacity to deliver the goods and services that are of value to the beneficiaries.

An example that is often relevant in the case of ecosystems divided by international boundaries is that of their capacity to produce and deliver water, that is, where watersheds are shared between countries. Well-managed watersheds offer vital services such as a sustained supply of good-quality water, the attenuation of flood events, prevention of soil erosion and reduced sediment loads in water courses and dams and the maintenance of dry season baseflows,[25] not to mention food from sustained fish populations, cultural services such as recreation and spiritual values related to religious beliefs, reduced costs on health care due to reduced risks of waterborne diseases, to name but a few. The substantial values that ecosystem services have to contribute to human well-being are well illustrated by the MEA as captured in Figure 2.3.

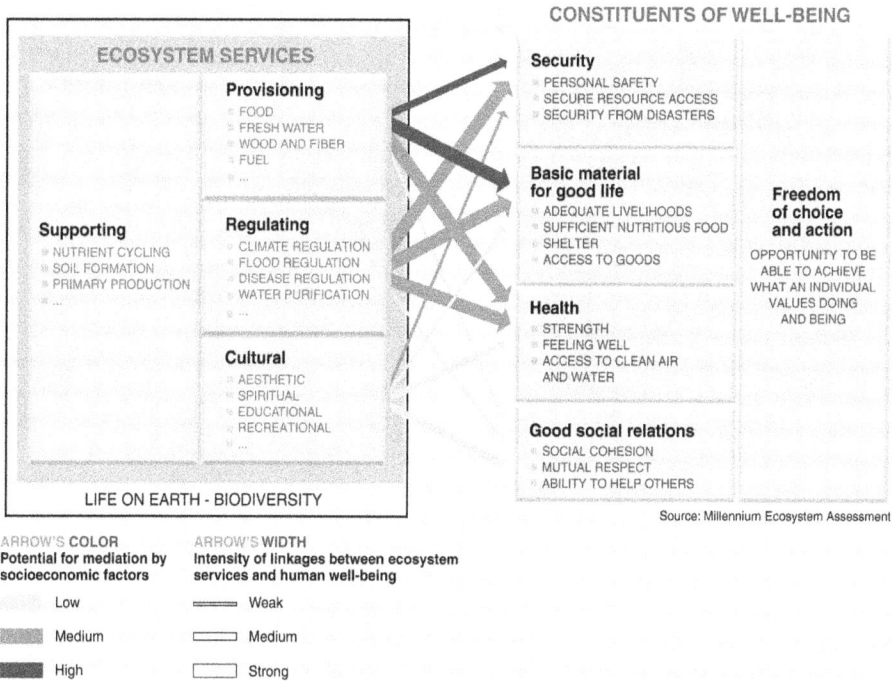

Figure 2.3 The relationship between ecosystem goods and services emanating from healthy, functioning ecosystems and human well-being.
Source: MEA, 2005.

It is important to highlight at this point that the value that this approach has in "selling" TBC to decision makers and stakeholders lies in the acceptance and application of social ecological thinking and in the linking of people back to nature for their own good. Where a business-as-usual approach persists, it is likely that other economic development or unsustainable land use options will prevail. Under these circumstances, it is unfortunate that nature will ultimately issue an invoice of costs to society and these will relate directly to increased vulnerabilities and shocks such as droughts, floods, tsunamis and disease outbreaks. However, where the social ecological paradigm and alternative measures of prosperity are embraced,[26] ecological and social resilience will be the outcome, irrespective of the quantification of an ecosystem goods and services assessment.

A Mechanism to Promote Peace in Border Regions

Among the benefits that may emerge from successful TBC initiatives is the notion that they may work to facilitate peace or to sustain political stability in volatile border regions. At one point in the history of TBC, the notion of peace parks (or Parks for Peace) was strongly promoted,[27] but the recent IUCN WCPA Guidelines[28] sees this as a special designation that may be applied to any of the three potential configurations discussed earlier in this chapter and is not a stand-alone TBC type. It is perhaps the unfortunate reality that political stability and peace are one of the more tenuous outcomes from a TBC process and that the achievement of conservation objectives will battle to hold sway over territorial disputes and conflicts. This is possibly most clearly demonstrated in the Korean DMZ, as alluded to earlier. Here the South Koreans have been hard at work for more than a decade, trying to have the DMZ established as a TBPA in the hope that it will catalyze reunification.[29] Thus far these efforts have not brought the North Koreans to the table, but perhaps in another decade or less, we will be able to look back and ascribe reunification to the TBC champions and this South Korean effort.

Another interesting case study is that of the Cordillera del Condor TBPA between Ecuador and Peru, whose establishment was an ongoing process over the period between 2002 and 2004. From a biodiversity perspective, it is held up as one of the richest and most diverse hotspots on the planet, but was subject to more than 150 years of conflict that ended in 1998; and, "after intense negotiation and the intervention of other countries (Argentina, Brazil, Chile, and the United States), a final agreement—the Acta Presidencial de Brasilia—was signed, finally resolving the border conflicts between the two countries."[30] This however had little to do with TBC effort, but the peace agreement did include a clause that paved the way for this in that it specified that bilateral cooperation between the two countries was to "aid the conservation of biological diversity and the sustainable use of the ecosystems of the common border."[31] What certainly does appear to be relevant to TBC and peace is that the channels of cooperation that have been opened for greater conservation efforts across the border and within this region of past conflict provide a platform from which lasting peace is built. The two countries have something to be proud of and to continue working toward, but it is an ongoing process that requires sustained effort with the following key areas of work identified:[32]

- Strengthen the planning processes and consolidate a binational vision.
- Promote an information network between protected areas within the Cóndor-Kutukú Conservation Corridor.
- Generate social, economic and biodiversity data to help prioritize conservation actions and sustainable development.
- Encourage a participatory process for the Cóndor-Kutukú Conservation Corridor.

These actions have been specifically listed here as they serve to illustrate important elements of the TBC processes as put forward by the IUCN WCPA Guidelines,[33] as well as the principles of a solid social ecological systems approach. If the TBC effort between Peru and Ecuador continues to enhance peaceful cooperation between the two countries, the peace park designation given to this TBC initiative will stand as a commemoration of the peace agreement.

The oldest TBPA, the Waterton-Glacier International Peace Park, was established in 1932 to celebrate the long-lasting peaceful relations between Canada and the United States and to further their friendship.[34] While no conflict situation was resolved through the establishment of the peace park, the designation has been used in a commemorative way, and perhaps within the context of social ecological systems, peace parks could be seen as proactive building blocks on which peace and political stability may be founded.

If people benefit from TBC and the establishment of cross-border conservation programs, whatever these may look like, then they will have a greater interest in the maintenance of peace. However, maintaining peace often comes at a price as illustrated by the fact that since 9/11, increased border restrictions between the United States and Canada have compromised previously enjoyed linkages between First Nations peoples with impacts on their ability to enhance their cultural similarities, thus highlighting the dynamic nature of TBC initiatives in the context of peace.

There is a school of thought that suggests that future conflicts will be over access to natural resources, especially water, but TBC offers a way in which these conflicts may be avoided. The work of the Friends of the Earth Middle East, as discussed earlier, demonstrates how the reconnection of divided nations to the value of collaboration around a shared resource such as water can actually facilitate peaceful coexistence. The same is true for the Southern African Development Community's (SADC) protocol on "shared water courses, where there is recognition for the need to work together towards the wise utilisation of this important commodity." The successful application of TBC as a tool to achieve this will, however, depend on the extent to which the champions, decision makers and participants understand and apply social ecological thinking and the principles discussed throughout this book.

NOTES

This author wishes to thank Maja Vasilijević, cochair of the Transboundary Conservation
  Specialist Group of the World Commission on Protected Areas of the IUCN, who provided
  valuable comments and feedback during the writing of this chapter.
1 IUCN Protected Areas Programme, "Management Planning for Natural World Heritage
  Properties" (Gland, Switzerland: IUCN, 2008), 35.
2 Maja Vasilijević, Kevan Zunckel, Matthew McKinney, Boris Erg, Michael Schoon and Tatjana
  Rosen Michel, *Transboundary Conservation: A Systematic and Integrated Approach. Best Practice Protected
  Area Guidelines*, Series No. 23 (Gland, Switzerland: IUCN, 2015), xii–107.
3 Ibid.
4 Ibid.
5 I. Lysenko, C. Besançon, and C. Savy, *UNEP-WCMC Global List of Transboundary Protected Areas*,
  2007, accessed on August 28, 2015, www.tbpa.net.
6 Ian Pulsford, David Lindenmayer, Carina Wyborn, Barbara Lausche, Maja Vasilijević and
  Graeme L. Worboys, "Connectivity Conservation Management," in *Protected Area Governance
  and Management*, ed. Graeme L. Worboys, Michael Lockwood, Ashish Kothari, Sue Feary and
  Ian Pulsford (Canberra, Australia: ANU Press, The Australian National University, 2015),
  851–88.
7 Will Steffen, Wendy Broadgate, Lisa Deutsch, Owen Gaffney and Cornelia Ludwig, "The
  Trajectory of the Anthropocene: The Great Acceleration," *The Anthropocene Review* (2015): 1–18
  (2015), accessed August 28, 2015, doi: 10.1177/2053019614564785.
8 Eun-Jin Park, *Whispers of the DMZ: All about the DMZ, a Symbol of Peace and Nature* (South Korea,
  Yeon Jun-hyug, 2013).
9 South Korea, Ministry of Foreign Affairs, *Diplomatic White Paper—2014* (Seoul: Ministry of
  Foreign Affairs, 2014), 44; Hyo-jin Kim, "Seoul Seeks International Support for DMZ Park
  Plan," *Korea Times*, January 26, 2015, accessed October 29, 2015, www.koreatimes.co.kr/
  www/news/nation/2015/01/116_172419.html.
10 Vasilijević, et al., *Transboundary Conservation*.

11 Adrian Phillips. Management Guidelines for IUCN Category V Protected Areas: Protected Landscapes/Seascapes (Gland, Switzerland and Cambridge: IUCN, 2002), xv–122.

12 Marc Hockings, Sue Stolton, Fiona Leverington, Nigel Dudley and José Courrau. *Evaluating Effectiveness: A Framework for Assessing Management Effectiveness of Protected Areas.* 2nd edition (Gland, Switzerland and Cambridge: IUCN, 2006): xiv–105.

13 IUCN Protected Areas Programme, 2008.

14 Matthew J. McKinney and Shawn Johnson. *Working across Boundaries: People, Nature, and Regions* (Cambridge, MA: Lincoln Institute of Land Policy and Center for Natural Resources and Environmental Policy, 2009).

15 Vasilijević, et al., *Transboundary Conservation.*

16 Kevan Zunckel, *Southern African Development Community Transfrontier Conservation Guidelines: The Establishment and Development of TFCA Initiatives between SADC Member States.* Guidelines compiled by Kevan Zunckel of Zunckel Ecological & Environmental Services in collaboration with the SADC TFCA Network (Gaborone, Botswana: SADC, 2014).

17 Vasilijević, et al., *Transboundary Conservation.*

18 Steffen, et al., "The Trajectory of the Anthropocene."

19 Ibid..

20 Johan Rockström and Mattias Klum, *The Human Quest: Prospering within Planetary Boundaries* (Stockholm: Langenskiöld, 2012).

21 Steffen, et al., "The Trajectory of the Anthropocene."

22 M. Georgina Mace, "Whose Conservation?" *Science* 345 (2014): 1558–60.

23 Ibid.

24 Millennium Ecosystem Assessment, Ecosystems and Human Wellbeing: Current State and Trends (2005), accessed on August 30, 2015, http://www.millenniumassessment. org/en/ Condition.aspx.

25 Julia Martin-Ortega, Robert C. Ferrier, Iain J. Gordon and Shahbaz Khan, *Water Ecosystem Services: A Global Perspective* (International Hydrology Series) 1st Edition (Cambridge: Cambridge University Press, 2015).

26 Tim Jackson, *Prosperity without Growth? The Transition to a Sustainable Economy* (Cardiff, Wales: Sustainable Development Commission, 2009).

27 Trevor Sandwith, Claire Shine, Lawrence Hamilton and David Sheppard, *Transboundary Protected Areas for Peace and Co-operation* (Gland, Switzerland and Cambridge: IUCN, 2001), xi–111.

28 Vasilijević, et al., *Transboundary Conservation.*

29 Park, *Whispers of the DMZ.*

30 Martín Alcalde, Carlos F. Ponce and Yanitza Curonisy, "Peace Parks in the Cordillera del Cóndor Mountain Range and Biodiversity Conservation Corridor," accessed on August 31, 2015, www.tropicalforests.ch/files/projects/PD_02_00_article_2005.

31 Ibid.

32 Ibid.

33 Vasilijević, et al. *Transboundary Conservation.*

34 Ibid.

BIBLIOGRAPHY

Alcalde, Martín, Carlos F. Ponce and Yanitza Curonisy. "Peace Parks in the Cordillera del Cóndor Mountain Range and Biodiversity Conservation Corridor." Accessed on 31 August 2015. www.tropicalforests.ch/files/projects/PD_02_00_article_2005.

Hockings, Marc, Sue Stolton, Fiona Leverington, Nigel Dudley and José Courrau. *Evaluating Effectiveness: A Framework for Assessing Management Effectiveness of Protected Areas.* 2nd edition. Gland, Switzerland and Cambridge: IUCN, 2006.

IUCN Protected Areas Programme. *Management Planning for Natural World Heritage Properties*. Gland, Switzerland: IUCN, 2008.

Jackson, Tim. *Prosperity without Growth? The Transition to a Sustainable Economy*. Cardiff, Wales: Sustainable Development Commission, 2009.

Kim, Hyo-jin. "Seoul Seeks International Support for DMZ Park Plan," *Korea Times*, January 26, 2015. Accessed October 29, 2015. www.koreatimes.co.kr/www/news/nation/2015/01/116_172419.html.

Lysenko I., C. Besançon and C. Savy. *UNEP-WCMC Global List of Transboundary Protected Areas*, 2007. Accessed August 28, 2015. www.tbpa.net.

Mace, Georgina M. "Whose Conservation?" *Science* 345 (2014): 1558–60.

Martin-Ortega, Julia, Robert C. Ferrier, Iain J. Gordon and Shahbaz Khan. *Water Ecosystem Services: A Global Perspective* (International Hydrology Series) 1st Edition. Cambridge: Cambridge University Press, 2015.

McKinney, Matthew, J. and Shawn Johnson. *Working across Boundaries: People, Nature, and Regions*. Cambridge, MA: Lincoln Institute of Land Policy and Center for Natural Resources and Environmental Policy, 2009.

Millennium Ecosystem Assessment. *Current State and Trends Assessment: Ecosystems and Human Wellbeing*. (2005). Accessed August 30, 2015. www.millenniumassessment.org/en/Condition.aspx.

Park, Eun-Jin. *Whispers of the DMZ: All about the DMZ, a Symbol of Peace and Nature*. Goyang City, Gyeonggi-do, South Korea: Wisdom House, 2013.

Phillips, Adrian. *Management Guidelines for IUCN Category V Protected Areas: Protected Landscapes/ Seascapes*. Gland, Switzerland and Cambridge: IUCN, 2002.

Pulsford, Ian, David Lindenmayer, Carina Wyborn, Barbara Lausche, Maja Vasilijević and Graeme L. Worboys. "Connectivity Conservation Management." *In Protected Area Governance and Management*, edited by Graeme L. Worboys, Michael Lockwood, Ashish Kothari, Sue Feary and Ian Pulsford, 851–88. Canberra, Australia: ANU Press, The Australian National University, 2015.

Rockström, Johan and Mattias Klum. *The Human Quest: Prospering within Planetary Boundaries*. Stockholm: Langenskiöld, 2012.

Sandwith, Trevor, Claire Shine, Lawrence Hamilton and David Sheppard. *Transboundary Protected Areas for Peace and Co-operation*. Gland, Switzerland and Cambridge: IUCN, 2001.

Steffen, Will, Wendy Broadgate, Lisa Deutsch, Owen Gaffney and Cornelia Ludwig. "The Trajectory of the Anthropocene: The Great Acceleration." *The Anthropocene Review*, 1–18 (2015). Accessed August 28, 2015. DOI: 10.1177/2053019614564785.

South Korea. Ministry of Foreign Affairs. *Diplomatic White Paper—2014*. Seoul: Ministry of Foreign Affairs, 2014.

Thomas, Lee and Julie Middleton. *Guidelines for Management Planning of Protected Areas*. Gland, Switzerland and Cambridge: IUCN, 2003.

Vasilijević, Maja, Kevan Zunckel, Matthew McKinney, Boris Erg, Michael Schoon and Tatjana Rosen Michel. *Transboundary Conservation: A Systematic and Integrated Approach. Best Practice Protected Area Guidelines*. Series No. 23, Gland, Switzerland: IUCN, 2015. https://portals.iucn.org/library/sites/library/files/documents/PAG-023.pdf.

The World Conservation Union–IUCN. "2003 Durban World Parks Congress." *Parks: The International Journal for Protected Area Managers*, 14 (2004): 1–57. Gland, Switzerland: World Commission on Protected Areas (WCPA) of IUCN–The World Conservation Union.

Zunckel, Kevan. *Southern African Development Community Transfrontier Conservation Guidelines: The Establishment and Development of TFCA initiatives between SADC Member States*. Guidelines compiled by Kevan Zunckel of Zunckel Ecological & Environmental Services in collaboration with the SADC TFCA Network. Gaborone, Botswana: SDAC, 2014.

Chapter Three

SOCIAL ECOLOGIES AND STRUCTURAL VIOLENCE: BOUNDARY-MAKING AS NATURE-MAKING IN A GATED GLOBE

Hilary Cunningham and Stephen Bede Scharper

Introduction: Boundary-Making as Nature-Making

This chapter builds on the idea that borders, boundaries and boundary-making are central to a social ecology approach—in terms of how we perceive nature, as well as how we understand natural and human-mediated biophysical processes. At a broad level, it could be argued that the Western legacy of compartmentalizing (e.g., bordering) the world into earth, air, fire and water underlies the nature–society binary itself.[1] Yet by insisting that we see nature and society as complexly interrelated, as well as all social and environmental issues as mutually embedded, social ecology challenges this dualistic legacy and invites a profound redrawing of nature–society boundaries. Additionally, social ecology's emphasis on justice, vulnerability, contingency and compassion provides a key—and, we argue, a *critical*—area of engagement for border studies.

Happily, as this volume attests, the project of redrawing nature–society boundaries appears to be surfacing with some vigor in recent border scholarship, prompting the field to engage more directly with interdisciplinary ways of thinking—especially across some of those tough epistemological divides that are often ignored or discounted when scholars remain firmly siloed within a discipline's parameters. This is particularly true of the border scholarship that is reaching out to ecology as a primary interlocutor. One noteworthy example is the University of Victoria's Borders in Globalization (BIG) project and its adoption of the Stockholm Resilience Center's (SRC) concept of a "planetary boundaries framework" as a guiding principle (i.e., a remapping of the planet in terms of its earth systems).[2] In so doing, BIG interdisciplinary border scholars have adopted a framework in which the traditional geopolitical borders of nation-states are contextualized within large environmental processes. The project now includes research on how atmospheric, terrestrial and aqueous phenomena might be integrated into the study of borders.[3]

Additional conceptual developments within border studies involve engagement with post-human ecology and its insistence on a relational approach to all beings (human and other-than-human). This has led, in some cases, to the reconceptualization of border environments and border zones as the "collective performances" of "embodied actors" (including not only security agents and human migrants, but also landscapes and endangered species).[4]

This turn to ecology within border studies, then, although still largely incipient, demonstrates the growing recognition that any discussion of cross-border management and governance cannot be treated outside of the deeply contingent ecological contexts that make up our now threatened planet.[5] A social ecology approach, therefore, challenges border scholars to step beyond merely thinking of society and nature integratively. Rather, this approach (following Murray Bookchin) embraces social ecology's original, emancipatory vision of just and harmonious relationships among, between and amid human and nonhumans, and trains a critical lens on existing border practices inimical to that vision.

A Sense of Urgency

Many scholars, policy makers and activists within border studies are experiencing a sense of urgency about the central role of borders and boundary-making in today's most pressing social and ecological issues. There is increasing recognition that the world's most urgent ecological problems run along the same fault lines of poverty, displacement, food insecurity, violent political upheaval and deteriorating health. Whether we are discussing climate change, ocean acidification or biodiversity loss, border scholars are recognizing that the real and future impacts of these ecological problems are not only global in scope, but also stratified in impact. Clearly, the planet's most vulnerable human and nonhuman populations are on the frontlines of social marginalization *and* ecological destruction. Loss of livelihood for millions of humans and loss of habitat for thousands of species of flora and fauna are now a growing, combined reality. It is for this reason that a social ecology approach to borders asks us to stay particularly attuned to those border landscapes in which the social and the ecological come together in highly consequential and contingent ways.

In this chapter, we explore the effects and implications—both social and ecological—of security fencing and border walls as a specific kind of (fortified) border landscape and as a landscape in which human/nonhuman suffering and environmental degradation interface in critical ways. While we include a discussion of how security fencing (as an expanding strategy for controlling illegal migration at international borders) generates both negative social and ecological impacts, we also discuss security fencing as a "nature-in the-making"—one in which security is the reigning constant and allows the bracketing off of the social and ecological costs of border walls, especially for the vulnerable humans and nonhuman populations most adversely affected by them. We develop the analytic of "edge effect" here—a scientific concept borrowed from biology and ecology—to incorporate a more ecologically politicized framework for thinking about security fencing, as well as to underscore the importance of an ecologically informed and engaged critical border studies.

Security Fencing

Whatever their geographical location, most of these walls are built out of a desire for security or to restrict migratory movements or smuggling. [...] Whether brick-built, fortified, electrified or militarized, these walls have the common objective of reinforcing a territorial limitation in order to control or even prevent the circulation of people.[6] (Lavorel quoted in *Borders, Fences and Walls: State of Insecurity?* p. 159)

In contemporary terms, "border wall" or "border barrier" describes a particular mode of partitioning at international borders. Such "walls" usually consist of fortified barricading (either continuous or segmented), and are intended to "seal off" a portion of the border so that people wishing to cross cannot do so without government inspection or permission. A border wall may include virtual as well as physical aspects such as cameras and sensor technology, multilayered fencing, antivehicle ditches, patrol roads on both sides of the barrier and exclusion areas (i.e., wide swaths of cleared land).

Morocco's "berm," for example, built from 1981 to 1987 and spanning an astounding 1,677 miles/2,700 km across the western Sahara, consists of a series of walls (usually 3 ft./1 m in height) made of sand and stone, with military bases, outposts and airfields spread out in intervals along the berm. (Much of the berm is also lined with landmines.) Israel's controversial "separation barrier" with Palestine (begun in April 2002 and projected to extend 430 miles/700 km when completed) has multilayered steel fencing, as well as concrete barricades (the latter up to 26 ft./8 m in height). Segments of the partition are also electrified and include exclusion zones that are 196 feet (60 m) wide on the Palestinian side of the border. Likewise, Spain's Melilla and Ceuta border fences (renovated in 2005 after thousands of sub-Saharan migrants climbed the fence in an attempt to enter Spain) include parallel, razor-wired fencing with a road running between the two barriers for patrol vehicles, as well as an underground system of cables connecting stadium lighting and motion detectors. The United States' post 9/11 "border wall" with Mexico (mandated by the 2006 Secure Fence Act) consists of several segmented portions of both virtual and reinforced fencing, with different kinds of barriers used to prevent pedestrian and vehicular traffic.

Security Fencing in a "Borderless" World

As geographer Elisabeth Vallet has noted, reinforced walls of the type just described are hardly a "new" feature of the human landscape. From the erecting of the Great Wall of China in the third century BCE, to Poland's Silesian Walls of the fifteenth century, to the Berlin Wall of the mid-twentieth century, "border fences" have been a constant in international relations.[7] Despite this historical legacy, however, the September 2001 terrorist attacks in the United States clearly have given the "border wall" new life. Today, highly fortified borders have assumed a signal saliency in post-9/11 social and ecological landscapes.

Such was certainly not the predicted trend for the twenty-first century, which many pundits prophesied would be the era of the post-national state and the concomitant decline in the importance of its territorial borders.[8] Some scholars, too, suggested that borders walls would give way to other security configurations. John Torpey's groundbreaking work on the passport (2000), for example, reflected on new twenty-first-century modes of "gating": his study explored the changing trajectory of state surveillance through a detailed and engaging history of the passport and the evolution of novel integrated surveillance technologies (e.g., new registration systems, improved personal identification techniques and new identity and travel documents), all of which enabled states to distinguish who "belonged" and who didn't with much greater "reach." Arguing that documentary controls were undergoing constant strengthening and rationalization, Torpey was not alone in speculating that *in the future* we might see a return to the private regulation of movement, one "rooted in the ownership of property within well-fortified and privately policed enclaves."[9] Walls, he suggested (referencing geopolitical borders and pointing to the 20,000 gated community enclaves in the United States in 2000, "up from a near zero figure only thirty-five years ago"),[10] might be giving way to more diversified surveillance technologies.

Scholars such as Torpey were certainly prescient in speculating that state surveillance would indeed generate many new forms of tracking, monitoring and managing human movement. But requiems for the so-called old-style fortified borders proved premature. These have not only persisted well into the twenty-first century—as we detail in this chapter—but in actual fact have dramatically proliferated alongside these other forms of state surveillance, especially in the past two decades.

The security fence's resilience and downright "popularity," not only at the US–Mexico border, in the Middle East, or in its proliferation throughout Europe in response to the Syrian refugee crisis, has been confounding for border scholarship, especially given that the field made a concerted effort to shift away from earlier conceptions of states as static, bounded entities in order to view them in more varied and undulating terms. Such a development was to provide a way to explore the state's permeable boundaries, as well as to interrogate the complex dynamics connecting margins and peripheries to centers.[11] Border zones, borderlands and border regimes,[12] for example, are some of the recent frameworks that have been developed to reflect the dually plastic and edge-like effects of state borders. Such concepts have also emphasized the fragmented nature of state sovereignty and allowed scholars to reconceptualize territorial borders as components within a much larger security toolkit consisting of (in addition to fortified fencing) stricter visa controls, accelerated deportations and forced returns. As a result, a nation's interior spaces can be seen as intricately connected to its edges through a network of security practices, as happened in the United States:

> [I]t is not only the borderline that became subject to an aggressive securing but also the [US] homeland's points of transit (airports, bus terminals, train stations, and subways), typically located in urban centers, as well its approach to immigration itself. The "border," it seems, has come to reside throughout the U.S. homeland—at both its edges and in its cities—so that the subway car (where one might just see something) apparently requires the same kind of vigilance as does a port of entry.[13]

Yet the stubborn presence of the highly fortified and securitized "border wall" well into the twenty-first century has raised questions about not only the resilience of a state's territorial edges, but also the possibility of a novel border formation. Does the border wall represent a unique "post-Westphalian" formation, incorporating features that are distinct from the ways in which earlier fortified borders operated? Is it better to think of these walls in *global* rather than national terms, particularly given that the fortified walls of the late twentieth and early twenty-first centuries have been spawned in the age of globalization?[14] Or is it better to view these border walls as cultural texts, landscapes of exclusion, that embody the deep anxieties (and fantasies) of a society governed through and coalescing around new security subjectivities?[15]

Security Fencing in a Bordering World: Walls and Gates

In 2007, Mike Davis used the term the "great wall of globalization" to describe the enclosed character of our newly globalizing world, one in which human movement was becoming increasingly stratified and dangerous, if not impossible, for migrants from the Global South. Cunningham (2004), arguing that international borders were playing the dual role of providing increased mobility for elites while denying mobility to the world's most impoverished populations, used the term "gated globe" to capture a similar dynamic.[16] From today's growing count of security fences, both of these metaphors seem apt.

As of this writing, there are approximately 65 fortified borders worldwide. Recent examples of border walls include Brazil's 2013 plan to build a 10,000-mile (16,000 km) virtual security fence, equipped with satellite technology, electromagnetic signaling, drone surveillance and an increased military presence.[17] In June 2015, the Hungarian government began construction of a 13-foot (4 m) fence along its 109-mile (177 km) border with Serbia (principally to prevent thousands of Syrian, Afghan and Iraqi migrants attempting to enter the country through Balkan land routes). Likewise in September 2015, the Bulgarian government—also citing illegal immigration and threats of terrorism—announced that it had completed 19 miles (31 km) of a projected 80 miles (129 km) of fortified fencing at its border with Turkey. In April 2015, after an attack at Garissa University by an anti-Christian militia, the Kenyan government began construction of a 440-mile (708 km) barricaded wall along its border with Somalia. Likewise, Saudi Arabia began construction of a 1,700 km (1,056 mile) fortified border with Yemen. Iran is currently erecting a 435-mile (700 km) fence along its border with Pakistan, and in September 2015, Malaysia and Thailand announced plans to build a common wall between the two nations.[18] Meanwhile, the Indian government is continuing its construction of fortified fencing at its borders with Bangladesh and Afghanistan—if it is ever finished, the latter will represent the longest security fence in the world: 2,500 miles (4,023 km).

Perhaps one of the most perplexing and disturbing features of these security fences or border walls is their remarkable increase in the first decades of the twenty-first century. After the Berlin Wall was razed (1989) and the Cold War declared to have come to an end (1991), there were 12 fortified borders internationally.[19] This means that—if we take 65 as a current total—there are now 53 more security borders than there were a quarter of a century ago—an almost fivefold increase. Equally disquieting (as we have alluded to) is the fact that increased security fencing has emerged alongside widespread claims that "we" are becoming a "borderless globe." The Schengen Agreement and the subsequent Maastricht Treaty (1992), for example, promised that the elimination of passport controls and border checkpoints among signatory states would generate greater freedom of movement for people, goods, services and capital. Instead, it has generated what many have referred to as Fortress Europe and a shift in emphasis to fortifying the external borders of the European Union, a development that has placed undue pressure on the EU's southern tier states to adopt security fencing. (These trends have only deepened since Britain's June 2016 Brexit vote.) Similarly, proponents of the North American Free Trade Agreement (NAFTA) (1994) claimed that trade and investment liberalization would bring greater cross-border economic prosperity to Mexico, Canada and the United States. Yet, beginning in 1993, the United States began an aggressive fencing off of its southern border with Mexico at high-traffic areas. Moreover, between 2006 and 2011 (according to US Department of Homeland Security data), 350 miles (563 km) of pedestrian fencing as well as 299 miles (481 km) of vehicle barriers were built as deterrents to illegal immigration. With the November 2016 election of Donald Trump, the campaign promise to build a wall across the *entire* US–Mexico border awaits implementation.

Fortified borders, then—often consisting of the multiple fences, trenches, watchtowers and death strips in the style of the Berlin Wall—have not receded, but in fact have proliferated at an astonishing rate. They have often done so often either alongside or in conjunction with widespread economic shifts to trade and investment liberalization as well as virulently racist anti-immigrant rhetoric. It appears, then, that the forecasted "borderless world" has indeed turned out to be a "gated globe."

Security Fencing as Structural Violence

With very few exceptions,[20] human and nonhuman actors, as well as a wide range of ecological habitats, are increasingly imperiled by the proliferation of security fencing. Yet to bring an ecological dimension to what are increasingly scenes of terrible human tragedy is not merely to add a variable: human displacement, migration and security fencing form a *social ecology* in which both the causes and patterns of human displacement come together in a border landscape—that is, one in which the social exclusions fostered by security fencing simultaneously generate ecological degradation. Given current and future trends of security fencing (including the standardization of its architectural features and policing strategies), these kinds of border walls might well be considered structural or institutionalized forms of social and ecological violence. Although structural violence concepts have focused on the systematic ways in which structures and institutions generate harm or disadvantage for human individuals, security fencing also points to some of the systematic ways in which the nonhuman world also suffers marginalization. We do not suggest, however, that nonhuman suffering is merely a "parallel" marginalization; rather we discern an integrated human/nonhuman "edge effect" in which socio-ecological degradation is constituted in and through the sociopolitical reality of security fencing.

Edge Effects: Reframing Human Displacement as Social Ecology

"Edge effect" is a concept we borrow from biology and ecology describing "the influences two bordering communities have on one another in a transitional area or eco-tone" (see also Cunningham 2012: 383). While these dynamics, ecologically speaking, can be quite complex, we highlight "edge effect" here as a way toward a more accountable (and hence critical and politicized) ecologically oriented border politics. An edge-effect analytic underscores that all borderscapes (and especially security walls) are not only generative of and generated by human–nonhuman "relations," but also engender highly differential, unequal and interconnected realities for both humans and nonhumans. The edge effects we focus on here are namely results of the profound vulnerabilities and tragedies that both precede and are intensified at these proliferating "edges" of our globe.[21]

Displacement: From "Homelessness" to "Globelessness"

Violent wars, economic collapse, ecologically devastated landscapes, species precarity and extinction and massive human flight are all factors connected to the rise and proliferation of security fencing. As we write this chapter, 4.8 million Syrian refugees have either sought or are seeking asylum after fleeing their country owing to civil war. (This is in addition to the 6 million internally displaced Syrians.) Thousands of other individuals and families are fleeing wars, poverty and persecution or environmental degradation in Libya, South Sudan, Eritrea, Nigeria, Iraq, Afghanistan, Kosovo, the Ukraine, Bangladesh and Myanmar. According to the UN High Commission on Refugees (UNHCR)'s *2015 Global Trends Report*, worldwide human displacement is at its highest level ever recorded: it is now 59.5 million people, up from 37.5 million a decade ago. Moreover, half of all displaced persons are children and 86 percent are from regions regarded as economically less developed. The UNHCR report underscores that globally one in every 122 humans is a refugee, internally displaced or seeking asylum.[22] Moreover, since 2008, environmental refugees now outnumber political refugees.[23]

The sheer magnitude of these figures is staggering, and it perhaps comes as no surprise that many of the twenty-first century's fortified borders coincide with migration routes.[24] Faced with a growing number of refugees, Bulgaria's new 80-mile (129 km) security fence (mentioned previously) was deliberately announced as an anti-migration measure. Similarly, in October 2015, Macedonia's foreign minister, Nikola Poposki, under pressure from other EU states, publicly discussed the need for "either soldiers or a fence […] or a combination of the two" as projections of asylum seekers for his country reached 4,000 daily.[25] Three months earlier, French and British authorities had announced the creation of a new "command and control" center in Calais, the French port at the mouth of the Channel Tunnel where thousands of asylum seekers gather and to "hitch" rides on the Chunnel trains. (Britain has agreed to finance a 9-foot × 2.74 m fence at that at the Eurotunnel railhead—flood lighting, mobile policing units, detection dogs and closed-circuit television are among the proposed security measures.) Such developments suggest that while displacement of human populations may begin with "homelessness" (as loss of both domicile and residency rights connected to a national jurisdiction), a new form of "globelessness" is increasingly characterizing the predicament of millions. In short, through aggressive and militarized border regimes, these security fences are the ultimate expression of disdain for vast swaths of the human community who are quickly becoming "planetary pariahs"—"unwelcome" *wherever* they attempt to settle and literally without a place on the globe.

Fatal Journeys

Border walls have been deeply implicated in the increased number of human fatalities on a number of fronts. While tracking the number of human lives lost during migration is a difficult and complex task, current estimates suggest 37,000 migrant border-related deaths occurred between 1996 and 2014 (based on seven regions).[26] Europe's external borders have registered the highest numbers (22,394 for the years 2000–14) with the US–Mexico border registering the second highest numbers (6,029 for the years 1998–2013).[27] According to the International Organization of Migration (IOM), 65 percent of migrants who died in transit during these periods came from Africa and the Middle East.[28]

The authors of this chapter first became aware of the tragic social costs of security fencing during their fieldwork at the US–Mexico border (1994–2009), a period that saw the construction of walled borders at four "high-traffic" points between Texas and California. The principal idea behind this style of border enforcement—termed "prevention through deterrence"—was to "plug" the major, trans-border cities[29] where the number of illegal crossings were high, and then let the harsh geography of the surrounding area "do the rest."[30] Post-9/11 security fencing, mandated, as noted earlier, by the US Congress through the Secure Fence Act (2006), expanded the border wall to 700 miles (1,127 km) of barricading.

Although the new security fencing has made illegal crossing at these points much more difficult, little evidence has surfaced to support the deterrence thesis.[31] It appears that migrants now take new "routes" through more remote areas of the desert where—often without proper food, clothing and water supplies, and in the hands of trafficking mafias—migrants are continuing to die. According to US Border Patrol statistics, the remains of at least 300 migrants have been found *annually* on the US side of the border since 2000. This pattern of migrant mortality has held firm despite a significant decrease in Border Patrol apprehensions for the same period.[32]

A similar pattern also characterizes Europe's current refugee crisis, as thousands of migrants opt for highly dangerous sea voyages in order to bypass the fortified fencing and stricter policing of terrestrial crossing points. The International Organization for Migration, for example, reported that 680,928 people had arrived in Europe by sea in 2015; at least 3,175 others had died or had gone missing in the attempt.[33]

Borders as Biotic Meeting Places

While escalating human fatalities provide compelling evidence of the underside of security fencing and border walls, Cunningham (2012) has explored a broader rubric for rethinking how socially inscribed boundaries might be re-envisioned across more ecologically informed conceptions of transboundary space (and time). She notes that borders are always located within "a complex set of relations with 'nature'":

> While nature always is—like a border or a boundary—a discursive formation produced in the context of many different kinds of human practices, natural systems themselves (as ecologists underscore) are also made up of complex kinds of boundaries, territorializations and agencies.[34]

Because all international borders map across and often utilize natural features, they are uniquely ecological as well as social sites. These borders therefore should be seen as biotic meeting places, that is, sites in which viruses, species and habitats (to name a few) intersect with patterns of human migration, commerce, security, tourism and governance.[35] International borders, however, can also be biotically fractured in that, as built environments, they can, for example, adversely impact not only a species' habitat, but also partition a species' reproductive geography, as well as impede access to food and water.

Although a growing body of research has focused on transboundary conservation issues (e.g., Busch 2007; Duffy 2007; Ramutsindela 2007; Wolmer 2003), comprehensive studies of the ecological footprint of security installations are few in number. Recently, however, important studies of the impact of security fencing on wildlife have been published, documenting the often adverse and frequently devastating effects of border walls for wildlife, including (especially but not exclusively) the impacts of habitat fragmentation and curtailment of mobility for large carnivores.[36]

In the following section, to demonstrate this point, we rely on studies conducted at the US–Mexico border where, at least since 2006, concerns about the ecological impacts of security fencing have been widely raised and debated.[37]

Nature and Structural Violence: Ecological "Footprints" at the US–Mexico Wall

There are approximately 670 miles (1,078 km) of fencing currently separating the United States and Mexico (most of which was constructed between 2006 and 2009). The current security fence bisects the natural ranges of many nonhuman animal species and has proved problematic on a number of ecological fronts. Among the direct ecological effects of the US–Mexico border wall are: degradation of wildlife habitat and habitat connectivity; increased roadside mortality for terrestrial animals; altered wildlife behavior owing to high-intensity lighting and operational noise; increased avian mortality owing to lighting towers and high fencing; soil erosion and flooding owing to non-permeable fencing;[38] disrupted migratory ranges for endangered, threatened or candidate species; removal and destruction of rare and fragile desert plants; increased possibility of inbreeding expression; and, in "human" terms, loss of ecological and cultural resources for local indigenous communities and loss of access to natural landscapes for local border communities.

While modest efforts have been made to address some of these ecological concerns and concessions have been made to accommodate certain species of wildlife,[39] security has remained a privileged and unquestioned construct, overriding concerns about the ways in which security fencing and border walls are fostering human rights violations as well as ecological degradation. The US–Mexico border, in particular, has witnessed the legislating of this security privilege in which local conservation considerations were explicitly made (and remain) subordinate to overarching "Homeland" security concerns. In May 2005, for example, the U.S. REAL ID Act gave the secretary for the Department of Homeland Security (DHS) the discretionary power to waive all environmental protocols, including those mandated in previous federal legislation. In December 2005, DHS secretary Michael Chertoff took advantage of this privilege to waive—"in their entirety"—the environmental protocols standing in the way of triple fencing planned for the Tijuana River National Estuarine Research Reserve near San Diego, California.[40] Treated by the DHS as a haven for illegal migration and drug traffickers, "Smugglers Canyon" was back-filled with 2 million cubic yards of soil (taken from nearby mountaintops) and a three-tiered wall, roads and stadium lighting were put in place. Local residents and ecologists vociferously protested these developments as the canyon drained directly into the estuary, one of the largest saltwater marshes in California and the breeding/nesting ground for more than 350 species of birds.[41] At present, the border wall at Tijuana has disrupted the migration habitats of several species, including jaguars[42] (listed as endangered since 1977), bighorn sheep, the California red-legged frog and the pygmy owl.

Additionally, many of these detrimental ecological impacts have been linked not only to the architectural features of the fortified fencing, but also to one of its secondary effects: namely, the rerouting of migrants into remote regions of the deserts mentioned earlier. Currently, there are hundreds of informal roads and thousands of footpaths, all of which are heavily traveled by migrants and human traffickers. The impacts of these informal human corridors, as well as the effects of campsites and discarded water and food packaging, are now adversely disrupting a variety of fragile desert ecologies. The current, proposed immigration reform under discussion in the United States does not recognize the border's role in generating such environmental effects. (Ironically, it instead calls for stiffer penalties for those involved in human trafficking that "degrades or harms the environment or natural resources" or "pollutes an aquifer, spring, stream, river, or body of water.")[43]

These observations, although focusing on the US–Mexico border, are also increasingly being borne out in new studies of border fence construction across Eurasia, especially during the post-9/11 era (see Trouwborst et al. 2016). Taken together, these studies point to the deeply negative effects of border walls for the nonhuman as well, including displacement, loss of home/habitat, diminishment of well-being and death. The rush to build security fencing as a method to divert and control people therefore positions both the human and nonhuman in the same "bordered reality," fostering interlocking injustices, vulnerabilities and inequalities for humans and nonhumans alike.

Conclusion

This chapter has explored the interface of the social and ecological across the landscape of security fencing by highlighting issues of human and nonhuman mobility, suffering and mortality. Security walls and gates are clearly a central feature of a growing number of global border landscapes. As a particular type of border entailing specific act(s) of bordering, they encompass a much larger geography of unprecedented human and nonhuman displacement, migration and social as well as ecological exclusion.

Border walls are also features in a larger political and economic landscape in which security has been granted metaphysical as well as legislative privilege over the lives and well-being of thousands of vulnerable human and nonhuman actors. The fortified borders that are proliferating at an alarming rate across the globe thus are antithetical to a social ecology approach in which human and ecological problems are understood as mutually primary and contingent.

The dramatic increase in walled borders over the past several decades, and the concomitant social and ecological oppression and unconscionable loss of life it has fostered, suggests that such security fencing along national boundaries constitutes a new form of institutionalized violence, a nature-making that is especially baleful for vulnerable human and nonhuman populations. In linking this dual oppression of human and ecological communities, the social ecology approach adopted here, it is hoped, will engender a sense of urgency in counteracting the structural and ideological wellsprings of such odious border barriers.

NOTES

1 Environmental philosopher J. Baird Callicott, for example, has suggested that Thales's (624–546 BC) delineation of "substance" as emerging from out of a borderless chaos (*apeirion*) is foundational to Western ideas about "nature" as something separate from the human. According to Callicott, Thales's metaphysical bordering of "nature" (as something from out of nothing) laid the epistemological groundwork for Aristotle's subsequent hierarchical ordering of life forms and hence to traditional Western scientific conceptions of "nature" as an object, an idea that remains powerfully present today (see Callicott 2007).

2 The SRC's interdisciplinary team identified nine "thresholds" that it considered essential to the future of human survival and well-being: 1) stratospheric ozone depletion; 2) loss of biosphere integrity (biodiversity loss and extinctions); 3) chemical pollution and the release of novel entities; 4) climate change; 5) ocean acidification; 6) freshwater consumption and the global hydrological cycle; 7) land system change; 8) nitrogen and phosphorus flows to the biosphere and oceans; 9) atmospheric aerosol loading. See also www.stockholmresilience.org/21/research/research-programmes/planetary-boundaries/planetary-boundaries/about-the-research/the-nine-planetary-boundaries.html. (Accessed October 1, 2015.)

3 BIG's agenda now includes international climate strategies and carbon trading, new structures of environmental governance and the co-management of defined geographical features (such as watersheds, rivers and aquifers), as well as wildlife corridors and invasive species.

4 J. Sunberg, "Diabolic *Caminos* in the Desert and Cat Fights on the Río: A Posthumanist Political Ecology of Boundary Enforcement in the United States–Mexico Borderlands," *Annals of the Association of American Geographers* 101(2011): 318–36.

5 See, for example, S. Dalby, *Security and Environmental Change* (Cambridge: Polity Press, 2009).

6 S. Lavorel, "Walls and Access to Natural Resources," in *Borders, Fences and Walls: State of Insecurity?* ed. E. Vallet (Burlington, VT: Ashgate Publishing, 2014), 159.

7 E. Vallet, "Introduction." In *Borders, Fences and Walls: State of Insecurity?* ed. E. Vallet (Burlington, VT: Ashgate Publishing, 2014), 1. See also M. Chaichian, *Empires and Walls: Globalization, Migration and Colonial Domination* (Boston, MA: Brill, 2014).

8 A. Appadurai, *Modernity at Large* (Minneapolis: University of Minnesota Press, 1996); K. Ohmae, *The End of the Nation State* (New York: Free Press, 1995).

9 J. Torpey, *The Invention of the Passport: Surveillance, Citizenship and the State* (Cambridge: Cambridge University Press, 2000), 157.

10 Ibid, 157.

11 V. Das and D. Poole, eds. *Anthropology in the Margins of the State* (Santa Fe, NM: School of America Research Press, 2004).

12 See H. Donnan and T. Wilson, eds. *Borders: Frontiers of Identity, Nation and State* (Oxford: Bloomsbury Academic Publishing, 1999); B. Korf and T. Raeymaekers, "Introduction: Border, Frontier and the Geography of Rule at the Margins of the State." In *Violence on the Margins: States, Conflict and Borderlands,* eds. B. Korf and T. Raeymaekers (New York: Palgrave Macmillan, 2013), 3–28; and Markus Euskirchen, Henrik Lebuhn and Gene Ray, "From Borderline to Borderland: The Changing European Border Regime, *Monthly Review* 59 (2007): 41–52. For an interesting critique, see S. Elden, "Land, Terrain, Territory." *Progress in Human Geography* 34(2010): 799–817.

13 J. Maskovsky and H. Cunningham, "Fragmented" Security: Protecting the Homeland in the 21st Century US," in *Rethinking America: The Imperial Homeland in the 21st Century,* eds. I. Susser and J. Maskovsky (Boulder, CO: Paradigm Publishers, 2009), 195. Also see R. Nieto-Gomez, "Walls, Sensors, Drone: Technology and Surveillance on the US–Mexico Border." In *Borders, Fences and Walls: State of Insecurity?* ed. E. Vallet (Burlington, VT: Ashgate Publishing, 2014), 191–2010; D. Millis and S. Nicol, "Borderlands at Risk." In *The Border Militarization Reader,* ed. J. Jordan (Tucson, AZ: Alliance for Global Justice, 2013), available at https://afgj.org/border-militarization-study-guide; M. Coleman, "From Border Policing to Internal Immigration Control in the United States." In *A Companion to Border Studies,* eds. T. Wilson and H. Donnan (Oxford: Wiley-Blackwell, 2012), 419–37; Donnan and Wilson, *Borders*; Paasi 2009; A. Pratt, *Securing Borders: Detention and Deportation in Canada* (Vancouver, BC: UBC Press, 2005); D. Newman and A. Paasi, "Fences and Neighbors in the Postmodern World: Boundary Narratives in Political Geography." *Progress in Human Geography* 22(1998): 186–207.

14 Y. H. Ferguson and R. Mansbach, *Globalization: The Return of Borders to a Borderless World?* (New York: Routledge, 2012).

15 W. Brown, *Walled States, Waning Sovereignty* (New York: Zone Books, 2010).

16 Philosopher Wendy Brown uses "walls within walls" as a metaphor in her discussion of the increased number of gated communities in US Southwestern cities, especially in areas in close proximity to "the wall" with Mexico (2010: 19).

17 Five years earlier, Brazil built a 10-foot (3 m) steel and concrete wall along a short portion of its border with Paraguay.

18 Perhaps it comes as no surprise that a new report estimates that the global homeland security market is expected to be worth $544.02 billion USD by 2018 ("The Global Homeland Security and Emergency Management Market," published by Markets and Markets [M&M], 2015).

19 Vallet, "Introduction," 2. Vallet notes that in the 20 years following the end of the Cold War, the number of border walls has tripled.

20 Korea's Demilitarized Zone, erected in 1953, is one such exception in that the fortified border has had salubrious effects on local flora and fauna. The border wall in this region consists of multilayered fencing and is heavily patrolled by armed soldiers. According to ecologists, the absence of human activity in the area has made the zone attractive to thousands of species that are extinct or endangered elsewhere on the peninsula. The endangered White-napped and Red-crowned Cranes are examples of species who are making a comeback, as well as the Asiatic black bear, egrets and a subspecies of the Siberian tiger.

21 While for some scholars and activists, human concerns (and hence human ascendancy) must remain at the forefront of any analytic, "edge effect" suggests that these inequalities are multilayered, multi-specied and densely interconnected. In some ways this is to suggest that—following social ecology—marginalization is not merely a question of the human "subject," but is itself an entanglement of human and nonhuman. It follows that justice and liberation must be formulated as a new kind of human/nonhuman "entanglement." This is to say that—perhaps—justice itself is a kind of "edge effect."

22 See UN High Commissioner on Refugees (UNHCR): http://unhcr.org/556725e69.html#_ga=1.152371696.850573673.1445109388 UN. Also Amnesty International 2012.

23 See S. Lovgren, "Climate Change Creating Millions of 'Eco Refugees,' UN Warns." *National Geographic News.* Oct. 2005. 13 Mar. 2012: 18.

24 Frontex, for example, the agency that oversees the EU's borders, focuses on eight routes and collates statistics on the number of "detections" of migrants on each route. The result of this is the coordination of "joint operations" between Frontex and member states aimed at reducing the number of migrants on these routes. https://euobserver.com/justice/123681.

25 www.telegraph.co.uk/news/worldnews/europe/macedonia/11855675/Macedonia-plans-fence-and-troops-on-Greek-border-to-stop-migrants.html.

26 T. Brian and F. Laczko, *Migrant Deaths: An International Overview. Fatal Journeys: Tracking Lives Lost during Migration* (Geneva, Switzerland: International Organization for Migration, 2014), 24.

27 These are based on US Border Patrol statistics for bodies found only on the US side of the border.

28 Brian and Laczko, *Migrant Deaths.*

29 Early on, Ciudad Juarez-El Paso, Tijuana-San Diego and Ambos Nogales were identified as key sites for security fencing.

30 H. Cunningham, "Nations Rebound? Crossing Borders in a Gated Globe," *Identities: Global Studies in Culture and Power* 11(2004): 329–50; J. Maskovsky and H. Cunningham, 'Fragmented' Security: Protecting the Homeland in the 21st Century US," in *Rethinking America: The Imperial Homeland in the 21st Century*, ed. I. Susser and J. Maskovsky (Boulder, CO: Paradigm Publishers, 2009), 193.

31 See D. E. Martínez, J. Slack and P. Vandervoet, "Methodological Challenges and Ethical Concerns of researching Marginalized and Vulnerable Populations: Evidence from Firsthand Experiences of Working with Unauthorized Migrants." In *Unchartered Terrains: New Directions in Border Research and Methodology, Ethics and Practice*, eds. A. O. O'Leary, C. M. Deeds and S. Whiteford (Tucson: University of Arizona Press, 2013), 101–20; D. E. Martínez, R. Reineke, R. Rubio-Goldsmith and B. A. Parks, "Structural Violence and Migrant Deaths in Southern Arizona: Updated Data from the Pima County Office of the Medical Examiner, 1990–2013." *Journal of Migration and Human Security* 2 (2014): 257–86.

32 Over the past three fiscal years, US Border Patrol statistics show that there were 100 migrant deaths per 100,000 apprehensions. A decade ago the rate was 40 per 100,000. See R. Reineke, and D. E. Martínez, "Migrant Deaths in the Americas (United States and Mexico)," in *Fatal Journeys: Tracking Lives Lost during Migration*, ed. Tara Brian and Frank Laczko (Geneva, Switzerland: International Organization for Migration, 2014), 54.

33 https://www.iom.int/. Accessed October 25, 2015.

34 H. Cunningham, "Permeabilities, Ecology and Geopolitical Boundaries," in *A Companion to Border Studies*, eds. T. Wilson and H. Donnan (Oxford: Wiley-Blackwell, 2012), 374.

35 See A. Smart and J. Smart. "Biosecurity, Quarantine and Life Across the Border." In *A Companion to Border Studies* (Oxford: Wiley-Blackwell, 2012), 354–70.

36 See A. Trouwborst, F. Fleurke and J. Dubrelle, "Border Fences and Their Impacts on Large Carnivores, Large Herbivores and Biodiversity: An International Wildlife Law Perspective." Review of European, Comparative and International Environmental Law 25(3):1–16. Also Linnell et al. "Border Security Fencing and Wildlife: The End of the Transboundary Paradigm in Eurasia?" *PloS Biology*. Published: June 22, 2016 /http://dx.doi.org/10.1371/journal.pbio.1002483.

37 We rely here on a recent 2011 published study (Lasky et al.), as well as research fostered by a 2006 conference held in Tucson, Arizona, where ecologists focused on the biological effects of the wall and its consequences for wildlife.

38 In 2008, for example, the border fence at Organ Pipe Cactus National Monument in southern Arizona began to dam up water after heavy rainfall and a severe monsoon thunderstorm. After the event, the National Park Service conducted a study and concluded that the pooling of water against the fence had caused soil erosion and damage to riparian vegetation. See "Effects of the International Boundary Pedestrian Fence in the Vicinity of Lukeville, Arizona, on Drainage Systems and Infrastructure, Organ Pipe Cactus National Monument, Arizona,"

National Park Service. 1 (August 2008). Note 13. www.nps.gov/orpi/naturescience/upload/FloodReport_July2008_final.pdf.

39 Bollard fencing, used in washes in Arizona, for example, consists of interlocking poles. The spacing between the poles allows people, some animals and water to pass through, but not vehicles.

40 The "Borderlands" website—a campaign launched by the Sierra Club that focuses on the ecological impacts of the US–Mexico wall—claims that this waiver of law is the largest in US history, encompassing 37 federal laws protecting land, air, water, wildlife, public health and religious freedom. See www.sierraclub.org/borderlands. (Accessed August 15, 2015.)

41 In 2007, Chertoff also invoked the waiver in the construction of a 35-mile (56 km) wall in an area adjacent to Arizona's Cabeza Prieta National Wildlife Refuge (where the Sonoran Pronghorn is near extinction) to build a 15-foot (4.6 m), impermeable steel barrier along the edge of the San Pedro River in Arizona. The river is recognized as one of North America's most biologically diverse areas. The waiver was invoked again in April 2008 for a suite of border infrastructure projects spanning Texas, New Mexico, Arizona and California. See "Laws Waived on the Border." www.sierraclub.org/borderlands/laws-waived-border. (Accessed September 2, 2015.)

42 See H. Hebert, "US Jaguar Plan Foiled by Border Fence, Critics Say," *National Geographic*, January 18, 2008. http://news.nationalgeographic.com/news/2008/01/080118-AP-jaguars.html. (Accessed September 1, 2015.)

43 See S. 744, the "Border Security, Economic Opportunity, and the Immigration Modernization Act" (Senate Bill).

BIBLIOGRAPHY

Amnesty International. *Hostile Terrain: Human Rights Violations in Immigration Enforcement in the US Southwest*, 2012. www.amnestyusa.org/research/reports/usa-in-hostile-terrain-humna-rights-violation-in-immigration-enforcemnt-in-the-us-southwest.

Appadurai, A. *Modernity at Large*. Minneapolis: University of Minnesota Press, 1996.

Brian, T. and F. Laczko. *Migrant Deaths: An International Overview. Fatal Journeys: Tracking Lives Lost during Migration*. Geneva, Switzerland: International Organization for Migration, 2014.

Brown, W. *Walled States, Waning Sovereignty*. New York: Zone Books, 2010.

Busch, J. "Gains from Configuration: The Transboundary Protected Area as a Conservation Tool." *Ecological Economics* 67(2007): 394–404.

Callicott, J. B. "Lamarck Redux: Temporal Scale as the Key to the Boundary Between the Human and Natural Worlds." In *Nature's Edge: Boundary Explorations in Ecological Theory and Practice*, edited by C. S. Brown, 19–40. Albany: State University of New York Press, 2007.

Chaichian, M. *Empires and Walls: Globalization, Migration and Colonial Domination*. Boston, MA: Brill, 2014.

Coleman, M. "From Border Policing to Internal Immigration Control in the United States." In *A Companion to Border Studies*, edited by T. Wilson and H. Donnan, 419–37. Oxford: Wiley-Blackwell, 2012.

Cunningham, H. "Gating Ecology in a Gated Globe: Environmental Aspects of Securing Our Borders." In *Borderlands: Ethnographic Approaches to Security, Power, and Identity*, edited by H. Donnan and T. Wilson, 125–42. Lanham, MD: University Press of America, 2010.

Cunningham, H. "Nations Rebound? Crossing Borders in a Gated Globe." *Identities: Global Studies in Culture and Power* 11(2004): 329–50.

Cunningham, H. "Permeabilities, Ecology and Geopolitical Boundaries." In *A Companion to Border Studies*, edited by T. Wilson and H. Donnan, 371–86. Oxford: Wiley-Blackwell, 2012.

Das, V. and D. Poole, eds. *Anthropology in the Margins of the State*. Santa Fe, NM: School of America Research Press, 2004.

Davis, M. *In Praise of Barbarians: Essays against Empire.* Chicago, IL: Haymarket Books, 2007.

Donnan, H. and T. Wilson, eds. *Borders: Frontiers of Identity, Nation and State.* Oxford: Bloomsbury Academic Publishing, 1999.

Donnan, H. and T. Wilson, eds. *Ethnographic Approaches to Security, Power, and Identity.* Lanham, MD: University Press of America, 2010.

Duffy, R. "Peace Parks and Global Politics: The Paradoxes and Challenges of Global Governance." In *Peace Parks: Conservation and Conflict Resolution*, edited by S. H. Ali, 55–68. Cambridge, MA: MIT Press, 2007.

Elden, S. "Land, Terrain, Territory." *Progress in Human Geography* 34(2010): 799–817.

Euskirchen, M., H. Lebuhn and G. Ray, "From Borderline to Borderland: The Changing European Border Regime, *Monthly Review* 59 (2007): 41–52.

Ferguson, Y. H. and R. Mansbach. *Globalization: The Return of Borders to a Borderless World?* New York: Routledge, 2012.

Hebert, H. "US Jaguar Plan Foiled by Border Fence, Critics Say." *National Geographic*, January 18, 2008. Accessed September 1, 2015. http://news.nationalgeographic.com/news/2008/01/080118-AP-jaguars.html.

Heyman, J. "Environmental Issues at the US–Mexico Border and the Unequal Territorialization of Value." In *Rethinking Environmental History: World System Theory and Global Environmental Change*, edited by A. Hornborg, J. R. Mitchell and J. Martinez-Alier, 327–44. New York: Altamira Press, 2007.

Korf, B. and T. Raeymaekers. "Introduction: Border, Frontier and the Geography of Rule at the Margins of the State." In *Violence on the Margins: States, Conflict and Borderlands,* edited by B. Korf and T. Raeymaekers, 3–28. New York: Palgrave Macmillan, 2013.

Lasky, J. R., W. Jetz and T. H. Keitt. Conservation Biogeography of the US–Mexico Border: A Transcontinental Risk Assessment of Barriers to Animal Dispersal. *Diversity and Distributions*, 17: 673–87, 2011. doi:10.1111/j.1472-4642.2011.00765.x.

Linnell, J., A. Trouwborst, L. Boitani, et al. "Border Security Fencing and Wildlife: The End of the Transboundary Paradigm in Eurasia?" *PloS Biology*. June 22, 2016: http://dx.doi.org/10.1371/journal.pbio.1002483

Lavorel, S. "Walls and Access to Natural Resources." In *Borders, Fences and Walls: State of Insecurity?* edited by E. Vallet, 159–74. Burlington, VT: Ashgate Publishing, 2014.

Martínez, D. E., R. Reineke, R. Rubio-Goldsmith and B. A. Parks. "Structural Violence and Migrant Deaths in Southern Arizona: Updated Data from the Pima County Office of the Medical Examiner, 1990–2013." *Journal of Migration and Human Security* 2 (2014): 257–86.

Martínez, D. E., J. Slack and P. Vandervoet. "Methodological Challenges and Ethical Concerns of researching Marginalized and Vulnerable Populations: Evidence from Firsthand Experiences of Working with Unauthorized Migrants." In *Unchartered Terrains: New Directions in Border Research and Methodology, Ethics and Practice*, edited by A. O. O'Leary, C. M. Deeds and S. Whiteford, 101–20. Tucson: University of Arizona Press, 2013.

Maskovsky, J. and H. Cunningham. "'Fragmented' Security: Protecting the Homeland in the 21st Century US." In *Rethinking America: The Imperial Homeland in the 21st Century*, edited by I. Susser and J. Maskovsky. Boulder, CO: Paradigm Publishers, 2009.

Millis, D. and S. Nicol. "Borderlands at Risk." In *The Border Militarization Reader*, edited by J. Jordan. Tucson, AZ: Alliance for Global Justice, 2013. Available at https://afgj.org/border-militarization-study-guide.

Newman, D. and A. Paasi. "Fences and Neighbors in the Postmodern World: Boundary Narratives in Political Geography." *Progress in Human Geography* 22(1998): 186–207.

Nieto-Gomez, R. "Walls, Sensors, Drone: Technology and Surveillance on the US–Mexico Border." In *Borders, Fences and Walls: State of Insecurity?* Edited by E. Vallet, 191–210. Burlington, VT: Ashgate Publishing, 2014.

Ohmae, K. *The End of the Nation State.* New York: Free Press, 1995.

Passi, P. "Bounded spaces in a 'Borderless' World: Border Studies, Power, and the Anatomy of Territory," *Journal of Power* 2 (2009): 213–34.

Pratt, A. *Securing Borders: Detention and Deportation in Canada.* Vancouver, BC: UBC Press, 2005.

Ramutsindela, M. *Transfrontier Conservation in Africa: At the Confluence of Capital, Politics and Nature.* Boston, MA: CABI Publishing 2007.

Reineke, R. and D. E. Martínez. "Migrant Deaths in the Americas (United States and Mexico)." In *Fatal Journeys: Tracking Lives Lost during Migration,* edited by T. Brian and F. Laczko, 45–83. Geneva, Switzerland: International Organization for Migration, 2014.

Sierra Club. "Laws Waived on the Border." Accessed September 2, 2015. www.sierraclub.org/borderlands/laws-waived-border.

Sifford, B. and C. Chester. "Bridging Conservation across *La Frontera*: An Unfinished Agenda for Peace Parks along the US–Mexico Divide." In *Peace Parks: Conservation and Conflict Resolution,* edited by S. H. Ali, 205–26. Cambridge: MIT Press, 2007.

Smart A. and J. Smart. "Biosecurity, Quarantine and Life Across the Border." In *A Companion to Border Studies,* edited by T. Wilson and H. Donnan, 354–70. Oxford: Wiley-Blackwell, 2012.

Sunberg, J. "Diabolic *Camino*s in the Desert and Cat Fights on the Río: A Posthumanist Political Ecology of Boundary Enforcement in the United States–Mexico Borderlands." *Annals of the Association of American Geographers,* 101(2011): 318–36.

Torpey, J. *The Invention of the Passport: Surveillance, Citizenship and the State.* Cambridge: Cambridge University Press, 2000.

Trouwborst, A., F. Fleurke and J. Dubrelle. "Border Fences and Their Impacts on Large Carnivores, Large Herbivores and Biodiversity: An International Wildlife Law Perspective." *Review of European, Comparative and International Environmental Law,* 25(2016): DOI: 10.1111/reel.12169.

U.S. Congress. Senate. *Border Security, Economic Opportunity, and Immigration Modernization Act.* S. 744. 113th Cong., 1st sess. (June 7, 2013).

Vallet, E. "Introduction." In *Borders, Fences and Walls: State of Insecurity?* edited by E. Vallet, 1–7. Burlington, VT: Ashgate Publishing, 2014.

Wolmer, W. "Transboundary Conservation: The Politics of Ecological Integrity in the Great Limpopo Transfrontier Park." *Journal of Southern African Studies,* 29(2003): 261–78.

Part II

BRIDGES: RESILIENCE, RESTORATION AND RECLAMATION

Chapter Four

BORDERS AS ZONES OF EXPERIENTIAL LEARNING: THE CASE OF THE BALKANS PEACE PARK PROJECT

Todd Walters and Saleem H. Ali

Introduction

National borders are synthetic constructs that may be defined by some geographic features such as rivers or mountain ranges, but essentially remain figments of political expediency. However, social systems evolve around them to provide a unique context for learning the interface between society and ecology. This chapter provides a concise historiography of the development of an initiative in the western Balkans that sought to harness such learning opportunities "between the lines" through experiential field education. The challenges and criticism faced by the progenitors of this initiative are considered in the post-conflict reconstruction and reconciliation landscape of the Balkans. Conflict transformation requires empowerment of agents of change, and this is a core component of the experiential peace-building process, especially in terms of helping participants understand the shared meaning of their experience. Such empowerment is often the goal of small-scale peace-building initiatives that target people with influence in divided communities, so that they will be able to apply what they have learned in their home constituencies. This is often done through joint cooperative initiatives or projects that allow a transformed group of people from each side of the divide to have a platform to reach out and extend their transformation to others in their communities. In our understanding, this approach to peace building rests on four criteria: (1) the responsibility and judgment of being empowered; (2) the conscious use of symbolism and ritual to create meaningful images, metaphors and experiences; (3) the transference of individual transformation back into the community; and (4) the reframing of community relationships so as to counter prevailing stereotypes and to inspire a positive notion of the "other" through a real-world example. The Balkans Peace Park Project (B3P) sought to use such a framework to further its goals of peace education and also to foster a better appreciation of the social ecology of this complex border landscape.

The Birth of the Balkans Peace Park Project (B3P)

The story starts with a flash of inspiration from one intrepid woman following her wanderlust in the footsteps of a famous British explorer, Edith Durham, who trekked by horseback through the Dinaric Alps at the turn of the century—before communism lowered its Iron Curtain of isolationism and paranoia. Inquisitive young British anthropologist Antonia Young surrendered to her inner adventurer and began exploring Tito's Yugoslavia in the 1960s. Using her curious personality and depth of anthropological knowledge, she accepted the phenomenal hospitality of the region's people, all the while keeping her keen eye open to social and cultural nuances, particularly in the remote, rugged and stunningly beautiful communities tucked away in the valleys of these limestone mountains. Those mountains and those people kept drawing her back; year after year, decade after decade, she continued to return. Friendships turned into adopted families, children grew up and had their own families, political systems transitioned, and conflict gripped the region more than once.

Through it all, Antonia Young studied, wrote and continued to explore. Her book *Sworn Virgins*[1] won international acclaim—unveiling the unique cultural phenomenon that allowed a widowed woman or eldest daughter who lost her father or the man of the house to assume a man's role in patriarchal Albanian society. Talking, dressing, acting as a man and assuming the man's duties around the home and in the community were all part of this phenomenon. Adopting a new name to go with the new role, these women earned acceptance from their communities as they demonstrated their abilities to assume the gender role responsibilities of a man. The cultural anthropologist was fascinated, and dug deeper, exploring the shadowy world of retribution killings through "blood feuds," whereby the eldest male of the family was expected to commit a revenge killing of a murderer, the murderer's male child or the family patriarch— and thus the tit-for-tat murderous exchanges between families extended throughout generations. Antonia Young was in the region when Albanian communism came to an end in the 1990s, as well as during the scandal of the financial pyramid schemes, which bankrupted as many as 70 percent of Albanian families. Shortly thereafter, Slobodan Milosevic and his ethnocidal brand of Serbian nationalism swept the Balkans, leaving a conflict-torn region with internally displaced people, refugees, a mined landscape scarred with environmental damage, hardened ethnic identities and a general psychological profile of posttraumatic stress. It was during this point in time that Antonia Young learned something new from her husband, Dr. Nigel Young, a peace studies scholar and a former professor at the University of California, Berkeley, who was then the founder of the peace studies program at Colgate University. She learned about the idea of an international peace park.

In June 2001, the idea of a transboundary conservation area for peace and reconciliation in the region began to coalesce. An open meeting in York, UK, led to the formation of a UK-based project committee working toward the creation of a peace park in the Balkans. This small group of ordinary citizens, many of them Quakers and peace activists, resolved that they would undertake this project to help support the people of the region and help bring peace to the opposite side of Europe. After compiling a shared list of contacts throughout the region, the early strategy focused on cultivating a growing network of contacts who were encouraged to form nongovernmental organizations (NGOs) while simultaneously working to publicize the region and the concept of a "Balkans peace park" in the UK and internationally, in order to draw attention to the plight of the people still struggling to recover and rebuild in the wake of the Yugoslav conflict and dissolution of the nation. One of the first spotlights shone when Rosie Swale,[2] the internationally renowned explorer and travel writer, set out alone, on foot, to explore by running the approximate boundaries of the proposed Balkans peace park, while sharing the idea with anyone who would listen. And so the idea began to grow.

The summer of 2003 saw the "inaugural trek"[3] from Rugova (in present-day Kosovo, which declared independence on February 17, 2008), through the Prokletije Mountain range (and into present-day Montenegro, which achieved independence June 3, 2006) and onward to Vermosh and Thethi (remote villages in northern Albania). Comprised of B3P committee members, international adventurers and US college students from Colgate University, and jointly organized with NGOs in the region, the trek brought together local people interested in transcending political boundaries and further exploring this idea of what it would mean to have a peace park in their region.

After receiving official recognition as a charity from the UK government in 2004, the B3P committee helped to organize a 550-kilometer cycle tour from Podgorica (the present-day capital of Montenegro) through all three regions, broadening the growing local constituency supporting the Balkans peace park concept.[4] This momentum led to a weekend workshop held in the Yorkshire Dales National Park, UK, with local NGO representatives from Albania, Kosovo, Serbia and Montenegro, who were increasingly committed to embracing the idea of a Balkans peace park and wanted to learn more about how they could make it their own. The group developed and wrote a formal proposal for the establishment of the "First Balkans Peace Park," intending to secure sponsorship and financial support, while also formally introducing the idea to the governments in each country. The Ministry of the Environment in Kosovo was the first government entity to fully support the idea. Additionally, the small group of committed citizens in the UK realized that the project was starting to take shape. Shortly thereafter, in March 2005, Nigel Young secured the opportunity to meet with Harald Egerer, the UN Environment Program (UNEP) liaison officer in Vienna, Austria. By the conclusion of that conversation, the proposed Balkans peace park was declared the "First Cross-Border Balkans Peace Park." Though largely symbolic, this international institutional declaration was another critical step toward broadening global recognition and support for the idea.

While things were progressing on the conceptual level, Antonia Young could not ignore her close connections with the people on the ground, and was excited to return in 2005 and head a three-year ethnographic study as part of the Shala Valley Archaeological Project[5] within Thethi National Park in Albania. Being back in her element allowed her to not only study in depth the nuances of the evolution of the unique mountain culture that spanned the political boundaries in the post-conflict era, but also to share the progress made on the Balkans peace park concept, and to introduce the concept to thousands of other individuals. The seeds were beginning to take root. Later that summer Fatos Lajçi, a dedicated Kosovar environmentalist, led a trek of local and international participants through the region, which he called the Long Walk for Peace.[6] The trek culminated in the first international conference to explore the idea of a Balkans peace park with local and international actors, held in the flashpoint region of Mitrovica, Kosovo. Lajçi was able to secure the support of the Kosovan Ministry of Youth, Culture and Sport, further inserting the idea into the political system in Kosovo, and actively completing the first project acknowledging the Balkans peace park idea sponsored by a local government and championed by a local stakeholder.

These successes were harnessed to develop a more comprehensive, integrated vision with practical projects, which could initiate the environmental peace-building process on multiple levels of society simultaneously. In April 2006, UNEP committed to funding the first phase of this integrated vision for the purpose of promoting the development of strong local democratic procedures, fostering better cross-border cooperation, and promoting harmonious trans-border environmental protection in the proposed Balkans peace park region. The support of UNEP went a long way toward establishing the legitimacy of the B3P committee, both in the UK and in the Balkans, and lent considerable weight to the idea. It also initiated a new stage in the evolution of implementation. In November 2006, a coalition of local NGOs in the region hosted a conference in the Grand Hotel in Prishtina, Kosovo, bringing together the mayors and other municipal leaders of the communities that would be considered in or around the B3P area, inviting them to commit themselves publicly to supporting the development of a transboundary peace park.[7] The mayors or their deputies from five of the six municipalities in the proposed Balkans peace park region addressed the conference and signed a Letter of Good Intent to work together to support the creation of the peace park within their municipalities in partnership with their counterparts across the border. The sixth mayor gave his signature at a later ceremony.[8]

Since 2006, the B3P has collaborated with other international NGOs and government development organizations, including UNEP, the International Union for the Conservation of Nature (IUCN), European Green Belt, the Austrian Development Cooperation and the SNV Dutch Development organization, as well as with local and regional NGOs and government organizations; and more recently in 2011, with the German Organization for International Cooperation (GIZ). The start of 2007 saw additional cross-border trekking expeditions,[9] including a multi-activity, borders-crossing trip organized by B3P committee member Richard Hargreaves, which also introduced the concept of "ecotourism." Hargreaves held this expedition to attract attention to the region and the symbolic cross-border efforts of environmental peacebuilding. The expedition crossed the Albania–Montenegro border twice and included climbing, hiking and mountain biking activities with international participants and local guides from each country.[10] During 2007, academic publications and conference presentations began to illustrate the progress of the Balkans peace park concept with the broader international academic community focused on peace studies, environmental studies and border studies. Abbey Radis, assistant to Antonia Young, presented her own paper, "The Role of

Resource Sharing Initiatives in Peacebuilding," on behalf of the B3P at the Parks, Peace and Partnerships Conference in Waterton Lakes National Park, Alberta, Canada, as part of the celebration of the seventy-fifth anniversary of its cross-border collaboration with Glacier National Park. Ann Kennard made a presentation about the B3P, marking the formal close of EUROPARC's Nature–Bridging Borders conference held in Cesky Krumlov in the Czech Republic. Every year since November 2007, B3P colleagues have addressed the Royal Geographical Society (RGS) on some aspect of B3P's work at its annual seminars. A busy 2007 closed with an accolade, as the B3P received a Highly Recommended Certificate from the British Guild of Travel Writers as part of the Best Overseas Tourism Project.

At this point, the B3P had built a robust network of contacts throughout the region at multiple levels of society, including the central government, several international government organizations, regional government, municipalities, NGOs and other organizations from Albania, Kosovo and Montenegro. In March 2008, the B3P helped to convene 60 of these stakeholders in a two-day workshop in Shkodra, Albania, for the purposes of planning the next steps toward the creation of the transboundary Balkans peace park. Specialist groups were formed around key topic areas from ecotourism and organic food certification, to development projects and addressing environmental challenges. This meeting formalized the process adopted by this diverse group of stakeholders, introduced the concept and all of its players to new participants, and established a superordinate regional goal for all stakeholders. After this conference, the B3P returned to the region in summer 2008 for the first annual B3P Summer Programme. The Summer Programme signaled the first occasion in which the organization implemented a project in the region that was not a conference or an ecotourism trek. The Summer Programme demonstrated a direct, concrete contribution to the community in the remote Shala Valley where Antonia Young had completed her ethnographic work with the Shala Valley Project. (This was also the project that coauthor Todd Walters coordinated for 10 weeks in the village of Thethi, Albania.)

Through Antonia Young's ethnographic studies, members of the Shala Valley community identified the necessity of English-language instruction and practical skill development. The B3P Summer Programme brought 17 international volunteer teachers and five local Albanian teachers to instruct more than 80 youths in English and environmental education.[11] To complement the formal classes, the volunteers also harnessed their passions to provide extracurricular instruction in art, music, drama and sports activities, while also contributing to the development of sustainable tourism in the Shala Valley by living with local families and supplementing their income. These families were learning how to adapt their traditional notions of hospitality to the concept of hosting foreign travelers in their homes, providing meals and supplies and offering local guide service to sites of environmental, cultural or historical significance. The Summer Programme has also served to provide a presence in the region for the B3P when other activities take place such as first ascents of mountains within the region. Partners can synergize publicity and co-promote each other's activities. This synergy took place when US rock climber John Ely and his team pioneered a new route to the summit of Maya Arrapit in Thethi, Albania, and a Polish team named its new route up Maya Lagojvet the "Balkans Peace Park Route." Ely and his team even collected signatures at their base camp in support of the creation of a Balkans peace park.[12]

The Summer Programme in Thethi has continued each summer since 2008, and expanded to include the Rugova Valley in Kosovo in 2010, when B3P volunteers participated in a summer camp organized by the Environmentally Responsible Action (ERA) group. In 2012, the B3P expanded its activities to the village of Vermosh and developed a sister program across the border in Plav, Montenegro, in 2015, after formally establishing a partnership with Prokletike National Park in Montenegro. Teaching both environmental education and English-language classes supports intergenerational skills that will foster ecotourism as a livelihood opportunity as well as increase environmental awareness and activism targeted to youth within the region. In order to foster greater local ownership of the B3P concept and process, the UK-based committee has worked hard to build the capacity of local supporters and local partners, culminating in 2011 with the formal founding and recognition by the Albanian national government of B3P Albania. B3P Albania is a local NGO committed to the creation of a peace park in the tri-border region, founded and operated by Albanians, which now organizes the Summer Programme with financial and volunteer support from B3P UK. Further reflecting the global growth of the concept, there has also been some momentum toward creating a 501(c)3 nonprofit B3P USA; however, the formal application to the US federal government has not been filed at the time of this chapter's completion.

In 2011, other organizations working in the region in conjunction with the B3P made significant progress; GIZ arranged for 40 members of mountaineering clubs in the three countries to trek from Rugova to Plav, then from Vusanje to Thethi, Valbona and Cerem. This signaled a significant development: a cross-border trek route, which has now been mostly waymarked and become the "Peaks of the Balkans Trail." Polish climbers returned to make a route up the Maja Shkurt peak in Prokletije which they named "Peacehammer," while a party of UK climbers enjoyed what they called "adventure climbing" from a camp between Qafa e Pejës and Runic meadows in Albania. Finally, International Peace Park Expeditions in partnership with the University of Vermont, United States, focused on transboundary environmental cooperation, sustainable development projects and ecotourism initiatives—this allowed students to experience firsthand the link between the theory of the classroom and how it plays out in the real world.[13]

International Peace Park Expeditions continues to return to the region on an annual basis, having now completed four expeditions bringing more than 40 students from the United States, Canada and Japan to the proposed Balkans peace park region to learn about environmental peacebuilding through experiential learning. In 2015, International Peace Park Expeditions partnered with the US Embassy in Kosovo and the US National Park Service Office of International Affairs to bring a delegation of Kosovars and Montenegrins to the United States for a National Park Capacity Building Expedition to support the sustainable development of Bjeshket e Nemuna National Park in Kosovo and Prokletije National Park in Montenegro.

Figure 4.1 Thethi National Park, Albania. Students from the 2015 Accredited Academic Expedition, "Environmental Peacebuilding and Sustainability in Washington, DC, and the Balkans," climb the transboundary ecotourism trail "Peaks of the Balkans" on a border-crossing trek from Albania to Montenegro. Photograph by Todd Walters, May 2015.

Organizational Structure

The B3P is a UK-based, registered charity,[14] comprised of a group of people who passionately believed in an idea, and after a decade of challenging work remains determined and committed to bring their idea to fruition. According to the B3P website, "B3P is a genuine grassroots network bringing together a diverse selection of people: academics, artists, environmental activists both in the Balkans, and around the globe, and of course involving local people living and working in the valleys and villages of Northern Albania, Eastern Montenegro and Western Kosovo/a."[15] The organization has fostered the development of a Balkans Peace Park Project Albania—B3P Albania—closely tied to the UK charity, but comprised of a board of directors and members who are all local Albanians who have embraced the mission. Each organization is an NGO that is recognized locally and nationally, and is built on a shared vision, relying on the hard work of volunteers. In addition to internal member fundraising, B3P applies for grants from embassies, foundations, regional/national banks and companies. The organization actively seeks partnerships with other people, organizations, institutions, ministries and international agencies that share the vision of the Balkans peace park. B3P Albania is expected to operate in much the same manner.

Figure 4.2 Lake Plav, Montenegro. Students from the 2015 Accredited Academic Expedition titled "Environmental Peacebuilding and Sustainability in Washington, DC, and the Balkans" participate in a lecture on transboundary water resource management on the dock of Lake Plav, Montenegro, located on the outskirts of Prokletije National Park. Photograph by Geoff Dabelko, May 2015.

Sir Graham Watson, Liberal Democrat Member of the European Parliament for South West England and Gibraltar, is a patron of the B3P and places the BPP in its context:

> The European Union has done a great deal to secure peace and prosperity for its members, but has been deeply troubled by conflict in South East Europe. Whilst EU membership remains a beacon of hope for Balkan countries, schemes like the Balkan Peace Park Project are vitally important to peace in Europe. The Project rises above the politics that have plagued the region, and instead focuses on the issues that are common to Albanians, Kosovars and Montenegrins alike; protecting the shared natural environment and promoting a sustainable economic prosperity for all those living in the area. For me, this embodies both the spirit of liberalism and European integration, and I am therefore proud to be a Patron of the Balkans Peace Park Project.[16]

Strategy Evolves—Future Activities

Working through the co-leadership of SNV and GIZ, two larger professional international development agencies with paid staff and sizeable budgets, a new strategy emerged for consideration. The Austrian Development Agency (ADA) proposed a partnership between SNV, GIZ and the B3P, and local NGOs in each country in order to combine the B3P volunteer grassroots approach with the funded, professional top-down approach of SNV and GIZ. The aim was to develop accommodations, information centers, way-marking of trails, map production, training of local guides and procedures for obtaining official border-crossing permission from the relevant government agencies of the three countries.

SNV developed the following leadership and organizational structure (which was considered confidential at the time) to more effectively coordinate and monitor all of the stakeholders involved in transboundary environmental cooperation, and all of their projects. The key donor for this proposal, ADA determined that the approach was too "top down," and did not include the B3P in a meaningful way beyond participation in the advisory board—which carried only "recommendation power" and not decision-making power. The latter would be maintained by SNV and GIZ. Recognition of the grassroots approach of the B3P and its lack of a clearly defined role in this new strategy is what led to its ultimate demise. ADA stipulated that funding would only be granted should the structure and approach be changed to focus on the bottom-up approach, with a top-down administration process, and that the B3P become a member of the steering committee and not just the advisory board. Neither SNV nor GIZ agreed to these terms, and this structure and the proposal was withdrawn from consideration and never enacted. Indeed, according to B3P chair Ann Kennard, GIZ decided to not even contribute its part of the proposal, with its page remaining blank. Both GIZ and SNV went on to develop alternative proposals that included pieces of this initiative that never came to fruition, and they solicited other donors in order to fund their plans.

This aborted initiative highlights the challenges of a multi-stakeholder approach to transboundary collaboration and brings into focus the different operating approaches, the different budget sizes, the differences between professional development agencies and volunteer-based NGOs and the difficulty in agreeing on a common strategic approach despite sharing similar goals and objectives. Perceived power discrepancies between different stakeholders can derail an initiative before it even begins.

Challenges and Dynamics

Like any initiative that involves fundraising, volunteers and coordinating on an international stage with stakeholders from many different countries, the B3P has faced a number of challenges over the course of its first decade of evolution. Obvious language barriers and lost-in-translation moments, as well as cultural nuances of invitations exchanged and hospitality returned, have both developed positive collaboration while also creating misunderstandings, which have generated distrust. Communication styles that fail to recognize power dynamics have contributed to this distrust among stakeholders of different levels (from embassies and international development agencies to the national government ministries and the local NGOs), often alienating potential local partners. There are inevitable challenges when people seek to transition from a way of life built on rural agriculture, livestock raising and traditional village life to another lifestyle built on adapting notions of hospitality toward the eco-tourist, and that includes guest houses, restaurants/bars/cafes and locals offering guide services in mountain trekking, mountain biking, whitewater rafting, fly fishing, motor-cycle tours etc. These challenges include adapting to discrepancies and disagreements between local people and organizations, and the unintended consequences of selecting some people and organizations to receive funding to spur this transition, while others receive nothing and harbor resentment.

Internal challenges with local partner NGOs included the need to overcome initial distrust of these outsiders and the perception that the B3P was "all talk and no action" as the initial years of engagement were based around conferences and vacation treks before the on-the-ground projects began with the B3P Summer Programme in 2008. Also lacking was a long-term strategic vision for the region with an understanding of all three countries' national development priorities, as well as the large-scale infrastruc-ture development projects interconnected at the regional level through international development priorities. These would create practical and meaningful livelihood oppor-tunities from civil engineer to construction laborer positions. The B3P recognized that collaboration with GIZ and others who could provide leadership, funding and dedi-cated, paid, full-time staff was the best way to facilitate cross-border collaboration on the regional level. Such collaboration could address multiple issues simultaneously (includ-ing national park creation and capacity building in all three countries), and allow the B3P to contribute its grassroots strengths. These strengths include a sizable network of contacts, expertise in anthropology, geology, cross-border cooperation, management, knowledge and background of Eastern European cultures and languages and author-ship of numerous articles and chapters, while being able to maintain its original vision and contribute to a long-term strategic development plan coordinated and managed by other organizations.

Communication across cultures is both critical to success and one of the most common potential pitfalls. A complex, nuanced, underlying communication challenge occurs with the evolution of technology options that are now increasingly prolific with the ubiquitous mobile phone culture, the rising smartphone culture and the infinite number of Internet-based communication tools, ranging from email, VoIP (Voice over Internet Protocol like Skype) and smartphone apps (like Vibr and WhatsApp) to instant messaging, Facebook chat, Twitter and SMS. These technological tools have all broken down the cost barrier in terms of money, but have erected a knowledge barrier, in terms of a generational gap. In 2011, B3P leadership indicated directly that it did not feel comfortable keeping pace with the current pace of technology evolution and adoption, and it has made the deci-sion to consciously limit the tools with which it communicates on an everyday basis to email and phone calls—both while in the Balkans and when working from the UK. The B3P secretary began using Facebook, but the general feedback indicates that it has not been at all useful. Locals in this border region rapidly embrace various new communica-tion tools and, since 2014, B3P has begun to accept social media and now has an active manager of its Facebook page. Nevertheless, for external stakeholders, there is simply too much noise of competing, better-resourced charities capturing attention through more aggressive marketing tactics.

Albania, Kosovo and Montenegro form a region suffering from a demographic bulge due to the conflict in the 1990s, as most starkly displayed in Kosovo, where 70 percent of the population is under the age of 30. Youth unemployment is stratospheric throughout the region, including among the college educated. Security experts call the interaction of the "youth bulge" with the high unemployment rate a toxic mix. Scholars have long linked youth bulges to historical instances of social instability and even wars, especially when combined with high unemployment, though Bloom cautions that the empirical evidence is shaky.[17] The European Commission, under the EU Instrument contributing to Stability and Peace (IcSP) is currently gathering data using more rigorous methodology to better understand if this "toxic mix" is trending toward greater social instability or even a return to conflict. As the B3P works to attract younger volunteers, including some from the region, it is actively working to address this intergenerational communication/technology gap. Initial steps along this path include eight master's students who have used the B3P as their thesis topic, and others who have volunteered in the Summer Programme in Thethi, Albania for their university internship. Some local organizations also struggle with the word "peace" and the designation of the mountains around their homes as a "peace park." Their primary rationale is that "we were not involved in the conflict; we do not need to build peace; [and] we are already peaceful." This perspective can be countered with Galtung's positive peace theory,[18] which states that negative peace is just the absence of violence, while a positive peace is active collaboration for mutual benefit.

We can build peace in a region that already considers itself peaceful—the example of Waterton-Glacier International Peace Park between the United States and Canada reflects this notion of positive peace. This charged terminology of "peace" is avoided altogether in the Peaks of the Balkans initiative, and partially for that reason, has received wider acceptance than the Balkans peace park term despite being more than a decade younger as an initiative. Of course, this new terminology changes the focus of the cross-border collaboration, yet the fact remains that cross-border collaboration is being stimulated and issues like environmental conservation, ecotourism opportunities and waste management make this project an environmental peace-building initiative—whether or not it is named a peace park.

Another major challenge that prevented the achievement of a formal declaration of the proposed Balkans peace park was the status of the national parks in each country. In 2012, Prokletja National Park in Montenegro and in 2014, Bjeshket e Namuna National Park in Kosovo became functional. Previously, the Prokletja National Park system had been critiqued by many as a "paper park" existing only in law since 2010 but without any infrastructure, without understood or demarcated boundaries or management structures. However, substantial progress has been made through concerted efforts by Enes Dreshkovic, who was appointed the first park director in 2012 (having served also as president of the HRID Mountaineering Club). Within a year of his appointment, a park office was opened and, in 2014, a visitor center was established.

In Albania, Thethi National Park has existed since before the end of communism in 1992, yet it remains woefully understaffed with just two local rangers for the entire Shala Valley.[19] Through the efforts of the B3P coalition, GIZ and others, another major challenge in forming a peace park was overcome when, in the summer of 2015, Thethi and

Valbona National Parks' borders were officially extended all the way to the border with Montenegro and Kosovo. This pivotal expansion will allow for connectivity to establish transboundary environmental protection.

In Kosovo, the initiative to formally gazette Bjeshket a Namuna National Park system went through many challenges and was defeated twice. Some politicians suggested that the Kosovar constitution required a 20-year moratorium before it could be proposed again if it was defeated a third time. The reason that the bill failed twice was directly related to the lack of knowledge by local people surrounding the potential benefits and the multiuse regulations of the national park. Past proposals failed to inform local people of these benefits, and they were under the misconception that creating a national park would displace them from their land and mountain homesteads, to which they have territorial family or clan claim, but not legal title. In addition, they also feared the removal of their traditional grazing rights for livestock. However, through concerted efforts from domestic and international movements, a legal mechanism was found to enable the establishment of Bjeshket National Park in December 2012, with Fatmir Morina appointed as its first director in 2014.

Despite these advances, the park is not welcomed by everyone. Ripped-up trail markers and anti-park graffiti on maps and kiosks are not uncommon. Rights for landowners was a new and confusing issue when the park was first established, and loggers have spread rumors about the government trying to take over private land and to prohibit traditional lifestyles and land use. Poaching and illegal logging is lucrative and continues, though it has been dramatically reduced through stricter monitoring of the single access road, which provides access to Rugova Gorge at the heart of the park.

The B3P has attempted to operate on the national park level by arranging study tours for professionals from the region to Yorkshire Dales National Park in the UK and Brecon Beacons National Park in Wales to understand how these national parks are managed. Even when national-level issues can be addressed, the hurdle of the official Track 1 political context with all of its layers of international diplomatic intrigue remains—from the relationship with Serbia, to UNMIK, and later EULEX (which replaced UNMIK in December 2008) in Kosovo maintaining its capacity building presence, to the competition to achieve EU accession status and eventually full membership. All of these issues make it politically unlikely that a formal peace park agreement is feasible in the short term. However, the political situation changes so rapidly that there may be a ripe moment in the future when a multi-track approach will build a critical mass of support and be applied effectively during the right window of opportunity.[20] The B3P has been effective, working at many different levels of society and politics in the region, but has yet to muster the cachet to influence Track 1 diplomacy and international policy.

Fundraising has long been a challenge for all charities, and it remains a challenge for the B3P, which continues to be a committed volunteer organization without an endowment, with fundraising efforts implemented on a project-to-project basis through proposal writing and grassroots campaigns. Several emerging international actors present the potential to be part of a greater international project, a network of organizations, institutions and local actors and a strategic, coordinated funding body and project implementation process. This recent development of large international actors further embracing the transboundary collaborative process includes GIZ and its Peaks of the

Balkans Initiative—"A Hiking Trail between Albania, Kosovo and Montenegro." This initiative won the World Tourism and Travel Council Award for the top sustainable destination in 2013, leading to a 10-fold increase in tourists within two years. This has been a blessing and a bane as the infrastructure does not have the capacity to absorb such numbers, leading to increased pollution of the air and waterways and a proliferation of garbage, particularly single-use plastic bottles and bags.

SNV has been working with the World Wildlife Fund (WWF) and the International Union for the Conservation of Nature (IUCN) Offices for South Eastern Europe on The Dinaric Arc Initiative.[21] Erg explains that

> Environment for People in the Dinaric Arc is a project designed to promote the natural and cultural values of the area while enhancing local livelihoods through improved regional cooperation and strengthened environmental governance. It aims at fostering sustainable development and building capacity of rural communities in the transboundary areas in the region.[22]

The B3P Committee has embraced the GIZ/SNV lead "Peaks of the Balkans" project and is actively collaborating on strategic steering committee decisions as well as sharing project information concerning the B3P Summer Programme plans. Initial collaboration in this next phase of the relationship began in earnest in November 2011.

Educational efforts from international organizations have definitely assisted in catalyzing domestic collaboration between conservation management organizations. Albania's park authority signed a regional park agreement with Kosovo at the end of 2014, alongside the expanded Thethi and Valbona national parks that now contiguously border both Kosovo and Montenegro without any missing pieces. The Balkan Lynx Recovery Program, initiated by an Albanian conservation organization called Protection and Preservation of Natural Environments in Albania (PPNEA) has also proven to be a new driver of cooperation. It uses biodiversity monitoring through camera trapping in Albania and Macedonia, and recently expanded into Kosovo and Montenegro, following the transboundary habitat of the Balkan Lynx's range known through GPS tracking collars. The role of charismatic megafauna in social systems and in fostering positive media for conservation efforts is well known,[23] and this case further illustrates their salience in border ecologies as well.

Critiques: Pitfalls of Peace Park Development

A critique that local partner organizations have expressed directly is a disconnect that the B3P is now addressing. In spite of the conferences, meetings and publicity events in the early years (2001–7) of the proposed Balkans Peace Park development, locals felt there was not enough sufficient on-the-ground action and practical projects/programs that would actively make a difference in people's lives. Border communities do not simply want to be studied; instead, they hope to directly benefit from the experiential learning and see an improved quality of life and increased livelihood opportunities. Successive B3P Summer Programmes (2008–15) have demonstrated a commitment to on-the-ground projects, and their expansion into Kosovo and Montenegro further galvanizes this long-term commitment to service learning and shared experiences for mutual benefit. B3P is no longer viewed as an organization that is "all talk and no action."

Other local partner critiques include unintended consequences and the B3P's lack of ability to adapt to quickly address them—including responding to damage to local partner vehicles in the field and determining whose responsibility it was to pay for repairs. Other unintended consequences include not working to create real partnerships in the early days of cross-border trekking, and not sharing the experiences together as peers, but rather treating local guides as mere service providers. This has been addressed in recent years through the expansion of the Summer Programmes to Montenegro, where they now see a direct benefit on the ground in their country, and in a more collaborative planning process with local leadership like the B3P Albania NGO, which shifted the relationship away from "service provider" to "partnership."

A final local partner critique revolves around an oft-cited challenge faced by small international organizations—the impossible necessity of being a foreigner who is not a local. No matter how deep a connection one develops with a place over time, short of living there, one cannot possibly understand the nuance of local politics in each of the three countries. Therefore, international organizations/NGOs often unknowingly choose a path that ignores regional, local and national political structures and procedures, and instead focus on the international and community levels. This pitfall harkens back to this book's Introduction, where the reader is reminded by Singh and colleagues of the importance of organizational scales and the role of hierarchy in social ecological systems. A prime example centered around efforts to create the international peace park, when there was no existing national park in Kosovo, or bringing the mayors together to sign the Letter of Good Intent, but not being able to bring this initiative to the regional or national level. Now that Bjeshket e Nemuna National Park in Kosovo and Prokletije National Park in Montenegro have been formally established, park directors have been appointed and professionalization is under way, and Thethi and Valbona National Parks in Albania have been extended to the borders, a real possibility exists to actually connect them into the transboundary international peace park. Local partner organizations have realized many positive interactions and collaborations with the B3P. Despite the aforementioned critiques, B3P members are adapting, and changing their behavior and seeking to redress the mistakes of the past and to avoid committing similar ones in the future.

French scholar Juliet Fall at the University of Geneva is one of the most outspoken critics of the proposed Balkans peace park and the idea of peace parks in general. Fall asserts that the concept of borders is inherently violent, and that creating a collaborative framework to manage transboundary areas is only entrenching the concept of the border itself, and its inherent ability to divide, demarcate and separate. Through her historical review of the ontological derivation of the words "border" and "protected area," she uncovers international communities' evolution of the concepts over time, but continually highlights the inability to deal with this inherent dichotomy. She views international peace parks as a new name for an old concept—the ontological evolution of using the symbolism of words to create divisions in the real world.

In her 1999 article "Transboundary Biosphere Reserves: A New Framework for Cooperation," Fall examines the idea of cross-border environmental conservation and highlights the challenges and barriers to successfully setting up management structures for transboundary cooperation, asserting that "management of protected areas adjacent to political borders is rarely thought of as a common necessity for neighbouring countries."[24] The argument becomes more nuanced in her 2003 article "Planning Protected Areas across Boundaries: New Paradigms and Old Ghosts." This article drills down to the definition of a coherent planning unit for protected areas, and she explores the differences between the natural and social science approaches to defining the boundaries of transboundary protected areas; she then applies that analysis to explore how natural and social science approaches have influenced planning.[25] This line of thought continues in her 2010 coauthored article "Unbounded Boundary Studies and Collapsed Categories: Rethinking Spatial Objects."[26]

She asserts in a 2004 article, "Constructing the Carpathians: The Carpathian Convention and the Search for a Spatial Ideal," that "what is missing is an appropriate internationally-recognised legal framework." We completely agree with this critique.[27] International peace parks appear to be a concept that is applied differently around the world based on local legal norms, local cultures and locally available assets of the natural world. A standardized, accepted, international legal framework would benefit the field greatly and provide a basic roadmap of required steps to be accomplished in order to reach international peace park recognition.

Conclusion

The B3P exemplifies the distinctive feature of national border areas that can provide opportunities for reflecting on conflict and peace and experiential learning. Even though the ultimate goal of a peace park in this region remains to be realized, the social movements around this process provide an opportunity for instructive engagement. The genesis of this initiative from both external and internal agents of change also exemplifies the comparative lesson drawing that border landscapes have the potential to provide.

As the four criteria for peacebuilding outlined in our introduction remind us, border landscapes indeed inspire a positive notion of "other" through their real-world examples. Experiential learning is an important frame through which contemporary discourse on borders should be considered. Architectural clinics have previously followed such an approach with key border landscapes in terms of landscape design (most notably in the Jordan River Valley and the Korean Peninsula).[28] However, the linkage of such learning efforts as a means of galvanizing broader change in perceptions about the linkage of social and ecological systems deserves greater attention.

NOTES

1 Antonia Young, *Women who Become Men: Albanian Sworn Virgins* (New York: Bloomsbury Publishing, 2000).

2 Antonia Young writes: "Rosie Swale has written six books and numerous articles. Her achievements are truly remarkable: she sailed the Atlantic alone in a boat only 6 meters long (70 days); she rode two horses alone, the length of Chile (5,000 kms.—8 months). She has run, for

charities, across Romania, Iceland, Cuba and in the Sahara Desert marathon, then Nepal. She is currently running round the world for charities; you can check her progress at: www. rosiearoundtheworld.co.uk." Source: Antonia Young, "Establishing the Balkans Peace Park (Albania, Montenegro and Kosova/o) Overcoming Conflicts through Negotiation on Cross-Border Environmental Protection," *Central & Eastern European Review* 2(2008): 1–34.

3   See Richard Hargreaves's comment on the inaugural trek: "In 2003 the 'Inaugural trek' took place. 36 people from 8 countries embarked on mountain walks in Kosovo, Montenegro, and Albania, finishing with a conference for 80 people in Shkodër, organized by Blendi Dibra of IRSH. Transport was used between countries because border crossings were not open. The walks included the wonderful mountain walk from Lepushë near Vermosh to Thethi via Qafa Koprishtit and Qafa e Pejës, said to be the first time this route had been walked for 15 years." Source: Richard Hargreaves, Report on Trekking from Thethi to Curraj Eperm, Albania (Unpublished 2006), http://balkanspeacepark.org.

4   See Richard Hargreaves's full comment: "Cycle ride by 8 people from 5 countries: 550km. Podgorica – Kolashin – Andrijevica – Cakor Pass – Drelaj – Peja – (Transport to Berane) – Plav – Gusinje – Vermosh – Koplik – Thethi – Shkodër – round Lake Skadar – Virpazar – Podgorica. Trucks had to be hired for parts of the route, especially in Albania where the gravel mountain roads defeated those not on mountain bikes. Great help was provided by Branko Hajdukovic, President of the Yugoslav Cycling Federation." Source: Richard Hargreaves, Report on the 2007 two week multi-activity, borders-crossing trip (Unpublished 2007). http:// balkanspeacepark.org.

5   Shala Valley Project. www.millsaps.edu/svp/.

6   In his commentary, Rossi writes: "2003 signaled 'A Long Walk for Peace,' sponsored by the Kosovar Ministry of Youth, Culture and Sport, for 21 people, mostly from Kosovo but with two participants from the UK and three Albanians. The group embarked on mountain walks in each country." Source: Chris Rossi, "A Long Walk for Peace: The Balkans Peace Park Project," http://groups.colgate.edu/cews/archives/2004–2005/Chris%20Rossi%20Panel%201%20 balkans.pdf.

7   As it was not locally driven, this coalition of local NGOs quickly dissolved after this event, and "ERA Group" is now the only NGO from this original group that still exists.

8   Rossi offers more details: "Conference in Pristina in November at which mayors or leaders from 5 of the 6 municipalities serving the B3P region, Peja, Decan, Rozaj, Plav, Shkodër and Bajram Curraj, signed a Letter of Good Intent to support the concept of the Balkans Peace Park—organized by a Coalition of local environmentalists from Kosovo, Montenegro and Albania." Rossi, "A Long Walk for Peace."

9   Hargreaves adds that "A group of 15 did the two day roundtrip trek from Okol (above Thethi) in Albania to Zastan Kabila above Vusanje (Montenegro)." Hargreaves, "Report on the 2007 two week multi-activity, borders-crossing trip."

10 Hargreaves elaborates further: "July: 'Multi-activity, borders-crossing trip' from Plav: 4 day trek on foot into Albania from Ropojana valley (Vusanje), Qafa e Pejës, Thethi, Valbona, Kukaj, Qafa Valbona, Zastan Kabila, Plav. 5 day mountain bike tour to Kosovo: Cakor Pass, Drelaj, Peja, Decan, Qafa Bogicevica, Babino Polje, Plav. The group climbed a peak in each country: Maja Arapit (Albania), Ochnyak from Grbaje (Montenegro), Hajla Peak (Kosovo/ Montenegro border) and also raised a B3P banner on Trimedra, c.2365m, the mountain point where Albania, Kosovo and Montenegro meet." Ibid.

11 Jonathan Todd Walters, "B3P Summer Programme 2008 Report," Paper presented at the 2008 B3P Annual Meeting at Coventry University–Peace & Reconciliation Centre, September 20, 2008, Coventry, United Kingdom.

12 See Hargreaves's observation: "Rock climbing developments: Polish climbers made a new route and possible first ascent of Mt. Lagojvet in Prokletije, which they named 'Balkans Peace Park route.' John Ely from US and climbers from Germany and Albania made a major new

route up the 1000m face of Maja Arapit. They also visited the Summer Programme in Thethi and collected names for a petition to promote B3P at their base camp by the spring at the start of the Qafa e Pejës path." Source: Richard Hargreaves, *B3P Newsletter*, 8(2011), http://balkanspeacepark.org.

13 Conservation Beyond Borders: Exploring the Prospects for a Peace Park in the Balkans. http://newswatch.nationalgeographic.com/2011/09/28/conservation-beyond-borders-balkans-2011-academic-expedition/.

14 According to its website (B3P Website), accessed April 15, 2012, http://balkanspeacepark.org.

15 Ibid.

16 MEP Graham Watson: 2010, B3P website. http://balkanspeacepark.org.

17 David E. Bloom, "Youth in the Balance," *Finance and Development*, 49 (2012): 7–11, www.imf.org/external/pubs/ft/fandd/2012/03/bloom.htm.

18 J. Galtung, *Peace by Peaceful Means: Peace and Conflict, Development and Civilization* (London: Sage, 1996).

19 Shala Valley Project, www.millsaps.edu/svp/.

20 Refer to the Institute for Multi-Track Diplomacy, www.imtd.org/index.php/about/84-about/131-what-is-multi-track-diplomacy, for a graphic explanation of the multi-track approach. The graphic includes seven sequential tracks as follows: government, professional conflict resolution, business, private citizen, research/training/education, peace activism, religion, funding and media/public opinion.

21 B. Erg, Dinaric Arc Initiative to boost transboundary cooperation in the Western Balkans, (Gland, Switzerland: International Union for Conservation of Nature, April 16, 2010), www.iucn.org/about/union/secretariat/offices/iucnmed/?5059/Dinaric-Arc-Initiative-to-boost-transboundary-cooperation-in-the-Western-Balkans.

22 Ibid.

23 Emma Marris, "Charismatic Mammals Can Help Guide Conservation," *Nature* 24 (2013), doi:10.1038/nature.2013.14396.

24 Juliet J. Fall, "Transboundary Biosphere Reserves: A New Framework for Cooperation," *Environmental Conservation* 26 (1999): 252–5.

25 Juliet J. Fall, "Planning Protected Areas across Boundaries: New Paradigms and Old Ghosts," *Journal of Sustainable Forestry* 17 (2003): 81–102.

26 Bernard Debarbieux, Juliet J. Fall and Marius Schaffter, "Unbounded Boundary Studies and Collapsed Categories: Rethinking Spatial Objects," *Progress in Human Geography*, 34 (2010): 254–62.

27 Harald Egerer and Juliet J. Fall. "Constructing the Carpathians: the Carpathian Convention and the Search for a Spatial Ideal," *Revue de Géographie Alpine*, 92 (2004): 98–106.

28 Cornell University ran an architectural clinic on the DMZ border zone in 2010. Yale University ran a similar clinic. Refer to *National Geographic Online* article by Yehre Suh. "Designing Ecological Peace in the Koreas," http://voices.nationalgeographic.com/2011/12/23/designing-ecological-peace-in-the-koreas/, December 23, 2011.

BIBLIOGRAPHY

Bloom, David E. "Youth in the Balance." *Finance and Development*, 49 (2012): 7–11. www.imf.org/external/pubs/ft/fandd/2012/03/bloom.htm.

Conservation Beyond Borders: Exploring the Prospects for a Peace Park in the Balkans. (2001). http://newswatch.nationalgeographic.com/2011/09/28/conservation-beyond-borders-balkans-2011-academic-expedition/.

Debarbieux, Bernard, Juliet J. Fall and Marius Schaffter. "Unbounded Boundary Studies and Collapsed Categories: Rethinking Spatial Objects." *Progress in Human Geography* 34 (2010): 254–62.

Egerer, Harald and Juliet J. Fall. "Constructing the Carpathians: The Carpathian Convention and the Search for a Spatial Ideal." *Revue de Géographie Alpine*, 92 (2004): 98–106.

Erg, B. Dinaric Arc Initiative to boost transboundary cooperation in the Western Balkans. Gland, Switzerland: International Union for Conservation of Nature. April 16, 2010. www.iucn.org/about/union/secretariat/offices/iucnmed/?5059/Dinaric-Arc-Initiative-to-boost-transboundary-cooperation-in-the-Western-Balkans.

Fall, Juliet J. "Planning Protected Areas across Boundaries: New Paradigms and Old Ghosts." *Journal of Sustainable Forestry* 17 (2003): 81–102.

Fall, Juliet, J. "Transboundary Biosphere Reserves: A New Framework for Cooperation." *Environmental Conservation* 26 (1999): 252–5.

Galtung, J. *Peace by Peaceful Means: Peace and Conflict, Development and Civilization.* London: Sage, 1996.

Hargreaves, Richard. *B3P Newsletter.* 8(2011). http://balkanspeacepark.org.

Hargreaves, Richard. "Report on the 2007 two week multi-activity, borders-crossing trip." (Unpublished, 2007). http://balkanspeacepark.org.

Hargreaves, Richard. "Report on Trekking from Thethi to Curraj Eperm, Albania." (Unpublished, 2006). http://balkanspeacepark.org.

Marris, Emma. "Charismatic Mammals Can Help Guide Conservation." *Nature.* 24 (2013), doi:10.1038/nature.2013.14396.

Rossi, Chris. "A Long Walk for Peace: The Balkans Peace Park Project." (2004–5 archives). www.colgate.edu/portaldata/imagegallerywww/3661/ImageGallery/Chris%20Rossi%20Panel%201%20balkans.pdf.

Shala Valley Project. www.millsaps.edu/svp/.

Suh, Yehre. "Designing Ecological Peace in the Koreas." December 23, 2011. http://voices.nationalgeographic.com/2011/12/23/designing-ecological-peace-in-the-koreas/.

Walters, Jonathan Todd. "B3P Summer Programme 2008 Report." Paper presented at the 2008 B3P Annual Meeting at Coventry University–Peace & Reconciliation Centre, September 20, 2008, Coventry, United Kingdom.

Watson, MEP Graham. B3P Website. (2010). http://balkanspeacepark.org.

Young, Antonia. *Women Who Become Men: Albanian Sworn Virgins.* New York: Bloomsbury Publishing, 2000.

Chapter Five

SOCIAL ECOLOGIES IN BORDERLANDS: CRANE HABITAT RESTORATION AND SUSTAINABLE AGRICULTURE PROJECT IN THE DEMOCRATIC PEOPLE'S REPUBLIC OF KOREA

Hall Healy, George Archibald and Arthur H. Westing

Introduction

One of 15 crane species around the world, the Red-crowned Crane (*Grus japonensis*) of northeast Asia, is divided into a migratory population on the mainland (about 1,400), and a resident population in northern Japan (approximately 1,500), for a total of around 2,900 birds in the wild. Consequently, the International Union for Conservation of Nature (IUCN) considers the Red-crowned Crane Endangered. About 1,000 of the migratory cranes winter on the Korean Peninsula, of which its borderlands within and contiguous to the Demilitarized Zone (DMZ) connecting the two countries are crucial to this species' continued survival.[1]

Cranes are firmly embedded in Asian culture and have been spiritual icons for millennia, as exhibited in the art of China, India, Russia, Japan and Korea. They symbolize happiness, longevity and loyalty in human societies globally. They are a consummate example of what Edward O. Wilson calls "biophilia," the "innately emotional affiliation of human beings to other living organisms"[2]—a social ecological concept that gives hope to efforts like the ones described in this volume to reintegrate humankind with nature. In spite of that affection, however, 11 of the 15 species are Vulnerable or Endangered, according to IUCN. Similar threats confront them everywhere: habitat degradation and loss owing to development, pollution, chemically based fertilizers and pesticides, hunting and illegal trade. Murray Bookchin, a father of social ecology, would certainly cite cranes as an unwitting victim of ecological problems caused by practices of human society, which also possesses solutions to these challenges.

This chapter explores the context creating the separation of the two Koreas, its resulting new borderlands and the plight of migratory cranes there; specifics of unique crane habitat restoration and sustainable agriculture work in the Democratic People's Republic of Korea (DPRK) within that setting; project successes to date; and next steps.

All aspects of the project have social ecology underpinnings and implications. And they provide one response, in the context of a farm cooperative in North Korea and the Korean Demilitarized Zone, to questions Bookchin poses, of what has been and could be "humanity's place in nature" and "society's relationship with the natural world,"[3] both in creating the divide between humans and nature and in helping to close that gap. The project demonstrates the impacts of redrawn borderlands on the natural world. What we also trust will be shown through the North Korean work is that wildlife, in this case cranes, can coexist with humans, not in some "ecological wilderness zone," but in an integrated manner.[4] In continuation of and expansion on themes developed in the prior chapter, it is likewise possible to see the North Korean project and the DMZ, as Verena Conley puts it, as an "intertwining" of cultures, and to view the DMZ as a larger version of her *Jardin d'Essai* (test garden), emphasizing "the need for people to cooperate with one another."

Partners in this project were the State Academy of Sciences, DPR Korea (SAOS); Pisan Cooperative Farm in Anbyon County, DPRK; International Crane Foundation (ICF), Baraboo, Wisconsin, USA, a private, nongovernmental organization; BirdLife International (a global partnership of conservation organizations)—Asia Division and Korea University, both in Tokyo; and Hanns Seidel Stiftung, a foundation in Munich, Germany.

The Korean Peninsula: Social Ecological Perspectives

Political, Geopolitical Contexts

The Korean War of 1950–3 ended with an armistice agreement—and with both the DPRK/North Korea and the Republic of Korea (ROK)/South Korea avowedly looking forward to achieving a peace treaty, and ultimately reunification, though there is no such treaty as of yet.[5] The Military Demarcation Line (MDL) established at the time to separate the two Koreas was 248 kilometers (154 miles) long, bisecting a Demilitarized Zone (DMZ) four kilometers (2.5 miles) wide—the established DMZ thus covering an area of 99,200 hectares (245,130 acres = 383 square miles). An informal Civilian Control Zone (CCZ) was also established directly south of the DMZ that averaged 5.4 kilometers (3.4 miles) in width; a CCZ of similar width is said to exist immediately north of the DMZ. Consequently, the combined area of the DMZ plus its two associated CCZs is perhaps 367,000 hectares (907,000 acres = 1,417 square miles).

In 1953, the DMZ was placed under the control of the Military Armistice Commission (MAC) consisting of China, North Korea and the United Nations (UN) Command (composed of 16 UN member states, including and represented by the United States), but not including South Korea. At various times since then, China, North Korea (these two in 1994) and most of the UN Command nations have resigned from MAC (either formally or in practice). MAC, now renamed the United Nations Command Military Armistice Commission (UNCMAC), has in recent years become primarily a US operation carried out in cooperation with South Korea.[6]

Relations between North and South Korea have waxed and waned markedly since 1953; they reached a high point of cooperation during the 1990s, as manifested especially by their 1991 Agreement of Reconciliation, Non-aggression, Exchanges, and Cooperation. Among a host of other pledges, the two Koreas thereby committed themselves to working together to carry out peaceful uses of the DMZ, and also to cooperate in diverse fields, including the environment. In early 1991, North Korea approached the United Nations to explore the possibility of a DMZ-centered bio-sanctuary, a request South Korea repeated soon thereafter. The action agency here became the United Nations Environment Programme (UNEP).

North Korea drew back from its initial interest in 1992, although later reiterating its commitment to preserve the biota and ecology of the DMZ. South Korea maintained its commitment, dealing with UNEP and subsequently also with the United Nations Development Programme (UNDP). In 1997, President Kim Young-Sam of South Korea, in addressing the United Nations General Assembly, specifically expressed his hope that the two Koreas would cooperate to protect and preserve the DMZ, turning it into a zone of peace and ecological integrity.

Also in 1997, MAC for the first time invited South Korea to participate directly in its negotiations. In 2000, the heads of state of both countries (North Korea's Kim Jong-Il and South Korea's Kim Dae Jung) met for the first time ever. Also in 2000 Kim Dae Jung was awarded the Nobel Peace Prize for his burgeoning "sunshine policy" toward North Korea. More recently, former president Park Geun Hye of South Korea announced in 2013 her intent to pursue making the DMZ a "world peace park," as part of the "Trustpolitik" program. This plan, an incremental trust-building process, focuses more on ordinary people and civil society, while increasing trust and cooperation between the two Koreas.[7]

The aim of a country to protect its borders from outside intrusion—the traditional definition of national security—has evolved considerably in recent decades. The notion of national security has increasingly come to encompass such additional national obligations as rights to health care and an environment of a quality permitting a life of well-being and dignity. It was concomitantly recognized ever more fully that those expanded national obligations also require a respect for nature, some species of which are not confined by national borders.

That respect translated on one hand into sustainably managed agricultural, forest, wetland and other rural areas. On the other, it meant setting aside some modest fraction of the world for plants and animals making up the biosphere. Soon, additionally recognized was the incongruity between eco-region boundaries and national boundaries, leading to the realization that here was yet another reason countries had to eschew at least some level of isolationism to achieve expanding security obligations. So it is that societal security is dependent on environmental security—which, in turn, cannot be achieved without social awareness of the connection between the two, and the necessary actions that follow from such linkage.[8]

Social Ecological Perspectives: Transfrontier Park's Potential to Help Reintegrate Humans and Nature

In looking at the potential for borderlands to contribute to a more ecologically integrated world even in such a conflicted region, one possible link is joint designation of the DMZ as a transfrontier park for the mutual benefit of nature, both countries and their people. As a by-product and irony of the Korean War, and off-limits to most human activity for more than 60 years, it now contains up to an estimated 3,500 plant, bird, mammal and fish species. At the moment, the DMZ represents a *de facto* isolated "wilderness park." But these species and their accompanying natural resources of wetlands, five major rivers and forested land (the latter covering 75 percent of the DMZ) have the potential to provide much-needed materials and services to both Koreas, in the form of ecosystem services such as pollution control, carbon sequestration, ecotourism and sustainably harvested fish and lumber,[9] and this without the necessity of "exploitation" described as a concern by Bookchin, but of sustainable and mutual benefit.[10] The DMZ borderlands, while now a "black belt" prohibiting interchange and integration of people and nature, could become a "green belt" allowing nutrition, access, transit and respite, in essence the way the cranes now treat it, unfettered by human constraints, while also facilitating a "green approach" to conflict resolution.[11]

The notion of transfrontier parks for peace and nature is not new. In 1924, representatives of Poland and the former Czechoslovakia established two pairs of cooperating, contiguous nature reserves in the Tatra Mountains straddling what is now the Polish–Slovakian border, for the express purpose of rebuilding bilateral trust as an approach to settling a World War I border dispute. In 1999, Ecuador and Peru established the demilitarized transfrontier Cordillera del Condor Peace Park to celebrate postwar settlement of a boundary dispute and to commemorate fallen soldiers of both sides. More than two dozen formal bilateral transfrontier reserves for peace and nature now exist around the world, with many more at various levels of informality.

North and South Korea have been independently exploring establishment of park space on either side of the DMZ, the North in South Hwanghae Province, the South in Yeoncheon and Paju. Mount Keumgang, near the DMZ in the DPRK, was designated as a United Nations Educational, Scientific and Cultural Organization (UNESCO) Biosphere Reserve in 1982, submitted for UNESCO World Heritage status and subsequently placed on the Tentative World Heritage List in 2000. South Korea's Mt. Seorak, while not a "Biosphere Reserve," was submitted for World Heritage status and then placed on the Tentative World Heritage List in 1994. Short of being able to designate the DMZ or portions of it as some form of biosphere or transboundary reserve, action has been taken to ameliorate the tenuous status of certain species. Contiguous to the DMZ, in Hwacheon County, ROK, the Korea Otter Research Center has been conducting monitoring, research and release of otters (*Lutra lutra*). Habitat for these animals is the Bukhan (North Han) River that extends from North Korea into South Korea. The otters' electronic tracking collars poignantly demonstrate that political boundaries are no obstacle to their wanderings. They are even less so for migratory birds.

The borderlands depicted in other chapters of this book all have their unique aspects, but none is as fortified as is either side of the DMZ, nor has been in its current state as long. The DMZ now is the most heavily fortified border in the world, with very little communication passing between the two neighbors. This presents its own obstacles in realizing a social ecological reintegration of humans and nature, but it also provides opportunities.

One would be to allow sharing of DMZ resources in a sustainable fashion, including fishing, timber harvesting and water. A "water fund" could be established that has South Korea paying North Korea to supply a consistent quality and quantity of water to the South, as has been done by New York City for years to farmers in the Catskill Mountains, thereby avoiding billions of dollars of investment in treating water full of agricultural chemicals and cow manure. Another possibility is to have the relatively pollution-free North Korea receive pollution credits from the more industrialized nations, à la carbon trading in some Western countries. All of these approaches could exemplify a more harmonious relationship politically and between humans and nature. In fact, such sharing could help establish necessary trust between the parties and serve as a useful metaphor for more integration of humans and nature later on. In that way, the DMZ borderlands would offer a bridge, not a barrier, to further cooperation.

Spiritual and Symbolic Components

Cranes have been iconic throughout Asia and many parts of the world for centuries, as demonstrated in sculpture, paintings and on clothing. Numerous crane sculptures and paintings adorn the ancient Forbidden City of Beijing, China. Paintings in the temples and tombs of Japan contain cranes. Cave art depicting cranes has been discovered in Spain, Britain and Sweden going back 5,000, 6,000, perhaps even 12,000 years,[12] in short, rooting the cultural in the natural.[13] Perhaps the cranes, owing to their long history with humans, also could be a connector between Bookchin's "first nature" and "second nature."[14]

In the corporate world, cranes are used as logos by Air Koryo, North Korea's national air carrier, Japan Airlines and Lufthansa of Germany, implying stability and strength. Millennium Pharmaceutical Company has used its "Thousand Cranes of Hope" project to bring attention to its commitment to develop drugs for treating cancer.[15] Numerous other companies, sports teams and countries also use the crane name or its representation. The Ugandan flag contains a crane, and cranes are the national bird of Nigeria, South Africa and Uganda.

Social and Cultural Components

A famous Japanese legend, with numerous renditions, about a "Crane Maiden" tells of a poor farmer who rescued a wild crane from a trap. In one version, the crane flies away, only to return as a beautiful young woman. The maiden wove resplendent cloth for the farmer on condition that she never be viewed while she worked. When this was disregarded and he saw a crane plucking her own feathers to make the cloth, she flew away, never to come back.[16] Through this story the crane embodies fragility, loyalty and beauty and reminds the reader of the importance of integrity.

Schoolchildren in Hiroshima, Japan, have made thousands of paper origami cranes as symbols of peace, part of the Japanese tradition of *Senbazuru*, which maintains that anyone who folds 1,000 origami cranes will receive one wish, such as long life or recovery from illness.[17]

Going back hundreds of years in Korean culture, people have practiced "mountain worship" called *San-shin*, in which the character is portrayed achieving a highly enlightened state of being. Its most common representation is that of a tiger. Although cranes do not represent San-shin, they do appear in San-shin paintings and those of *Dokseong* ("The Recluse"), a popular shaman deity found in Korean Buddhist temples. According to San-shin expert David Mason in Seoul, "The second most common object that San-shin is shown holding is a fan made of white crane feathers, a symbol of San-shin's power to marshal wind or other spirits, bringing Taoist and Confucian associations with cranes into these icons as enhancements of spiritual powers."[18] Being able to command forces of nature and spirits is reminiscent of Korean King Wang Kôn of the Koryo Dynasty (91–1392 CE), who in 935 CE said in one of his *Ten Injunctions*, "I carried out the great undertaking of reunifying the country by availing myself of the latent virtue of the mountains and streams."[19] Not a bad image to evoke support for redressing disparities described by social ecologists.

Depictions of San-shin are found in temples throughout South Korea, and the practice is known in North Korea as well, where there are a number of temples containing San-shin paintings. Mason also notes that "San-shin became the central figure of all Korean religious culture, the most common deity, nearly universally revered. This process [...] is still evolving and enjoying a widespread revival. Owing to its association with all of the major religions to which Koreans subscribe, mountain worship is flourishing in [South] Korea," perhaps even beginning to serve as a symbol for a greener future.[20]

Both South and North Korea have a system for designating "Natural Monuments," which can be species, places or cultural traditions they deem worthy of protection. In South Korea, the Red-crowned Crane is one such monument, National Natural Treasure #202, as is the White-naped Crane (*Grus vipio*) as Treasure #203.[21] In North Korea, both Red-crowned and White-naped Cranes are Natural Monuments, as are various locations vital to cranes, including Mundok on the west coast and Kumya and the Anbyon Plain in the southeast.[22] Many Koreans, North and South, bear the name "Hak," one of the Korean words for crane. Numerous town names in North Korea, including some near the project site (described later in this chapter) in Anbyon, contain the word for crane. Another cultural treasure in the DPRK is the centuries-old "Crane Pavilion" in Anbyon Town.

The wall of the massive compound containing the mausoleum of the DPRK founder, Kim Il Sung, and his son Kim Jong Il also features a flock of cranes in flight.

Cultures throughout the world have created legends, Aesop's fables among them, about cranes and their interaction with humans, usually supporting the role of cranes as symbols of marital fidelity, mate and parental devotion, vigilance, luck, intelligence or deep contemplation and weather omens. As renowned naturalist and writer Peter Matthiessen said: "Every land where they appear has tales and myths about the cranes."[23] In one more social ecological nod of appropriateness to this project, the etymological origin of the English word *congruent*—agreeing, accordant—derives from the Latin word for crane—*grus*.[24]

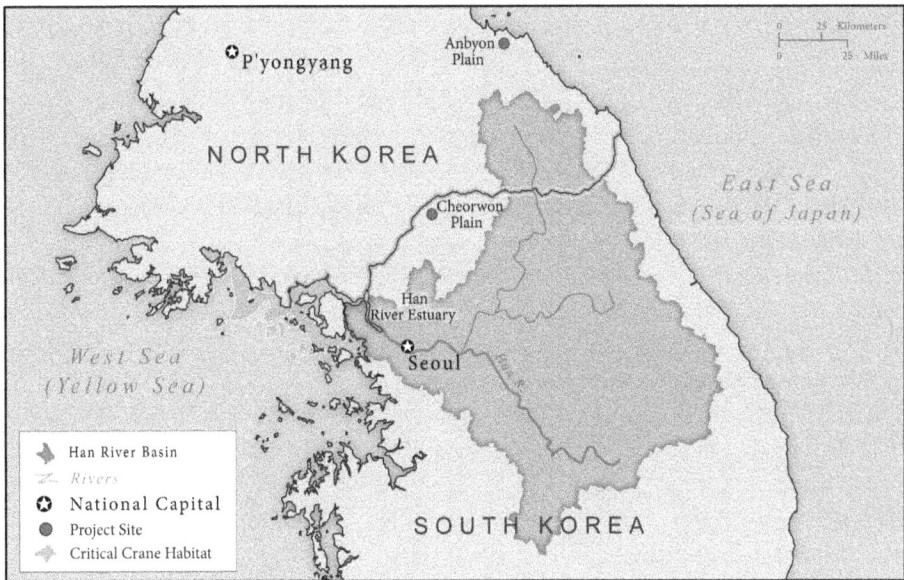

Figure 5.1 Crane Habitat Restoration and Sustainable Agriculture Project Area—Anbyon, DPRK. Courtesy of the International Crane Foundation, 2014.

Crane Habitat Restoration and Sustainable Agriculture Project

Background

Red-crowned Cranes migrate to the Korean Peninsula in late autumn and depart in late winter. Once common on lowlands throughout southern portions of North Korea and northern portions of South Korea, they are now primarily restricted to wintering in valleys within and near the DMZ. Wetlands and agricultural fields of the Cheorwon Basin in the ROK, near the center of the peninsula, support the majority of the cranes. Their flyway from Cheorwon to breeding grounds in eastern China and southeast Russia passes over the Anbyon Plain just south of Wonsan on the east coast of the DPRK.[25] Until food shortages in North Korea in the 1990s, the Anbyon Plain was a wintering area for as many as 244 cranes, and a transient stopover for numerous other species. Since 2008, the International Crane Foundation has collaborated with BirdLife International and the State Academy of Sciences, DPRK, in efforts to restore the Anbyon Plain as a crane wintering area.

By the early 1990s, North Korea's soil productivity had diminished owing to flooding, drought and reduced imports of fertilizer. These factors led to significant declines in farm yields. Subsequently, food supplies for people and therefore gleanings in the fields, previously a major food source for cranes, also decreased. It is unlikely that the cranes as individuals were harmed during these times, since they are strictly protected in North Korea, and only the military can maintain firearms.

Project Goals

Goals of the Anbyon project are to help local farmers improve crop yields and food supplies, while restoring habitat and food supplies for migratory cranes and other birds within an agricultural setting on the Pisan Cooperative Farm (PCF), Anbyon, DPRK. George Archibald, ICF cofounder, "has always felt that you can't help cranes without also helping people who live near them [...] that their [cranes' and peoples'] fates are intertwined,"[26] a fact underscored from a social ecological perspective. The PCF is part of the former crane wintering area on the Anbyon Plain, about 100 kilometers (62 miles) northeast of the Cheorwon Plain, that extends from the DPRK across the DMZ and into the ROK, where the birds go after leaving Anbyon.

The project contributes to implementation of numerous Ramsar Convention 2009–15 Strategic Plan Goals. Ramsar is the International Wetland Treaty [*UNTS* 14583] signed in 1971 and ascribed to by 169 nations, including ROK, though not yet the DPRK.[27] These goals include but are not limited to: Wise Use (Strategies and Key Result Areas including flood defense, food security, poverty eradication, cultural heritage, scientific research and science-based management); International Cooperation (Strategies including synergies and partnerships, regional initiatives and international assistance); and Institutional Capacity and Effectiveness. The project also supports the DPRK's "Conservation of a Natural Monument," program and one of that country's top three science goals—food security.

Project Objectives

To achieve the mutually beneficial goals of more food for humans and cranes, and restored habitat for the birds, is a series of interwoven objectives (i.e., interdependence between cranes and humans) relating to training, equipment and supplies. This series of objectives includes: increasing food production by training leaders and farmers in organic farming; providing machinery needed by the farmers such as a rice-seed sorter; providing seeds of nitrogen-fixing vetch (genus *Vicia*), a legume used to improve soil quality; and providing fruit tree seedlings for planting on hillsides to reduce erosion and flooding, while also offering another source of nutrition and income. It also includes: encouraging wild cranes to return and stay in the area by educating farmers and local residents on the importance of cranes and biodiversity in general; using a pair of cranes furnished by the Chinese State Forestry Administration as decoys to attract the wild ones; and educating people on the integral link with their own health and well-being.

These objectives are progressing positively, with assistance from the national and local DPRK governments, the Pisan Cooperative and modest annual financial help from ICF and Hanns Seidel Stiftung.

Helping Farmers Develop Sustainably Productive Agricultural Practices

Fortuitously for the Anbyon project, a 2008 edict from the DPRK central government mandated an increase in organic farming practices throughout the country. Organic farming (the practice of adding natural materials such as straw, manure, peat and

Table 5.1 Anbyon, DPRK experimental plots: Crop yield from organic versus chemical fertilizers.

Year	% Yield of Organic Fertilizer Versus Chemical Fertilizer
2008	74.7
2009	86.4
2010	89.6
2011	91.2

Source: Table developed by International Crane Foundation based on data provided by State Academy of Sciences, DPR Korea, Pisan Cooperative Farm, Anbyon, DPRK, 2011.

clay—and sowing nitrogen-fixing plants—to the soil) provides needed nutrients without human-made chemicals.

PCF has about 500 hectares (ca. 1,240 acres) on the plain and hillsides, of which 250 hectares (620 acres) are arable. Demonstrating the challenge to agriculture in general on the Korean Peninsula, only 16 percent of North Korea and 22 percent of South Korea is arable.[28] The Anbyon Plain encompasses about 10,000 hectares (ca. 24,700 acres) of land, divided among 11 cooperatives.

At the project's initiation in 2008 and 2009, SAOS and workers at the PCF introduced organic farming by planting 3,000 apricot, plum, nut and other tree seedlings on the hills; establishing a demonstration plot of organically grown rice; teaching organic farming techniques; and providing much-needed machinery. Many seedlings in the initial planting perished, mostly owing to a lack of water and poor soil quality. In 2011, ditches were dug to retain water; since then, soil quality also has been improving through the use of organic fertilizers. Another planting of seedlings will be made when conditions have improved adequately.

Since 2008, there have been four hectares (10 acres) at the PCF where only organic farming has been practiced. It takes several years before adequate nutrients are established to achieve crop yield equal to that with chemical fertilizers. In 2008, crop production from the organic plots was 74.7 percent of what it would have been on chemically fertilized areas. It had increased to 91 percent by 2011. As Table 5.1 demonstrates, there has been steady progress in productivity with organic fertilizers.

In terms of actual production achieved, Table 5.2 shows how successful the experimental plots have become.

Organic Farming Practices

At Pisan Cooperative, there are three sources of organic fertilizer produced in a new facility built with the help of Anbyon County, all of which support more ecologically focused crop production. One is made mainly with manure, in abundance at the cooperative. Another, called "humic acid," is created by isolating components of naturally occurring peat in the area. The peat currently is brought from 12 kilometers (ca. seven and a half miles) away by oxcart. A third type is made from animal fur, poultry feathers, microbiological elements,

Table 5.2 Anbyon, DPRK experimental plots: Actual 2011 yields from organic versus chemical fertilizer [1 kg/ha = 0.892 lb./acre. 1 g = 0.0353 oz.].

Experimental Plot Variable	Organic Farming Plot	Control (40 kg/Hectare with Chemical Fertilizer)
Seed Type	Pingdu No. 12	Pingdu No. 12
	Hamju-chal No. 2	Hamju-chal No. 2
Transplant Date	May 25	May 22
	June 20	June 18
Heading Date	July 30	July 27
	August 10	August 10
Number of Ears	670	710
(per hectare)	830	850
Weight of 1,000	28.0	28.0
Grains (g)	27.0	27.5
Harvest Date	October 3	October 1
	October 8	October 7
Yield per Hectare (kg)	5,100	5,590
	5,700	6,100

Source: Table developed by International Crane Foundation based on data provided by State Academy of Sciences, DPR Korea and Pisan Cooperative Farm, Anbyon, DPRK, 2011.

sulfuric acid and sodium hydroxide and used as a supplement for added nutrition. The PCF hopes to sell surplus production of these fertilizers to other cooperatives in the area. All these methods harken back to a time of greater harmony between agricultural outputs and inputs, with less detrimental side effects on the surrounding environment.

To achieve even greater food production, farmers have recently initiated double cropping—that is, planting of two crops during the growing season, generating attractive yields for various plants, including potatoes, rice planted after the potato crop, rape plant and rice planted in late June.

It is premature to claim that these new practices in organic farming at Pisan have achieved an "ecological society." However, a case can be made that the activities are creating more sustainable food supplies for humans and wildlife, and that if were maintained, could lead to less "pain and suffering,"[29] and where once again, cranes and humans can live in symbiosis. The project also has generated many varied social ecological benefits, including improved soil fertility and decreased soil acidity; improved food security and crop yield without the detrimental effects of chemical fertilizers; greater carbon content (from organic matter) in the soil and improved soil structure that is lighter, more able to absorb water and better aerated, through the addition of compost; and lower cost (not to mention the sheer availability) of organic over chemical fertilizers. Pisan purchased a full-cycle rice-milling machine to automate the de-husking process, in order to increase productivity, yield and food availability (by almost double). Several ponds have been constructed to grow water lettuce [*Pistia stratiotes*] for farm animals and to raise mud snails and crabs for cranes. A seven-seat vehicle (the "crane van") has also been purchased to transport farmers and supplies in and around the cooperative.

These accomplishments are enough in themselves. But they are just the tip of the iceberg in demonstrating the magic of thinking ecologically, "with its emphasis on the organic, holistic, and developmental."[30] The small amount of annual funds, $25,000–$50,000, provided by the International Crane Foundation since 2008, has been leveraged many-fold by the cooperative, local and national governments. The national government has invested in a livestock breeding facility at Pisan. Ditches have been dug to furnish irrigation of crops. Forty new homes have been built, as have new dirt roads and an office building. An old administration building has been converted to a kindergarten. A 300-person lecture hall has been constructed, allowing the cooperative to train more than 40,000 people from all over the DPRK in organic farming techniques. Training in organic farming techniques also has occurred in China for key project staff, along with the publishing of a book by Hanns Seidel Stiftung on organic farming practices.

Because of all this activity, a science and technology study team visited Pisan to collect information on and film the PCF, which was nominated as a model demonstration farm for all of the DPRK; and, national and local newspapers published articles on the farming techniques.

Crane Habitat Restoration

As a backdrop for this project, it should be noted that with the Anbyon area's centuries of farming, natural wetlands have long since disappeared, not surprising in the annals of social ecology.

Figure 5.2 Photo of Red-crowned and White-naped Cranes in Korea's Demilitarized Zone. Photograph by Dr. George Archibald, 2013.

In the 1980s, Professor Hiroyoshi Higuchi and others conducted research using radio transmitters on Red-crowned and White-naped Cranes to learn the cranes' migratory paths.[31] Their data correlated well with research by North Koreans on Anbyon Plain from the 1970s, showing that crane numbers peaked in early December and late February to early March. Higuchi and his colleagues found that several Red-crowned Cranes, equipped with transmitters at breeding areas in China and Russia, migrated south along the east coast of the Peninsula, stopping over in Anbyon. Some spent winters there for many years. Others continued southwest to Cheorwon Basin, adjacent to the DMZ, in the western part of Gangwon Province (ROK). A few birds moved back and forth between the two sites during winter. Concurrent with the decline of cranes in Anbyon owing to food shortages in the 1990s, there was an increase on ROK's Cheorwon Basin from about 300 to approximately 1,000 Red-crowned Cranes. This demonstrates the pivotal role the borderlands created by the Korean War play in this species survival.

At present, Cheorwon provides secure wintering for waterbirds. However, assuming relations improve between the Koreas and there is eventual reunification, that situation could well change for the worse. With peace, the ROK hopes to transform the Cheorwon Plain into "Reunification City," which would have the unintended consequence of eliminating the winter habitat for 1,000 Red-crowned Cranes, 3,000 White-naped Cranes, 250,000 geese and many other birds, certainly a huge step back in reintegrating humans and nature. Consequently, crane experts believed that an alternative site was needed. Anbyon was selected because of its prior history as an important wintering area for the birds, a choice that ties in well with the cultural importance people in the area have placed on cranes.

A pair of captive Red-crowned Cranes was used as decoys to attract migrating wild cranes to land. In November and March 2008–9, large flocks of cranes circled the Anbyon Plain, called to the captive cranes and then continued their migration to the Cheorwon wetlands.

In mid-November 2009, the captive cranes, seven wooden decoy cranes and amplification of recorded crane calls were all employed to attract the migrating wild cranes. Ninety-three White-naped and 91 Red-crowned Cranes flew overhead. Of those, 41 Red-crowned Cranes landed near the captive birds and remained for several days. In 2010, only the captive cranes were used to lure the wild cranes, none of which landed.

In October 2011, after the rice harvest, water was pumped into 63 hectares (156 acres) of paddies to create wetlands near the captive cranes to attract wild ones. The wooden decoy and crane call luring techniques were again utilized. One hundred twenty cranes circled the area as if interested in landing. Gratifyingly, 22 landed in small groups and stayed for varying times. One group of five remained for three weeks before leaving for Cheorwon. In addition, about 20 White-naped Cranes, 1,000 Greater white-fronted and Bean Geese [*Anser albifrons* and *A. fabalis*], Grey Herons [*Ardea cinerea*] and several species of egrets and shorebirds used the flooded rice paddies. In 2012, almost 70 Red-crowned Cranes landed at Anbyon, with 35 landing in 2013, and 18 landing in late 2014, and, incredibly, 116 landing in 2015. SAOS researchers feel that flooded paddies and live cranes are the most important factors in attracting wild cranes.

Two major food sources for the cranes, mudfish and crabs, are increasing as a result of organic farming and the ponds built in 2011. Crabs increased by 130 percent in the 12 experimental plots. Cranes have trailed people putting out corn, rice residue, fish and crabs for them.

Cranes continue to fly over the Anbyon Plain in spring and autumn, and as a result of the project to date, upwards of 100 have landed for several days or weeks since 2008. A lack of food, inadvertent disturbance from an increasing human population and perhaps crane "memories" of disturbances during the 1990s and an abundance of food and protection in and near the DMZ all conceivably coalesce to influence the cranes to spend most of the winter in the Cheorwon Basin. As local people become increasingly aware of the cranes and their needs, researchers are hopeful that the Anbyon Plain will once again become a major wintering site. In early 2015, Pisan farmers constructed a fence around the perimeter of the crane sanctuary to reduce disturbances from humans and domestic animals. An artificial feeding station for cranes will also be established in the fenced area. During upcoming winters, guards will be placed at strategic points to prevent humans from approaching the cranes. It is hoped that as cranes learn to trust humans, they will become more tolerant of their presence, as has happened in the Cheorwon Basin. Eventually, the hope is that these artificial means of sustaining the crane populations won't be needed, as, indeed they are not, in other parts of the world, like India, where humans and cranes coexist peacefully on very small plots of land, assuming there is sufficient food and security.

Public Education

Since 2008, captive cranes have served to educate the public about the birds' intrinsic value. Now farmers are anxious to bring back the wild cranes. After receiving a SAOS-created brochure on crane conservation, local schoolchildren were encouraged to collect many kilograms of grasshoppers to feed them. The PCF manager feels cranes have been a catalyst, making Pisan well known and bringing them "good luck."

Presentations have been made to Pisan and SAOS project leaders on the life history of the Red-crowned Crane and the biology and conservation of cranes on their wintering grounds in South Korea. These discussions have emphasized that development pressures on crane populations in the ROK necessitate restoration of former crane wintering sites in North Korea.

Project Funding

To date, ICF has collected monies for the project from private individuals and foundations. Needless to say, without these modest funds, totaling about $300,000 in cash as of 2015, the project would not be possible. Several hundred thousand more dollars of "in kind" support also have been provided.

Future Steps and Needs

Owing to its progress up to now, the project has created attention at the national and local levels in the DPRK and brought additional resources, though much remains to do. North Korean colleagues are pleased with the advances in organic agriculture and initial responses of the wild cranes.

Although there are many benefits to organic farming, there are substantial costs related to the transport of materials. Major PCF requirements include: equipment to transport peat, clay and organic deposits to processing sites and farm fields and construction of greenhouses and fertilizer storage tanks. SAOS also needs funds to publish and distribute books about biodiversity that are important to the public education process.

Considering the impressive accomplishments to date and the dedication and expertise of SAOS and PCF personnel, there is high optimism about the future of the project and the potential for expanding it to other known crane areas in the DPRK, such as Kangryong, Mundok and Kumya. There also is hope that relations between the Koreas will improve, providing more opportunities for significant financial assistance to Anbyon.

Many incentives exist for enhancing agricultural output in Anbyon, not the least of which is a basic human need for sustenance. By improving food supplies for humans, more also will be available for cranes and other migratory birds. The crane, as famed American naturalist Aldo Leopold said, is "worthy of protection in its own right as an enduring symbol of peace [...] When we hear his call we hear no mere bird. [...] He is the symbol of our untamable past, of that incredible sweep of millennia which underlies and conditions the daily affairs of birds and men. [...] *Upon the place of their return*, [in this case, Anbyon] *they confer a peculiar distinction* (emphasis added)."[32] Because of the organic agricultural successes up to this point at the PCF, it has become a model throughout the DPRK. It is the authors' fervent hope that Pisan and Anbyon also become a place of distinction for return of the Red-crowned Cranes and other migratory birds and a place where successful reintegration of humans and nature can occur. The area will never return to that of the cranes' ancient past. Hopefully it can offer an example to people in Peru, as we will read in the next chapter, of treasures their Amazon still has that they do not want to lose, and to those in Cyprus (Chapter 7) and Lebanon (Chapter 8) of how species and peoples can be brought back from the precipice.

NOTES

1 Curt Meine and George Archibald, IUCN/SSC Crane Specialist Group, *The Cranes: Status Survey and Conservation Action Plan* (Gland: International Union for Conservation of Nature (IUCN), 1996) accessed August 6, 2015. https://portals.iucn.org/library/efiles/documents/1996-022.pdf, 194–204.

2 Edward O. Wilson, *In Search of Nature* (Washington, DC: Island Press, 1996), 165.

3 Murray Bookchin, *The Philosophy of Social Ecology, Essays on Dialectical Naturalism* (Montreal: Black Rose Books, 1990), 16.

4 Ibid., 177.

5 The 1953 Armistice Agreement (Panmunjom, July 27, 1953) was unilaterally "declared invalid" by North Korea on March 11, 2013 (Alastair Gale and Keith Johnson, "North Korea Declares

War Truce 'Invalid,'" *Wall Street Journal*, March 12, 2013, A10). The significance and ramifications of that declaration are as yet uncertain.

6 UNCMAC retains only a tenuous connection with the United Nations, its two most recent periodic reports having been submitted on September 10, 1998 (UN Security Council, *Letter Dated 9 September 1998 from The Permanent Representative of the United States of America to the United Nations Addressed to the President of the Security Council, Document No. S/1998/844* (New York: UN Security Council, September 10, 1998), 1–17; and on November 7, 2000 (*UN Security Council, Letter Dated 6 November 2000 from The Permanent Representative of the United States of America to the United Nations addressed to the President of the Security Council, Document No. S/2000/1070* (New York: UN Security Council, November 7, 2000), 1–11. Moreover, on January 14, 2013, the DPRK submitted a detailed report to the United Nations making its case that UNCMAC has become a United Nations organ in name only (UN Security Council, *Letter Dated 14 January 2013 from the Permanent Representative of the Democratic People's Republic of Korea to the United Nations addressed to the President of the Security Council, Document No. S/2013/20* (New York: UN Security Council, January 14, 2013), 1–9.

7 Zachary Keck, "The Three Faces of Park's Trustpolitik," *The Diplomat*, May 3, 2013, accessed April 6, 2014. http://thediplomat.com/2013/05/the-three-faces-of-parks-trustpolitik/presidents-approach-to-north-korea.

8 Arthur H. Westing, "Regional Security: The Case of the Korean Demilitarized Zone (DMZ)," in *From Environmental to Comprehensive Security* (Heidelberg: Springer, 2013), 87–110.

9 Hall Healy, "Korean Demilitarized Zone: Peace and Nature Park," *International Journal on World Peace* 24 (2007): 62.

10 Bookchin, *Philosophy of Social Ecology*, 145.

11 Ke Chung Kim, "Preserving Korea's Demilitarized Corridor for Conservation: A Green Approach to Conflict Resolution," in *Peace Parks: Conservation and Conflict Resolution*, ed. Saleem H. Ali (Cambridge, MA: MIT Press, 2007), 239–59.

12 Betsy Didrickson, *The Quality of Cranes: A Little Book of Crane Lore* (Baraboo, WI: International Crane Foundation, 2010), 11.

13 Bookchin, *Philosophy of Social Ecology*, 118.

14 Ibid., 41–44.

15 "The Promise of 1000 Origami Cranes," Millennium Pharmaceutical, accessed March 31, 2014, www.1000cranesofhope.com/about-the-project/.

16 www.iksd.org/lksd1/outreachact/FormsDocumment/Pamfiles/Japanese%20Art%20and%20Cultures/7%20The%20Story%20of%20a%20Crane%20Wife.doc. 2012.

17 Didrickson, *Quality of Cranes*, 113.

18 David Mason, email message to author, January 17, 2012.

19 Bruce Cumings, *Korea's Place in the Sun, A Modern History* (New York: W.W. Norton & Company, 1997), 237.

20 "David Mason's San-Shin Website." Accessed 2012. www.san-shin.org/index3.html.

21 Didrickson, *Quality of Cranes*, 115.

22 The Compilation Committee of the Illustrated Book of the Korean Natural Monuments, *The Illustrated Book of the Korean Natural Monuments (Animals Part)* (Pyongyang, DPRK, 2007), 76–89.

23 Didrickson, *Quality of Cranes*, 15.

24 *Webster's New Universal Unabridged Dictionary* (New York: Barnes & Noble Books, 1996), 430; Didrickson, *Quality of Cranes*, 16.

25 Hiroyoshi Higuchi, Yuri Shibaev et al., "Satellite Tracking of the Migration of the Red-Crowned Crane *Grus Japonensis*," *Ecological Research* 13 (1998): 275–80.

26 Eric Wagner, "Living on the Edge," *Smithsonian Magazine* 42 (2011): 58.

27 Ramsar Convention Secretariat, *The Ramsar Strategic Plan 2009–2015, as adopted by Resolution X.1 (2008) and adjusted for the 2013–2015 triennium by Resolution XI.3 (2012) (Gland, Switzerland: Ramsar Convention Secretariat, 2012)*, accessed March 31, 2014, www.ramsar.org/pdf/strat-plan-2009-e-adj.pdf.

28 "Arable Land in South Korea," Trading Economics, accessed March 31, 2014, www.trading-economics.com/south-korea/arable-land-hectares-wb-data.html; "Arable Land in North Korea," Trading Economics, accessed March 2012, www.tradingeconomics.com/north-korea/arable-land-hectares-wb-data.html.
29 Bookchin, *Philosophy of Social Ecology*, 45.
30 Ibid., 137, 141.
31 Jong Ryol Chong, Hiroyoshi Higuchi and U Il Pak, "The Migration Routes and Important Rest-Sites of Cranes on the Korean Peninsula," in *The Future of Cranes and Wetlands: Proceedings of the International Symposium Held in Tokyo and Sapporo, Japan in June 1993*, ed. Hiroyoshi Higuchi, Jason Minton and Reiko Kurosawa, 41–2 (Tokyo: Wild Bird Society of Japan, 1994); and, Hiroyoshi Higuchi, Kiyoaki Ozaki et al., "Satellite Tracking of White-Naped Crane Migration and the Importance of the Korean Demilitarized Zone," *Conservation Biology* 10 (1996), 809.
32 Aldo Leopold, *A Sand County Almanac, with Essays on Conservation* (New York: University Press, Inc., 2001), 160.

BIBLIOGRAPHY

Bookchin, Murray. *The Philosophy of Social Ecology, Essays on Dialectical Naturalism*. Montreal: Black Rose Books, 1990.
Chong, Jong Ryol, Hiroyoshi Higuchi and Pak U Il. "The Migration Routes and Important Rest-Sites of Cranes on the Korean Peninsula." In *The Future of Cranes and Wetlands: Proceedings of the International Symposium Held in Tokyo and Sapporo, Japan in June 1993*, edited by Hiroyoshi Higuchi, Jason Minton and Reiko Kurosawa, 41–50. Tokyo: Wild Bird Society of Japan, 1994.
Compilation Committee of the Illustrated Book of the Korean Natural Monuments, *The Illustrated Book of the Korean Natural Monuments (Animals Part)*. Pyongyang, DPRK, 2007.
Crane maiden: www.iksd.org/lksd1/outreachact/FormsDocument/Pamfiles/Japanese%20Art%20and%20Cultures/7%20The%20Story%20of%20a%20Crane%20Wife.doc. 2012.
Cumings, Bruce. *Korea's Place in the Sun: A Modern History*. New York: W.W. Norton & Company, 1997.
"David Mason San-Shin Website." Accessed 2012. www.san-shin.org/index3.html.
Didrickson, Betsy. *The Quality of Cranes: A Little Book of Crane Lore*. Baraboo, Wisconsin: International Crane Foundation, 2010.
Gale, Alastair and Keith Johnson. "North Korea Declares War Truce 'Invalid.'" *Wall Street Journal*, March 12, 2013.
Healy, Hall. "Korean Demilitarized Zone: Peace and Nature Park." *International Journal on World Peace* 24 (2007): 61–83.
Higuchi, Hiroyoshi, Ozaki Kiyoaki, Go Fujita, Minton Jason, Ueta Mutsuyuki, Soma Masaki and Mita Nagahisa "Satellite Tracking of White-Naped Crane Migration and the Importance of the Korean Demilitarized Zone." *Conservation Biology* 10 (1996): 806–12.
Higuchi, Hiroyoshi, Shibaev Yuri, Minton Jason, Ozaki Kiyoaki, Surmach Sergey, Go Fujita, Momose Kunikazu, Momose Yuria, Ueta Mutsuyuki, Andronov Vladimir, Mita Nagahisa and Kanai Yutaka. "Satellite Tracking of the Migration of the Red-Crowned Crane Grus Japonensis," *Ecological Research* 13 (1998): 273–82.
Keck, Zachary. "The Three Faces of Park's Trustpolitik." *The Diplomat*, May 3, 2013. Accessed April 6, 2014. http://thediplomat.com/2013/05/the-three-faces-of-parks-trustpolitik/.
Kim, Ke Chung. "Preserving Korea's Demilitarized Corridor for Conservation: A Green Approach to Conflict Resolution." In *Peace Parks: Conservation and Conflict Resolution*, edited by Saleem H. Ali, 239–59. Cambridge, MA: MIT Press, 2007.
Leopold, Aldo. *A Sand County Almanac, with Essays on Conservation*. New York: Oxford University Press, 2001.
Mason, David. Email message to author. January 17, 2012.

Meine, Curt and Archibald, George, IUCN/SSC Crane Specialist Group. The Cranes: Status Survey and Conservation Action Plan. Gland: International Union for Conservation of Nature (IUCN), 1996. Accessed August 6, 2015. https://portals.iucn.org/library/efiles/documents/1996-022.pdf, 194–204.

Millennium Pharmaceutical. "The Promise of 1000 Origami Cranes." Accessed March 31, 2014. www.1000cranesofhope.com/about-the-project/.

Ramsar Convention Secretariat. *The Ramsar Strategic Plan 2009–2015, as adopted by Resolution X.1 (2008) and adjusted for the 2013–2015 triennium by Resolution XI.3 (2012)*. Gland, Switzerland: Ramsar Convention Secretariat, 2012. Accessed March 31, 2014. www.ramsar.org/pdf/strat-plan-2009-e-adj.pdf.

Security Council, United Nations. *Letter Dated 14 January 2013 from The Permanent Representative of the Democratic People's Republic of Korea to the United Nations addressed to the President of the Security Council, Document No. S/2013/20*. New York: UN Security Council, January 14, 2013.

Security Council, United Nations. *Letter Dated 6 November 2000 from The Permanent Representative of the United States of America to the United Nations addressed to the President of the Security Council, Document No. S/2000/1070*. New York: UN Security Council, November 7, 2000.

Security Council, United Nations. *Letter Dated 9 September 1998 from The Permanent Representative of the United States of America to the United Nations Addressed to the President of the Security Council, Document No. S/1998/844*. New York: UN Security Council, September 10, 1998.

Trading Economics. "Arable Land in South Korea." Accessed March 31, 2014. www.tradingeconomics.com/south-korea/arable-land-hectares-wb-data.html. "Arable Land in North Korea." Accessed March 2012. www.tradingeconomics.com/north-korea/arable-land-hectares-wb-data.html.

Wagner, Eric. "Living on the Edge." *Smithsonian Magazine* 42 (2011): 54–9.

Webster's New Universal Unabridged Dictionary. New York: Barnes & Noble Books, 1996.

Westing, Arthur H. "Regional Security: The Case of the Korean Demilitarized Zone (DMZ)." In A. H. Westing, *From Environmental to Comprehensive Security*. Heidelberg: Springer, 2013, 87–110.

Wilson, Edward O. *In Search of Nature*, Washington, DC: Island Press, 1996.

Chapter Six

SOCIO-ECOLOGICAL TRANSFORMATIONS IN RIPARIAN ZONES: THE PRODUCTION OF SPACES OF EXCLUSION AND THE UNEVEN DEVELOPMENT OF RESILIENCE IN THE SONORAN BORDERLANDS

Lily A. House-Peters

Uneven development is the hallmark of the geography of capitalism. […] It is the geographical expression of the contradictions inherent in the very constitutions and structure of capital.[1]

In August 2014, the Buenavista del Cobre copper mine, owned and operated by Grupo México, the third largest copper producer worldwide, with 2012 sales of more than $10 billion, experienced a major tailings dam collapse. The resulting spill caused 40,000 cubic meters of toxic sulphuric acid and heavy metals to spill into the Rio Sonora, which flows south from its headwaters in Cananea into the capital city of Hermosillo. Following the spill, 22,000 people in seven towns were left without access to water. Exposure to the polluted water also proved devastating for livestock and agricultural operations, damaged the local riparian ecology and caused wildlife mortalities. Hardly one month later in September 2014, the Buenavista del Cobre mine experienced a second spill, this time sending water contaminated with toxic tailings materials into the binational San Pedro River (Figure 6.1).

The San Pedro River flows north from its headwaters in the mountains near Cananea, crossing the international border and flowing into Arizona. In light of the spills, there have been calls throughout Sonora and beyond, even echoing in the chambers of Mexico's national congress, to cancel Grupo México's concession to operate the Buenavista del Cobre mine in Cananea. However, the cancelation of the concession is highly unlikely due to the strong relations of economic and political dependence between Grupo México and the Mexican government.

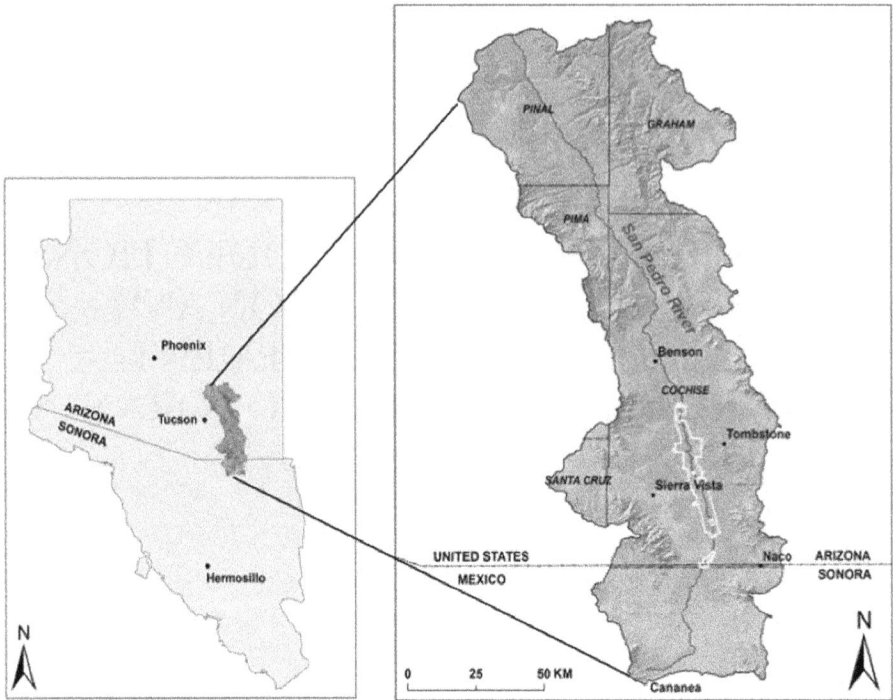

Figure 6.1 Map of the binational San Pedro River watershed. Figure created by author. *Source:* San Pedro River Basin Data Browser.

The power the mine wields over local land and water resources today represents a major shift from previous arrangements of power in rural Sonora, organized around populist agrarian reform. On February 4, 1959, an unusual delegation of high-level Mexican officials convened on the rural outskirts of Cananea, Sonora, less than 100 kilometers from the US border. Gathering on the Martinez Ranch, surrounded by the golden grasslands and forested riparian corridors of the San Pedro River and its tributaries, the president of Mexico, Adolfo López Mateos, the governor of the state of Sonora, and the leaders of the nation's Department of Agriculture stood before a crowd of hundreds. López Mateos, barely two months into his presidency, stepped forward to greet the assembled landless peasants, ranchers, agrarian reform leaders and local mine laborers. In a brief speech steeped in patriotic prose extolling the revolutionary virtues of the 1917 Mexican constitution, the president symbolically transferred 256,507 hectares (633,843 acres) of recently expropriated land to the people's representative, Ruben Peralta y Peralta, for the creation of seven collective ranching *ejidos* (communities that manage and cultivate land in common) benefiting 853 formerly landless peasants. The expropriated *latifundio* (land privately owned as a large estate), representing nearly the entire surface area of the Mexican portion of the San Pedro watershed, had previously been under the exclusive ownership of American mining and ranching magnate Colonel William Greene and his heirs. During his six-year presidential term, López Mateos distributed more land to the peasants than any president since Lázaro Cárdenas (1934–40), a total of 30 million acres, signaling a period of strong state intervention in the economy.[2]

The expropriation of the American-owned *latifundio* in the summer of 1958 and the subsequent *reparto* (redistribution) of the land to local *campesinos* (peasants) in early 1959 marked a watershed moment for the establishment of commons land management in the Sonoran borderlands. However, contemporary shifts in the political-economic and ecological conditions in the region have led to a series of acts of (re)enclosure. The term *enclosure* emerged from the sixteenth- and seventeenth-century process of creating boundaries using hedgerows to demarcate private property in the English countryside. Nicholas Blomley defines the process of enclosure as the "conversion of commonable lands, whether on wastes, commons, or village fields, into exclusively owned parcels, and the concomitant extinction of common rights."[3] In agrarian systems of production, enclosure is closely tied to dispossession. The enclosure and conversion of commonly managed land to private property serves to exclude certain users, thus divorcing certain agrarian producers from their means of production (i.e., land and water).[4] In the riparian zones of the San Pedro River, enclosure is accompanied by the imposition of severe limitations to accessing surface and groundwater resources, fodder and forage materials for cattle, and nutrient-rich, irrigable cropland.

In the binational San Pedro River watershed, the dispossession and alienation of small-scale ranchers and farmers from land and water in the riparian zone via various mechanisms of enclosure have also contributed to a significant shift in the balance of power, particularly in the Sonoran portion of the watershed. In Mexico, neoliberal shifts in law and policy over the past two decades strongly favor the privatization of land and water resources. These shifts have chipped away at the ability of the *ejidos* and the *ejidatarios* (members of the *ejido* community) to maintain their common management of land and water resources, instead favoring industrial-scale mining operations and private, capital-intensive agriculture. In the Arizona portion of the watershed, the implementation of ecological conservation policies that exclude working landscapes, such as farms and ranches, serve to displace local producers.

This chapter traces the shifting politics of access to land and water within a binational riparian corridor in the Sonoran borderlands. This research reveals the effects of changes in political, institutional and environmental management regimes on producers dependent on access to riparian resources. I identify distinct mechanisms functioning on both sides of the international border to enclose riparian space and unevenly restrict access to conditions of production. In Sonora, I focus on changes in riparian relations in the decades following the 1959 redistribution of the Greene *latifundio* to create the seven collective ranching *ejidos* (Figure 6.2).

Specifically, I interrogate the contested processes of privatization and expropriation attending to how these processes have affected the livelihoods of small-scale producers. In the Arizona portion of the San Pedro River riparian corridor, I draw attention to the

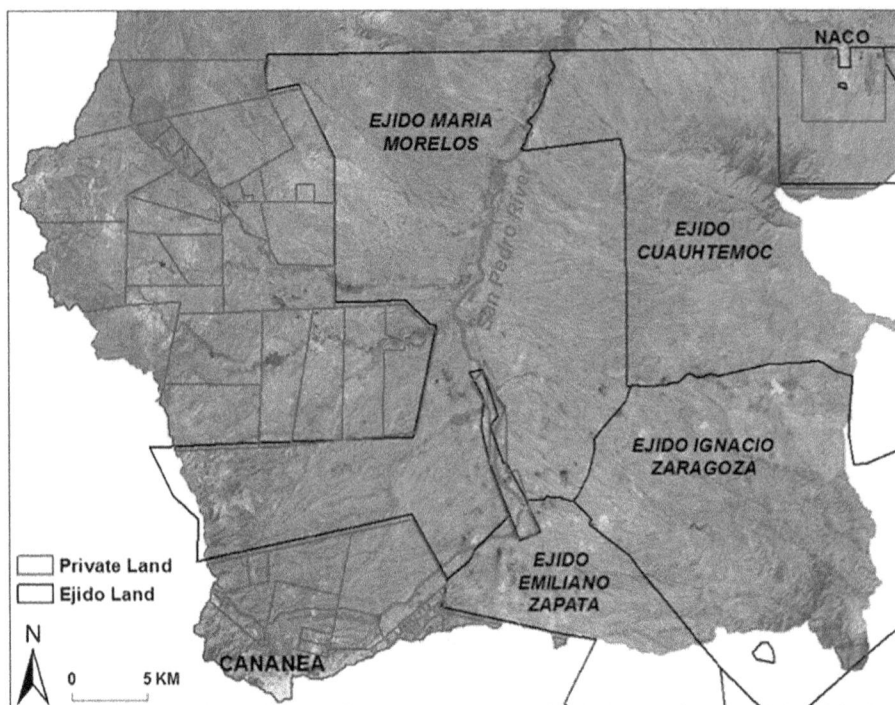

Figure 6.2 Map depicting *ejido* property boundaries (black lines) and private property boundaries (red lines) in the Mexican portion of the binational San Pedro River watershed. Figure created by author.
Data source: San Pedro River Basin Data Browser.

politics of conservation, illustrating the winners and losers of the creation of an exclusionary riparian conservation area in 1989 and demonstrating how conservation may become enrolled in programs of securitization in the context of increasingly militarized US–Mexico border relations.

   This research is guided by two main questions. What are the political-economic mechanisms through which riparian space is enclosed and certain actors become excluded from access to land and water resources? How do shifts in property rights regimes in the borderlands affect the transformation of human and ecological relations in the riparian zone of the transboundary San Pedro River? To answer these questions, I draw on archival and field research conducted in the Mexican cities of Hermosillo and Cananea and in the US state of Arizona in 2013 and 2014. This chapter presents findings based on the analysis of primary and secondary sources, including land titles, agrarian records, policy papers, legal documents and newspaper articles and interviews with key informants. Weaving theoretical insights from scholarship in Marxist political economy, political ecology and resilience theory through the empirical evidence, I identify three mechanisms that serve to enclose riparian resources throughout the binational San Pedro River watershed. The mechanisms are: (1) privatization—the exclusive, alienable rights to land and water resources; (2) expropriation—the seizure of land and transfer of property rights to another individual or government entity; and (3) conservation—based on a Western conservation logic of species-by-species habitat management that excludes human livelihood activities from occurring within the conservation area. To illustrate this argument, I present three empirically based vignettes that highlight the current shift toward limiting access to high-value land and water resources located within the riparian corridor. This research is significant because it elucidates the complicated social and ecological dynamics that characterize this unique landscape and the human and nonhuman communities who inhabit it.

I argue that the identification of these three mechanisms of enclosure is key to elucidating the interrelations among law, global political economy and social-ecological transformation in riparian spaces in the Sonoran borderlands. Furthermore, I present an approach that is sensitive to power relations and recognizes the social production of nature and biophysical landscapes.[5] Attending to the operation of power in socio-ecological landscapes requires attention to both the explicit and hidden forms and workings of power. Drawing inspiration from Michel Foucault, I understand power as relations of force that produce outcomes and consequences that materially transform both social and ecological spaces.

The consequences of enclosure are significant in the watershed, contributing to a shift in the balance of power in the binational watershed and to transformations in social-ecological relations within a highly valued borderland riparian zone. In the Sonoran portion of the watershed, shifts in property rights regimes and law have chipped away at the power of the *ejidos* and the members of *ejido* communities to maintain their land in common. Recent legal reforms, for example, the 1992 PROCEDE land reform and the updated National Waters Law, serve the natural resources exploitation needs of industrial capital through establishing legal precedent for the privatization of *ejido* lands and the legal separation of land and water. This research reveals that in Sonora, small-scale agricultural producers and ranchers are losing control over land and water resources as the Buenavista del Cobre copper mine's power has increased rapidly in the region over the past 20 years. As the world's third largest copper producer located in Cananea, Sonora, at the San Pedro river's headwaters, it has consolidated control over land and groundwater resources. As copper prices continue to soar on the global market due to increasing demand, the mine is currently undergoing a 3.4 billion USD expansion with the aim of doubling its production capacity to 1.3 million tons of copper annually by 2017. This doubling of capacity will increase production from the current 90,000 metric tons per day to 200,000 metric tons per day, requiring substantial increases in water consumption, in particular the proliferation of deep, high-capacity groundwater wells in the riparian zone (Figure 6.3).

The power wielded over resources today by the mine represents a major shift from February 4, 1959, when President López Mateos created seven collective ranching *ejido* communities through the redistribution of the Greene *latifundio* landholdings.

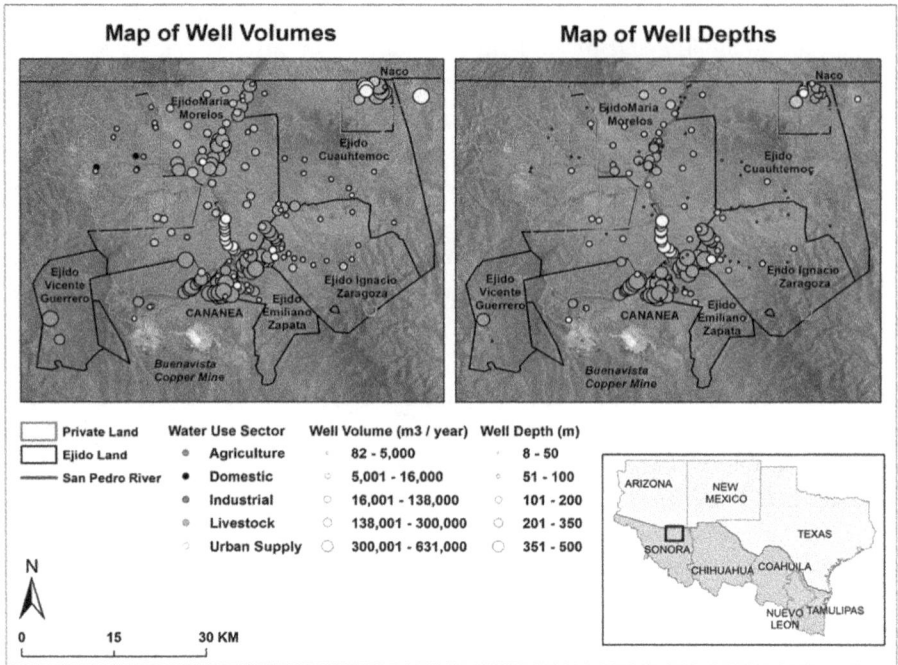

Figure 6.3 Groundwater concessions for the Mexican San Pedro, represented by type and size of use (left-hand map) and by well depth (right-hand map). Figure created by author. Data source: Mexico CONAGUA Agency REPDA database.

Contextualizing the San Pedro River in the Sonoran Borderlands

The San Pedro River, a transboundary waterway, originates in northern Sonora, Mexico, in the mountains near the copper mining center of Cananea and flows north, crossing the international border into southern Arizona. Rivers, central protagonists in the history of human settlement and agricultural development in a water-limited US–Mexico border region, have long been objects of conflict, their narrative marked by alternating cycles of water scarcity and abundance.[6] Historically, in Sonora's river valleys, the narrow alluvial floodplains along a river's banks were one of the few locations where irrigated agriculture was possible, resulting in a long history of social and ecological entanglements in these areas. The location of freshwater played a central role in the history of settling the semiarid Sonoran borderlands; rivers influenced the location of areas of cultivation and habitable spaces for settlement and productive agrarian activities. Thus, access to water resources and riparian spaces is characterized by a long history of shifting political-economic conditions, natural resource policies and transformations in social-ecological relations.

The San Pedro River riparian corridor—the forested floodplains adjacent to the river—supports multiple competing demands for water that outpace available supply. The deep interrelations between riparian ecology, coupled with groundwater-surface water hydrology and social institutions of law and property, necessitate a brief introduction into the social-ecological dynamics of riparian corridors. In arid and semiarid regions, riparian ecosystems are sights of both disproportionately high biodiversity and intensive human activity. These narrow bands of dense forest are significant biodiversity hotspots and provide a range of critical environmental services, including freshwater availability, flood protection, nutrient deposition, carbon sequestration and groundwater recharge. Additionally, these resource-dense zones support a wide range of crucial economic activities, including ranching, agriculture, mining, recreation and tourism.

In the riparian corridor, biodiversity is critically dependent on hydrologic processes, specifically surface flow, shallow groundwater levels and water quality. Riparian corridors are dependent on access to both surface and subsurface water flows and are highly influenced by coupled groundwater-surface water hydrology. Riparian corridors exist in areas of discharge from the shallow alluvial zones of the aquifer where the stream channel incises the top of the saturated zone. In these areas, the water table is high and vegetation can easily access groundwater, leading to dense canopies predominately comprised of cottonwood-willow forests and mesquite *bosques*. Water availability from surface flow and high groundwater tables is a major determinant of riparian vegetation presence, diversity and composition. The distribution of streamside plants is dependent on numerous factors, including depth to the water table, rooting characteristics and the riparian substrate geology, all of which are sensitive to the processes of land use change, including nearby agricultural activities, resource extraction, industry and urban development.

Hydrologic processes are influenced in complex ways by both direct human intervention and broader climatic and landscape-scale processes. For example, aquifer depletion, due to excessive groundwater pumping to sustain agriculture and urban development, reduces the amount and timing of water available to ecological communities in the riparian corridor. Land uses adjacent to rivers deeply impact riparian systems. Surface water extraction, groundwater pumping, livestock grazing, nutrient inputs and the replacement of riparian forest with agricultural crops lead to a loss of riparian habitat complexity, increased stand mortality and the reduced ability of species to successfully reproduce. Urban growth is responsible for increased runoff and sediment, the replacement of riparian habitat with roads and infrastructure, habitat fragmentation, increased levels of point and non-point source pollution and the introduction of invasive species. Furthermore, the type and amount of water available in semiarid-region riparian systems varies by season due to influences from precipitation variability, recharge processes and human activities that impact surface water diversion, groundwater pumping and wastewater discharge.

The strong coupling between visible surface water and invisible (or less visible) groundwater in riparian zones presents persistent challenges to effective land and water management regimes. This unique constellation of social-ecological relations eludes the full comprehension of scientists, experts and practitioners, complicating the penetration of the gaze of scientific and state knowledge production, and remains only partially understood today. The inability of experts to model this complex system and make visible its hidden dynamics continues to render the landscape fugitive to contemporary environmental governance regimes. The invisible qualities of groundwater and the only partial understanding of the dynamics between surface and groundwater that occur in the riparian zone present a persistent challenge to effective governance.

Theorizing Uneven Resilience and Riparian Enclosure

To elucidate social-ecological relations in the riparian corridors of the binational San Pedro River watershed, I draw insights from resilience theory, political ecology and historical-geographical materialism. I argue that the explanation of socio-ecological transformation offered by traditional resilience theory[7] is inadequate because it fails to elucidate power relations that impact coupled social and ecological dynamics. Instead, I introduce an approach informed by political ecology's sensitivity to the operation of power and historical materialism's grounded approach to understanding relations of property and political economy with a reinterpretation of resilience theory. This marrying of diverse theoretical approaches serves to bridge a critical gap in understanding the relationship between social-ecological transformations, the production of spaces of exclusion and the uneven development of resilience.

Resilience theory presents a comprehensive framework for examining the ability of socio-ecological structures (SES) to absorb and withstand disturbance while maintaining existing SES and functions. However, there is a tendency for analyses formulated through resilience thinking[8] to conceal, rather than reveal, politics and power relations. This tendency has led to descriptions of flat resilience landscapes, rather than recognition and further interrogation of uneven topographies of resilience within a single socio-ecological system. The rich empirical scholarship in political ecology demonstrates that complex relations between natural resources and power intersect to shape differential rather than similar outcomes, in particular uneven access to natural resources within and between communities.[9]

This case study illuminates the production of an uneven topography of riparian resilience, where policies that promote the resilience of one set of actors actively undermine the resilience of another group. For example, in riparian SES, groundwater pumping is a key variable of system behavior due to its impact on shallow groundwater tables, a critical source of water for human and ecological communities in semiarid climates. In the shallow alluvial sub-flow zones of the riparian corridor, groundwater pumping is directly linked to local decreases in water table levels. As the industrial mining sector consolidates power and resources and is able to access deeper supplies of groundwater, the mining industry is insulated from the negative impacts of increasing water scarcity in the region. However, small agricultural and ranching producers and ecological communities that only have access to and thus depend on surface water flow, shallow groundwater wells and high water table levels are exposed to the negative externalities that result from the steady expansion of capital accumulation in the mining sector. Thus, as aquifer depletion affects local water table levels, crisis conditions are experienced unequally, leading to increased resilience for some at the expense of decreased resilience for others.

Historical-geographical materialism understands human–environment relations as both historical and political and imbued with power. Informed by the work of Karl Marx and a century of materialist scholarship, David Harvey presents a refined historical-geographical materialist approach. Harvey argues that "we must have critical ways to think about how differences in ecological, cultural, economic, political, and social conditions get produced (particularly through those human activities that we are in a position in principle to modify or control) and we also need ways to evaluate the justice/injustice of the differences so produced."[10] The historical-geographical materialist framework is useful for rethinking resilience through its grounded approach, which focuses attention explicitly on the "concrete historical and geographical conditions in which human action unfolds."[11] Following this approach, I attend to the "connection of the social and political structure with production"[12] and argue for a central focus on processes of production. Denying the bourgeois argument that social processes follow natural, apolitical trajectories, the historical materialist argument instead employs political-economic analysis to reveal the mechanisms through which "changes in the land"[13] have come to be. This type of analysis demonstrates how benefits and risks are distributed differentially both within and between groups of actors. The uneven distribution of benefits and risks is neither natural nor externally dictated, but rather internal to the system, a material representation of capitalism's inherent contradictions. Following this approach, it is necessary to analyze social and political institutions that structure the conditions of production, which transform natural materials from use-value objects into commodities inhered with surplus value for market exchange.

It is through material processes that communities are conjured into being, set together or torn apart, and come to experience cooperation or conflict. Law and property are powerful institutions that structure social and political relations between people and relations between humans and nonhumans, through control over the transformation of nonhuman nature through processes of production. By recognizing the material basis of history, it is also possible to recognize that a certain mode of production is always combined with a certain mode of cooperation. For example, shifts in land and water property rights regimes affect how both social and ecological arrangements take shape, impacting which actors have access to the benefits provided by land and water resources and which actors are excluded. Thus, a historical-geographical materialist approach provides a useful analytical framework to examine social and ecological transformations in riparian spaces.

Transformations of raw materials via the production process engender socio-ecological transformations, famously coined by Neil Smith as the "production of nature."[14] The transformation of nature through human labor and technology is necessary to produce surplus value, thus creating an entanglement between labor, value, property and power. The emphasis on examining the conditions and processes of production brings property relations into focus. Property rights regimes represent a critically important factor in determining who has access to the benefits derived from natural resources, such land and water, in semiarid region riparian zones. Thus shifts in law, policy and property rights serve to transform how actors experience space, as insiders or outsiders, included or excluded.[15] Property is a powerful institution that creates, mediates and maintains political relations between people.[16] Furthermore, property influences relations between social and ecological actors, through control over the transformation of nonhuman nature through labor and processes of production.[17] Shifts in law and policy that restructure property rights regimes serve to redefine the rules, norms and conventions that mediate access to the benefits provided by land and water resources.[18] Property rights function as legally protected control over resources, which gives the property holder the power to make decisions over the allocation of scarce resources. This decision-making power renders property and property reform a thoroughly political issue.[19]

Enclosure serves as a useful theoretical framing device for understanding contemporary transformations in riparian spaces in the US–Mexico borderlands. Through an examination of acts of enclosure, it is possible to link property rights, producers' control (or lack thereof) over labor and the modes of production and peoples' experiences of dispossession and exclusion. In *Capital Volume 1*, Karl Marx presents his oft-cited definition of primitive accumulation: the historical process of divorcing the producer from the means of production.[20] In the century since Marx's writings, scholars have reworked definitions and understandings of primitive accumulation. For example, Alice Kelly offers an expanded definition, arguing that primitive accumulation is "neither simply accumulation via violent means nor a necessarily immediate process [...] it involves the act of enclosure of a commons, whether that be the enclosure of land, bodies, social structures, or ideas."[21] Thus, the process of enclosure of previously communally managed lands represents not only an economic shift, but also a transformation in socio-ecological relations and practices. Enclosure is not a monolith; rather, enclosure can take different forms and can occur through various practices and mechanisms. Feminist scholar Silvia Federici argues that neoliberal capitalism has introduced changes to processes of social reproduction and the reproduction of labor power that has led to a new round of enclosures via dispossession though debt, development programs and technological modernization.[22] In addition to enclosure, commodification serves as a central method of capital expansion into new territories.

The commodification of nature—defined as the penetration of capitalist relations of production into nature—presents a conceptual approach for theorizing the production of unequal risk in contemporary environmental politics in the San Pedro River watershed, where certain actors become beneficiaries of risk, while others become bearers of risk. In Mexico, the penetration of the market into the allocation and distribution of land and water resources is responsible for far-ranging implications for social and environmental justice that are only just beginning to be understood. Under the market environmentalism paradigm—characterized by the introduction of market institutions to natural resource management—tensions arise due to the head-on collision of the desire to devolve state resource control and the contradictory requirement of the existence of a strong state that can defend and enforce private property rights. The scientific administration of nature, a phenomenon that is crucial in market-based environmental governance, due to the need for ecological appraisal and monitoring, has further resulted in the expansion of the modern state's power.[23] In the case of the "uncooperative commodity" of water,[24] the commodification process is complicated by water's geographical, sociocultural and biophysical properties. In Bakker's definition, a commodity is "a *standardized* good or service, with *interchangeable* units, sold at a price determined through market exchange."[25] The biophysical, cultural and spatial characteristics of water, namely, its properties as a life-giving, continually circulating, scale-linking resource, do not easily succumb to messages of ecologic and economic reductionism, violating the conditions necessary for well-functioning markets and thus rendering water particularly resistant to commodification.[26]

Yet, the commodification of biophysical elements raises an inherent contradiction: the simultaneous requirement for standardization and interchangeability and the impossibility of achieving these required characteristics. In the attempt to standardize, the process of commodification produces and promotes certain types of knowledge. Morgan Robertson examines and problematizes the production of scientific knowledge that is translatable to the logics of law and capital.[27] Ecological assessments and monitoring programs become requirements of projects seeking to produce nature as suitable for commodification. Furthermore, for the translation from ecological logic to market logic to be complete, the representations of ecology that result must be noncontroversial, transportable and commensurable. On this point, Robertson states, "The difference between selling ecosystem services and selling loaves of bread is that legal and capital logics require information about ecosystem services that scientists *cannot provide* in a noncontroversial way. Furthermore, the uniqueness of ecology to particular spaces ruptures the spatial abstraction that allows commodification to work in the first place."[28]

In the San Pedro River watershed situated in the Arizona–Sonora borderlands, shifts in property rights regimes are restructuring the organization of access to and management of land and water resources in riparian spaces. Contemporary legal and policy shifts governing the management of land and water have created mechanisms for the re-privatization of access to riparian resources and encouraged private forms of ownership and individual management of resources. The enclosure of collectively managed resources is most often accomplished through a transition to private property. The dissolution of the commons in favor of privatization and titling of land often leads to marginalization of smallholders and the poorest subsistence farmers. Expropriation, the seizure of land and transfer of property rights, serves to restructure social relations and power dynamics within and between communities, while the creation of protected conservation areas may remove land and water from productive activities in the name of ecological protection. For example, the designation of the San Pedro Riparian National Conservation Area (SPRNCA) in 1989 followed a traditional Western approach to conservation based on species-by-species accounting, rather than more holistic approaches to ecosystem-based conservation that allow for and value the maintenance of working landscapes as part of rather than contrary to conservation goals. In the case of the SPRNCA, within the conservation boundary, covering 57,000 acres of riparian habitat and high-elevation grassland, agricultural and ranching operations and cattle grazing became prohibited. The result of these shifts is an erosion of collective resource management with the effect of significantly re-scripting social and ecological relations within riparian social-ecological systems.

Three Mechanisms of Riparian Enclosure

This section draws on archival research conducted in Arizona and Sonora to present three brief vignettes that illustrate how the processes of privatization, expropriation and conservation are being deployed in the binational San Pedro River watershed to produce enclosures and spaces of exclusion in the riparian zone.

Privatization

The stark erosion of power of the agrarian reform sector began in earnest in the early 1980s, when the Mexican economy was marred by the 1982 financial crisis and the devaluation of the peso, followed by a phase of national debt restructuring programs and austerity measures. The subsequent retraction of state support for special programs, such as price guarantees for staple crops, marked a sharp decrease in the political power of the *ejido* sector. In 1986, President Miguel de la Madrid signed the General Agreement on Tariffs and Trade (GATT), which led to a reduction in agricultural subsidies by 13 percent per year. BanRural bank slashed credit to *ejidatarios*, compounding the negative effects for small producers associated with the subsidy reductions. Beginning in 1988, President Carlos Salinas de Gotari's *sexenio* (six-year term) marked the shift toward a neoliberal understanding of land and water as economic rather than public goods. Furthermore, Salinas reframed natural resources management through the neoliberal governance concepts of deregulation, liberalization and privatization.

In 1991, citing the low productivity of *ejido* and other communally managed lands, Salinas introduced plans to transform the agrarian structure in Mexico, effectively ending a 70-year period of interventionist, state-led agrarian reform. The 1992 introduction of the Programa de Certificacion de Derechos Ejidales (PROCEDE) indicated a major shift in land tenure law and marked the transition from the period of state-led agrarian reform beginning in 1917 to a period of market-led agrarian reform.[29] PROCEDE ended the redistribution of land for the creation of new *ejidos* and fundamentally altered land tenure laws. Previously *ejido* land was considered usufruct property, meaning the right was only for the use of the land, not for full ownership. As such, *ejido* land was inalienable, signifying that the land could not be sold or rented (though scholarship points to widespread illegal renting of land and exchange of titles that occurred). PROCEDE formally initiated the process of legal certification and titling of parcels for privatization, transfer and sale. The year 1992 also ushered in the implementation of the Ley de Aguas Nacionales (National Water Law), which reformed the 1917 water law, significantly conferring the ability to rent, sell and transfer water right concessions, which was previously not allowed.

In the mid-1990s, the first stages of the PROCEDE process were carried out in the seven ranching *ejido* communities formed in 1959. On October 9, 1994, the first PROCEDE meeting, titled the Assembly of the Delimitation, Destiny, and Allocation of Ejido Lands, was held in the *ejido* community of Emiliano Zapata. In addition to the *ejido* ruling body, consisting of the president, secretary, treasurer and vigilance council, the meeting was attended by a visiting representative of the Agricultural Tribunal, a representative from the national census bureau (INEGI), a notary public and 68 *ejidatarios* with legally recognized rights to common property. The order of the day was to vote on the ending of the regime of collective ranching, which would allow *ejidatarios* to obtain certificates for land tenure. The next step forward in parcel certification would be the official surveying and delineation of the spatial boundaries of each parcel, which had to be recognized as correct by the voting members of the *ejido* assembly.

In nearby *ejido* Vicente Guerrero, the assembly of *ejidatarios* met in May 1995 regarding a solicitation by Minera María to purchase approximately 950 *hectáreas* (385 acres) of commons land (Figure 6.4).

Figure 6.4 Privatization and sale of riparian land and water rights to Minera María from an *ejidatario* turned private landholder in *ejido* Vicente Guerrero. Photograph by author, May 2014.

The open pit mine, owned by Grupo Frisco, a company within Mexican billionaire Carlos Slim's holdings, stated that the land would be used for the construction and installation of processing plants and industrial installations, to continue the exploration and exploitation of mineral ores and to drill and install three wells. Originally, the mine began its operations in 1980 solely producing copper concentrates. However, the ability to expand operations to produce cathode copper (which began in 1999) required additional land, and more importantly, additional water resources.

During a following general assembly meeting of *ejidatarios* on June 16, 1995, a disagreement erupted with some *ejidatarios* claiming *"Protestamos lo necesario"* (necessary protest) against the mine's plan. In September 1995, the case was transferred to the Agricultural Tribunal. The trial, attended by 29 percent of the *ejidatarios*, heard arguments from a faction of community members who sought to challenge the allocation of land to the mine and called for the nullification of an earlier agreement that had been negotiated with the mining company. However, the judge, Maximiliano Figueroa Romero, decided against the protesting *ejidatarios* and Minera María eventually gained access to the land and the accompanying water resources. In 1997, the mine obtained concessions to pump 1,102 acre-feet of groundwater per year. Although this quantity of water is dwarfed by the 25,554 acre-feet per year (AFY) of groundwater concessions under the control of the Buenavista copper mine in Cananea (today owned by Grupo México), it represents a significant strain on a community already experiencing water scarcity.

Previous research has clearly shown that groundwater pumping directly within the riparian corridor is strongly tied to local decreases in groundwater levels, leading to high mortality rates for cottonwood-willow forests.[30] The Gila River Adjudication determined that wells located in the sub-flow zone of the saturated floodplain alluvium significantly impact the quantity of surface water available in the river channel. Increasing demands for groundwater have caused the binational San Pedro River aquifer to become over-exploited, resulting in significantly decreased groundwater levels. Stretches of the river that historically were perennial, meaning they contain water all year long, now flow only following precipitation events, and small lakes and ponds have experienced visible drying over the past decade as a result of the combined impacts of unsustainable pumping and long drought cycles.

In northern Sonora, a major outcome of the PROCEDE process has been the fenc-ing of land to demarcate plots, although full privatization and certification of titles has been more limited. Importantly, these outcomes of the PROCEDE process are being implemented most intensely in the riparian zone. This is a result of the high value of riparian land, which is highly productive, especially for irrigated agriculture and animal husbandry due to access to surface water and the existence of shallow groundwater lev-els. The process of mapping and parceling land in the San Pedro River watershed has had the effect of rendering land tenure configurations increasingly visible (e.g., fences) and legible (e.g., maps and registered GPS coordinates) to the Mexican state. Yet, the "fugitive" qualities of baseflow (a natural, visible discharge of groundwater) remain a persistent challenge. Baseflow is notoriously difficult to measure and sensitive to a num-ber of factors, including season, changing evapotranspiration demands of vegetation and near-stream pumping. Although overall average daily baseflow volume at one point in the San Pedro River is measured at 19,900 cubic meters, the flow is highly differentiated based on season. For example, average winter daily baseflow volume is 35,750 m^3 but average daily baseflow volume in June (pre-monsoon) is a mere 8,661 cubic meters per day. During political conflict, actors have enrolled these dynamic measurements to either support or challenge the state of the groundwater overexploitation in the basin.

For example, in 1999, José Manuel Barcelo, president of the local *ejido* Zapata, argued that "while the ejido's wells are dry, the mine has enough water for its activities." However, Isaac López, director of operations of the mine, immediately countered that "preliminary results [of a hydro-geologic study] indicate that system recharge is greater than previously believed, thereby indicating that the aquifer is underexploited."[31] López does admit that "accurate assessments of evapotranspiration, flow toward the San Pedro River, and the underground flow through the divide toward the United States have not been determined," thus highlighting the partial state of knowledge that continues to be a problem in the basin. In 1999, the mine also began implementing an "ambitious project in global hydrological control" that included constructing channels to divert captured rainwater to specific areas of the basin. Informants mentioned that they believed one strategy of the mine to keep up the appearance of steady groundwater levels was to reen-gineer water flows to the small lakes in the northern reaches of the basin, where dropping water levels were visible and often created the greatest backlash from watershed residents toward the mine's exploitation of the aquifer.

In 2008, a ranching support program called PROGAN (Programa de Producción Pecuario Sustentable y Ordenamiento Ganadero y Apícola) was established with the aim of enhancing natural resources conditions in livestock areas by boosting productivity through technology adaptation and ranch improvements, such as fencing. PROGAN has served to reinforce the shift toward fencing land, which followed the implementation of PROCEDE. This articulation of PROCEDE and PROGAN has created a veritable fencing boom in the Sonoran borderlands. PROGAN disfavors *ejidatarios* ranchers in multiple ways. First, making the necessary improvements to grazing land to qualify for financial support through PROGAN is more feasible for private landholders with fenced parcels than for those who remain part of grazing commons. Second, as fencing of land intensifies, collectively managing cattle becomes increasingly difficult. Once open tracts of grazing land have been transformed into mazes of enclosures, producers are denied access to water resources and highly productive forage in the riparian corridors.

Expropriation

The process of expropriation (colloquially defined as the taking of something from another's possession for one's own use) occurs when a public agency, such as a government, takes property, such as land, for a purpose deemed to be in the public interest. Expropriation can take both politically progressive and conservative forms. The expropriation and subsequent redistribution of the Greene *latifundio* in the late 1950s was an example of a progressive expropriation that benefited hundreds of landless peasants and wage laborers. During the past two decades, extractive industries, in particular mining, have expanded rapidly in the Cananea region. This expansion in operations has necessitated an accompanying expansion of access to land and water resources, leading to cases of expropriation of land, causing enclosure of commons grazing land and areas within the riparian zone.

On November 5, 1990, a presidential decree ordered the expropriation of 566 *hectáreas* (1,400 acres) of commons grazing land from the territory of *ejido* Emiliano Zapata for use by Minera de Cananea (the Cananea Mine company). The Commission of National Asset Evaluation assigned a value of 1,018,275 Mexican pesos per *hectárea* of expropriated land, equivalent to approximately US $345, due to extreme inflation in Mexico in 1990. The decree justified the expropriation of the land under Article 121 of the Federal Agrarian Reform Law, which states that *ejidal* and communal lands can be expropriated for a public utility only where the new social benefit will exceed the benefits of its current use. On May 7, 1991, the expropriation was finalized during an official meeting held in Hermosillo, Sonora. The meeting, attended by engineers from the Agrarian Delegation of the State of Sonora, a representative from the National Bank of Works and Services (Banco Nacional de Obras y Servicios), and a lawyer from the Cananea mine formalized the measurement and demarcation of the boundaries of the expropriated land and transferred the compensation payment to the *ejido*'s general fund.

Conservation

In the 1980s, scientists measured rapidly declining groundwater levels of one to two feet per year in southern Arizona, which were linked to declining surface water flows in the San Pedro River. As a response to pressure from environmental agencies and as an attempt to mitigate widespread environmental degradation in the riparian corridor, in

1988, the US Congress designated a 40-mile conservation area in the Arizona portion of the river. Within the boundaries of the San Pedro Riparian National Conservation Area (SPRNCA) agrarian activities were eliminated, explicitly creating a zone of exclusion for livestock grazing and agricultural production. The designation of the SPRNCA further fragmented an already internationally divided riparian space, establishing asymmetrical land management practices on either side of the border; part of the river flowing through Arizona was designated a "livestock-free" landscape, while open-range cattle grazing and livestock production continues in Sonora.

Kelly contends that conservation serves as a mechanism for the "legalized seizure" of property in the form of protected areas.[32] Powerful narratives that privilege the conservation of wildlife and natural resources through the exclusion of certain groups serve to legitimate the creation of these protected areas. In the case of the SPRNCA, the exclusion of cows is a technology of government founded on a very particular understanding of nature based on expert discourse and Western understandings of conservation science. This understanding of nature as a system external to humans, with an internal equilibrium that has been thrown off balance, allows for environmental policy decisions that restrict certain subjects from having access to nature, under the justification that conservation through exclusion is the only method that can reestablish the system to equilibrium.

Furthermore, the role of the Bureau of Land Management (BLM), the designated manager of the SPRNCA, has recently begun to shift. Although an original task of the BLM was to manage and monitor the trespass of cattle in the SPRNCA corridor, this role has transitioned to include the management and monitoring of migrants who pass through the SPRNCA, which is a major travel corridor. Where cattle were originally considered the largest threat to environmental conservation in the riparian zone, monitoring the movement of migrants through the corridor is increasingly part of the BLM's activities.

The Southern Arizona Project (SAP) and Operation Restore Our Arizona Monuments (ROAM) are ongoing efforts by the BLM to address the impacts of illegal immigration and drug smuggling on public lands in southern Arizona. Operation ROAM establishes a partnership between the BLM and the US Border Patrol, the Alliance to Combat Transnational Threats, the Arizona Department of Public Safety, and the local county sheriff's department. The BLM's 2011 SAP report states that fiscal year 2011 marked a major shift in the emphasis and approach of the BLM toward the management of border issues through the expansion of Operation ROAM. This marks a transition of BLM activities from being mainly reactive clean-up and restoration activities to proactive tactics to monitor migrants moving through the riparian corridor. Operation ROAM is described as a resource protection and restoration program with the goal of "enhancing the protection of natural and cultural resources on public lands and improving coordination and cooperation with border law enforcement and land management partners."[33] To meet these goals, the BLM Arizona rangers partner with other law enforcement officers for two-week periods as part of law enforcement "surges."

Thus, the shifts to conservation and more recently securitization, based on the logic of exclusion, has enrolled new actors and agencies in riparian management and served to rescript power relations in the region. Where ranchers had long enjoyed a privileged position, the new politics of exclusion in the SPRNCA have shifted privilege away from ranchers to land management agencies, urban residents, recreationists and military and border security forces. Under the justification of regional economic growth, ecological conservation and border securitization, the riparian zone of the San Pedro River has become a corridor of exclusion and an object of the state's scrutiny.

Discussion

These vignettes illustrate the development of increasing inequality in power relations in the riparian spaces of the Sonoran borderlands. Transformations in the political economic and ecological conditions in the borderlands have led to restructuring of property rights regimes for productive natural resources, such as land and water. Though no less dramatic in its impact, the return to exclusive ownership of riparian resources has been signaled by far less pomp and circumstance than the 1959 presidential visit to transfer the lands of the Greene *latifundio* to local *campesinos*. In the subsequent 50 years, most of the gains made during earlier periods of agrarian reform activism have been severely eroded in favor of private property rights, the expansion of extractive industries and border securitization.

David Harvey asserts that "[A]ll socio-political projects are ecological projects and vice versa. […] All critical examinations of the relation to nature are simultaneously critical examinations of society."[34] In *Changes in the Land*, William Cronon demonstrates the critical importance of interrogating the social and ecological processes that shape transformations in material conditions.[35] Cronon shows how the transition from a subsistence economy to capitalism alienated both the products of the land and the products of human labor, resulting in profound transformations in both human and more-than-human communities. Shifts in property regimes are key to these political-economic transitions. The move from a claim to the use of things on the land (i.e., usufructory rights) to a claim to the land itself (i.e., private, alienable rights) serves to erode social obligations and to deny the possibility for collective solutions in favor of solutions that support individualistic, permanent, alienable and exclusive rights to resources.

In Sonora, Mexico, following the 1992 land and water law reforms, there has been a reconsolidation of groundwater resources under mining company control. Access to very deep supplies of groundwater serves to insulate the industrial mining sector and its economic profits from the negative impacts of water scarcity when groundwater levels drop and shallow wells become inoperative. In contrast, local rural residents, agricultural producers and ecological communities who depend on shallow groundwater tables for their subsistence and survival are exposed to the negative externalities that result from the steady expansion of capital accumulation in the mining sector.

In riparian SES, groundwater pumping is a key variable of system behavior due to its impact on shallow groundwater tables, a critical source of water for human and ecological communities in semiarid climates. Thus, as local water table levels drop, crisis conditions are experienced unevenly. Emily Yeh contends that enclosure often serves to compound rather than to alleviate grazing problems for communities and ecosystems.[36]

The exclusion of individuals and communities from accessing land and water resources necessary for maintaining their livelihoods has serious negative implications. Examining the intersections of water management and property rights regimes with social relations, political economy and ecology exposes the often-concealed sites where the contradictory dynamics of capitalist accumulation penetrate systems of natural resource production, producing subjects differentially excluded from the benefits of natural resources, especially land and water.

Conclusion: Toward a Socio-ecological Approach to Management

This chapter examines how shifts in property rights regimes intersect with social and ecological transformations in riparian spaces in the binational San Pedro River watershed, leading to varied outcomes for producers in the region. Political-economic conditions are responsible for producing the current configurations of uneven access to and distribution of resources. As the art of governance continues to shift in favor of neoliberal strategies for resource governance, negative social and ecological consequences abound. Further compounding the situation is the fact that vulnerability to and responsibility for coping with hardship are being transferred from societal-level concerns to individual obligations. Scholars of neoliberalism point out that individualized, market-based solutions come to appear in lieu of collective political solutions and that the ideal of the fundamentally self-interested individual comes to limit the sense of what is politically possible.[37]

Processes and events that reconfigure social-ecological power relations often result in the exacerbation rather than the amelioration of difference and marginalization. Henri Lefebvre argues that "the dominant form of space, that of the centers of wealth and power, endeavors to mold the spaces it dominates, and it seeks by violent means, to reduce the obstacles and resistances it encounters there."[38] Transformations of social-ecological relations thus serve to differentiate individuals and communities vis-à-vis access to natural resources. The contradictions inherent to capitalism are expressed in the production of spaces of exclusion whereby some bodies and ecologies are unevenly exposed to scarcity, vulnerability and harm. Said another way, "contradictions in the social relations entail social contradictions on the land."[39] Thus, attending to modern forms of enclosure, exclusion and dispossession provides new and necessary avenues of critical research into social-ecological transformation and social and environmental justice in landscapes of resource conflict. This intervention unlocks new conceptual avenues for proposing forms of management that more equitably redistribute the negative effects of capitalist accumulation, such as falling water tables and aquifer depletion.

Reconciling conflicts that arise over multiple, competing uses of water in semiarid watersheds with over-allocated supplies is an ongoing challenge facing resource managers worldwide. Scholars of human-environment geography argue that in addition to the recognition of power and politics as central to resource struggles, ethics must also be explicit for resource management to achieve success. While scholars such as Peter Linebaugh call for the development of an ethic of human solidarity that transcends social divisions and instead recognizes commonality in the human experience,[40] post-humanist-inspired scholars such as Bruce Braun draw attention to the need for an environmental ethic grounded in the inescapable entanglement of human and nonhuman bodies and objects.[41]

A return to thinking about ethics provides new ways to imagine reconciling conflicting interests and reviving strategies of collective resource management. Rather than eliding and ignoring social and ecological difference, it is imperative to recognize and value the multiple perspectives, interests and knowledge present in riparian zones. In contrast to laws, policies and practices that manage through exclusion, I argue that management approaches based in an inclusive environmental ethic may open new political possibilities. If we approach relations between diverse human communities and the multiple nonhuman entities that exist in riparian systems as webs of intricate relations, impossible to disentangle, then it becomes possible to locate affinities, cultivate solidarity and build coalitions across social and ecological boundaries. An approach based on coalitions and cooperation creates opportunities to move beyond contentious narratives and assignations of blame toward management decisions grounded in collective responsibility in opposition to the individualist ontology of risk management presented by neoliberal environmental management models. Furthermore, instead of dedicating attention solely to economic growth, which favors unsustainable industrial-scale mining and agriculture with little regulation, a social-ecological approach rooted in ethics takes seriously broader considerations including social reproduction, human and nonhuman community health and well-being and food and water security.

In *Fugitive Landscapes*, Samuel Truett highlights enduring tensions present through the historical development of the Sonoran borderlands.[42] Although Truett's analysis focuses primarily on the nineteenth century, his conclusions continue to echo through the region today. The promise of enormous mineral wealth and large open grassland spaces simultaneously attracted adventurous spirits, risk-taking entrepreneurs and foreign capital investment. Yet, these same spaces also presented the very obstructions that impeded and arrested the successful implementation of large-scale development projects. Throughout history, those who aspired to control the appealing, yet elusive and dangerous Sonoran spaces found their dreams dashed. Truett paints these binational spaces as both highly fluid and utterly bordered, defined by mutual suspicions and overlapping histories, periods of intractable conflict interspersed with fleeting moments of cooperation. Drawing attention to the deviant storylines that haunt the borderlands, Truett reminds the reader of the lengthy list of dreams that never came to fruition in the Sonoran borderlands, the futures that failed to take shape and the human ability to ignore and forget historical failures.

NOTES

1 Neil Smith, *Uneven Development: Nature, Capital, and the Production of Space, 2nd Edition* (Athens: University of Georgia Press, 2008), 4.
2 Steven E. Sanderson, *Agrarian Populism and the Mexican State: The Struggle for Land in Sonora* (Berkeley: University of California Press, 1985).
3 Nicholas Blomley, "Making Private Property: Enclosure, Common Right and the Work of Hedges," *Rural History* 18 (2007), 2.

4 Blomley, "Making Private Property"; Michael Hardt and Antonio Negri, *Commonwealth* (Cambridge, MA: Belknap Press of Harvard University Press, 2009); Peter Linebaugh, *Stop Thief! The Commons, Enclosures, and Resistance* (Oakland, CA: PM Press, 2014).

5 Smith, *Uneven Development*.

6 Thomas Sheridan, "The Limits of Power: The Political Ecology of the Spanish Empire in the Greater Southwest," *Antiquity* 66 (1992), doi:10.1017/S0003598X00081163.

7 Crawford S. Holling and Lance H. Gunderson, "Resilience and Adaptive Cycles," in *Panarchy: Understanding Transformations in Human and Natural Systems*, ed. Lance H. Gunderson and Crawford S. Holling (Washington, DC: Island Press, 2002); Jeremy Walker and Melinda Cooper, "Genealogies of Resilience: From Systems Ecology to the Political Economy of Crisis Adaptation," *Security Dialogue* 42 (2011), doi:10.1177/0967010611399616.

8 Brian Walker and David Salt, *Resilience Thinking: Sustaining Ecosystems and People in a Changing World* (Washington, DC: Island Press, 2006).

9 Eric Swyngedouw, "Modernity and Hybridity: Nature, *Regeneracionismo*, and the Production of the Spanish Waterscape," *Annals of the Association of American Geographers* 89 (1999), doi:10.1111/0004-5608.00157; Michael Ekers and Alex Loftus, "The Power of Water: Developing Dialogues between Foucault and Gramsci," *Environment and Planning D: Society & Space* 26 (2008), doi:10.1068/d5907; Trevor Birkenholtz, "Irrigated Landscapes, Produced Scarcity, and Adaptive Social Institutions in Rajasthan, India," *Annals of the Association of American Geographers* 99 (2009), doi:10.1080/00045600802459093; Trevor Birkenholtz, "'On the Network, Off the Map': Developing Intervillage and Intragender Differentation in Rural Water Supply," *Environment and Planning D: Society & Space* 31 (2013), doi:10.1068/d11510; Karen Bakker, *Privatizing Water: Governance Failure and the World's Urban Water Crisis* (Ithaca, NY: Cornell University Press, 2010); Farhana Sultana, "Producing Contaminated Citizens: Toward a Nature-Society Geography of Health and Well-Being," *Annals of the Association of American Geographers* 102 (2012), doi:10.1080/00045608.2012.671127; Jessica Budds and Farhana Sultana, "Exploring Political Ecologies of Water and Development (Guest Editorial)," *Environment & Planning D: Society & Space* 31 (2013), doi:10.1068/d3102.

10 Harvey, *Justice, Nature, and the Geography of Difference*, 5.

11 Ibid., 8.

12 Karl Marx, "The German Ideology," in *Karl Marx: Selected Writings*, ed. David McLellan (Oxford: Oxford University Press, 1977), 164.

13 William Cronon, *Changes in the Land: Indians, Colonists, and the Ecology of New England* (New York: Hill and Wang, 1983).

14 Smith, *Uneven Development*.

15 David Delaney, "Running with the Land: Legal-Historical Imagination and the Spaces of Modernity," *Journal of Historical Geography* (2001), doi:10.1006/jhge.2001.0352; Nicholas Blomley, "Simplification Is Complicated: Property, Nature, and the Rivers of Law," *Environment and Planning A* 40 (2008), doi:10.1068/a40157.

16 C. B. Macpherson, "The Meaning of Property," in *Property: Mainstream and Critical Positions*, ed. C. B. MacPherson (Toronto: University of Toronto Press, 1978); James William Hurst, *Law and Economic Growth: The Legal History of the Lumber Industry in Wisconsin, 1836–1915* (Cambridge, MA: Belknap Press of Harvard University Press, 1964).

17 Smith, *Uneven Development*.

18 Macpherson, "The Meaning of Property"; Emily Yeh, "The Politics of Conservation in Contemporary Rural China," *The Journal of Peasant Studies* 40 (2013), doi:10.1080/03066150.2013.859575.

19 Hurst, *Law and Economic Growth*.

20 Karl Marx, *Capital Volume 1: A Critique of Political Economy* (New York: International Publishers, 1967).

21 Alice B. Kelly, "Conservation Practice as Primitive Accumulation," *The Journal of Peasant Studies* 38 (2011): 685, doi:10.1080/03066150.2011.607695.

22 Silvia Federici, *Caliban and the Witch* (Brooklyn, NY: Autonomedia, 2004).
23 James McCarthy and Scott Prudham, "Neoliberal Nature and the Nature of Neoliberalism," *Geoforum* 35 (2004), doi:10.1016/j.geoforum.2003.07.003.
24 Karen Bakker, *An Cooperative Commodity: Privatizing Water in England and Wales* (Oxford: Oxford University Press, 2004); Karen Bakker, "Neoliberalizing Nature? Market Environmentalism in Water Supply in England and Wales," *Annals of the Association of American Geographers* 95 (2005), doi:10.1111/j.1467-8306.2005.00474.x.
25 Bakker, "Neoliberalizing Nature," 552, emphasis added.
26 Bakker, "Neoliberalizing Nature."
27 Morgan Robertson, "The Nature that Capital Can See: Science, State and Market in the Commodification of Ecosystem Services," *Environment and Planning D: Society and Space* 24 (2006), doi:10.1068/d3304.
28 Robertson, "The Nature that Capital Can See," 382.
29 Eric Perramond, "The Rise, Fall, and Reconfiguration of the Mexican *Ejido*," *The Geographical Review* 98 (2008), doi:10.1111/j.1931-0846.2008.tb00306.x.
30 Julie C. Stromberg, R. Tiller and Brian Richter, "Effects of Groundwater Decline on Riparian Vegetation of Semiarid Regions: The San Pedro, Arizona," *Ecological Applications* 6 (1996); Arizona Department of Water Resources (ADWR), "Subflow Technical Report, San Pedro River Watershed: In Re the General Adjudication of the Gila River System and Source", (2002); S. J. Lite and Julie C. Stromberg, "Surface Water and Groundwater Thresholds for Maintaining *Populus-Salix* Forests, San Pedro River, Arizona," *Biological Conservation* 125 (2005), doi:10.1016/j.biocon.2005.01.020.
31 Stephen McElroy, "San Pedro Conference Proceedings/ Memoria Descriptiva de la Conferencia San Pedro" (Tucson, Arizona: Semi-arid Land-Surface-Atmosphere (SALSA) Research Program, 2000), 14.
32 Kelly, "Conservation Practice as Primitive Accumulation."
33 Bureau of Land Management (BLM), "Southern Arizona Project to Mitigate Environmental Damages Resulting from Illegal Immigration," Fiscal Year 2011 Report (2011), 1.
34 Harvey, *Justice, Nature, and the Geography of Difference*, 174.
35 Cronon, *Changes in the Land*.
36 Yeh, "The Politics of Conservation."
37 Wendy Brown, "American Nightmare: Neoliberalism, Neoconservatism, and Democratization," *Political Theory* 34 (2006), doi:10.1177/0090591706293016; Jason Read, "A Genealogy of Homo-Economicus: Neoliberalism and the Production of Subjectivity," *Foucault Studies* 6 (2009).
38 Henri Lefebvre, *The Production of Space* (Malden, MA: Blackwell, 1991), 49.
39 Harvey, *Justice, Nature, and the Geography of Difference*, 185.
40 Linebaugh, *Stop Thief!*, 140.
41 Bruce Braun, *The Intemperate Rainforest: Nature, Culture, and Power on Canada's West Coast* (Minneapolis: University of Minnesota Press, 2002).
42 Samuel Truett, *Fugitive Landscapes: The Forgotten History of the US–Mexico Borderlands* (New Haven, CT: Yale University Press, 2006).

BIBLIOGRAPHY

Arizona Department of Water Resources (ADWR). "Subflow Technical Report, San Pedro River Watershed: In Re the General Adjudication of the Gila River System and Source." Report (2002).

Bakker, Karen. *An Uncooperative Commodity: Privatizing Water in England and Wales*. Oxford: Oxford University Press, 2004.

Bakker, Karen. "Neoliberalizing Nature? Market Environmentalism in Water Supply in England and Wales." *Annals of the Association of American Geographers* 95 (2005): 542–65. doi:10.1111/j.1467-8306.2005.00474.x.

Bakker, Karen. *Privatizing Water: Governance Failure and the World's Urban Water Crisis*. Ithaca, NY: Cornell University Press, 2010.

Birkenholtz, Trevor. "Irrigated Landscapes, Produced Scarcity, and Adaptive Social Institutions in Rajasthan, India." *Annals of the Association of American Geographers* 99 (2009): 118–37. doi:10.1080/00045600802459093.

Birkenholtz, Trevor. "'On the Network, Off the Map': Developing Intervillage and Intragender Differentiation in Rural Water Supply." *Environment & Planning D: Society & Space* 31 (2013): 354–71. doi:10.1068/d11510.

Blomley, Nicholas. "Making Private Property: Enclosure, Common Right and the Work of Hedges." *Rural History* 18 (2007): 1–21. doi:10.1017/S0956793306001993.

Blomley, Nicholas. "Simplification Is Complicated: Property, Nature, and the Rivers of Law." *Environment & Planning A* 40 (2008): 1825–42. doi: 10.1068/a40157.

Braun, Bruce. *The Intemperate Rainforest: Nature, Culture, and Power on Canada's West Coast*. Minneapolis: University of Minnesota Press, 2002.

Brown, Wendy. "American Nightmare: Neoliberalism, Neoconservatism, and Democratization." *Political Theory* 34 (2006): 690–714. doi:10.1177/0090591706293016.

Budds, Jessica and Farhana Sultana. "Exploring Political Ecologies of Water and Development (Guest Editorial)." *Environment & Planning D: Society & Space* 31 (2013): 275–9. doi:10.1068/d3102.

Bureau of Land Management (BLM). "Southern Arizona Project to Mitigate Environmental Damage from Illegal Immigration." Fiscal Year 2011 Report (2011).

Cronon, William. *Changes in the Land: Indians, Colonists, and the Ecology of New England*. New York: Hill and Wang, 1983.

Delaney, David. "Running with the Land: Legal-Historical Imagination and the Spaces of Modernity." *Journal of Historical Geography* 27 (2001): 493–506. doi:10.1006/jhge.2001.0352.

Ekers, Michael and Alex Loftus. "The Power of Water: Developing Dialogues between Foucault and Gramsci." *Environment & Planning D: Society & Space* 26 (2008): 698–718. doi:10.1068/d5907.

Federici, Silvia. *Caliban and the Witch*. Brooklyn, NY: Autonomedia, 2004.

Hardt, Michael and Antonio Negri. *Commonwealth*. Cambridge, MA: Belknap Press of Harvard University Press, 2009.

Harvey, David. *Justice, Nature, and the Geography of Difference*. Malden, MA: Blackwell, 1996.

Holling, Crawford S. and Lance H. Gunderson. "Resilience and Adaptive Cycles." In *Panarchy: Understanding Transformations in Human and Natural Systems*, edited by Lance H. Gunderson and Crawford S. Holling, 25–62. Washington, DC: Island Press, 2002.

Hurst, James Willard. *Law and Economic Growth: The Legal History of the Lumber Industry in Wisconsin, 1836–1915*. Cambridge, MA: Belknap Press of Harvard University Press, 1964.

Kelly, Alice B. "Conservation Practice as Primitive Accumulation." *The Journal of Peasant Studies* 38 (2011): 683–701. doi:10.1080/03066150.2011.607695.

Lefebvre, Henri. *The Production of Space*. Malden, MA: Blackwell, 1991.

Linebaugh, Peter. *Stop Thief! The Commons, Enclosures, and Resistance*. Oakland, CA: PM Press, 2014.

Lite, S. J. and Julie C. Stromberg. "Surface Water and Groundwater Thresholds for Maintaining *Populus-Salix* Forests, San Pedro River, Arizona." *Biological Conservation* 125 (2005): 153–67. doi:10.1016/j.biocon.2005.01.020.

Macpherson, C. B. "The Meaning of Property." In *Property: Mainstream and Critical Positions*, edited by C. B. MacPherson, 1–13. Toronto: University of Toronto Press, 1978.

Marx, Karl. *Capital Volume 1: A Critique of Political Economy*. New York: International Publishers, 1967.

Marx, Karl. "The German Ideology." In *Karl Marx: Selected Writings*, edited by David McLellan, 175–207. Oxford: Oxford University Press, 1977.

McCarthy, James and Scott Prudham. "Neoliberal Nature and the Nature of Neoliberalism." *Geoforum* 35 (2004): 275–83. doi:10.1016/j.geoforum.2003.07.003.

McElroy, Stephen. "San Pedro Conference Proceedings/ Memoria Descriptiva de la Conferencia San Pedro." Tucson, Arizona: Semi-arid Land-Surface-Atmosphere (SALSA) Research Program, 2000.

Mexican National Commission for Water (CONAGUA). Public Registry for Water Rights (REPDA). www.conagua.gob.mx/Repda.aspx?n1=5&n2=37&n3=115.

Perramond, Eric P. "The Rise, Fall, and Reconfiguration of the Mexican *Ejido.*" *The Geographical Review* 98 (2008): 356–71. doi:10.1111/j.1931-0846.2008.tb00306.x.

Read, Jason. "A Genealogy of Homo-Economicus: Neoliberalism and the Production of Subjectivity." *Foucault Studies* 6 (2009): 25–36.

Robertson, Morgan. "The Nature that Capital Can See: Science, State and Market in the Commodification of Ecosystem Services." *Environment and Planning D: Society and Space* 24 (2006): 367–87. doi:10.1068/d3304.

Sanderson, Steven E. *Agrarian Populism and the Mexican State: The Struggle for Land in Sonora.* Berkeley: University of California Press, 1985. New Mexico State University (Las Cruces) and the Environmental Protection Agency (Landscape Ecology Branch, Las Vegas NV). San Pedro River Basin Date Browser. http://case.nmsu.edu/CASE/SanPedro/.

Sheridan, Thomas. "The Limits of Power: The Political Ecology of the Spanish Empire in the Greater Southwest." *Antiquity* 66 (1992): 153–71. doi:10.1017/S0003598X00081163.

Smith, Neil. *Uneven Development: Nature, Capital, and the Production of Space* (2nd Edition). Athens: University of Georgia Press, 2008.

Stromberg, Julie C., R. Tiller, and Brian Richter. "Effects of Groundwater Decline on Riparian Vegetation of Semiarid Regions: The San Pedro, Arizona." *Ecological Applications* 6 (1996): 113–31.

Sultana, Farhana. "Producing Contaminated Citizens: Toward a Nature-Society Geography of Health and Well-Being." *Annals of the Association of American Geographers* 102 (2012): 1165–72. doi:10.1080/00045608.2012.671127.

Swyngedouw, Eric. "Modernity and Hybridity: Nature, *Regeneracionismo,* and the Production of the Spanish Waterscape." *Annals of the Association of American Geographers* 89 (1999): 443–65. doi:10.1111/0004-5608.00157.

Truett, Samuel. *Fugitive Landscapes: The Forgotten History of the US–Mexico Borderlands.* New Haven, CT: Yale University Press, 2006.

Walker, Brian and David Salt. 2006. *Resilience Thinking: Sustaining Ecosystems and People in a Changing World.* Washington, DC: Island Press, 2006.

Walker, Jeremy and Melinda Cooper. "Genealogies of Resilience: From Systems Ecology to the Political Economy of Crisis Adaptation." *Security Dialogue* 42 (2011): 143–60. doi:10.1177/0967010611399616.

Yeh, Emily. "The Politics of Conservation in Contemporary Rural China." *The Journal of Peasant Studies* 40 (2013): 1165–88. doi:10.1080/03066150.2013.859575.

Chapter Seven

FROM NO-MAN'S LAND TO EVERY-MAN'S LAND: SOCIO-ECOLOGICAL APPROACHES TO RECLAIMING SHARED SPACES IN BORDER LANDSCAPES, WITH EXAMPLES FROM GERMANY AND CYPRUS

Anna Grichting

At its maximum of defiance, the frontier doubles itself inevitably into two lines, each turned toward the exterior, but which must also protect the interior against the threat not only of the other but also of this intermediary interstitial region, the no man's land, this geographical expression of misunderstanding, of rift, at first a corridor of death, desolation, and barbed wire, but which can sometimes soften and become the very image of the crossing of frontiers when that finally begins to occur.[1]

Introduction

This chapter highlights a shift toward human-centered conservation practices, in which nature conservation benefits from the inclusion and empowerment of human communities instead of their exclusion and marginalization and examines two cases: the Cyprus Buffer Zone and the Berlin Wall.[2] In both cases, nature and landscape have played a role in bridging communities across the divide—in Berlin, communities from both sides of the Wall collaborated to bring the Mauer Park into being, while in Cyprus, biologists collaborated on a biodiversity survey in the Buffer Zone. Ecosystems and landscapes must be seen as coupled social-ecological systems whose ability to respond to stresses and change derives from ecological and social characteristics, as well as from the link between these natural and human components. Additionally, many recent studies and literature examine the importance of nature in physical and psychological recovery through practices of active engagement.[3] Contemporary research in neuroscience also demonstrates the effects of settings on the brain, leading to significant developments in healing approaches enhanced by design and access to nature.[4]

The United Nations Buffer Zone (hereafter referred to as UNBZ) that divides the Mediterranean island of Cyprus is examined and proposed as a future shared social and ecological space for the Cypriot communities—a *third space* or *thirdscape* that must rise beyond the polarized sphere of the binary and of bicommunalism to embrace the mosaic of social and ethnic groups that inhabit and produce the landscapes of Cyprus.[5] Creating a shared space also implies a shared process, toward co-creating a landscape for the future coexistence of multiple ecologies and social groups. Addressing the contemporary theme of the spatial redevelopment of a post-military zone, it also refers to other border-lands that are undergoing or have undergone similar transformations—in particular in Germany and Berlin—and that have, as precedents, informed this speculative research.

The Cyprus Buffer Zone is of particular interest as a contemporary and transitioning boundary, as a marginal landscape and as a gateway to the European Union (EU). The island is historically situated along what we propose to name an East–West fault line, a geographical zone at the nexus of a tri-continental junction that has acted as a barrier and bridge, as a stage of cultural encounters and of military and ideological conflict between Eastern and Western cultures. The UNBZ, also named the *Green Line*, separates the Greek Cypriot communities in the south (Republic of Cyprus) from the Turkish Cypriot communities in the north (the de facto Turkish Republic of Northern Cyprus), and defines a range of varying boundary conditions—from urban and suburban edge conditions to landscape, ecological and maritime enclaves. This territory offers a series of unique sites for the investigation of borderscapes and their future socioecological transformations; the divided city of Nicosia and its marginalized historic core; the bicommunal village of Pyla enclaved within the British Sovereign Military Bases; the ghost town of Varosha, a modern suburb of the historic city of Famagusta; the ruined villages and unexplored archaeological sites within the Buffer Zone; the abandoned copper mines that adjoin the Green Line; and the recently recognized habitats for endangered species and migratory birds.

This chapter highlights some of the socio-ecological opportunities for reconciliation and co-creation of new, shared spaces and green commons by illustrating potential or existing projects and initiatives in the Buffer Zone. These include the preservation of endangered plant and animal communities that thrive in the Buffer Zone and are studied by biologists and ecologists; the Home for Cooperation (an initiative of the Association for Historical Dialogue) located in the Buffer Zone in the divided capital of Nicosia; and ephemeral actions and temporary events ("Occupy the Buffer Zone" and the German "Green Belt Event"). These projects position the Green Line Buffer Zone as a *space of possibilities* for ecological and social projects that can build future resilience and enhance biocultural diversity involving actors and stakeholders across the dividing line. Investigating the physical landscapes as well as the multiple civil society initiatives within and across the Buffer Zone, the Cyprus GreenLineScapes Laboratory is an interactive and participative platform that aims to reveal, reclaim and restore the landscapes of the Green Line. One project for the Green Line in Cyprus has been proposed and is being developed by the author, based on her PhD research.

Socio-ecological Approaches to Borders in Conflict Zones: Toward Rhizomatic Systems and Thirdscapes

Bookchin, who first theorized social ecology in the Anglo-Saxon world, declared that the real battleground on which the ecological future of the planet will be decided will clearly

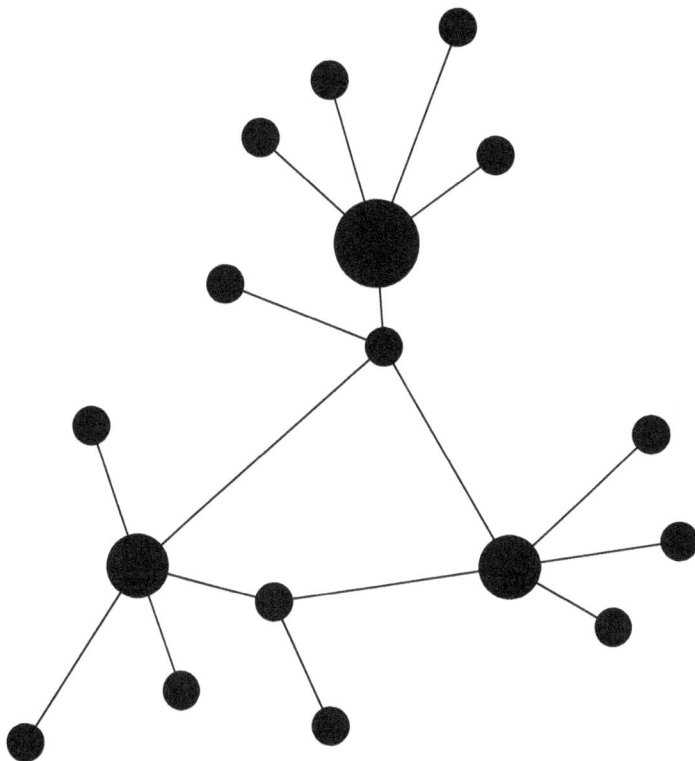

Figure 7.1 Structural representation of topology of the Rhizome.
Source: www.urbagram.net/microplexes/.

be a social one, underscoring that the way human beings deal with each other as social beings is crucial to addressing the ecological crisis.[6] Similar to Bookchin's principles for social ecologies, French philosophers Deleuze and Guattari address the necessity to move away from hierarchal relationships toward more mutualistic and transversal ones. They also argue that it is necessary to overcome the dualistic framework underpinning Western philosophy.[7] The dynamic and unhierarchical structures of these encounters and articulations are described and theorized by Deleuze as a *rhizomatic* relationship or structure.

Rhizome derives from an organic, underground structure that reproduces itself underground. A rhizome (from ancient Greek: *rhízōma* or "mass of roots") is a modified subterranean stem of a plant that is usually found underground, often sending out roots and shoots from its nodes. Rhizomes develop from axillary buds and are diageotropic, or grow perpendicular to the force of gravity. If a rhizome is separated into pieces, each piece may be able to give rise to a new plant. Deleuze and Guattari use the rhizome to describe "the connections that occur between the most disparate and the most similar of objects, places and people."[4] The rhizome has the capacity to map process, that is, to trace "networked, relational and transversal thought" without constructing the map as a fixed entity, and it creates a space for interdisciplinary thinking. The rhizome is a *moving matrix* that conceives how the different aspects of concrete, abstract and virtual entities can be seen as "multiple in their interrelational movements with other things and bodies." As *open systems of thought*, rhizomatic formations can serve to overcome, overturn and transform structures of rigid, fixed or binary thought and judgment—"the rhizome is 'anti'-genealogy."[5] As an alternative or opposition to the binary, and in its capacity to map process and connect elements, the rhizome is of particular interest in this work, which is concerned with the *reconnection* of disjointed territories and the deconstruction of the us/them binary that is the result of societies in conflict.

The concept of Thirdscapes is a neologism proposed as a *depolarizing* conceptual device and as an interdisciplinary framework for examining the interstitial space of the boundary.[8] Scape is used as concept that implies and describes depth and perspective— namely an extensive view, a wide and long view. It is also used in botany to describe a stalk or upshot arising at or beneath the surface of the ground, and in biology to describe the shaft of an animal part such as an antenna or a feather. It therefore contains the ver- tical, connective element that arises from the ground, as well as the deeply perspectival, evoking a backbone for future visions. This concept of Thirdscapes to approach border- lands in conflict is intended to extract us from the simplifications and entrenchments of the polarized discourses of conflict—We/They, Us/Them, Dominant/Other, Subject/ Object, West/East, Occident/Orient, Civilized/Barbaric, Progression/Regression, Modern/Primitive—in order to creatively connect different approaches to transforming and overcoming the boundary and the conflict. For Soja, Third*space* is the space of social practice, the space occupied by sensory phenomena, including products of the imagina- tion such as projects and projections, symbols and utopias.[9]

Homi Bhabha uses the concept of Thirdspace as a space for the negotiated reimagin- ing of cultural identity. As a cultural concept, it refers to a space for the constructing and reconstructing of identity, a space of fluidity, where identity is not fixed, where we nego- tiate identity and become neither this nor that, but our own. Bhabha asserts that "This third space displaces histories that constitute it, and sets up new structures of authority, new political initiatives. [...] The process of cultural hybridity gives rise to something different, something new and unrecognizable, a new area of negotiation of meaning and representation."[10] It is also a space of memory. For example, the Third Space of Commemoration is associated with a democratic and collaborative process of construct- ing memory.[11] In Germany, the collaborative art between East and West was seen as a cultural space, a pan-German third space, situated between the official programs of the Federal Republic and the Democratic Republic, where the work of commemoration could take place. Calico is particularly interested in this collaborative art between East and West.[12] Calico notes that "The cultures of East and West Germany were third spaces generated by the negotiations between indigenous (German) and occupying (American and Soviet) cultures, neither of which proved entirely sufficient for commemoration. That work required an additional, pan-German third space between the two states."[13]

In contemporary questions of landscape planning and design, dynamic or unexpected natures have become increasingly recognized for their ecological value and for their con- tribution to the preservation of biodiversity. Marginal sites abandoned to nature—also referred to as *terrain vague*—have been described as *Third Landscapes* (Gilles Clément).

These neglected areas where biodiversity thrives can be considered the earth's genetic reservoir, and Clément confers on the Third Landscape the role of a matrix (or *matriciel*), that is, of a global landscape *in becoming*. It is not a landscape that is designed and constructed; it is a landscape that *becomes* the privileged space of biological intelligence, with the capacity to constantly reinvent itself. Clément argues that there is more diversity where environments meet and overlap, and similar concepts can be found in the art of Permaculture that also refer to the *border effect* or the *margin effect*.[14] These interfaces have a biological depth; they comprise biological layers and their wealth is often superior to the environments that they divide. The Third Landscape also promotes stronger ecological health, becoming a territory for the multiple species, which find nowhere to be.

The concept of *terrain vague* was first theorized by Ignasi de Sola-Morales in the mid-1990s as a contemporary space of project and design that includes the marginal wastelands and vacant lots that are located outside the productive spaces of a city or territory, which Morales describes as oversights in the landscape that are mentally exterior in the physical interior of a geographical area. These liminal and forsaken spaces are often invested by human communities who create new futures and orchestrate these spontaneous natures, extracting or enhancing certain species to create an evolving landscape that is guided by the historical, cultural and ecological conditions surrounding the site. Social and ecological diversity can be articulated as social ecologies, as an intertwining of the theory of biocultural diversity and social-ecological resilience, also touching on the domains of systems theory and human–environment interactions.[15]

These Thirdscapes can provide us with new social and ecological lenses that can be activated to reconceptualize border landscapes. In order for the border to develop and evolve and to become a backbone of reconciliation and interaction, the space not only has to be a social space of debate and negotiation, a cultural space of commemoration, but also an ecological space of evolving nature. An action has to be deployed to engender a process of transformation, and an agency has to be activated.

Beuys, Berlin and the Border Effects: Third Pathways, Urban Ecology and the German Green Belt

German artist Joseph Beuys developed the concept of an "Action Third Path," which gives us insights into the activation of these social ecologies in the transformation and healing of conflict borders. Beuys considered art a political activity and, aside from being one of the founders of the German Green Party, he is considered a forerunner to the economic-political idea of the *Third Way*. Beuys's ideas for a new concept of economics were inspired by Wilhelm Schmundt (1898–1992) the anthroposophist Rudolph Steiner (1861–1925), who was also the inspiration for Beuys's expanded concept of art about a "threefold social organism." In connection with his art, Beuys introduced the anthroposophical concepts of space and counterspace, arguing that in all fields of knowledge and life, traditionally opposed, polar elements needed to be reintegrated to lead to expanded concepts and outlooks.[16]

Beuys's projects include "land healing" projects, and they prefigure ways in which contemporary German culture should still aspire above all to "bridging" and "helping others."[17] In 1984, Beuys attempted to neutralize the *spiritual barriers* brought about by the Berlin Wall by proposing that it be slightly altered in height—elevated by five centimeters—which he ironically considered better proportions. He explained that far from constituting literal endorsement of the Wall, his pleas for improved proportions function primarily to indicate the way in which what he rather ambiguously terms "realistic spiritual training" might liberate the young from a kind of entrenched fatalism.[18] His proposal to contemplate the Wall from an optical angle is a call to disarm the Wall and to annihilate it through inner laughter. Beuys calls for introspection by asking what part of man's character has contributed to the Wall coming into being and continuing to exist. He goes on to add: "Quintessence: The Wall as such is totally unimportant. Don't talk so much about the Wall! Establish through self-education a better moral in mankind and all walls will disappear. There are so many small walls between you and me."[19] Beuys's artistic and political approach to society and ecology can be foundational in our thinking about borders. We must not only externalize our efforts to break down walls and barriers, but also to internally examine what makes us build walls between ourselves and others.

Emmanuel Terray describes the landscapes of divided Berlin as "shadow spaces," and the *terrains vagues*, the no-man's lands or interstitial spaces, as the *shadows* of the city, as the *spaces of the possible*, as spaces outside the mainstream, official culture in which creation can take place.[20] It is the shadow of this gap, of the Wall—this breach in the psychological, political and physical landscape of Berlin—from which links and bridges are constructed. This shadow is a conceptual space in which actions of forgiving and projects for remembering can be constructed, outside the political and psychological web that imprisons populations in a polarized and fragmented identity. *Terrain vagues* are contemporary spaces of project and design that include the marginal wastelands and vacant lots that are located outside the city's productive spaces.[21] These negative, interstitial and marginal spaces—derelict lands, brownfields, voids, loose spaces, heterotopias, dead zones, urban wilds, countersites—have either been abandoned by economic forces or are in a flux of natural transformation or in danger of disappearance. If left fallow or encouraged to re-naturalize, they can become urban forests and/or havens for biodiversity, creating hybrid fabrics of wild and built lands in the city.

In the shadows of the more publicized and official Berlin Wall sites, some jewels of memory and pockets of wild landscapes have been salvaged from the rampant real estate ventures through the agencies of local ecological, artistic and spiritual communities. These include Mauer Park, a very popular green space between Prenzlauer Berg and Wedding, which resulted from a bottom-up, community-led initiative; the Chapel of Reconciliation and Berlin Wall Memorial initiated by the minster of the Evangelical parish whose land and church were swallowed up and demolished by the death strip; and the Lohmuehle Wagendorf, an ecological community of caravan dwellers who invested a segment of the former Wall. This narrow strip of barren land was reclaimed by nature and invested in by a border community that is experimenting with how to accommodate and cooperate with nature. It is a socio-ecological laboratory that experiments with new ways of living within a minimal ecological footprint and a maximum sociocultural output. This land emerges from these border spaces through the agency of a border community.[22] The members of the Lohmuehle community live totally off the grid, use solar and wind power, recycle water, plant their own food and experiment with microorganisms to fertilize the earth and ward off parasites. It is probably the most radically ecological and experimental space along the former Wall, and one that seeks to preserve, enhance and work with the natural wilderness that arose after the Wall's destruction.[23]

New ways of looking at these types of landscapes emerged, in particular in Berlin during the period of the Wall, where scientists and researchers in West Berlin, confined within the territory of their half city and without access to the countryside, began to concentrate their research and fieldwork on urban sites. Among them, Herbert Sukopp, professor at the Institute of Ecology at the Technical University of Berlin, developed a systematic approach toward urban ecology in the 1970s. The political mission of this ecological approach created new networks between scientists, institutions and resources, and, in the shadow of the Berlin Wall, Sukopp and his team became the leaders of German urban ecology and were called on to advise on matters of urban policies and planning. According to Lachmund, "There has probably never been any other city of a comparable size as thoroughly scrutinized for its urban wildlife as the walled city of West Berlin. [...] Ecologists in West Berlin turned their own city into their primary research object and practical fieldwork site."[24]

In the state of isolation of the half-city of West Berlin, urban green and natural spaces began to occupy a prominent place in the public policy agenda. Within the limits of the Great Berlin of the 1920s, a number of rural landscapes, including forests and rivers, lakes, bogs and wetlands, existed as classified natural landscape reserves since the founding of the metropolitan city. Part of Sukopp's research included comparing a number of plant species in 1945 and 100 years earlier, resulting in the elaboration of a "red list" of endangered species for West Berlin. The result of this work was the classification of a number of new natural reserves and increased restrictions for bathing and boating on the River Havel. He also carried out Biotope mapping between 1979 and 1983 for the West Berlin Senate, as a basis for a comprehensive landscape planning scheme for West Berlin, in which he mapped the entire city with regard to the flora and fauna. Sukopp's work was particularly interesting and innovative in that he also observed that new urban biotopes and ecologies were emerging in the city, and he developed a theoretical framework for an ecological approach to understanding cities during the 1950s and 1960s. This approach assumed that the interplay of human influence on a natural site resulted in new, stable forms of vegetation. Open spaces of particular interest to the researchers in Berlin were the *Trummerberg*, the rubble fields built with the debris of buildings destroyed during World War II. These were progressively naturalized and attracted bird and animal species. The liminal areas of the Berlin Wall as well as abandoned railway structures also became new urban wastelands, and the Berlin ecologists considered that these landscapes were also worthy of protection. Sukopp initiated the Mosaic metaphor, and he attributed different meanings and functions to the different urban and natural biotopes, from natural sanctuaries to urban parks, giving recommendations for more ecological gardening and for the greening of rooftops and courtyards.

After the fall of the Berlin Wall in 1989, a strip of land running through the center of Berlin was liberated and exposed to new territorialization. While the rapid reconstruction accompanied the speculative boom in the central locations and filled in the gaps between East and West Berlin, certain portions of the no-man's land escaped development and were left fallow. The linear landscape of the Berlin Wall was once a smooth strip of sand filled with pesticides and land mines, to prevent nature from growing and people from crossing, yet studies of the former death strip undertaken seven years after the fall of the Wall revealed naturally evolving landscapes.[25] Certain portions of the no-man's land, particularly those outside the city core, became wild landscapes, with young birch trees evoking the promise of a new forest landscape if left to the natural evolutions of a climax vegetation. This evoked the idea of Third Landscapes that Gilles Clément conceptualized around the same time.

Later, a red line was painted on the streets in the center of Berlin to inform curious and disoriented visitors of the location of the Wall that had so hastily disappeared. Toward the periphery of the city, fragments of the buffer zone have been officially or unofficially reclaimed as public space, while others lie fallow, waiting to be developed. The sterile sand and erased urban fabrics were progressively replaced by nature and the patrol path, although completely erased in the city center, has remained in some areas as a bicycle or pedestrian trail.[26] A Web site and guide now retraces the Wall and connects these elements to form a sort of necklace. In the city center, with the recent economic downturn, several parcels of the former Wall are still vacant as the projects to redevelop them have been stalled and are now used for temporary sculpture exhibitions. The Skulpturenpark Berlin Zentrum (Central Berlin Sculpture Park) is a particularly interesting site, with an irregular form that is a trace of the former baroque fortifications of the city, and where the Berlin Wall intersects the former historic walls.[27] The street that borders the area is named Wallstrasse, not because of the infamous Berlin Wall, but because of the first medieval and baroque walls. In the past century, the area has undergone drastic changes: from cosmopolitan buildings that lined its street in the late 1900s to their destruction in WWII; and from the 1961 construction of the Berlin Wall to its deconstruction in 1989. Since then the area has remained largely unused and vacant. With approximately five hectares of open lots, it offers a vast space and unique history to host various sociocultural activities, with tenants often renting spaces in adjacent buildings in order to provide a different perspective of the park. The Sculpture Park's exhibit organizers are interested in sculpture as a process that has the potential to reveal and critique the social, historical and structural contexts provided by the site. One exhibition held in 2009 by German artist Angela Melitpolous—*Möglichkeitsraum I*, which translates as *Space of Possibilities*—unfolds in a transnational, spatial act of montage.[28] Photographs of the ghost city of Varosha in Cyprus and around the Green Line in Nicosia were reproduced on billboards and planted into the derelict space of the Skulpturenpark in the former border strip dividing Berlin. Telephone numbers scratched into the ground invited visitors to call up and listen to voices that tell a few stories about other no-man's lands of Europe. After the last exhibition at Skulpturenpark in 2009, construction activities began to pick up again on the site. Concurrent to these new developments, artist Erik Smith has taken the area as a site of excavation and while hotels and condominiums shoot up, he continues his artistic work of uncovering an architecture of memory.

Figure 7.2 The Skulpturenpark Berlin Zentrum.
Source: www.skulpturenpark.org/.

While Berlin did not project or implement a project for the Berlin Wall, a visionary and large-scale ecological project was designed for the pan-German border along the Iron Curtain. This project for recycling the Iron Curtain, on both the national and transnational scale, is known as the Pan-European Green Belt, a memorial and environmental trail that runs for 8,500 kilometers from the Baltic Sea to the Mediterranean Sea. This Green Belt represents a valuable chain of biotopes that has become home to a number of endangered species such as the wolf bear and lynx.[29] A segment of this ecological corridor is the German Green Belt, which runs along the border that once separated East (Democratic Republic) and West (Federal Republic) Germany, extending from Travemuende on the Baltic Sea to the Czech border in the south.

Those that have planned, plotted or implemented walls, borders and buffer zones worldwide could probably not imagine that they were designing ecological corridors of biodiversity. If it were not for the people who had steadily and regularly been observing the wildlife and biodiversity in these fertile swathes of military land, and who recognized these ecological qualities, they would have disappeared after the fall of the walls.[30] Shortly after the fall of the Wall in November 1989, environmentalists from Friends of the Earth in Bavaria published a petition for a green belt project to protect the border areas as the ecological backbone of Central Europe. In collaboration with Friends of the Earth, the Department for Habitat Protection and Landscape Ecology at Germany's Federal Agency for Nature Conservation in Bonn began a database and inventory of the ecosystems and species along the green belt. Ornithologists, botanists and entomologists walked the hundreds of kilometers along the former border to collect data, which were complemented by observations from local birdwatchers and plant lovers, resulting in the identification of more than 1,000 species from Germany's Red List of endangered species. The green belt harbors a rich mixture of habitats, including forests, heathlands, sand dunes, salt meadows, riparian areas, green meadows and shorelines—with forests that had not been touched for 40 years.

In the marginal areas of the green belt, mostly beset by high unemployment and an exodus of the young, it was important to make the project truly sustainable and to generate income and jobs. Three pilot projects were developed with a mixture of ecotourism and sightseeing, connected by the former patrol path, which is now a cycling trail. Aside from sustainability, it is also important to maintain openness and accessibility as it was feared that the former border would become an exclusive or forbidden zone serving only environmentalism.

Co-creating Ecological and Social Shared Spaces for Increased Resilience in Cyprus and Beyond

Building on fieldwork, research and projects undertaken by the author on the Berlin Wall, the Korea Demilitarized Zone and the German green belt, transboundary peace parks have led to the hypothesis that the Cyprus Green Line should be investigated for its value as a preserve of biodiversity and endangered species. This speculation resulted in a project that was initially developed in association with the Harvard Program on Humanitarian Policy and Conflict Research, investigating the possibilities of human reconciliation and environmental cooperation in Cyprus through the Buffer Zone and that was presented in Cyprus to UN agencies and environmental nongovernmental organizations (NGOs).[31]

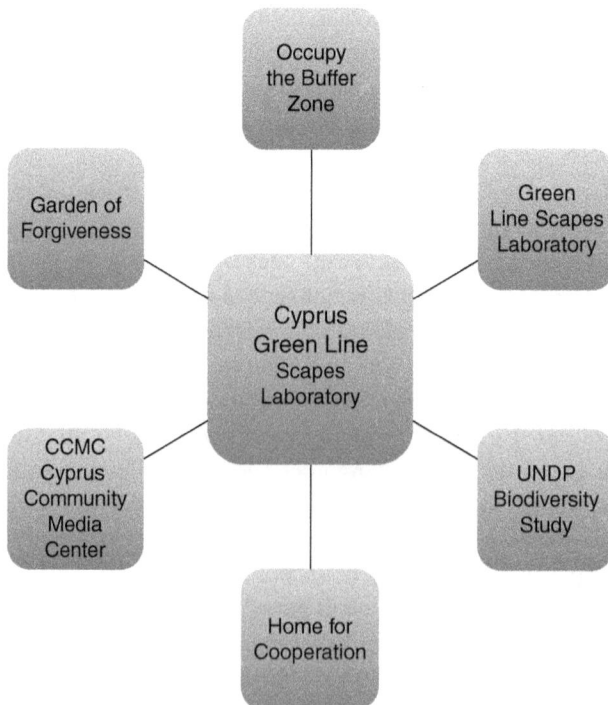

Figure 7.3 Cyprus GreenLineScapes Laboratory.
Source: Anna Grichting, 2014.

A year later, in 2007, investigations into the unexpected flourishing of nature in the Green Line—of flowers, birds, insects and mammals—were undertaken by scientists from both the Turkish and Greek Cypriot communities, confirming my hypothesis that the so-called *Dead Zone* of Cyprus was in fact a thriving landscape of biodiversity.[32] Species thriving in the 180-kilometer stretch of the Buffer Zone include 358 plant species, 100 bird species, 20 reptile and amphibian species and 18 mammal species. As nature has invaded abandoned structures, animals have moved into vacant villages within the Buffer Zone.

There are many sites of memory along the Green Line, many of them painful memories of the ethnic clashes of the 1960s and 1970s. There are still people grieving on both sides for the men, women and children who disappeared without a trace during the height of the conflict. According to UN data, more than 1,400 Greek Cypriots and 500 Turkish Cypriots are listed as missing, and after reaching a 2006 agreement, approximately 270 remains have been unearthed on both sides of the ceasefire line. While it may not be possible to locate the missing persons and their graves, it is important that they be honored and remembered; this remembrance and grieving will help to heal the wounds between the two communities. Irish-Cypriot Cyprus Broadcasting Corporation presenter Colette Ioannidou—who lived through the 1974 division of the island—reiterated this during a radio broadcast and noted that "The families of the Missing on both sides are the walking wounded whose aching hearts and souls need to be comforted. This can only happen when we realize that there is still even more to lose by not embracing each other's needs now, by not trying to forgive even if there are things that are so hard to forgive."[33] Intertwined with the recent memories of trauma are historical memories of coexistence that will work to reweave the Cypriot cultures, and these will also need to include the new evolutions and ethnicities that have shaped the identities of the island in the recent years. Abandoned cemeteries, ruined churches, centennial olive trees, individual memorials, collective monuments, traces and relics can be articulated through landscape sites of remembrance and forgiveness along the Green Line, such as the Garden of Forgiveness proposed hereafter.

Home for Cooperation, Temporary Occupations and Future Landscapes of Forgiveness

The lens of psychohistory and psycho-geography is relevant to a socio-ecological approach to borders and conflict. This lens underscores the importance for institutions and organizations to address and evaluate the history and narratives that are being taught to children in schools and communicated through media and other state channels. It also stresses the value of organizations such as the Association for Historical Dialogue that have set up the Home for Cooperation within the Buffer Zone to encourage cross-border meetings and activities that contribute to breaking down walls and barriers.[34] The Association for Historical Dialogue is a bicommunal NGO that established the Home for Cooperation as a shared space for dialogue in an abandoned house in the UN Buffer Zone. Funded by foreign embassies and EU monies, the space and organization are apolitical and offer structures to other initiatives and NGOs working within and across the border. It is an important node in the rhizomatic network and structure with which to overcome the social consequences of border conflict.

Figure 7.4 The Home for Cooperation in the Buffer Zone of Nicosia.
Photograph by Anna Grichting, 2011.

Nicosia, or Lefkosia/Lefkosa is advertised as the last divided capital in the world with the military buffer zone (UNBZ) running through the center of the walled city. Recently, with the Occupy movements that were taking place across the world, activists from both sides of the divide, including Turkish and Greek Cypriots, created Occupy the Buffer Zone in a set-up camp in the city's center within the UN-controlled no-man's land. For the activists, the division of their island is a domestic manifestation of international capitalism, the local symptom of a global problem, and (according to Michalis, one of the activists) it is now known that Britain and the United States encouraged the division of the island.[35] The Occupy group recognizes that the Cyprus problem is not a head-on clash between two peoples. The island was divided to be used as a military base for resource monopolization happening in the Middle East and has been described as "an unsinkable aircraft carrier anchored off the shores of the Levant." Being in no-man's land, the protesters were untouchable for both the Greek and Turkish Cypriot authorities. They were advocating for reunification of the island and asking for the departure of UN troops from the Buffer Zone as well as the removal of the British Sovereign Bases.[36] Ironically, the Occupy movement in the Buffer Zone was a movement to de-occupy Cyprus and remove foreign armies and military infrastructures. The Buffer Zone thus became a shared space for activists from both sides to promote their ideologies of reunification.

In Beirut, after the war, a Garden of Forgiveness was planned and designed, with communities from all Lebanese factions and faiths. Situated along the Green Line that formerly divided Beirut during the war, the Hadiqat As-Samah project was founded and developed by Alexandra Asseily and Solidere (the Lebanese Company for the Development and Reconstruction of the Beirut Central District). According to Asseily, "forgiveness is a liberating act that gives humans the capacity for peace," while the garden seeks a common ground outside religious and sectarian issues of the region.[37] The site is deeply layered with the traces of previous civilizations and it is a model and inspiration for a similar project proposed by the author on one of the Bastions of the walled city of Nicosia—the Flatro Bastion—which is currently enclosed within the UN Buffer Zone. Similar to the Beirut project location, the Flatro Bastion has many layers of history that include Nicosia's Hellenistic, Roman, Lusignan, Venetian, Ottoman and British pasts and multiple faiths—Muslim, Orthodox Christian, Catholic, Armenian, Maronite. Like the Hadiqat As-Samah garden in Beirut, the Nicosia Garden of Forgiveness is destined as a space for major healing and forgiveness for all, and no singular, prioritized view will be forced on its visitors.

Figure 7.5 (a) Flatro Bastion in Nicosia. Proposal for the Garden of Forgiveness in the Green Line Buffer Zone. *Source:* Anna Grichting GreenLinescapes/Google Earth, 2008. (b) Flatro Bastion in Nicosia on Google Earth. *Source:* Anna Grichting GreenLinescapes/Google Earth, 2013.

Conclusion

It is not really a line, not very visible, and not often Green. Between two frozen fronts that will not clear the storm, it forms an interstice of land that encapsulates much pain, weaving through landscapes of copper, sand, sea, and stone—crossing cities, roads, rivers, fields, orchards, plains and mountains. It is a landscape of memory in becoming, a necklace of archaeologies, a river of hope, a ribbon of fertile flora, a haven of mice and mouflon. A chasm of traumas, it will flourish into a beautiful scar, a peaceful paradise, an Eden of ecological wonders where the lemons will become less bitter and Aphrodite will converse with Venus, Mary and Umm Haram in a joyful song of Angels.[38]

Borderlands in conflict areas, while becoming negative, forsaken, forbidden and often highly militarized spaces, also become wildlands and havens for nature and biodiversity. In the absence of human development, nature can reclaim and restore its ecosystems and/or create new ones. In the contemporary fields of landscape design and planning, dynamic or unexpected natures have become increasingly recognized for their ecological value and for their contribution to the preservation of biodiversity.

Preserving the memories—personal and public—of these abandoned spaces, through interventions such as trails, parks and monuments, are ways to requalify and reactivate connections to past layers of landscape histories. We are looking at new ways to design with, and not against, the spontaneous, wild or *third* natures that emerge in abandoned sites, thereby increasing urban biodiversity. It is necessary to develop design processes in these dynamic and multilayered urban spaces that are not linear or confined, but circular, multidimensional, sociopolitical processes, often associated with a resistance to more conventional planning methods and landscape aesthetics. These processes—in the case of border landscapes in conflict zones—must also involve the communities on either side, as well as the stakeholders within the dividing line, co-creating relationships that are not hierarchical, but collaborative and rhizomatic.

The ambitions of a plan for the Buffer Zone will be, on the one hand, to connect the ecological patches and corridors of specific biodiversity to the existing network of nature reserves and priority biotopes. On the other, it will be to articulate the linear ecological infrastructure of the buffer with other existing or proposed infrastructures—that is, public transport (revive the old railway) and water networks. The former UN patrol path of the Buffer Zone will become a memorial bicycle and pedestrian path that will link the various cultural and ecological landscapes of the Green Line, forming the backbone of the project.

The linear structure of the boundary encompasses the diverse typologies and dimensions of landscapes, and will offer the opportunity for ecological planning at varying territorial scales, ranging from the large scale of the ecological and cultural region to which Cyprus belongs, to the island scale, and even down to the smallest scale of the parcel or lot in the historic city of Nicosia, or in the villages enclaved by the Buffer Zone. When national, regional and/or international scales

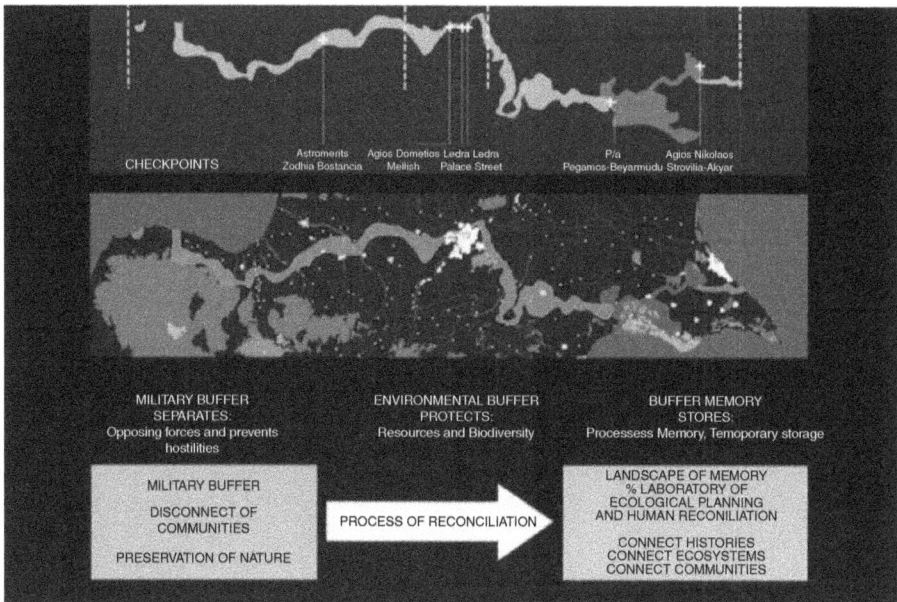

Figure 7.6 From military buffer to laboratory of ecological planning and human reconciliation.
Source: Anna Grichting, *Boundaryscapes, Recasting the Green Line of Cyprus*, 2008.

are considered, the links between biological diversity and diversity between cultures need to be considered. According to the United Nations Educational, Scientific and Cultural Organization (UNESCO), a multiscale approach is needed, and the issue of scale—spatial, temporal, historical and institutional—is crucial in assessing the links between biological and cultural diversity, and in considering their implications for research and policy.[39] Aside from the more obvious spatial scales, time scales and historical contexts are of high importance, particularly when it comes to understanding the process of change and developing adequate adaptation and/or mitigation strategies.

This vision is not a personal or individual creation. Rather, it is a *third vision* created through the (re)articulation of existing connections, collaborations and emergences in, along and across the *Third Landscapes* of the Green Line. It represents an alternate and possible future reality that is intended to accompany and inform a process of planning and reconciliation. To borrow the words of Gilles Clément:

> The important thing is to foster and achieve an equilibrium in which no one species has the upper hand. [...] The aesthetic for the third landscape (undeveloped plot, leftover fragment) is yet to come. [...] It resides in the astonishing biodiversity, the wonder and moment when we grasp the purpose and meaning of the Third Landscape and its transformative potential that we discover a new sort of beauty.[40]

NOTES

1 Michel Butor. *Frontiers*, trans. Elinor S. Miller (Birmingham, AL: Summa Publications, 1989), 100.

2 Frederik J. W. van Oudenhoven, Dunja Mijatovic and Pablo B. Eyzaguirre, "Social-Ecological Indicators of Resilience in Agrarian and Natural Landscapes," *Management of Environmental Quality: An International Journal*, 22 (2011): 154–73.

3 Keith G. Tidball and Marianne K. Krasny, eds., *Greening in the Red Zone: Disaster, Resilience and Community Greening* (New York: Springer-Verlag, 2014).

4 Esther M. Sternberg, *Healing Spaces: The Science of Place and Well-Being* (Cambridge, MA: Belknap Press of Harvard University Press, 2009), 193–214.

5 Anna Grichting, "Thirdscapes: Ecological Planning and Human Reconciliation In Borderlands," *International Journal of Environmental, Cultural, Economic and Social Sustainability* 5 (2009): 239–56.

6 Murray Bookchin, "What Is Social Ecology?" in *Environmental Philosophy: From Animal Rights to Radical Ecology*, ed. Michael Zimmerman (Englewood Cliffs, NJ: Prentice Hall, 1993), 462–78.

7 Gilles Deleuze and Felix Guattari, *A Thousand Plateaus: Capitalism and Schizophrenia*, trans. Brian Massumi (London: Athlone Press, 1988).

8 Anna Grichting, *Boundaryscapes. Recasting the Green Line of Cyprus*. Doctor of Design diss., Harvard University, 2008.

9 Henri Lefebvre, *The Production of Space*, trans. Donald Nicholson-Smith (Cambridge, MA: Blackwell, 1991).

10 Homi K. Bhabha, *The Location of Culture* (London: Routledge Classics, 2004).

11 Joy H. Calico, "Judische Chronik: The Third Space of Commemoration between East and West Germany," *The Musical Quarterly* 88 (2005): 95–122.

12 Calico, "Judische Chronik."

13 In 1960, composer Paul Dessau and compatriot poet Jens Gerlach initiated a collaborative project between East and West German artists that would become *A Jewish Chronicle*, a musical commemoration of the Warsaw Ghetto uprising of 1943, in response to a surge in anti-Semitic activity in West Germany. See Joy H. Calico, "Judische Chronik: The Third Space of Commemoration between East and West Germany," *The Musical Quarterly* 88 (2005): 95–122.

14 Permaculture is an approach to designing human settlements and agricultural systems that mimic the relationships found in natural ecologies.

15 Million Belay, *Participatory Mapping, Learning and Change in the Context of Biocultural Diversity and Resilience*. PhD thesis, Rhodes University, 2012.

16 David Adams, "Joseph Beuys: Pioneer of a Radical Ecology." *Art Journal* 51 (1992): 26–34.

17 Ibid.

18 Nicholas Zurbrugg, *The Parameters of Postmodernism* (Carbondale: Southern Illinois University Press, 1993).

19 Ibid., 121 and Adriani Götz, Winfried Konnertz and Karin Thomas, *Joseph Beuys: Life and Works*, trans. Patricia Lech (New York: Barron's Educational Series, 1979), 114, 116.

20 Emmanuel Terray, *Ombres Berlinoises: Voyage Dans Une Autre Allemagne* (Paris: Editions Odile Jacob, 1996).

21 Iganis De Sola-Morales, "Terrain Vague," paper presented at *Present and Future Architectures of the City*, XIX Congress of the International Union of Architects, Barcelona, 1996.

22 www.lohmuehle-berlin.de/.

23 Anna Grichting, "Landscapes of the Green Line. Healing the Rift," in *Climate Change: A Challenge for Europe and Cyprus*, eds. Engin Karatas and Eckart Kuhlwein (Hamburg, Germany: Tredition/Rotation, 2010), 36–47.

24 Jens Lachmund, "Ecology in a Walled City: Researching Urban Wildlife in Post-war Berlin," *Endeavour* 31 (2007): 78–82.

25 Anna Grichting. *Ruptures, Traces, Memoires. Reterritorialisation d'Une Friche De Frontiere. Le Cas De Berlin*. Diplomes d'Etudes Superieures en Urbanisme et Amenagement du Territoire, University of Geneva, Switzerland, 1999.

26 Ibid.

27 "Skulpturenpark Berlin_Zentrum, Exhibitions 2006–09," accessed June 6, 2014, www.skulpturenpark.org/.

28 Angela Melitopoulos, *Möglichkeitsraum I (The Blast of the Possible). A Transnational Space Montage*, accessed June 6, 2014, www.skulpturenpark.org/exhibit/wunderland/angela_melitopoulos_E.html.

29 In September 2005, the European Parliament called for the former border area to become part of an "Iron Curtain trail" stretching 4,250 miles (6,800 km) from the Arctic Sea to the Black Sea along the Cold War border between the Western and Soviet blocs.

30 Christian Schwägerl, "Along Scar from Iron Curtain, A Green Belt Rises in Germany," Report posted (April 4, 2011), accessed June 6, 2014, http://e360.yale.edu/feature/along_scar_from_iron_curtain_a_green_belt_rises_in_germany/2390/.

31 Anna Grichting, *The Green Line of Cyprus: Human Development and Reconciliation through Environmental Cooperation*. HPCR Harvard Program for Humanitarian Policy and Conflict Research, Harvard University, 2006.

32 Salih Gucel, et al., *Monitoring Biodiversity of the Buffer Zone in Cyprus* (Cyprus: Near East University, 2007).

33 Colette Ioannidou responding to a radio broadcast by Sevgul Uludag, a journalist from the Turkish Cypriot community, who has spearheaded the search for the mass graves, reporting on atrocities in both communities and risking her own safety in the process. See Sevgul Uludag, *Cyprus Missing*. BBC World Broadcast, April 21, 2008.

34 Vamik D. Volkan, *Cyprus—War and Adaptation: A Psychoanalytic History of Two Ethnic Groups in Conflict* (Charlottesville: University Press of Virginia, 1979).

35 Michalis, Cypriot Occupy activist, cited by Jonathan Socrates in "Occupy Buffer Zone," Blog Post March 2012, accessed June 6, 2014, http://theoccupiedtimes.org/?p=2636#sthash.rZS-4d0lI.dpuf/ and http://jonathansocrates.wordpress.com/.

36 Ibid.

37 Michael Spens, "Deep Explorations into Site/Non-site: The Work of Gustafson Porter," *AD: Architectural Designs* 77 (2007): 68.

38 Anna Grichting, "GreenLineScapes," in *Cyprus. Tracing the Non-visible*, eds. Babis Metaxas; Achilleas Kentonis, Maria Papacharalambous and Philippos Philippou (Place of publication not identified: Representation of the European Commission in Cyprus, 2012), 58.

39 United Nations Educational, Scientific and Cultural Organization (UNESCO), *Links between Biological and Cultural Diversity*. Report of the International Workshop, September 26–28, 2007 (Paris: UNESCO, 2007).

40 Gilles Clément, *Le Jardin En Mouvement*, accessed October 22, 2015, www.gillesClément.com/.

BIBLIOGRAPHY

Adams, David. "Joseph Beuys: Pioneer of a Radical Ecology." *Art Journal* 51 (1992): 26–34.

Belay, Million. *Participatory Mapping, Learning and Change in the Context of Biocultural Diversity and Resilience*. PhD diss., Rhodes University, 2012.

Bhabha, Homi K. *The Location of Culture*. London: Routledge Classics, 2004.

Bookchin, Murray. "What Is Social Ecology?" In *Environmental Philosophy: From Animal Rights to Radical Ecology*, edited by Michael Zimmerman, 462–78. Englewood Cliffs, NJ: Prentice Hall, 1993.

Butor, Michel. *Frontiers*. Translated by Elinor S. Miller. Birmingham, AL: Summa Publications, 1989.

Calico, Joy H. "Judische Chronik: The Third Space of Commemoration between East and West Germany." *The Musical Quarterly* 88 (2005): 95–122.

Clément, Gilles, *Manifeste du Tiers Paysage*. Paris: Collection "L'Autre Fable, Editions Sujet/ Object, 2004.

Clément, Gilles. *Le Jardin En Mouvement*. Accessed October 22, 2015. www.gillesClément.com/.

Deleuze, Gilles and Félix Guattari. *A Thousand Plateaus: Capitalism and Schizophrenia*. Translated by Brian Massumi. London: Athlone Press, 1988.

De Sola-Morales, Iganis. "Terrain Vague." Paper presented at *Present and Future Architectures of the City*, XIX Congress of the International Union of Architects. Barcelona, 1996.

Götz, Adriani, Winfried Konnertz and Karin Thomas. Translated by Patricia Lech. *Joseph Beuys: Life and Works*. New York: Barron's Educational Series, 1979.

Grichting, Anna. *Boundaryscapes. Recasting the Green Line of Cyprus*. Doctor of Design diss., Harvard University, 2008.

Grichting, Anna. "GreenLineScapes." In *Cyprus: Tracing the Non-visible*, edited by Babis Metaxas, Achilleas Kentonis, Maria Papacharalambous and Philippos Philippou, 58. Place of publication not identified: Representation of the European Commission in Cyprus, 2012.

Grichting, Anna. *The Green Line of Cyprus: Human Development and Reconciliation through Environmental Cooperation*. HPCR Harvard Program for Humanitarian Policy and Conflict Research, Harvard University, 2006.

Grichting, Anna. "Landscapes of the Green Line. Healing the Rift." In *Climate Change: A Challenge for Europe and Cyprus*, edited by Engin Karatas and Eckart Kuhlwein, 36–47. Hamburg, Germany: Tredition GmbH/Rotation, 2010.

Grichting, Anna. *Ruptures, Traces, Memoires. Reterritorialisation d'Une Friche De Frontiere. Le Cas De Berlin*. Master's Thesis, Diplomes d'Etudes Superieures en Urbanisme et Amenagement du Territoire, University of Geneva, Switzerland, 1999.

Grichting, Anna. "Thirdscapes: Ecological Planning and Human Reconciliation In Borderlands." *International Journal of Environmental, Cultural, Economic and Social Sustainability* 5 (2009): 239–56.

Gucel, Salih, Iris Charalambidou, Bayram Gocmen, Ahmet Karatas, Anif Ozge' Soyumert Ozden, and Wayne Fuller. *Monitoring Biodiversity of the Buffer Zone in Cyprus*. Cyprus: Near East University, 2007.

"The Iron-Curtain Trail: The Green Belt: A Unique Biotope along the Former 'death strip.'" Accessed June 6, 2014. www.ironcurtaintrail.eu/en/der_iron_curtain_trail/green_belt/index. html.

Lachmund, Jens. "Ecology in a Walled City: Researching Urban Wildlife in Post-war Berlin." *Endeavour* 31 (2007): 78–82.

Lefebvre, Henri. *The Production of Space*. Translated by Donald Nicholson-Smith. Cambridge, MA: Blackwell, 1991.

Melitopoulos, Angela. *Möglichkeitsraum I (The Blast of the Possible)*. A Transnational Space Montage, accessed June 6, 2014, www.skulpturenpark.org/exhibit/wunderland/angela_melitopoulos_ E.html.

Schwägerl, Christian. "Along Scar from Iron Curtain, A Green Belt Rises in Germany." Report posted (April 4, 2011). Accessed June 6, 2014. http://e360.yale.edu/feature/along_scar_ from_iron_curtain_a_green_belt_rises_in_germany/2390/.

"Skulpturenpark Berlin_Zentrum, Exhibitions 2006–09." Accessed June 6, 2014. www.skulpturen-park.org/.

Socrates, Jonathan. "Occupy BufferZone," Blog Post March 2012. Accessed June 6, 2014, http:// theoccupiedtimes.org/?p=2636#sthash.rZS4d0lI.dpuf/ and http://jonathansocrates.word-press.com/.

Sternberg, Esther M. *Healing Spaces: The Science of Place and Well-Being*. Cambridge, MA: Belknap Press of Harvard University Press, 2009.

Terray, Emmanuel. *Ombres Berlinoises: Voyage Dans Une Autre Allemagne*. Paris: Editions Odile Jacob, 1996.

Tidball, Keith G. and Marianne K. Krasny, eds. *Greening in the Red Zone: Disaster, Resilience and Community Greening*. New York: Springer-Verlag, 2014.

Uludag, Sevgul. *Cyprus Missing*. BBC World Broadcast, April 21, 2008.

United Nations Educational, Scientific and Cultural Organization (UNESCO). *Links between Biological and Cultural Diversity*. Report of the International Workshop, September 26–28, 2007. Paris: UNESCO, 2007.

Van Oudenhoven, Frederik J. W., Dunja Mijatovic and Pablo B. Eyzaguirre. "Social-Ecological Indicators of Resilience in Agrarian and Natural Landscapes." *Management of Environmental Quality: An International Journal* 22 (2011): 154–73.

Volkan, Vamik D. *Cyprus—War and Adaptation: A Psychoanalytic History of Two Ethnic Groups in Conflict*. Charlottesville: University Press of Virginia, 1979.

Zurbrugg, Nicholas. *The Parameters of Postmodernism*. Carbondale: Southern Illinois University Press, 1993.

Part III

CORRIDORS: CATALYSTS AND COLLABORATION IN CONFINED SPACES

Chapter Eight

ENSURING HOPE IN MILITARIZED LANDSCAPES: THE CASE OF LEBANON

Rabih Shibli

Introduction

For the academic year 2010–11, I compiled and edited a book featuring the works of final-year students in the Department of Landscape Design and Ecosystem Management at the American University of Beirut (AUB). The title and cover page needed to capture the core theme that linked the 22 narratives and reflect the work methodology adopted for each project. While reviewing the pictures I had taken of the different locations, one image instantly caught my attention—a magnolia tree planted on the side yard of a tire repair shop, located along Beirut's notorious former Green Line. The image perfectly captured the research. The leafless tree had been efficiently used to hang tires. Upon rendering the image, I filled the tires with soil and allowed climbing plants to reclaim the space; *Remodeling Harshscapes* thus became the title of the book.[1] The process of remodeling harshscapes adheres to Murray Bookchin's theory in social ecology that "nearly all our present ecological problems originate in deep-seated social problems."[2] Wars, protracted conflicts, internal political and sectarian divisions embody societal anxieties, which drop heavy shadows over the Lebanese landscape. Enclaves and gated zones, reminiscent of Hilary Cunningham's gated ecologies, manifest as postwar landscapes that produce an array of rigid and elastic borderlines and develop unique mechanisms to inject sustenance within every sclerotic setting.

This chapter studies two projects, designed and implemented by the Community Development Projects Unit (CDPU) at the American University of Beirut, that tackle militarized landscapes. The first project, titled *Reclaiming the Traditional Water Conservation Practices in Rural South Lebanon—Case of Marwaheen Village,* considers a South Lebanon village's ordeal in which farmers applied their deep-seated knowledge of local plains and gorges to sustain rootedness within an arid, ecological system that had been "assigned" as a war zone. The second project, titled *Urban Agriculture—Women's Vocational Training Center—Ein El Hilwi Palestinian Refugee Camp,* explores the aspirations of disenfranchised female groups. In a suppressed and gated environment, modest cultivation practices enabled the refugees to imprint upon the camp a landscape of hope for the future. I place the Marwaheen village project first, not for lack of recognition of the suffering incurred by the Palestinian refugees at Ein El Hilwi, but because Marwaheen lies near the Israeli

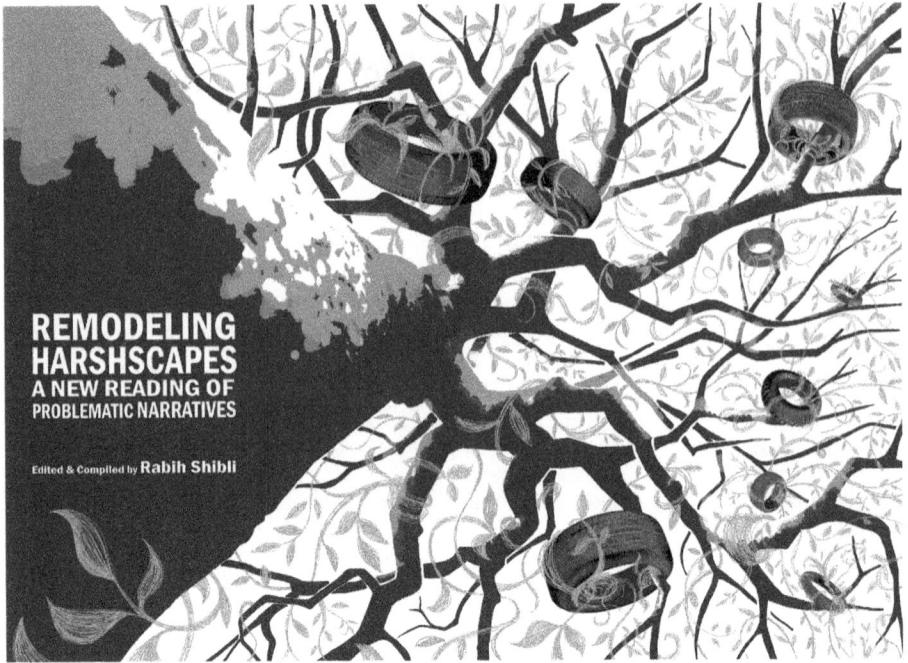

Figure 8.1 Schematic drawing of the cover page of a student's workbook, representing the theme of remodeling harshscapes. Photograph, courtesy Zarifi Haidar, 2011.

border and represents the true ironies of border life in a conflict zone. Nearly razed to the ground in 1976, Marwaheen is actually closer to an Israeli settlement than to other Lebanese villages, and so it has known its share of border violence. Hope is a positive attribute and forms a key element not only within these two projects, but also within other cases throughout this book. Bookchin writes that "social ecology is an appeal not for moral regeneration but also, and above all, for social reconstruction along ecological lines."[3]

Both case studies in this chapter will be examined using a three-part conceptual framework that incorporates the theoretical underpinnings of "social reconstruction," namely, that local inhabitants' desires, needs and wants be addressed in order to create an ecologically balanced landscape. An important caveat to this framework is that these projects fall within the volatile border zone that is South Lebanon.

1. The Morphology of Landscape[4]: defined by Carl Sauer as the symbiotic associations between nature and its inhabitants. *Morphology of Landscape* is a thorough reading of the socioeconomic and political dimensions that have evolved or radically transformed, measuring their impact on the natural environment and grasping the implications of the latter on the production of space.

2. Instigating Ecological Projects: incorporating local knowledge in the design and sustainability of community projects. The envisioned developmental

schemes contribute to empowering marginalized communities by providing them with mechanisms to sustain successful operations and adequate resources management.

3. Strategic Intervention: applied as a catalyst for inducing change in sclerotic landscapes. Sites that are chosen for the initiation of progressive visions recapitulate all factors that correspond to the multifaceted potential and limitations ingrained in people and their lands.

Reclaiming Traditional Water Conservation Practices in South Lebanon: The Case of Marwaheen Village

In the aftermath of the July 2006 War, three out of the dozens of NGOs and international agencies that poured into South Lebanon came to my village, which was one of the most destroyed, where they initiated a WATSAN project (water and sanitation). The municipality gave the approval for installing "concrete septic tanks," and 200 units were put next to the "unhygienic" old open tank systems. The problem with the new system was that, although it didn't cost the recipients a penny, it needed vacuuming every 3 months while the old ones endured the refuse of a lifetime. Accordingly, villagers with their intuitive behavior responded by altering the tanks' usage; they connected hoses that were fixed to their toilet seats onto the rooftops; they cleaned the roofs and started harvesting rainwater instead!

—Quote from Rabih Shibli, this chapter's author and director of the Center for Civic Engagement and Community Service at the American University of Beirut

Jabal Amel—A Militarized Landscape

With the demarcation of the 1916 Sykes-Picot line carving Jabal Amel (Lebanon) from Galilee (Palestine) and Mount-Haramoun (Syria), the hilly terrain and fertile coastal plains of the Litani River's southern watershed, currently known as South Lebanon, were transformed from a marginalized residual rural setting into a geostrategic abode of war. In the aftermath of the 22-year Israeli occupation of the "Security Belt" came the July 2006 War, which was stabilized by the deployment of 15,000 United Nations troops and 15,000 from the Lebanese army. This peacekeeping military presence distinguishes the area south of the Litani River with the "highest rate of soldiers to population in the world—that is, close to one soldier for every seven inhabitants!"[5] Jabal Amel has become a militarized landscape, a place fully charged with armaments, covert and overt.

This militarization has been realized alongside a tragic absence of strategic goals for planning, accompanied by an increased dependency on a shadowy, war-related economy. The state and nongovernmental organizations (NGOs) alike have tried to forge models for practice within this sociopolitically constructed and complicated matrix. On the one hand, a "Newtonian-mechanical" approach was adopted and practiced by the central government, characterized by framing wants and needs in a set of technical problems that materialized into a number of infeasible and shallow

Figure 8.2 Convoy of United Nations Interim Force in Lebanon (UNIFIL) patrolling in southern Lebanon. Photograph by Rabih Shibli, 2012.

projects.[6] Schools with empty desks, hospitals running at minimal capacity, roads traversing deserted mountains, retaining walls stretching beside solid rock and dried-out communal water reservoirs were but a few of the palpably futile attempts to achieve economic development. On the other hand, national and international organizations and NGOs became active on alternative tracks either to ensure modernity and peace as a path that "reduces all motives for militarized violence," or to reinforce "steadfastness" that is an integral composite of the "Lesser Jihad."[7] In this regard, very modest achievements were realized as a result of prohibitive security measures, disconnectedness from grassroots needs, weak institutional and management setups or parochial developmental views.

This miasma has triggered the exodus of southerners seeking security and livelihoods, while—for those who remained—tobacco became a main source of sustenance. As the youth migrated, the areas under cultivation radically decreased. Only one state-subsidized tobacco crop license is granted per family for the cultivation of 2,000 square meters of land. Municipalities of the border villages and hamlets, overwhelmed with burdens of security and poverty reduction, lacked the basic technical and financial resources to cope with rural development in such a volatile and marginalized context. Aware of the impotence of the state, mayors reacted with the available resources to secure some sense of rootedness, whenever possible, in this fragile environment.

Figure 8.3 An example of vacant structures funded by the Lebanese government to develop areas under Israeli occupation in southern Lebanon. Photograph by Rabih Shibli, 2012.

Steadfastness in a Homeland

Marwaheen is the epitome of the plight of southern border villages. In November 1976, Israeli proxy militias overran three southern border villages: Hanin, Yarin, and Marwaheen, forcing the population to flee and razing whole areas to the ground. This hostile act was a prelude to the March 1978 invasion of South Lebanon and the imposition of the security belt. The village fabric extends linearly along a ridge surrounded by terraced and hilly terrain overlooking the coastal plain from Tyre to Akko. The Israeli settlement Zaari't is closer in distance to Marwaheen than to any other Lebanese village, and the dividing line between the two stretches along the Blue Line.[8] Two days after the start of the Second Lebanon War, at dawn on July 15, 2006, loudspeakers resonating from Zaari't called on the Marwaheenese to flee their houses and evacuate the village. A few hours later, an open-topped pickup loaded with 27 children was hit by a rocket, which caused an atrocious massacre and fueled the divide with the *alien neighbors*. Out of the registered population of 3,500, fewer than 300 remain.

The Blue Line demarcating the border is, among other things, a spatial divide between vast areas of cultivated land on one side and moors on the other. The shockingly over-cultivated Israeli fields are irrigated by rainwater harvesting ponds, which is the same basic technique Arab villagers have adopted for centuries. On the Lebanese side, this rural heritage is disappearing. Open village reservoirs are being converted to roundabouts, village parks, town halls and the like. Marwaheen has kept its communal pond (*Birki*), which is the heart and soul of the village, according to Mayor Mohammad Obeid. With a rounded, cut-edged stone wall, the *Birki* encompasses an area of 4,000 square meters, with a volume of approximately 13,000 cubic meters.

This water junction has always been regarded as the source of livelihood for a community traditionally dependent on herding and cultivation. The current malfunction of Marwaheen's vital water hub is attributed to the interruption of watershed channels due to the opening of roads, the erection of walls and houses and excessive infiltration of harvested water via cracked walls and basin caused by the heavy bombardments on the village. Marwaheenese reminisce about the good old days when water would fill the pond to overflowing; those were seasons of good yields. For more than three decades, the village has witnessed a massive desertification process aided by three previously mentioned main factors: (1) the exodus of youth outside the security belt; (2) dependency on rain-fed, state-subsidized tobacco plantations; and (3) water shortage. Despite the years of violence and state incompetence, the Marwaheenese demonstrate remarkable attachment to their land. They terrace the steep, rocky terrain and set customary codes (*'urf*) for herding and land use. They clear their fields of landmines and cluster bombs after each invasion, and resort again to tobacco for sustenance. This antagonistic coexistence yields precarious results—agriculture and wars entwine and set normative strictures for life and death along the southern frontier, the landscape of a homeland.

Figure 8.4 Terraced hilly terrain showing shrubs, olive trees and the tobacco plantation in Marwaheen village. Photograph by Rabih Shibli, 2012.

Birkit Marwaheen

In August 2007, a team of AUB students camped in the village for 10 days. Early each morning, they accompanied farmers to pick tobacco. In the afternoons, they squatted next to women with their children as they shredded the leaves, and learned the practice of tobacco cultivation, which constitutes the main source of income for all permanent residents in the village. The Marwaheenese have become less dependent on rainwater due to the rise of tobacco cultivation, but farmers still depend on the *Birki* (communal pond) catchment to irrigate their other plants. The students spent their evenings listening to captivating stories about war, battles and permanent instability while armored Israeli Humvees roared overland during the night. One of the children encapsulated this bewildering environment in a mental-map sketch that illustrated him swimming in the *Birki*, while other children played on cultivated ground and birds floated next to warplanes. On another occasion, AUB students recorded a conversation with youngsters expressing their anger and hatred toward their country, revealing the trauma caused by the loss of those dearest to them.

Within this stressful context, the *Birki* represents a chink of hope and a source of sustenance. Many traditional water reservoirs in the south were damaged or under severe threat due to the impact of wars or uncontrolled urban sprawl. As a result, some have been filled with debris from demolished houses and converted into village parks. Thus,

Figure 8.5 AUB students working hand in hand with local farmers in the rehabilitation of Marwaheen pond. Photograph by Rabih Shibli, 2012.

traditional practices for efficient management of water resources are being abandoned or, at best, replaced by environmentally wasteful ones. In the project titled *Reclaiming the Traditional Water Conservation Practices in South Lebanon: The Case of Marwaheen Village*, the planning team drew on the significance of rainwater harvesting as a viable process for securing sustainable rural economic development, and rehabilitating and upgrading the vicinity of the *Birki* to a public-amenity landscape.

A restoration project was initiated to reinforce the walls and basin, and to upgrade the surrounding perimeter. The result was a significant enhancement of the storage capacity (the volume of the pond increased from 12,770 m³ to 26,000 m³), prevention of water infiltration and an increase of vegetated land (from 2.8 acres, or 1.1 hectare, in September 2011 to 6.2 acres, or 2.5 hectares, in September 2012). The pond serves the dual purpose of water source and junction point, where tractors from the village and surrounding areas fill their cisterns for irrigation purposes. The village well pumps additional fresh water into the pond during the dry season to compensate for the increased demand. A minimum charge is levied for each cistern by the municipality in order to cover the operational costs of the village's well. The elders and youngsters enjoy sitting around the *Birki* circumference. When dry, it functions as a sunken playground ideal for playing catch, hopscotch and children's soccer. Currently, the CDPU partners with a group of local donors and a cluster of 10 municipalities to build an agricultural extension center in Marwaheen. The center will cultivate *mashaa'* land (communal land), and enhance smallholder productivity through specific technical and management assistance that is sensitive to the particular agroecological environment in semiarid regions. The overarching premise of the center is to ensure rootedness in a militarized landscape.

Urban Agriculture and the Women's Vocational Training Center (WVTC) in the Ein El Hilwi Palestinian Refugee Camp

I grew up helping my father (may his soul rest in peace), who was a farmer from Tarsheeha, cultivating our front garden. In an instant, I decided to quit school and just focus on agriculture—business was going well for a 12 year old—but my father refused. Coriander was my specialty. With little attention it yielded great return. Following later additions to the house, the front yard was gone. I moved my garden to the rooftop and even set up a plastic green house on part of it. A few years ago, my nephew built on the roof. The new rooftop is made of corrugated sheets. With nowhere to plant, I opened a hole in the kitchen wall, fixed a wire mesh and a cover, and planted my climbers.[9]

—Quote from Em-Hosam, chief trainer in the WVTC

Ein el-Hilwi—Capital of the Palestinian Diaspora

For more than 64 years, since their *Nakba* (catastrophe) in 1948, Palestinian refugees have undergone violent phases in their attempt to adjust to the complex Lebanese landscape.[10] Out of the 425,000 registered refugees, 265,000 reside in 13 camps and 42 informal settlements, while enduring abject living conditions. Among this population, 66 percent live below the poverty line (less than $6/day), 6.6 percent live in extreme poverty (less than $2.17/day)[11] and 56 percent are unemployed.[12] *Tawteen*, the phobia against Palestinian integration, has proven effective in deactivating the civil rights act and creating an enormous socioeconomic and urban divide between the gated Palestinian refugee camps and their surroundings.

The expulsion of the PLO in 1982, which previously provided services to the camps, together with the unwillingness of the Lebanese government to replace these services, further exacerbated the misery in the camps. A population living under enforced confinement and constant surveillance and lacking urban planning regulations and service delivery has turned the camps into a "space of exception and space of void."[13] The largest (1.2 square kilometer area),[14] most congested (80,000–100,00 inhabitants)[15] and most turbulent of all these camps (18 armed Palestinian movements and factions),[16] Ein el-Hilwi is regarded by many as the "Capital of the Palestinian Diaspora" and by others as the "Stronghold of Outlaws." The camp is gated, confined and controlled by the Lebanese army forces. All means of access to the surrounding area is blocked, leaving only four gates guarded by soldiers with bulletproof shields sheltering behind reinforced concrete bunkers. The spatial definition of Ein el-Hilwi is a dense, contiguous fabric structured along two main vehicular roads—el-Fawqani Street and el-Tahtani Street. Hundreds of tiny alleys define its urban syntax.

Restraints imposed on the supply of building materials to the camp have not managed to contain the massive and wild densification of buildings lacking basic living standards with regard to ventilation, sanitation and safety regulations. The most alarming physical hazards encountered in Ein el-Hilwi are the failure of concrete slabs and the excessive network of overhanging water and electricity pipelines. There is no elected public authority in Ein el-Hilwi; however, there is a wide array of self-appointed individuals or groups claiming righteousness to represent the masses. Among these rivals, recognition is often achieved by military hegemony over sectors within the camp. Each faction nurtures a number of local NGOs that operate as service providers among Westoxinated—or West-centric—donations and ideologically enchanted beneficiaries. Provisions for a certain group often lead to confrontations with others, and eventually to project termination or radical adjustment to the initial scope of work. To recapitulate, Ein el-Hilwi is an overpopulated camp, gated and secured at the boundaries while chaotic and crumbling inside.

The Kingdom of Women

Dorai argues that solidarity and the shared feeling of the *Nakba* unite refugees and enable them to "recreate the geography of Palestine in exile."[17] This geography is noted in neighborhood and street names visible on walls festooned with graffiti and nationalistic slogans cherishing the Right to Return, and transmitted from one generation to the next as a collective psyche. Extreme living conditions call for innovative skills in adaptation and survival. Notions of solidarity and hope are the core premise of the documentary film *The Kingdom of Women*, narrated by seven women from Ein el-Hilwi who describe the reconstruction process led by the women in the aftermath of the 1982 Israeli invasion.[18] Ein el-Hilwi had been almost totally destroyed and its men detained in the Ansar camp.[19] Upon their return, armed men resumed patrolling the camp while women sought alternatives for public works through NGOs.

Figure 8.6 A "greenhouse" atop a corrugated metal roof improvised to secure natural lighting and ventilation that are necessary for plants' growth. Photograph by Rabih Shibli, 2013.

Through efficiency, determination and professionalism, female groups established six vocational training centers in the camp, which are still in operation today. The Women's Vocational Training Center (WVTC) is one such place, where group commitment and eager female activists alleviate the bleak prospects of living with uncertainty. Their United Nations Relief and Works Agency (UNRWA)-owned, two-story building is fenced in by high walls and barbed wire on the outer perimeter, and steel bars protect the windows from gunfire. Situated on El Fawqni Street, meters from the El-Kifah El-Mosallah (Armed Defiance) checkpoint, its façade is pitted with bullet holes volley-fired from processions, protest marches, clashes and commemorations for fallen fighters. All measures are set in place so that this facility does not become a foothold for any of the belligerents. Accordingly, the WVTC is a prison-like structure that has become a dynamic hub for 12—mainly volunteer—female trainers who work in shifts with more than 200 girls (12–18 years old) and teach skills such as hairdressing, cosmetology, sewing and typewriting.

These programs ensure financial sustainability for the center, which runs independently without donor aid, and provide employment opportunities for young women in the neighboring city of Sidon. In one corner of the center is a small garden where women gather to smoke or take coffee breaks. This *fool's paradise*, according to Em-Hosam, softens much of the frustration of increasingly difficult living conditions. Gardens are often highly valued in refugee camps, perceived as "Nostalgia to Palestine," according to Roberts, who states that the "complaint about lack of farmland reflects the nostalgia

Figure 8.7 High walls, barbed wires, metal fences and plastic sheets create a physical and visual buffer for the Women's Vocational Training Center (WVTC). Photograph by Rabih Shibli, 2013.

to return to Palestine to farm the land as Palestinians did before 1948."[20] Other more practical or more psychological concerns might be present too, such as a dire need for greenery, space or any other outlet.

Green Stories

Buildings have encroached upon the camp's spatial configuration, leaving green pockets strangled. Very few women in Ein el-Hilwi still hold on to the practice of cultivating anything. There are some accounts of greening being practiced for household consumption, but more significantly just for the sake of it. Cables are used as trellises for climbing plants; tin cans, car wheels and plastic boxes for growing herbs. These green spots—modest initiatives—represent a glimmer of hope in the eyes of their nurturers. Greening in Ein el-Hilwi is neither a necessity nor a luxury; rather, it is a way to soften the harshness of bitter reality. *Promoting Urban Agriculture in Ein el-Hilwi Palestinian Refugee Camp* is the title of the project CDPU envisioned as an attempt to spread greening to the rooftops, walls and any other urban pockets to create a "landscape of hope for the future."[21] The concept was gleaned from the camp's green narratives, summarized and realized at the Women's Vocational Training Center (WVTC). The center thus serves as a prototype to integrate agricultural practices as a learning module, and to showcase urban agriculture as a sustainable intervention.

Twelve women from the center participated in the training program on new cultivation techniques. Each of the participants then transferred the skills she had acquired to a wider group. The training sessions ended with the creation of a greening methodology—a technical guide for implementation and training materials specifically designed for the refugee camp environment. This serves as a pivotal tool to help realize the underlying objective of the initiative. The prescribed methodology incorporates local materials and techniques that are efficient and affordable. The training materials use a hands-on approach and demonstrate how participants can devise their own green space. This program is sustained through the set-up of a greenhouse where residents can buy green materials at a heavily subsidized rate.

Green Center

The design intervention involved remodeling the prison-like structure, enabling it to function as a sustainable green center, and maximizing the utility of cultivated areas on ground, walls and roof levels. Accordingly, the corner zone of the building was excavated and four underground reservoirs (10,000 cubic meters each) were installed for harvesting rainwater from the rooftop, which could be extracted using a hand pump. A concrete bed covers the tanks and serves as a convenient break-time terrace where the women sit next to four newly planted lemon trees, under the shade of a grapevine. Water is used to irrigate the ground-floor garden, fill the tin cans of the vertical greening units and supply the tank on the roof. A steel staircase was added on the side of the building, ensuring connection from the first floor to the roof, where a 3 x 12 meter greenhouse is used as an indoor workshop. An exhibition area, designed along the entrance level of the building, serves to display and sell in-house products. Climbing plants and a belt of trees were planted along the perimeter of the building, and form a soft buffer edge.

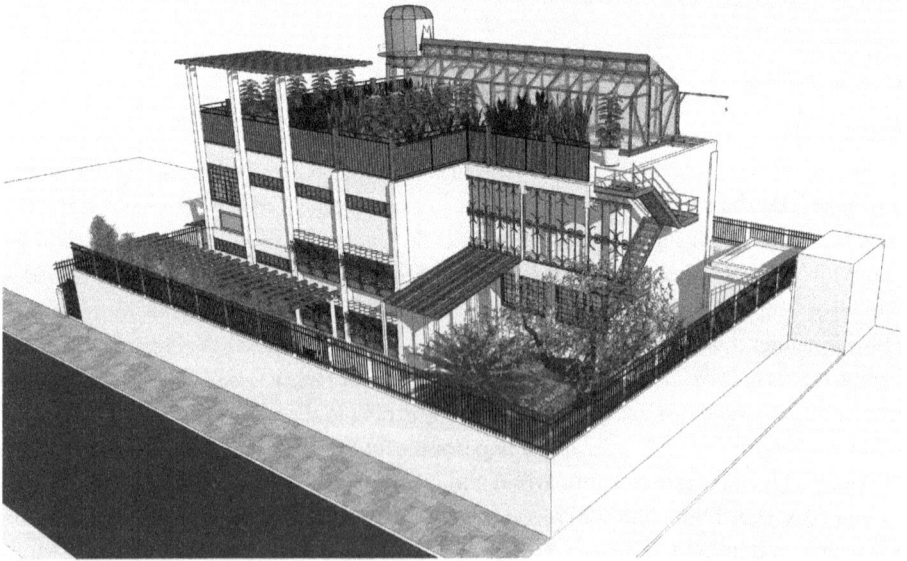

Figure 8.8 Three-dimensional model of the Urban Agriculture Center. Photograph by Rabih Shibli, 2013.

Conclusion

Ensuring hope is rendered insignificant if the projects presented in this chapter are compared to the sufferings as well as the aspirations of South Lebanon's inhabitants. Militarized landscapes operate in the covert. Understanding the dynamics of the underground trade requires unique skills that can penetrate an anxious collective psyche and assess its hidden dimensions. Social ecology, as a school of thought, is the mechanism that allows the human mind to analyze complex facts with compassion in order to plant the seeds for change within sclerotic settings such as those in South Lebanon, the Shu'fat Refugee Camp, or in Catholic–Protestant neighborhoods of Belfast, Northern Ireland.

In spaces with high levels of contestation, deprivation and marginalization, social ecology represents a progressive approach to dealing with complex socioeconomic and political tensions. Engaging local groups, utilizing existing resources and defining contextual management plans are instilled in the process.

Based on the results achieved in the two pilot projects, I endorse Bookchin's reasoning that "social ecology is an appeal not for moral regeneration but also, and above all, for social reconstruction along ecological lines."[22] These lines set the first milestones for change where wars and livelihoods intertwine to define patterns of engagement for land and people in militarized landscapes.

In such contexts, projects are initiated by securing consensus on a general theme, and develop when local knowledge is incorporated into the design process. Although clearly structured, the methodology of the work is highly flexible to accommodate the fluidity of various situations on the ground and is founded on a few guiding concepts. *Development planning*, as defined by Bollens, "seeks to integrate traditional spatial planning with social and economic planning […] [as well as to include] a participatory process that is aimed at empowering the […] marginalized."[23]

Next, *participatory design* leads to socially responsive projects. Because informal urban settlements, peripheral villages, gated neighborhoods, militarized landscapes and the like function mostly according to *'urf* (local customs) with limited adherence to written state codes, operating in such areas requires an in-depth understanding of local practices and knowledge. Local involvement in the decision-making and implementation process stimulates innovative ideas in terms of technical operations and resource management. Finally, *strategic intervention* targets short-term interventions with an immediate impact meant as a catalyst that induces complementary initiatives by the community itself.

The socioeconomic and political cleavages and tensions that dictate the majority of Middle Eastern geography foster gated communities, informal settlements and flawed natural ecologies. Uprisings and "Arab Springs" that have resulted in replacing fatigued dictators with updated versions and adopting outdated ideologies in lieu of imported ones exacerbate these cleavages. What is needed at this existential stage in the lives of millions in the Arab world—whether internally displaced, refugees or insecure citizens who are basically seeking dignity, equality and a better way of living—is a school of thought that Ibn Khaldoun realized 600 years ago and is now called social ecology![24]

NOTES

1 Rabih Shibli, *Remodeling Harshscapes: A New Reading of Problematic Narratives* (Beirut: American University of Beirut, 2011).

2 Murray Bookchin, "What Is Social Ecology?" in *Environmental Philosophy: From Animal Rights to Radical Ecology*, ed. Michael Zimmerman (Englewood Cliffs, NJ: Prentice Hall, 1993), 462–78.

3 Ibid.

4 C. O. Sauer, "The Morphology of Landscape," *University of California, Publications in Geography* 2 (1925): 19–53.

5 Gilbert Achcar and Michel Warschwski, *The 33-Day War: Israel's War on Hezbollah in Lebanon and Its Consequences*, (London: SAQI Books, 2007), 63.

6 Mark Duffield, *Global Governance and the New Wars: The Merging of Development and Security* (London: Zed Books, 2002), 14.

7 Erik Gartzke, "Globalization, Economic Development, and Territorial Conflict," in *Territoriality and Conflict in an Era of Globalization*, ed. Miles Kahler and Barbara F. Walter (New York: Cambridge University Press, 2006), 166.

8 Following every delineation process, the borderline has been named after the delegate in charge. Anglo-French, Newcombe, Tegart, Armistice, Purple, and the 2000 – UN Blue Line are representations of these processes.

9 Interview with Em-Housam, chief trainer in the Women's Vocational Training Center, Ein El Hilwi Palestinian Refugee Camp by Rabih Shibli, February 2012.

10 *Nakba* (catastrophe in English) is the term used in reference to the establishment of the state of Israel in 1948 and the forced migration of the Palestinian people from their land.

11 United Nations Relief and Works Agency, Lebanon Field Office, *Restoring Dignity: Responses to the Critical Needs of Vulnerable Palestine Refugees in Lebanon 2012–2016* (Beirut: UNRWA, Lebanon Field Office, 2011), 2.

12 J. Chaaban, H. Ghattas, R. R. Habib, S. Hanafi, N. Sahyoun, N. Salti, K. Seyfert and N. Naamani, *Socio-economic Survey of Palestinian Refugees in Lebanon*, Report published by the American University of Beirut (AUB) and the United Nations Relief and Works Agency for Palestine Refugees in the Near East (UNRWA), (Beirut: American University of Beirut, December 2010).

13 Sari Hanafi, "Palestinian Refugee Camps in Lebanon: Laboratories of State-in-the Making, Discipline and Islamic Radicalism," in *Thinking Palestine*, ed. Ronit Lentin (London: Zed Books, 2008).

14 Gray C. Gambill, "'Ain al-Hilweh: Lebanon's 'Zone of Unlaw,'" 5 (2003) *Middle East Intelligence Bulletin*, accessed April 15, 2014, www.meforum.org/meib/articles/0306_|1.htm.

15 The 80,000–100,000 estimate is before the Syrian crisis. For more about refugee estimates, see Doctors Without Borders/Médecins Sans Frontières (MSF), "From Damascus to Ain el-Helweh: Palestinians in Syria Flee to Lebanon," (May 2013), accessed April 15, 2014, www.doctorswithoutborders.org/article/damascus-ain-el-helweh-palestinians-syria-flee-lebanon/; and Franklin Lamb, "Lebanon: Why Focus on Scholarships for Ain al Hilweh Refugee Camp? Because It Exists," *Foreign Policy Journal* (November 15, 2013), accessed April 15, 2014, www.foreignpolicyjournal.com/2013/11/15/lebanon-why-focus-on-scholarships-for-ain-al-hilweh-refugee-camp-because-it-exists/.

16 Haitham Zoaiter, "Mokhayam Ein el-Hiwi a'simat al shatat al akthar maa'satan wa iktithathan [Ein el-Hilwi Camp, the Largest and Mostly Populated Capital of Refugees' Diaspora]," *Al-Liwaa* (Lebanon), August 13, 2010, 11.

17 Mohammad Kamel Dorai, "Palestinian Emigration to Lebanon from Northern Europe: Refugees, Networks and Transnational Practices," *Refuge: Canada's Journal on Refugees* 21 (2003): 26.

18 *The Kingdom of Women: Ein El Hilweh*, Documentary, 54 minutes; directed in Lebanon by Dahna Abourahme, 2010 (distribution at www.arabfilm.com and www.proactionfilm.com).

19 Ansar detention camp was established by the invading Israeli forces following the 1982 First Lebanon War.

20 Rebecca Roberts, *Palestinians in Lebanon: Refugees Living with Long-Term Displacement* (London: I. B. Tauris & Co Ltd., 2010), 151.

21 Julie Peteet, *Landscape of Hope and Despair: Palestinian Refugee Camps* (Philadelphia: University of Pennsylvania Press, 2005), 31.

22 Bookchin, "What Is Social Ecology?"

23 Scott A. Bollens, "Human Security through an Urban Lens," *Journal of Human Security* 4 (2008): 45–46.

24 See Ibn Khaldun, *The Muqaddimah: An Introduction to History*. Abridged and edited by N. J. Dawood. Translated from Arabic by Franz Rosenthal. (Princeton, NJ: Princeton University Press, 1969).

BIBLIOGRAPHY

Achcar, Gilbert and Michel Warschwski. *The 33-Day War: Israel's War on Hezbollah in Lebanon and Its Consequences*. London: SAQI Books, 2007.

Bollens, Scott A. "Human Security through an Urban Lens." *Journal of Human Security* 4 (2008): 45–6.

Bookchin, Murray. "What Is Social Ecology?" In *Environmental Philosophy: From Animal Rights to Radical Ecology*, edited by Michael Zimmerman, 462–78. Englewood Cliffs, NJ: Prentice Hall, 1993.

Chaaban, Jas, Hala Ghattas, Rima Habib, Sari Hanafi, Nadine Sahyoun, Nisreen Salti, Karin Seyfert and Nadia Naamani. *Socio-economic Survey of Palestinian Refugees in Lebanon*. Report published by the American University of Beirut (AUB) and the United Nations Relief and Works Agency for Palestine Refugees in the Near East (UNRWA). Beirut: American University of Beirut, December 2010.

Doctors Without Borders/Médecins Sans Frontières (MSF). "From Damascus to Ain el-Helweh: Palestinians in Syria Flee to Lebanon" (May 2013). Accessed April 15, 2014, www.doctorswithoutborders.org/article/damascus-ain-el-helweh-palestinians-syria-flee-lebanon/.

Dorai, Mohammad Kamel. "Palestinian Emigration to Lebanon from Northern Europe: Refugees, Networks and Transnational Practices." *Refuge: Canada's Journal on Refugees* 21 (2003): 23–31.

Duffield, Mark. *Global Governance and the New Wars: The Merging of Development and Security*. London: Zed Books, 2002.

Gambill, Gray C. "Ain al-Hilweh: Lebanon's 'Zone of Unlaw.'" 5 (2003) *Middle East Intelligence Bulletin*. Accessed April 15, 2014. www.meforum.org/meib/articles/0306_|1.htm.

Gartzke, Erik. "Globalization, Economic Development, and Territorial Conflict." In *Territoriality and Conflict in an Era of Globalization*, edited by Miles Kahler and Barbara F. Walter, 156–86. New York: Cambridge University Press, 2006.

Hanafi, Sari. "Palestinian Refugee Camps in Lebanon: Laboratories of State-in-the Making, Discipline and Islamic Radicalism." In *Thinking Palestine*, edited by Ronit Lentin, 82–100. London: Zed Books, 2008.

Housam-Em. Interview with Em-Housam, chief trainer, Women's Vocational Training Center, Ein El Hilwi Palestinian Refugee Camp by Rabih Shibli. February 2012.

Khaldun, Ibn. *The Muqaddimah: An Introduction to History*. Abridged and edited by N. J. Dawood. Translated from Arabic by Franz Rosenthal. Princeton, NJ: Princeton University Press, 1969.

Lamb, Franklin. "Lebanon: Why Focus on Scholarships for Ain al Hilweh Refugee Camp? Because It Exists." *Foreign Policy Journal* (November 15, 2013). Accessed April 15, 2014. www.foreignpolicyjournal.com/2013/11/15/lebanon-why-focus-on-scholarships-for-ain-al-hilweh-refugee-camp-because-it-exists/.

Peteet, Julie. *Landscape of Hope and Despair: Palestinian Refugee Camps*. Philadelphia: University of Pennsylvania Press, 2005.

Roberts, Rebecca, *Palestinians in Lebanon: Refugees Living with Long-Term Displacement*. London: I. B. Tauris, 2010.

Sauer, C. O. "The Morphology of Landscape." *University of California, Publications in Geography* 2 (1925): 19–53.

Shibli, Rabih. *Remodeling Harshscapes: A New Reading of Problematic Narratives*. Beirut: American University of Beirut, 2011.

The Kingdom of Women: Ein El Hilweh, Documentary, 54 minutes; directed in Lebanon by Dahna Abourahme. Distribution at www.arabfilm.com and www.proactionfilm.com. 2010.

United Nations Relief and Works Agency (UNRWA), Lebanon Field Office. *Restoring Dignity: Responses to the Critical Needs of Vulnerable Palestine Refugees in Lebanon 2012–2016*. Beirut: UNRWA, Lebanon Field Office, 2011.

Zoaiter, Haitham. "Mokhayam Ein el-Hiwi a'simat al shatat al akthar maa'satan wa iktithathan [Ein el-Hilwi Camp, the Largest and Most Populated Capital of Refugees' Diaspora]." *Al-Liwaa* (Lebanon), August 13, 2010.

Chapter Nine

DOMESTICATING AND ENLARGING ONE'S TERRITORY: DAY-TO-DAY POLITICS IN A CONFINED SPACE—THE SHU'FAT REFUGEE CAMP IN EAST JERUSALEM

Sylvaine Bulle

The Israeli–Palestinian conflict is frequently raised from a geopolitical or sometimes an ideological angle. A number of critical, illustrated works have extensively analyzed the logic of domination of one people over another and the relational cleavages resulting from security-based politics, that led, for example, to the creation of a separation wall (or barrier) between Israel and the Palestinian territories. Within this logic, geography, cartography and knowledge/power become the dominant modes of representation. They often foster an abstract vision of vertical power that erases all human relations. Anthropological and phenomenal aims disappear. The Palestinian landscape can be described as comprising security walls, camps, settlements and checkpoints—a place where a disconnect between the persons, the group and their environment is radically witnessed. Instead of beginning with a description of the total sense of domination faced by these walled-in inhabitants, the current study examines the resources to which they have recourse. These resources enable inhabitants to adjust to a problematic situation brought about by the wall and its enclosure. By thus focusing not only on relations of domination, but also on actors' attitudes, this chapter shifts attention to ordinary forms of denunciation. These are a way to read, not only the critical capabilities of people, but the way in which inhabitants adapt to and shape their environment.

The investigation briefly presented here[1] concerns the small refugee camp of Shu'fat situated along the security barrier in Jerusalem, where the citizens, all residents of Jerusalem, are more or less enclosed within an enclave. However, these citizen-refugees are no less motivated by the bonds or attachments that give value to local scale and property. The role of a personal logic of comfort for these walled-in refugees and their ways of acting locally can be understood as an attempt to organize their environment or surroundings. An entire series of practices and activities expresses the capacity of individuals to identify—and value the existence of and attachment to—refugee camps, which currently exist in legal limbo. It is through such a perspective that we seek to understand the meaning of these practices both cognitive and material—as the creation and enlargement of one's environment.

Practices such as building, gardening, planting and the creation of cottage industries and small businesses establish a vast physical and human experience that introduces an "ecology" of social activities[2] and the environment into the political arena. Social ecology addresses the complex and interrelated relationship between environment and inhabitants and offers a perspective on how familiar space is embedded in a social and political context, where the separation is transformed into one interface reminiscent of the edge effect highlighted in this book's introduction. In ways that are barely visible, relations between loved ones are a means to value the common good and show concern for social and spatial justice. Here, social ecology is an appeal not for moral regeneration or political recognition, but above all as a methodological approach for such spaces, where people's practical involvements with one another and with their environments in their everyday lives create new forms and discourses.

The Regime of Perception and the Familiar World

Residents of the Shu'fat camp face a series of difficult dilemmas as they pursue their daily lives—that is, how to improve their lives and construct livable spaces from which to act and communicate when war, restrictions and dispossession penetrate so deeply into daily life. Shu'fat camp residents are Palestinian refugees, registered with the United Nations Relief and Work Agency (UNRWA), and thus receive social and educational services, as well as a food ration card. Paradoxically, they are also residents of Jerusalem and, under certain conditions, benefit from city-residential status. The erection of the security barrier—or Wall—in 2005 has profoundly modified the civic status of Jerusalem's residents and the small camp of Shu'fat with its registered population of fewer than 11,000 persons. The camp is now girded by two sections of the Wall, which also divides East Jerusalem into two parts. Those who find themselves on the "good" side of the Wall have maintained their rights of residence and mobility and their civic rights. Shu'fat, as in other nearby communities, was historically governed by exchanges and proximity to Jerusalem or the hinterland of Ramallah. The construction of the Wall tore apart families and ripped familial and economic fabrics. Spatial position has determined individual fates, dictating social vulnerability for some and "luck" for others who maintain their freedom of movement and their social advantages. For those behind the Wall, it is a story of political and civil invisibility where refugees nonetheless act to build and produce their own spaces.

In these extreme conditions, we consider every local act as having the ability to reposition the actor in relation to his environment, to react to it and finally to enlarge it through cognitive, emotional or mental adjustments. For refugees confined within an enclave, such an act is a significant temporal event that offers possibilities for action and narration. In a dynamic where the environment is appropriated, the patriot and the refugee efface themselves for the benefit of the individual, and withdraw from essentialist representations— those that are called for by patriotism, or those that are reductionist, upheld by the fatalism of confinement. On the contrary, local engagement is represented by people who abolish the *essence* of the camp to create a livable human establishment—not only a refuge, but also an environment that pushes against the limits of enclosure. Thus at Shu'fat, within an enclosed world, a whole series of operations makes it possible to enlarge frontiers. Such actions reveal a new way of relating to the world and its domestication that can be understood either through a pragmatic perspective or through ecology of perception.[3]

The ecology of perception developed by Gibson (1979) proposes a cognitive and perceptive continuity between humans and their environment. Perception implies active engagement by human organisms in the world. The system that incorporates the "human-object-environment" also perceives and encourages agency or active engagement. This continuity can be regarded as a group of resources for individual action. It is understood to be a discernible *milieu* that provides perceptual orientations and ways of moving within specific situations. The availability of resources and the environment motivate the "exploration of a world at hand."[4] Objects, landmarks and private staff reestablish the link between intimacy and the external world. In other words, the perceptible and material environment offers potential for reaction, and motor or mental action, which can become political or social acts. Understood in this way, the construction of an environment cannot be thought of as a strict, mechanical adaptation to the constraints posed by the limitation of the right to circulate, work and interact under circumstances in which neighbors are rendered inaccessible. Instead, a pragmatic approach—based on the ecology of perception—takes into account the way people mobilize, identify resources, use such resources and make them visible and accessible. The world of the ecology of perception is a world of the distribution of intelligence that offers people the possibility and ability to explore this world when they so desire. The world of affordances is therefore communal and not private. It domesticates and enlarges a territory through communicative and practical competences.

Figure 9.1 Israeli security wall surrounding Shu'fat camp, which is on the left side. Photograph courtesy of Nora Akawi, 2010.

Living and Living Better: A Political Meaning

It is the *regime of the local* that awakens the cognitive and emotional qualities of a space, making it possible to configure an environment and to reestablish continuity between the world and things (or objects). In particular, the domestic level contains affective qualities that must assert their relation of belonging to the world. To build a home engages practical steps that have universal characteristics such as the need for protection and controlled exchange,[5] as well as civility and human community. Property presents itself as a measure of justice and as a home base of law.

The capacities for communication of stricken citizens are no different from those who are fully operational within the world and its shared language.[6] Any anthropology of an enclosed *milieu* must move beyond describing a given order dominated by violence, and instead turn toward human capacities and individual potential. On one level, the local scale appears through its existential and phenomenological aspect. At various levels of the home, the frontier and the wall, we see the forms of a weakened life, an ontology or experience of the war. Even in the divided city of Jerusalem, some interconnectivity always exists between subjects and objects and the environment that characterizes the composition or internal meshwork of objects, events and places.[7] The attachments and qualities given to domestic objects express a will and an act—that is, individual capacities to identify and value the meaning embodied within the very existence of life's daily elements. Physical surroundings as a condition of practical activity[8] become a support for confidence as well as for criticism. The environment makes possible actions and adjustments. The reality of confinement makes visible a bundle of operations from which citizens and their families must choose to support themselves, accessing these possibilities through the support of family networks and local relations. It is therefore possible to link the local with the political horizon.

"We will stay here; we will not be driven away a second time," say the residents of Shu'fat. For the refugees who stayed, they maintain first and foremost their right to build, to plant, to improve and beautify their surroundings—that is, to live as fully as possible. In other words, the attachment to the camp, which is largely absent from institutional discourses, but found in individual narratives, remains or appears as a form of attachment to individual life and the sense of privacy. It also expresses the wish for a future.

The Shu'fat camp has become a city. It pushes ceaselessly against its initial perimeter and against the instability of its very first structures. It is now made of a mixture of material and vital elements—inhabitation, interaction, work or rest. We can situate this mixture within the ontology of inhabitation[9] at the intersection of symbols, cognitive landmarks and actions affecting what existed beforehand. The ontology is reflected here in the way that inhabitants express and act on their connections to the space, their sense of belonging and attachments to their spaces. Feeling, remembering, acting or intending are all aspects of this ontology, seen here as the sum of all these permanent or discontinuous engagements.

Taking control of one's homeland is ever more visible and durable as a metaphysical condition without perpetuating distinction between nature and culture, housing and environment. Palestinians in the Shu'fat camp invest above all in the domestic as well as the common space, and work to attain material comfort for their families. They affirm their attachment to place, privacy and security through these investments, which are not always taken into account in the conventional discourse of resistance. Their attachment to domesticity (nearness), privacy and individual rights appear here as a tangible commitment and mode of action. Both commitment and action are responses to the fear of some future dispossession. The people of Shu'fat have already had their land expropriated twice, once in 1948 (their villages or places of origin) and again in 1967.[10] In addition, the profound crisis of the national political project contaminates property in the present, whereby one finds oneself currently attached to a property whose dispossession is anticipated in the near future. These forms of engagement with home and its surroundings—expressed as "pride of ownership"— are aimed less at publicly registering the condition of the refugee and more at affirming social life. The sensation of privacy (which is a universal value), and the sense of attachment to familiar things and space, also marks the emergence of individualism and subjectivity, which are potentially linked to the notion of self-realization or freedom and reflexivity.

Domesticating the Environment

The house for Shu'fat residents is primarily a domestic space providing stability and relief from the hardships and stresses of daily life. Recently, after the Wall was built, we observed considerable activity related to home improvement (furniture decoration, renovations of the façade, enlargement of the gardens and windows). Significantly, initiatives to improve homes occur especially in areas bordering the Wall. Beyond the home interior, one also finds expressions of "house pride." Since the Wall was built, these include investments and small property improvements such as gardens and the addition of stories and terraces. For each property, residual spaces are cultivated, even landscaped. Dividing walls between neighbors and delimitation fences are being built. The refugee creates a domestic environment while simultaneously reconfiguring his or her relationship with the outside world. Collective stairs to access gardens at the bottom of a slope were also built by residents or by the camp committee.

The configuration of an environment at the scale of a house and a neighborhood makes a sense of context possible. It changes the relation with the world, created by material conditions and actions. Beyond material concerns, the search for well-being translates into adjustments that can result concurrently in private demands and a shared will. The conditions of well-being that have appeared since the creation of the Wall do not compensate for the absence of mobility, but consolidate social activities, exchange and communication in a problematic situation.

The environment is an important source of creativity.[11] A marriage hall, popularly called the "Palace," has appeared in the middle of the camp. Financed by contributions from camp residents and the camp's youth center, this vast marriage hall, colorful and festive, legitimizes the camp as a place of civility, even happiness. On Fridays, Shu'fat refugees celebrate their weddings, and non-camp residents may also celebrate inside "the

Figure 9.2 Garden inside the camp, opposite the settlement of Pisgat Zeev. Photograph courtesy of Nora Akawi, 2010.

Palace." At other times, the hall is used for shows, ceremonies and local assemblies. The Palace is also utilized as a youth center where *dabkeh* (traditional Levantine folk dance) is taught along with classes in rap. It is a place where each person feels a sense of belonging, a haven, and not only a place of survival. The cognitive and bodily resources mobilized by song and theater describe confinement in a critical mode while at the same time rendering experiences possible. Live performances comprise real moments of public self-presentation. The bodily register that is given over through dance or song displays an intensity of being and of emotions—the loss of imprisoned loved ones, the humiliation of military control, the loss of family honor through unemployment and sometimes the denunciation of the Palestinian political authorities. These personal engagements are attempts to create a narrative of the collective trials suffered by the walled-in community. They take form or are translated into scenes that have a strongly dramatic or comedic character.

From the moment that it becomes public, the body possesses a mediating function. It is the seat of emotion and a spring of potential energy for relating to the world, and for engaging in practical acts aimed at recognition. As a space configured by interaction and communication, the Palace approaches the definition of a shared good where comfort becomes part of both private and collective norms. The Palace required sacrifices—the opening up of a large block and the demolition of a dwelling. These acts that put in place a lasting facility contradict the prevailing discourse about the camp's ontological precariousness. Camp leaders[12] came to an agreement on the demand for social relations and for facilities made by the inhabitants. This type of shared facility opens up an interstice between patriotic representation and the individual scale, between the institutional organization of the camp and the pragmatic action to expand its territory.

In Shu'fat, there has also been investment and growth in the areas of personal health and well-being, such as the construction of fitness centers, and shops selling cosmetics, furniture and sports products. Once again, the place created by the body or by celebratory events underlines the demand for security or well-being that is understood as an underlying, or inferred, asset.

We observe a high level of land speculation in the camps, and a dynamic market for land acquisition and construction especially for housing and commercial development that borders the Wall. Before the Wall was erected, some second-generation refugees— entrepreneurs who had succeeded in their business enterprises—moved from the camp to Jerusalem. They held their property in the camp as a second residence close to their families, thereby both demonstrating the process of mobility from the camp to the city, and keeping a foothold in the camp. Today, the movement is reversed. Since the Wall's construction, many residents have returned to Shu'fat in order to maintain their Jerusalem resident rights. In addition, many young people from other West Bank towns who hold Palestinian identity cards come secretly to look for work. Quite simply, Shu'fat and East Jerusalem are less shattered than the northern regions of the West Bank such as Nablus and Jenin.

In all of these operations, the domestication of the environment opens a large framework of personal or communal interactions that serves to deconstruct the notion of enclosure in favor of the legitimization of residents. These activities can be contrasted with the political representation of the camp as a place of resistance against occupation and Israeli institutions. Consequently, such activities serve to enlarge and change the public domain and sphere. Actions to improve life in the camp are regarded as advancing the common good of all. "We are all united as the fingers on a hand, refugees or not," say the residents of Shu'fat.[13] Neighborhood politics, intimate attachments and close relations with loved ones create bonds with the overall political structure in a way that is based on shared engagements that are realized within the sphere of public space.[14] These relations consist of enlarging the political question through local actions and behaviors.

Proximity and Politics: The Political Aims of an Ecology of Social Activities

Everyday policies and practices not only focus on commercial or housing development. Investments also extend to the urban sphere and infrastructure development, some of which takes place near the Wall. This is the case in local individual, family or group initiatives to install sewage systems that may not be a formal collective effort through the camp committee or the administrative heads (i.e., UNRWA). Instead, such initiatives rely on separate contracts, mediated by external parties such as the Jerusalem municipality. Requests for the installation of a water pipe on a new property, construction of a building at the camp's edge or appeal of an administrative decision (such as the denial of a

Figure 9.3 Extension and improvements in the camp. Photograph courtesy of Nora Akawi, 2010.

permit for building or movement) require personal involvement with the Israeli administration in Jerusalem, which is viewed as the enemy. While these are not formal collective efforts, they do result in communal activity. Responding to residents' demands for better transportation into Jerusalem, for example, the camp committee negotiated directly with the East Jerusalem Bus Company in order for residents to have to their own line without having to transit through the West Bank.

Getting together informally to obtain information, thus creating an association, implies that these regimes of engagement[15] possess the ability to make and justify an argument, and defer hostile judgment toward the Israeli *enemy*. The creation of an environment therefore makes tacit accords possible, and enhances compromise between actors reputed to be hostile, that is, Israelis and Palestinians. These agreements are neither permanent nor certain, but do consolidate a community of trust[16] based on targeted action. Local engagement thus creates compromise that can involve public negotiation without recourse to public mobilization resulting in participation *as* public mobilization.[17]

Finally, the existence of such transactions in a confined and enclosed place allows us to take another look at the local scale. The range of concrete, formal or informal operations taking place within Shu'fat appears to be a way of transforming an enclosed universe into one of intimacy and safety and sometimes into a form of common good. The way of acting in this enclosed space, the different and huge encroachments on daily life, proceed from some strategy of denunciation, but actors creatively address the situation using the existing environment. Like a struggle for the recognition of what is "already present" (*déjà là*), the actors operate and recognize the current space of life, shaped by personal and affective attachments. These intimate actions widen and enrich the surroundings to produce a collective space marked by various ways of engaging people—that is, a form of political reawakening. Activities at the domestic scale concern common good and politics by weaving the fabric of a livable environment without relying on any public institution.

Actions do not imply recognition of civil rights by others, especially Israel and the municipality of Jerusalem. Rather, the vulnerable citizen seizes opportunities, confronts multiple worlds and establishes relations beyond frontiers. Local actions do not persist merely to soften the hardships of social life. Such actions also establish a larger experience that inserts a social and environmental ecology within the moral and political landscape. The domestication of environmental elements responds to an aim, which is that of social ecology. This goes beyond the breach between politics and the moral—both domestic and public—by leading to responsible actions.

We must also view this ecology of social and physical activities through the lens of its political aspects, and recognize the plurality of citizens' engagements. These citizens find material support that allows them to temporarily break out of their walled-in condition, and create activist, communitarian injunctions, or ponder the question of citizenship. Within tensions between the attachment to an "already existing" place—fidelity toward community and concern for oneself—the actors destabilize ideological principals of a space conceived around initially constituted assets. Such principals include the mythic tale of exile, the promotion of the refugee camps' precarious character or the refugees' human condition and ontology. Furthermore, the attention paid to regimes of locality establishes a social ecology that we cannot disassociate from the activity of recognition. Recognition is based on respect and trust and is considered a key element of refugee action.[18] In the accomplishment of an action, the citizen, devoid or stripped of rights or civic status, affirms himself or herself as a person recognized for being capable and responsible. In these actions, enclosed "citizens" express the desire for safety, autonomy, trust and confidence. The mixture of fear and hope that Palestinians also call "pessoptimism" provides here a theoretical starting point for the notion of dignity and recognition.

It is perhaps through the domestication and enlargement of the environment that the concept of recognition can emerge. The regime of familiarity, if extended to different publics (notably, international institutions, NGOs and local administrations), could progressively lead to judicial recognition of the Palestinian people's individual right to coexist and circulate. Within these conditions, the local level could rise up as one body politic to foster human decency and recognition. It is also the way to express a judgment and an ordinary critique of existing institutions.[19]

In sum, the explosion worldwide of walls and security fences does not signify the extinction of spontaneous human activities. In the contemporary era of security, immigration, market flows and the surveillance state (i.e., the Israeli case) people deal with boundaries, often drawing their own lines, and connect their environment through collaborative practice.

This chapter highlights but one lesson drawn from the Shu'fat experience and complements what others write in this volume about divided or confined spaces. We must not forget that when humans act, react or rebel, they are often one step ahead of social analysts, experts and policy makers.

NOTES

1 The current investigation is part of a series of studies that took place in Shu'fat between 2006, the date of the security wall's creation, and 2010.

2 The notion of social ecology used in this chapter is that of Isaac Joseph, French philosopher and sociologist, who himself borrowed the idea from pragmatic philosophy in the United States—especially that of John Dewey. See John Dewey, *Le Public et Ses Problèmes* (Paris: Gallimard, 2010).

3 James Gibson, *The Ecological Approach to Visual Perception* (Boston: Houghton Mifflin, 1979).

4 Isaac Joseph, "L'athlète moral et l'enquêteur modeste. Parcours du pragmatisme," in *La Croyance et l'Enquête*, ed. Bruno Karsenti, et al. (Paris: EHESS, 2004), 18–52.

5 According to Georges H. Mead, private property is a form of social institution that articulates economic acts, like buying and selling. It is often accompanied by a set of shared acts like respect and conservation. See Georges H. Mead, *L'esprit, le Soi et la Société* (Paris: Presses Universitaires de France, 2006).

6 Acts of language are institutional phenomena. See John Searle, *Les Actes de Language* (Paris: Hermann, 1972).

7 See Tim Ingold, *The Perception of the Environment: Essays in Livehood, Dwelling and Skill* (London: Routledge, 2003).

8 Philippe Descola, *Par Delà Nature et Culture* (Paris: Gallimard, 2005).

9 Ingold, *The Perception of the Environment*. Descola and Ingold see the ontology of dwelling as the non-separation of culture and nature, practices and languages.

10 Refugees come mostly from the old city of Jerusalem (Moghrabi quarter) from where they were expelled after the 1967 War and the reunification of Jerusalem.

11 We could also refer here to the notion of interagentivity. According to Sen, development is fundamentally an empowering process, and this power can be used not only to preserve and enrich the environment, but also to decimate it. Therefore, we must not think of the environment exclusively in terms of conserving preexisting natural conditions, since the environment can also include the results of human creation. See Amartya Sen, *The Idea of Justice* (London: Penguin Books, 2010).

12 The administrative heads work for the UNRWA; the political head, or camp leader, works for Fatah, the majority political party in power.

13 Interview with a Shu'fat inhabitant, October 2009.

14 We borrow here from the notion of "public" using Dewey's approach, in which actors of any sort—individuals or institutions—engage in efforts of self-definition and attempt to control problematic situations and public affairs, based on procedures for managing disagreement.

15 Engagement comprises an implied dimension unrelated to programming, and assumes nearly spontaneous treatment, within the situation: "There is engagement as soon as the situation is active and not simply one that we are subject to." See Louis Quéré, "Confiance et engagement," in *Les Moments de la Confiance. Connaissance, Affects et Engagements*, ed. Albert Ogien et Louis Quéré (Paris: Economica, 2006), 117–41.

16 According to James, the notion of trust is a social intelligence that gradually allows relations to develop. See Williams James, *Essai d'Empirisme Radical* (Marseille: Agone, 2003).

17 There is no representative political body for either the inhabitants of Shu'fat or within the Palestinian community of Jerusalem in the municipality of Jerusalem, because the Palestinian political institutions (Fatah, OLP) refuse any cooperation with Israel.

18 Axel Honneth maintains that war often represents a collective event, capable of establishing bonds of solidarity beyond social barriers. See Axel Honneth, *La Lutte Pour la Reconnaissance* (Paris: Cerf, 2000).

19 On ordinary language, see, for example, Ludwig Wittgenstein, *Investigations Philosophiques* (Paris: Gallimard, 1990). For a theory of social critique, see Luc Boltanski, *De la Critique. Précis de Sociologie de l'Emancipation* (Paris: Gallimard, 2009).

BIBLIOGRAPHY

Boltanski, Luc. *De la Critique. Précis de Sociologie de l'Emancipation.* Paris: Gallimard, 2009.

Descola, Philippe, *Par Delà Nature et Culture.* Paris: Gallimard, 2005.

Dewey, John. *Le Public et Ses Problèmes, Œuvres Philosophiques.* Publications de l'Université de Pau, Farrago: 2003. Originally published in John Dewey, *Later Works,* vol. 2, edited by Jo Anne Boydston et al. Carbondale: Southern Illinois University Press, 1977.

Gibson, James. *The Ecological Approach to Visual Perception.* Boston: Houghton Mifflin, 1979.

Honneth, Axel. *La Lutte Pour la Reconnaissance.* Paris: Cerf, 2000.

Ingold, Tim. *The Perception of the Environment: Essays in Livehood, Dwelling and Skill.* London: Routledge, 2003.

James, William. *Essai d'Empirisme Radical.* Marseille: Agone, 2003. Originally published in William James, *Essays in Radical Empiricism.* New York: Longman Green, 1912.

Joseph, Isaac. "L'athlète moral et l'enquêteur modeste. Parcours du pragmatisme." In *La croyance et l'enquête,* edited by Bruno Karsenti, et Louis Quéré, 18–52, Paris, EHESS, 2004.

Mead, Georges H. *L'esprit, le soi et la société. Paris* : Presses Universitaires de France, 2006. Originally published in Georges H. Mead, *Mind, Self and Society.* Chicago: University of Chicago Press, 1934.

Merleau-Ponty, Maurice. *Phénoménologie de la Perception.* Paris: Gallimard, 1976.

Quéré, Louis. "Confiance et Engagement." In *Les Moments de la Confiance. Connaissance, Affects et Engagements,* edited by Albert Ogien et Louis Quéré, 117–41, Paris: Economica, 2006.

Searle, John. *Les Actes de Langage.* Paris: Hermann, 1972. Originally published in John Searle, *Speech Actes: An Essay on Philosophy of Language.* Cambridge: Cambridge University Press, 1966.

Sen, Amartya. *The Idea of Justice.* London: Penguin Books, 2010.

Wittgenstein, Ludwig. *Investigations Philosophiques.* Paris: Gallimard, 1990. Originally published in Ludwig Wittgenstein, *Philosophische Untersuchungen. Philosophical Investigations.* Oxford: Blackwell, 2009.

Chapter Ten

URBAN ALTERNATIVES AND COLLABORATIVE ECONOMICS IN BELFAST'S CONTESTED SPACE

Brendan Murtagh

Introduction

The transformative social and physical character of cities coming out of conflict has attracted increasing attention from academics as well as urban managers.[1] In particular, the potential to reengineer borderscapes via local development and land use policies focuses attention on the normative possibilities and the type of practices that might create new forms of integration and spatial diversity. For Yiftachel,[2] these transitional cities can be understood through the interplay of ethnocracy, capital and governance. He does not posit a new theory of urban change, but suggests that borderscapes can be best understood as a dynamic in which different forces compete for authority, legitimacy and, ultimately, spatial hegemony. Social ecology rejects the fixity of geographic boundaries by emphasizing the need to understand spatial reproduction via multi-scalar processes that "drop down" to local territories, communities and border formations. Thus, ethnocratic forces bolster racial elites and their capacity to reproduce authority via territorial control, separation and interfacing. Land becomes a signifier of security and conquest, and a vital resource in wider national struggles for identification and survival. The national is intimately connected to the local and the space for negotiation or collaboration becomes highly constrained.[3]

However, the end of conflict can also de-risk cities and facilitate accumulation, although capital is selective in seeking certainty, political endorsement and, crucially, the places that enable its reproduction. Governance thus helps and as Peck and Tickell[4] have pointed out, planning, urban policy and economic development are geared to extending the "viral" reach of the neoliberal project even into areas that were previously incubated by violence and insecurity. Yiftachel's framework helps to explain the cities that have negotiated their way out of conflict to join the market, global circuits of wealth and exchange and some form of civic stability. It also identifies the cities that remain dominated by an ethnocratic regime where identity trumps the market and resource competition, violence and the rigid control of territory endure in the socio-spatial construct of the borderscapes.

This chapter argues that these processes can operate simultaneously at the urban scale to explain the spatial proximity of reterritorialization and deterritorialization, especially in cities moving between violence to some form of ethnic accommodation. The 1998 Belfast Peace Agreement ended nearly 30 years of violence between Protestants and Catholics and set in motion a process of economic modernization stimulated by foreign direct investment, flagship urban regeneration projects and a booming housing market. Residential desegregation in the growth city was, however, also accompanied by increasing segregation in areas left untouched by peace and engagement within a neoliberalizing economy. Indeed, there were more physical *peace lines* separating Protestant and Catholic communities built in the 10 years after the Agreement than in the 10 previous years.[5] There are now 42 peace lines mainly in the north and west of the city, and these are also the poorest, most violent and least stable neighborhoods, which are easily exploited by ethnic entrepreneurs, extant paramilitaries and racketeers.[6] The main response has been to securitize, not transform these *wicked* spaces where poor, environmentally degraded and sectarianized landscapes are more tightly regulated via closed-circuit television (CCTV), security buffers and intensified policing.

It is thus important to locate any analysis of integrated and segregated space in the wider economic restructuring of cities, at least in the global North. Increased interfacing cannot be understood separately from the neoliberal tendencies that accompanied peace, and it is argued here that economics similarly need to be central to discussions about spatial liminality. The next section of this chapter develops Yiftachel's analysis by focusing in particular on the interplay between neoliberalism and spatial restructuring in ethnically divided cities. This sets off twin-speed processes in which proximate interfacing and integration reveal deeper instabilities in post-conflict urban recovery. The impact of these processes in Belfast is discussed with a particular focus on interface communities and the nature of their disconnection from the metropolitan economy. This sets the context for a case study in one peace line, Suffolk/Lenadoon in west Belfast, where cross-interface collaboration has created a social enterprise jointly owned by local Protestant and Catholic communities. The analysis shows that collaborative governance at the local level has widened interstitial space and offers some form of resistance to sectarian and market hegemonies. This chapter concludes by arguing that local activism and alternative economics have enabled gateways to puncture the peace wall and create new spatial relations based on the use and ownership of community assets, jobs and social enterprises.

The Neoliberal City

Boal[7] maintained that the Northern Ireland conflict stems from competing national ideological versions of the constitutional future of the region. These are not pure ethnic differences, but they are characterized by binary religious politico-cultural histories and claims. For Boal, there are two primary ethno-religious blocs: one Unionist, Loyalist and Protestant intent on maintenance of the union with Great Britain; and the other, a Nationalist, Republican and Catholic identity demanding reunification with the rest of Ireland. The establishment of the Northern Ireland state in 1921 had built-in instabilities reflected in episodes of Republican violence that culminated in the outbreak of The

Troubles in 1969. Associated with these processes is what Boal[8] termed the "segregation ratchet" whereby the rate of separation increased rapidly at times of violence, but rarely returned to their pre-conflict levels. Rampant ethno-nationalism characterized the 1970s and 1980s, as Protestants and Catholics scattered to their respective heartlands, secured and policed by new physical peace lines, especially in the inner city.

Knox[9] argued that part of the problem with the Agreement was that it was negotiated by the political elites at a macro level, but failed to effectively engage the local level. This was increasingly reflected by a disconnect between stabilized institutions at the regional level and uncertainty, fear and low-level incidence of violence concentrated in poorer neighborhoods. The explanation of segregation as a largely internal response to identity difference and violence no longer holds true in the uncertain process of post-conflict transition. The global effects of capital, culture and technology, of course, impact how places change, and, to some extent, risk and uncertainty insulated Northern Ireland from what Peck and Tickell[10] term the "viral effects" of neoliberalism. However, peace, a comparatively well-educated labor force and a determination to reengage the new world order saw the city reformed and twin processes of mixing and segregation reflect very different social and economic currents.

Peck and Tickell[11] described the features of neoliberalism as: the promotion of growth-first strategies; the naturalization of market logics; deregulation; a withdrawal from welfare; and a preference for privatization. Moreover, it is rolled out and over national economies and sovereign boundaries and is indifferent to welfare regimes or state regulation. Critics argue that this analysis is too simplistic and the current crisis renders neoliberalism largely redundant as a theoretical or political construct.[12] For Peck and colleagues,[13] however, neoliberalism is simply adjusting, like a "crises driven makeover" and can adapt and reform with its ideologies and practices left largely intact. Castree[14] also points out that it has always been *path-dependent* and conditioned by the institutional, cultural and regulatory frameworks in each particular context. It is, in Brenner and Theodore's[15] term, "actually existing neoliberalism" and in post-conflict Northern Ireland, urban renaissance, elite commercial projects and (over) speculation in the housing market were important signifiers of normalcy and an albeit hollow version of progress. In Belfast, this has taken shape in new waterfront developments, heavily subsidized by the state but led by private developers. Shirlow and Murtagh highlighted the way in which Belfast, as with other late industrial cities, has rebranded itself, in this case around the *Titanic*, which was built in the city.[16] Titanic Quarter is a 185-acre, mixed-use development proposed for the former shipyard, which is linked to the University Quarter and the Cathedral Quarter to create a cosmopolitan landscape that is safe for tourists, investors and the emerging professional class.

In the nearly three decades of conflict (approximately 1969–96), the rate of residential segregation between Protestants and Catholics accelerated to its highest level, but between 1991 and 2001, it largely stabilized and between 2001 and 2011, it was significantly reversed.[17] Areas of ethno-religious mixed housing expanded, but these were concentrated in middle-class areas, especially to the south of the city. Deindustrialization, the rise of the service economy, fair employment legislation and increasing public-sector jobs helped to expand the middle class both socially and spatially. Gating and gentrification accelerated a particular form of disaffiliation as the emergent consumption class recolonized apartment developments in the city center and in a rebranded waterfront. In reality, Belfast has caught up with the neoliberalization of urban space familiar in other late capitalist cities, but in more selective and potentially unstable ways. As mixing increased in the south of the city, segregation and periods of intercommunal violence intensified in the north and west where the new economy and the high-skilled jobs it demanded left little imprint.

This process of splintering is evident in the changing levels of ethno-spatial segregation and especially in how they intersect with class and tenure. For example, Shuttleworth and Lloyd[18] showed that the Dissimilarity Index for Belfast rose from 0.56 in 1971 to 0.66 in 1991, but only to 0.67 by 2001 (1.0 would be complete spatial segregation and 0 would represent complete spatial integration). However, the most recent calculations from the 2011 Census of Population show that the Index had declined substantially in the past decade to 0.58, primarily because of the expanded zone of middle-class housing in the south of the city.[19] Catholics now make up 45 percent of the Northern Ireland population (1.8 million) and Protestants 48 percent, but ethno-religious identities are breaking down with new economic migrants, a degree of security in the post-Agreement state and—it is argued here—the impact of class. This process of labor market restructuring and class restratification have also reshaped space, social relations between Catholics and Protestants in mixed areas and growing competition in poor neighborhoods.

Table 10.1 sets out the main spatial demographic changes between 2001 and 2011. It shows that there has been a comparatively modest increase in the number of electoral wards (582 wards in Northern Ireland) where no community has a majority of more than 50 percent from 13 (2.2 percent) to 18 (4.8 percent). However, there is a substantial decrease in the number of single-identity wards (where one community has more than 80 percent of the ward population) from 55.5 percent of all wards to 37.1 percent. In other words, the most segregated areas have remained broadly segregated, but already mixed areas appear to have become even more integrated. Yet, as the mixed city has become more prosperous with better-skilled jobs and services, the poor city has become more fatalistic and is increasingly characterized by ethnocratic tendencies.

Table 10.1 Residential segregation and mixing in Northern Ireland, 2001–11.

Either Religion	2001 Wards		2011 Wards	
	No	**%**	**No**	**%**
Less than 50%	13	2.2	28	4.8
50–59%	88	15.1	98	16.8
60–69%	94	16.2	106	18.2
70–79%	93	16.0	134	23.0
80–89%	146	25.1	153	26.3
90%	148	25.4	63	10.8

Source: Paul Nolan, *Peace Monitoring Report Number 2* (Belfast: Community Relations Council, 2013), 120.

Yiftachel and Ghanem[20] argued that ethnocratic regimes use power, economics and space to assert group rights over citizenship entitlements. They necessarily enhance the process of ethnicizing contested territory and their key features include:

- Ethnicity, and not citizenship, forms the main basis for resource and power allocation.
- The dominant ethnic nation appropriates the state apparatus and shapes the political system, public institutions, geography, economy and culture, so as to expand and deepen its control over state and territory.
- Political boundaries privilege the co-ethnic of the dominant group over minority citizens in order to squeeze out a clearly defined *demos*.
- Politics are ethnicized, as the ethnic logic of power distribution polarizes the body politic and party system.
- Rigid forms of ethnic segregation and socioeconomic forces are maintained, despite countervailing market forces.[21]

Writing on the Middle East, Yiftachel and Graham were especially interested in the way in which the Israeli state used a program of planned settlements to colonialize and control Arab territory. They saw ethnocracy linked to sovereign state interests, but cities coming out of conflict also exhibit variegated forms of ethnocratic features and practices. Post-conflict places do not change in linear ways, away from violence and toward an universal liberal peace, but retain fragments of ethnicity and sectarianism at the same time as they modernize infrastructure, housing markets and the wider economy. Moreover, the people and places not material to market adjustment are left behind but also regressively conditioned by ethnocratic competition and reterritorialization. In Belfast, the legacy is 99 peace lines and related physical artifacts (gates, closed roads or neutral buffer zones) that form the interface between Protestant and Catholic communities. Table 10.2 shows that three-quarters of these (77) are in the north and west of the city, with only one in south Belfast. The Belfast Interface Project[22] groups the 99 structures into 13 clusters where a number of peace lines are linked to form more concentrated and contested geographies. These are also summarized in Figure 10.1, which again illustrates that they are more prominent in the north and west of the city.

Table 10.2 Interface structures in Belfast.

Type	Total	Central	East	North	South	West
Metal fence	35	5	1	18	0	11
Wall with metal fence above	23	3	4	8	1	7
Buffer with fence	14	4	3	3	0	4
Road closed pedestrian access only	12	1	0	10	0	1
Solid wall	8	0	2	5	0	1
Gate with vehicle access	7	1	0	0	0	6
Total	**99**	**14**	**10**	**44**	**1**	**30**

Source: Belfast Interface Project (BIP). *Security Barriers and Defensive Use of Space* (Belfast: Belfast Interface Project, 2011), 9.

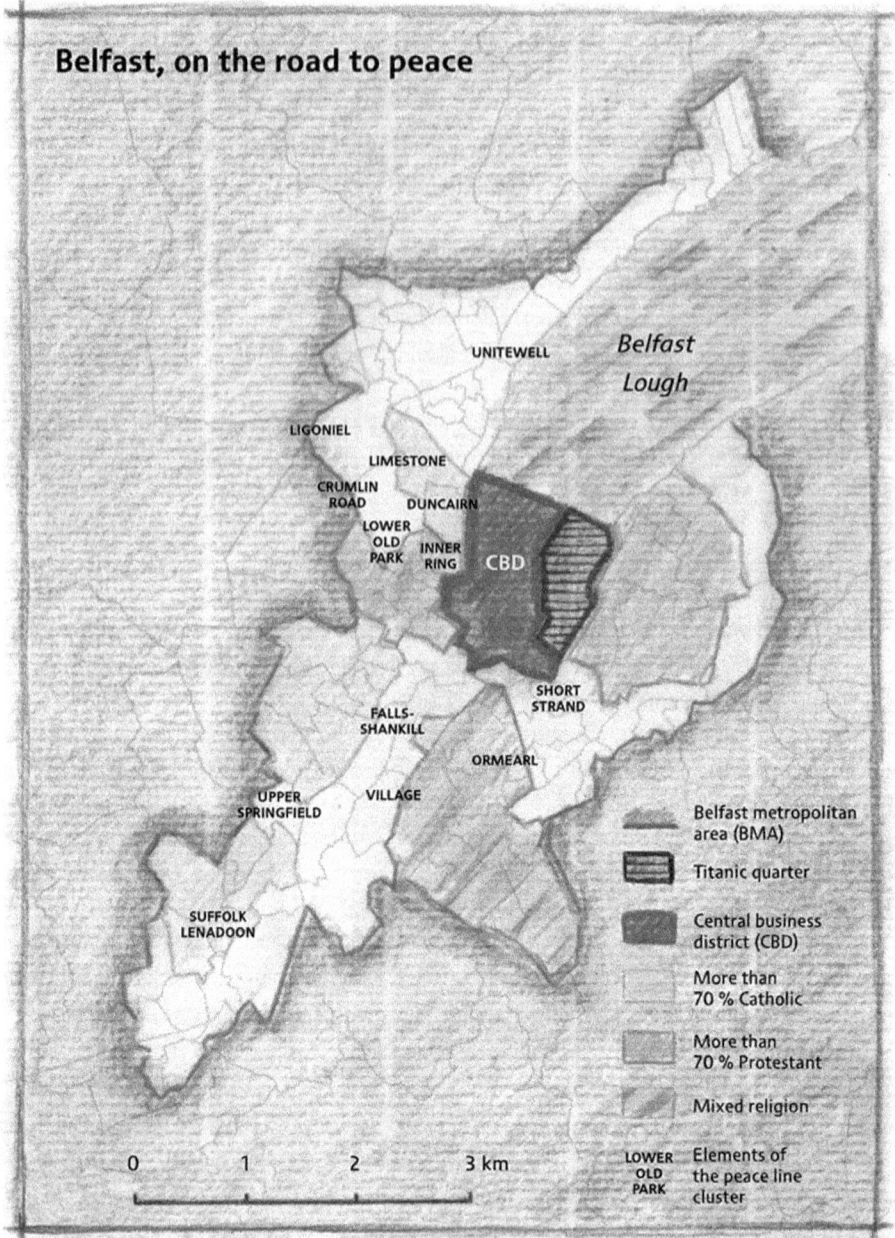

Belfast, on the road to peace

UNITEWELL

Belfast Lough

LIGONIEL

LIMESTONE

CRUMLIN ROAD

DUNCAIRN

LOWER OLD PARK

INNER RING

CBD

SHORT STRAND

FALLS-SHANKILL

ORMEARL

UPPER SPRINGFIELD

VILLAGE

SUFFOLK LENADOON

Belfast metropolitan area (BMA)

Titanic quarter

Central business district (CBD)

More than 70 % Catholic

More than 70 % Protestant

Mixed religion

LOWER OLD PARK — Elements of the peace line cluster

0   1   2   3 km

Figure 10.1 Religious distribution and neighborhoods within Belfast. Drawing by Philippe Rekacewicz, 2014.

Shirlow and Murtagh[23] audited the social ecology of the interfaces and showed that they experience multiple disadvantages, especially because of their disconnection from the wider metropolitan economy. Interface and poor areas generally face what economists refer to as a spatial and skills mismatch.[24] In the first, investment wants the prime sites, close to knowledge production and especially the main university in the south of the city. They no longer need—and have little interest in—former sites of industrial production, which have been degraded by decades of capital flight. In the second, the types of skills investors demand are also knowledge intensive, while the poorest areas exhibit depressingly low educational attainment and significant failings in even basic literacy and numeracy standards. Thus, O'Hearn[25] showed that—of the seven inward investments in west Belfast since 1997—only one remained by 2007, employing just 27 people. The financial cost of segregation has also been high on the British government's attempt to reshape the interface as an economic discourse. A government-commissioned report suggested that the diseconomies of the segregation could mount to £1.5 billion per annum in direct, indirect and opportunity costs, especially in lost jobs, investment and impact on tourism.[26] Interaction between segregated communities is minimal as fear causes each to seek the protection of its own shops, schools, health care services and entertainment.

Investors are also unlikely to be attracted to a deteriorating environment that has been blighted by disinvestment, violence and demographic instability. Only those with the least power in the housing market live near the interface, reproducing a residualized population of the unemployed, unemployable and poor. As Shirlow[27] showed, extant paramilitaries have reformed and criminalized to exploit the most vulnerable; sectarianize and control through intimidation and fear; and stamp on any progressive contact with the other. Houses and land are abandoned, especially in Protestant neighborhoods where lower birth rates, smaller family sizes and aging all reduce the population's capacity for self-renewal. Peace lines are also not especially useful at producing peace as 67 percent of all deaths during the violence happened less than 500 meters from an interface.[28] Ethnocracy is deeply embedded and hard to shift as these places are problematized as deviant, untreatable and socially regressive.

Collaborative Economics on the Interface

The challenge for the most disadvantaged and divided places is how to resist, adapt and sustain alternatives to these conditions and the hegemony of the market, sectarian politics and boosterist urban policies. Interface work has been slow to develop into a coherent response and has been, almost inevitably, reactive and concerned with management rather than transformative change. The dominant narratives indicate that these are spaces that need to be securitized and better policed, especially with more effective dividing strategies using the built environment as a buffer to separate communities. They need to be safely contained and prevented from infecting the growth economy in the *good* city, which in turn, enables them to be written down in policy terms.

However, there are some practices of resistance based on pragmatic forms of collaborative exchange especially focused on the development of alternative community-owned economies and social enterprises. McGarry and O'Leary[29] argued that community relations practice in Northern Ireland is often based on a simplistic form of liberal collaboration. The Contact Hypothesis suggests that prejudice, bolstered by segregation in schools, housing and employment, can be reduced, if not eliminated, by a deeper understanding of the other community. Certainly, such reciprocation helps, but it tends to devalue the complexities of ethnocracy and the way in which segregation is manipulated as a political resource. The collaborative paradigm is, however, deeply embedded in Anglo-Saxon approaches to spatial planning and conflict resolution.[30] Healey argues that spatial contests can be resolved via collective mediation in which the perspectives of different stakeholders are acknowledged, debated and worked through to an accommodation that satisfies the protagonists. For Yiftachel[31] and Pløger,[32] such prescription is simplistic, crucially because it fails to acknowledge the way in which power (economic, political, paramilitary and ethnic) is constitutive of socio-spatial relations. Yiftachel thus argues for a more specific engagement with planning's dark side, the inevitable competition between spatial interests and especially the uneven distribution of resources. Pløger highlights the centrality of agonism, which acknowledges how power works within and between communities; between communities and politicians; and between the neighborhood and the market. Negotiation, he claims, needs to be shaped around a purpose or limited agreement that finds common cause on which transformative change can be based. This acknowledges and addresses inequalities and also shapes discursive practice scripted around mutual negotiated outcomes, not the dissolution of differences.

The social economy has been traditionally strong in Belfast, supported by community-based credit unions, a culture of self-help (especially linked to Protestant and Catholic churches) and service provision, particularly in social care. Disinvestment and welfare displacement has left a space for communities to expand services and grow profitable business in working-class neighborhoods. For some, this has implicated social enterprises in the same neoliberal welfarism they purport to resist, but for others, it has radicalized local services, enabled social profit and created new circuits of neighborhood production and consumption.[33] If economics, at least in part, explains life chances in segregated neighborhoods, then local accumulation and redistribution is an option worthy of further exploration. One successful model, and there are not many, is a social enterprise that was formed after a decade of collaboration on a west Belfast interface. The role of collaborative economics in restructuring borderscapes also emphasizes the value of researching how local agency can disrupt, reconfigure and open real as well as figurative gateways, even in apparently solid dividing walls.

Suffolk is a small Protestant housing estate of approximately 800 people surrounded by the mainly Catholic neighborhood of Lenadoon of around 3,000 people. The interface was formed as the population shifts of the 1970s left residual pockets of minority enclaves bounded by physical peace lines. Initial contacts between the two communities centered on the very mundane need for traffic lights across the Stewartstown Road that formed part of the interface, but this stimulated a debate, especially between women's groups concerned with child safety. The gendered nature of the work was important and focused attention on a range of related problems such as childcare places, women returning to work and the need to draw children away from interface violence. Relationships remained delicate with intercommunity conflict flaring up at times of heightened political tension, such as during disputes over traditional Loyalist parades in the mid-1990s. The impact of this wider context was explained by a Protestant community worker:

> Even though things eventually did die down it looked as if the whole interface initiative was finished. People were interviewed in the media, saying that after what they went through how could they ever be expected to trust the other side. So it did look as though the whole thing was near to collapse.[34]

After a cooling-off period, tentative meetings were resumed, but with the risk that issues such as parading had the potential to destabilize relationships. As a result, a mobile telephone network was established among community workers. Thus, any signs of violence were identified and dealt with by activists on both sides of the interface, which consolidated trust building between a wider group of community workers. A joint statement helped to prepare both sides to handle disputes and laid the foundation for further cross-community dialogue. This reengagement led to the formation of the Suffolk-Lenadoon Interface Group (SLIG) to deal with two very specific issues: the need to address the physical environment of the Stewartstown Road interface; and the development of durable cross-community governance structures.

In this context, Yiftachel's concern with governance is again instructive as it emphasizes the importance of more useful and lasting arrangements to manage conflict and deliver change. A social enterprise company was formed called the Stewartstown Road Regeneration Project (SRRP), managed by four members of the Lenadoon Community Forum, four from the Suffolk Community Forum, and four independent members recruited for their expertise in urban regeneration. In essence, each of the two communities owned a one-third shareholding in the company with independents retaining the remaining one-third. Any profits would be redistributed evenly between the three sets of interests. The company focused on a single project to rebuild a two-story block of shops and offices on the Stewartstown Road. Retailing on the ground floor generated commercial rent while the upper story was allocated for offices for the community groups and local service businesses. The development of the project was supported by an external facilitator to help address the legal, financial and constitutional aspects of the project. This resulted in a written agreement on the use of sectarian symbols, flags and emblems and processes for dealing with intercommunity conflict.

The next challenge involved bringing the wider communities more deeply into the process using public presentations of the plans and civic engagement on both sides of the divide. SLIG again highlighted the role of women in this activity, especially in Suffolk, where they negotiated with Loyalist paramilitaries and a fairly fatalistic community, often at considerable personal risk:

> These women were all very vocal and made themselves very unpopular with some of the things that they said and some of the things they did, but they were prepared to step out and try something.[35]

Despite these reservations, a public meeting produced almost unanimous support for the project as a mutually successful solution to local development needs. This led to the

Peace-Building Plan as a physical statement agreeing to the use of contested spaces and development priorities: "The Plan will respect the positions and values of each community while specifically seeking to:

- Identify shared spaces that can be accessed by both communities;
- Identify activities that are required to provide security and build confidence within and between communities; and,
- Identify and respect that some activities, services and spaces will not be addressed in the short term but may form part of future options."[36]

Several mutual advantages were advanced to both communities to gain endorsement for the project, with an emphasis placed on potential mutual benefits. The Plan argued that:

- The redevelopment would help to ensure the longer-term sustainability of the Suffolk community and a survey with teenagers showed that the majority of young people planned to leave the estate as soon as they could;
- The redevelopment would secure existing services (a grocery store and post office) and provide much-needed new services;
- Job opportunities and investment would result from the redevelopment of the site; and,
- Community ownership and gain so that any profits generated from the social enterprises would be reinvested equally between the company and each community forum.[37]

Funding for the project came from the government, the European Union (EU) and US philanthropists and, when opened in 2002, the £1.5 million center completely reshaped the interface, physically as well as socially. It comprised a mix of commercial, retail and community uses: shop units, including a post office, convenience store, pharmacy and restaurant; health and social care services; and community meeting space. The police reported a significant drop in interface violence, the rental units were fully occupied and commercial confidence was reflected in the construction of a new private retail store on an adjacent site on the Stewartstown Road. The second phase of the project involved the development of a 50-place childcare center supported by EU Structural Funds and by £70,000 from the company's own profits. This profit had accumulated from rental income from the first phase and enabled the SRRP to leverage EU and government capital funding for the facility.

Table 10.3 shows the local economic impact of the new interface complex. Nearly 24,000 square feet of floor space provided 12 new services, more than 90 jobs and nearly £200,000 in rental income per annum. The organization was financially sound, holding £1.7 million worth of assets and more than £200,000 of unrestricted reserves to reinvest in new projects (including the second-phase development of the childcare center). The complex created nearly £1.5 million per annum in salaries in the neighborhood economy, which in turn supported services housed in the center. This minimized financial leakage from the area and helped the SRRP to recycle income and expenditure to create local multiplier effects.

Table 10.3 SRRP performance indicators.

Performance Indicator	Number
Size of development	22,370 square feet
Rental units	12
Tangible assets	£1,700,404
Rental income	£198,493
Total reserves	£202,080
Childcare places	50
Total employment	92
Salaries generated in the community	£1,493,000
Surplus for community reinvestment	£60,015

Source: Stewartstown Road Regeneration Project (SRRP). *Annual Report and Financial Statements 31 May 2012* (Belfast: Stewartstown Road Regeneration Project, 2012).

This approach also extends to the development and use of profits. The financial accounts for 2011–12 showed that the SRRP generated nearly £100,000 surplus in the previous financial year.[38] As noted earlier, under its governance rules one-third was retained by the company and one-third was allocated to the Suffolk and Lenadoon Forums, respectively. This supported community development projects, which in the prior year reflected the everyday concerns of residents in both areas. For example, it supported a locally based advice service specifically linked to recent welfare reform proposals, which will have a disproportionate effect on disadvantaged neighborhoods. The program set out the implications of reform and the rationalization of payments, taught how to maximize entitlements and provided practical support in relation to the new regulations. Similarly, the Forums were able to support 20 scholarships to a university access program, youth contact schemes and initiatives to strengthen mutual understanding across different cultures in local schools.

Knox[39] surveyed the residents on both sides of the interface and showed that 90 percent supported the Peace-Building Plan, although this was higher in Catholic Lenadoon (95 percent) than in Protestant Suffolk (83 percent), where insecurities and vulnerabilities connected with their comparative size persist. The Stewartstown Road is still an interface, but the interface has been revalorized as a service site, place of employment and a safe space to meet. In what Amin[40] referred to as the "engineering of endless tasks of interaction between adversaries," the social enterprise has created economic value, locally accountable ownership and the shared use of surpluses. Knox[41] showed that only 14 percent of residents (13 percent in Lenadoon and 15 percent in Suffolk) felt that the complex and peace-building process had not brought benefits, and he concluded that it had changed social relations, cross-community attitudes and a preference for sharing.

Conclusions

Belfast has changed remarkably in the past 15 years. Violence has effectively ended, there is new investment and, for the educated, there is a decent chance of a good job.

The Agreement and the stabilization of political institutions have brought a degree of economic growth and new spaces for sharing and residential mixing. However, the social, economic and spatial selectivity of these processes has the potential to destabilize the city and even the wider peace process. The recent increase in attacks by dissident Republican paramilitary groups and local disputes over Loyalist parades and how to deal with the past reflect uneasiness about how peace is experienced in the areas that suffered most in the conflict. Where capital has failed to assert itself or is not interested in doing so, eth-nocracy in the form of sectarian competition, interfacing and poverty has filled the space. Urban policy has pump-primed major investment sites, especially along the waterfront, following the standard regeneration models used in nearly every other late-industrial city in the global North.

The same cannot be said for the interface, which does not have a dedicated spatial policy, resources or ambitious governance to tackle its complex problems. Its residents are ignored, securitized or held responsible to pull themselves out of poverty and sectarian-ism. It is interesting that the Suffolk-Lenadoon initiative was financially supported more by the EU and the United States than by the local administration. It has not removed the peace line, but it has fundamentally altered it, possibly on the way to being something less divisive. The community owns the asset, manages it effectively, creates local multiplier effects and reinvests in the social, cultural and environmental life of its neighborhoods. It is an interstitial space that needs to be understood more deeply: is it simply a form of local pragmatism or a meaningful gateway through a previously impermeable peace wall? It does reflect a degree of political agency expressed through a more collaborative approach to economic exchange and the use of local assets and a different set of rela-tionships than the self-censorship that existed before. Whether this has altered the social ecology in a more deeply structural sense and whether such change can be scaled and replicated to other borderscapes is an area of potential research across contested cities.

NOTES

1 Wendy Pullan and Britt Baillie. *Locating Urban Conflicts: Ethnicity, Nationalism and the Everyday* (Basingstoke: Palgrave, 2013).
2 Oren Yiftachel, "Theoretical Notes on 'Gray Cities': The Coming of Urban Apartheid?" *Planning Theory* 8 (2009): 88–100.
3 Vanessa Watson, "Deep Difference: Diversity, Planning and Ethics." *Planning Theory* 5 (2006): 31–50.
4 Jamie Peck and Adam Tickell. "Neoliberalising Space." *Antipode* 34 (2002): 380–404.
5 Belfast Interface Project (BIP). *Security Barriers and Defensive Use of Space*. Belfast: Belfast Interface Project, 2011.
6 Peter Shirlow, *The End of Ulster Loyalism?* Manchester: Manchester University Press, 2012.
7 Frederick Boal, "Belfast: Walls Within." *Political Geography* 21 (2002): 687–94.
8 Ibid., 689.
9 Colin Knox, "Peace Building in Northern Ireland: A Role for Civil Society." *Social Policy and Society* 10 (2010): 13–28.
10 Peck and Tickell, "Neoliberalising Space," 381.
11 Ibid.
12 John Clark, "Living With/in and Without Neoliberalism." *Focaal* 5 (2008): 135–47.

13 Jamie Peck, Nik Theodore and Neal Brenner, "Postneoliberalism and Its Malcontents." *Antipode* 4 (2010): 94–116.

14 Noel Castree, "Crisis, Continuity and Change: Neoliberalism, the Left and the Future of Capitalism." *Antipode* 41 (2009): 185–213.

15 Neal Brenner and Nik Theodore, "Cities and the Geographies of Actually Existing Neoliberalism," *Antipode* 34 (2002): 349–79, 349.

16 Peter Shirlow and Brendan Murtagh, *Belfast: Segregation, Violence and the City* (London: Pluto Press, 2006).

17 Paul Nolan, *Peace Monitoring Report Number 2*. Belfast: Community Relations Council, 2013.

18 Ian Shuttleworth and Christopher Lloyd. "Are Northern Ireland's Two Communities Dividing? Evidence from the Census of Population Data 1971–2001." *Environment and Planning A* 41 (2009): 213–29.

19 Nolan, *Peace Monitoring Report Number 2*.

20 Oren Yiftachel and Asad Ghanem. "Understanding 'Ethnocratic' Regimes: The Politics of Seizing Contested Territories," *Political Geography* 23 (2004): 647–76.

21 Ibid., 650.

22 Belfast Interface Project (BIP), *Security Barriers and Defensive Use of Space*.

23 Shirlow and Murtagh, *Belfast*.

24 Simon Bridge, Brendan Murtagh and Kenneth O'Neill, *Understanding the Social Economy and the Third Sector* (Basingstoke: Palgrave, 2013).

25 Denis O'Hearn, "How Has Peace Changed the Northern Irish Economy?" *Ethnopolitics* 7 (2008): 101–18.

26 Deloitte. *Research into the Financial Cost of the Northern Ireland Divide* (Belfast: Deloitte, 2007), 90.

27 Shirlow, *The End of Ulster Loyalism?*

28 Shirlow and Murtagh, *Belfast*, 73.

29 John McGarry and Brendan O'Leary, "Power Shared after Deaths of Thousands," in *Consociational Theory: McGarry and O'Leary and the Northern Ireland Conflict*, ed. Rupert Taylor (London: Routledge, 2009), 15–84.

30 Patsy Healey, *Making Better Places: The Planning Project in the 21st Century* (Basingstoke: Palgrave, 2010).

31 Yiftachel, "Theoretical Notes on 'Gray Cities,'" 88–100.

32 John Pløger, "Strife: Urban Planning and Agonism." *Planning Theory* 3 (2004): 71–92.

33 Bridge, Murtagh and O'Neill, *Understanding the Social Economy and the Third Sector.*

34 Michael Hall, *Building Bridges at the Grassroots: The Experience of Suffolk-Lenadoon Interface Group.* Belfast: Island Publications, 2007, 21.

35 Ibid., 26.

36 Suffolk Lenadoon Interface Group (SLIG) *Peacebuilding Plan*, Belfast: Suffolk Lenadoon Interface Group, 2.

37 Ibid., 3.

38 Stewartstown Road Regeneration Project (SRRP). *Annual Report and Financial Statements 31 May 2012*. Belfast: Stewartstown Road Regeneration Project, 2012.

39 Knox, "Peace Building in Northern Ireland," 21.

40 Ash Amin, "Ethnicity and the Multicultural City: Living With Diversity." *Environment and Planning A* 34 (2002): 959–80, 969.

41 Knox, "Peace Building in Northern Ireland," 22.

BIBLIOGRAPHY

Amin, Ash. "Ethnicity and the Multicultural City: Living With Diversity." *Environment and Planning A* 34 (2002): 959–80.

Belfast Interface Project (BIP). *Security Barriers and Defensive Use of Space*. Belfast: Belfast Interface Project, 2011.

Boal, Frederick. "Belfast: Walls Within." *Political Geography* 21 (2002): 687–94.

Brenner, Neal and Nik Theodore. "Cities and the Geographies of Actually Existing Neoliberalism," *Antipode* 34 (2002): 349–79.

Bridge, Simon, Brendan Murtagh and Kenneth O'Neill. *Understanding the Social Economy and the Third Sector.* Basingstoke: Palgrave, 2013.

Castree, Noel. "Crisis, Continuity and Change: Neoliberalism, the Left and the Future of Capitalism." *Antipode* 41 (2009): 185–213.

Clark, John. "Living With/in and Without Neoliberalism." *Focaal* 5 (2008): 135–47.

Deloitte. *Research into the Financial Cost of the Northern Ireland Divide.* Belfast: Deloitte, 2007.

Hall, Michael. *Building Bridges at the Grassroots: The Experience of Suffolk-Lenadoon Interface Group.* Belfast: Island Publications, 2007.

Healey, Patsy. *Making Better Places: The Planning Project in the 21st Century.* Basingstoke: Palgrave, 2010.

Knox, Colin. "Peace Building in Northern Ireland: A Role for Civil Society." *Social Policy and Society* 10 (2010): 13–28.

McGarry, John and Brendan O'Leary. "Power Shared after Deaths of Thousands." In *Consociational Theory: McGarry and O'Leary and the Northern Ireland Conflict*, edited by Rupert Taylor, 15–84. London: Routledge, 2009.

Nolan, Paul. *Peace Monitoring Report Number 2.* Belfast: Community Relations Council, 2013.

O'Hearn, Denis. "How Has Peace Changed the Northern Irish Economy?" *Ethnopolitics* 7 (2008): 101–18.

Peck, Jamie, Nik Theodore and Neal Brenner. "Postneoliberalism and Its Malcontents." *Antipode* 4 (2010): 94–116.

Peck, Jamie and Adam Tickell. "Neoliberalising Space." *Antipode* 34 (2002): 380–404.

Pløger, John. "Strife: Urban Planning and Agonism." *Planning Theory* 3 (2004): 71–92.

Pullan, Wendy and Britt Baillie. *Locating Urban Conflicts: Ethnicity, Nationalism and the Everyday.* Basingstoke: Palgrave, 2013.

Shirlow, Peter. *The End of Ulster Loyalism?* Manchester: Manchester University Press, 2012.

Shirlow, Peter and Brendan Murtagh. *Belfast: Segregation, Violence and the City.* London: Pluto Press, 2006.

Shuttleworth, Ian and Christopher Lloyd. "Are Northern Ireland's Two Communities Dividing? Evidence from the Census of Population Data 1971–2001." *Environment and Planning A* 41 (2009): 213–29.

Stewartstown Road Regeneration Project (SRRP). *Annual Report and Financial Statements 31 May 2012.* Belfast: Stewartstown Road Regeneration Project, 2012.

Watson, Vanessa. "Deep Difference: Diversity, Planning and Ethics." *Planning Theory* 5 (2006): 31–50.

Yiftachel, Oren. "Theoretical Notes on 'Gray Cities': The Coming of Urban Apartheid?" *Planning Theory* 8 (2009): 88–100.

Yiftachel, Oren and Asad Ghanem. "Understanding 'Ethnocratic' Regimes: The Politics of Seizing Contested Territories." *Political Geography* 23 (2004): 647–76.

Part IV

PORTALS: DIALOGUE, EXCEPTION AND RETERRITORIALIZATION

Chapter Eleven

AUSTRALIA DAY: A SOCIAL ECOLOGY DIALOGUE ACROSS ABORIGINAL AND WHITE CULTURES

Carol Birrell and Stuart B. Hill

Australia Day, January 27, 2011, is a big event in the Australian calendar. It is a public holiday much anticipated and dreaded by parents and children, respectively, as it indicates the end of the long summer school holidays. The general populous sees it as a time to don the cloth of nationalism in the proclamation of the nation-state. Overall, it is a day of raw exuberance and celebration, but sometimes it gets ugly; it is the irruption of a nationalist sentiment that influences who is wanted and who is not wanted on these shores.

There is a little cove on the shores of Sydney Harbour, a favored haunt of tourists and Japanese brides alike, where the Sydney Harbour Bridge and the Opera House vie for prime camera attention. A small but significant crowd gathers in the pre-dawn. Uncle Max is only slightly nervous. He has been locked up with 30 or so dancers for the past four days, refining the performance that will tell the stories of his *country*[1]—Yuin country (which extends from Merimbula to Port Jackson)—about five hours' drive south of Sydney. They will dance the stories of the sacred mountain Biamunga. The dance is new, the original one long lost in the colonial dismemberment of Aboriginal culture. Today Australia "celebrates" more than 200 years of white occupancy.

Uncle Max Harrison is known as Dulumunmun, the tribal name both his son and grandson also hold. It was a privilege to bestow that name on his blood. There is no language now—just a few words, the odd expression. He's an aged Elder with a silver grey beard, longish hair to match and a plump, firm belly that hangs over his tightened belt. He is diabetic like most of his *mob*.[2] He knows today is important, not for the reasons that most people think, but for the fact that he will soon see an enactment of his culture that has been absent on this land for at least 150 years.

It has been no easy process to fill the gaps in the story and to let the choreographers translate it into dance. He had to trust and shape the product as if he was softening and working the ochre or white clay that he smears on the dancers' bodies to indicate Yuin affiliation, even though (because of the impacts of colonization) most of them are not Yuin. He fidgets with his belt, knowing his job is now done, and looks expectantly toward the hill from which the officials will come. The governor-general and the premier of the state are the regal and legal representatives that add weight to the day. He has put on a shirt and long pants instead of his ubiquitous shorts, and black tight shoes instead of his flattened brown sandals. The empty chairs begin to fill, except for the front two rows saved for the dignitaries, their RESERVED signs printed in bold type. Uncle Max watches each person closely as they arrive and fluff out their feathers before alighting on their nests.

It's his friend the lyrebird, the great imitator, who is here now. Not only can the lyrebird mimic the songs of a myriad of other birds, but also the sounds of all that modern life brings: the chainsaw, tractor, motorbike and even a child's shout of laughter. Uncle Max laughs as he recalls the day he found one's nest on the top of Biamunga. He got the shock of his life to discover that it was not just sound the bird could reproduce. There was the bird, strutting a traditional dance that had not been seen in many years. Someone in the crowd sees Uncle Max laugh, his body flinching with the movements of the lyrebird. His right wing has not the flexibility it once had, but it still holds proud. A few of his *mob* on Biamunga that day had tried to learn the dance from that bird, determined to capture it with gratitude and respect for the transmission of knowledge between bird and human.

Uncle Max knows that the people here today will gather to watch a dance, a token gesture of acknowledgment for a day that makes invisible the lived reality of other lives. Then they will move on, with scarcely another thought about the Yuin Elder and the performance, and what it all might mean.

He thinks back to Biamunga, the sacred initiation site that fills him with such grief. He sees the sanctified pools where he was led as a young man, taken through *law*[3] by his grandfather and four other Elders. He was snatched out of the bush camp to be trained in the knowledge of his people, and then thrown into the white world feeling full of incomprehension. That day his ochre-painted body slid down the smoothed granite slide into those pools where the blood from the initiation process was washed off, a replication of what had been done by thousands of young men before him—dumped into the big, deep, freezing pool of ceremony. His body shivers in remembrance.

But now look at all those white kids loving the same slide; their shrieks and giggles are no less infectious than in his day. Suddenly, he is taken to the base of the mountain, to the swathe of forest that has been cut down by the latest round of hungry Japanese logging. The sickness returns right in his liver, the nausea that won't leave. He knows the logging has cut right through the spiritual connection of that mountain, removing the scales from the back of the serpent. His despair makes him want to turn and leave this place beside the harbor, the false haven of security. There is weariness in his being from a lifetime of trying to get Whitefellas, and often also his own Blackfellas, to understand what this culture really means to him and his people—to sense the mountain itself, to know the spirits of the old ancestors that sit there making their presence felt even today. They are here now too, watching over his liver and the spirits of all the dancers who have become the ancestral snake. They also watch over the elegance and beauty of the lyrebird.

Another image presents itself to Uncle Max, one that restores health rather than threatens it. It is a gathering of another kind on that mountain, right below the smashed boulders at the top—a healing ceremony of whites and blacks determined to enable another story. It had been years since he had been here. This time the pain was in his heart, like someone had removed an essential part. He has brought the group here, to this place of powerful communication that now stands mute as a result of the officially sanctioned rock smashing. Once these rocks at the top of this mountain transmitted messages to other *mobs*, far, far away, beyond these shores even, through the potency of a quartz microchip in the swiftly cooled volcanic rock. But once those Whitefellas found it to be a hindrance to their own communication towers, they put an end to it. Blow up the rocks and smash the interference once and for all. Those gathered stand here now in two rows opposite each other, desperately trying to cut out the noxious humming of the giant communication towers, ignoring the pain in their hearts. They perform a simple request for healing by throwing dirt into the center of the rows, so that it can be picked up by Kurakarai Wind Spirit and taken deep into the heart of the mountain. It is over before it has hardly begun, but the small group stands there, not moving. The pain in his heart dissolves.

The dancers are ready to begin. Uncle nods. The dignitaries settle on their nests, preening in the heat and casually glancing at time-ticking wrist watches. The white-painted bodies begin to move to the rustle of leaves as the python rises, head blurred in a puff of white ochre. The ground is pounded with the hard feet of men and nurtured by the soft feet of women; the tough scaly snake caresses the soft earth. Dust rises in a blanket of spirit. The important front-row guests cough into white handkerchiefs. Uncle Max grins as the serpent digs down into the clay, forming sinuous rivers, reeling back up into the mountain, pushing it further and further into Father Sky.
Biamunga lives!

Carol: I wrote this story based on real events in 2011 in Sydney, on a day of national pride and sentiment called Australia Day. Aboriginal people refer to it as Survival Day. The dancers worked with Yuin Elder and Senior Lawman Uncle Max Dulumunmun Harrison over several weeks to hear the stories of his country, to go to the sacred mountain and to translate the stories into dance. Many of the original dances long ago disappeared in the process of colonization and cultural dismemberment.

Stuart: I'm interested in reflecting on this story through a social ecology[‡] lens and thinking about how it might help us find practical solutions for a world in crisis. The role of story has a strong place in any social ecology framing. This emphasizes the possibility of such stories being able to support holistic improvement—where personal, social, environmental and spiritual wellbeing are considered—when seeking to make things better. Also important is the role of the edges or borders between conflicted cultures. One may also think of them as "green lines" or corridors.

Carol: Yes, this story could be construed as yet another take on the contested space between whites and blacks that has played out for more than 200 years on this land. I wanted to show the underbelly, the richness of that space, rather than the toxicity that has often characterized it. This is not to deny the reality of the situation in Australia today, where Aboriginal people are still the dispossessed.

I agree that it's important to bring the notion of time and space into our conversation. Time has a way of collapsing in on itself here in the story, as does place. The Aboriginal concept of *the dreaming* conflates past, present and future into a moment wherein all are bound, called "everywhen" by Stanner.[5] In the story, we move from a time of ancient ceremony on this land, then to the sacred mountain being logged for Japanese pulp mills, and on to a healing ceremony enacted in more recent times that includes Indigenous and non-Indigenous persons. The story sits in the "green line" in your terms, or what we could designate as the liminal space.

Stuart: It's important to ask what might be the ingredients for improvement, to pinpoint the elements that enable reflection, understanding and eventually effective action. For example, Uncle Max is one of these ingredients. In his role as Elder, as the holder and transmitter of knowledge, he carries the culture and its embodied wisdom forward. He "enables" the persistence of his culture and its "gifts" for today's society.

Carol: Uncle Max has this expression, "You gotta give it away in order to keep it" (Max Harrison quoted by Birrell).[6] He is differentiating the role of a "holder" from a "keeper." If a keeper does not transmit his or her knowledge to the next generation, as is his or her responsibility, then the knowledge dies. Such keeping is destructive of culture. So paradoxically, the holder is only able to keep his or her culture alive by passing it on. This is no easy matter in our contemporary economic and political climate. Since white occupation, there has been much distortion of the norm around cultural transmission. There is much complexity here surrounding how many young Aboriginal people refuse or resist that knowledge transmission, or else they are just unable to fit it into a life of sheer survival. In the 15 years I have been working with Uncle Max, I have seen this played out with his children and grandchildren. I have witnessed them growing into roles as knowledge holders for a time, only to throw it all away at another time. This story brings out the weariness of the Elder who has had to struggle to keep his culture alive. It resonates with many other Indigenous cultures, as well as those people who are transplanted into a foreign culture.

Stuart: Well, I think it is worthwhile to draw out issues of similarity and difference here. There are those who are hurt and unhealed, and those who are in a process of ongoing healing. There is a parallel set of experiences in everyone: we are to varying extents all colonized, hurt and discounted and also liberated, healed and with a voice. To communicate those stories, we need to acknowledge similarities and utilize them to stimulate reflection on similar stories in the listener. When things are always expressed as difference, then we can reject them as being other, as being not-of-me.

Carol: What did you make of this story when you first read it?

Stuart: Initially, I felt that it emphasized difference. I think one always has to ask the question, "So what?" What values does the story have attached to it? One needs to respect the landscape and context of the story. Within all cultures there are things that come with those places that have imperatives embodied within them.

Carol: I am now thinking of the notion of *Ganma*[7] or meeting place that has been shared by the Yolngu people in Arnhem Land (Northern Territory). The estuary is the place of the meeting of freshwater and saltwater, a rich source of ecological diversity and productivity. The Yolngu people say that this very productivity, in the heart of the estuary, is also indicative of relations between blacks and whites. The salty brine, which is the product of the intermingling of those two waters, is the *Ganma*. Is this the place that accounts for both similarities and differences?

Stuart: Biological and ecological processes are most intense at the edges between different components and systems. Permaculture, for example, focuses on the vertical and horizontal edges in the design of productive sustainable systems.[8] In all organisms, including humans, membranes of cell walls are the edges where nearly everything goes on.

Carol: Well, the edge in the story between Aboriginal and non-Aboriginal people in contemporary Australia is very much like that cell membrane. It is semipermeable and although it may appear that the flow is primarily in one direction, it is clear that both cultures are touching, the membranous self of one rubbing against the membranous self of another. It is a point of interchange, as the Yolgnu claim, in relation to their process of *Ganma* (referred to earlier); although much of this interchange goes on below the surface, often unnoticed and overlooked.

When the dignitaries arrive in the story, to take up their important positions to watch the Aboriginal dance, little do they know of their transformation into the lyrebird, fluffing out their feathers as they settle on their individual nests. And then the bird transforms itself into Uncle Max, his body flinching with the movements of the lyrebird. Now, some may see this as a metaphorical device, but we are speaking of ancestral presence, as real and palpable in this moment as it was when the stories first emerged. For the surviving Yuni people, these stories are part of their country and their culture. It matters not who "gets" it—it insinuates itself regardless.

Another edge aspect is that the story itself is a fictionalized account—I was not there in person. While I was on the sacred mountain when it was being danced, I was only told part of what went on that day by Uncle Max. Since he has been my teacher over many years, it was not difficult to read between the lines and to imagine this story. Nonetheless, to express myself as a non-Indigenous woman in this way is taking a risk.

Stuart: I also experience the risk of being a white person commenting on this story, and I do so tentatively and with a sense of appreciation of being able to share my thoughts. I am aware also that such Indigenous stories have so often been trivialized with comments such as: "this is just a story"; "this is just art"; or "this is just a dance."

I like the way the story is told from different positions: the conventional way, from the perspective of Uncle Max, from the position of the first-time dance and from the snake itself. I think this is part of what I mentioned earlier as adding value through the multiple layers and expressions of creativity. There is an edge aspect here, too. It is edgy to speak of something that could be dismissed as being unreal, as fictional.

Carol: It seems we are speaking about a systemic view endemic to the social ecology perspective, whereby issues cannot be considered as separate from the whole. So is it possible to hold the multiple positions simultaneously, from the specific to the general? In this case, is the unique situation of Aboriginal people in postcolonial

Australia, at the same time similar to what David Orr calls membership of "a still larger whole, the global commons, indivisible by nation, tribe, religion, ethnicity, language, culture, or politics"?[9] Perhaps this is the role of the liminal place. I find it interesting to think of one of the earliest articulations of the liminal by Arnold van Gennep in the early 1900s.[10] He characterized it as a critical psychological state in traditional cultures that is in between worlds: the newly initiated young adult stands on the threshold of leaving behind the old ways of childhood freedom and irresponsibility before stepping into the roles of adulthood responsibility. As such, it is a site of pleni-potentiality that still holds both worlds, just as the estuary initially holds the freshwater separate from the saltwater, until the two merge and mix into a new substance, the brine. It is a place of flux, and of creativity and development.

Stuart: We are speaking here about change: the moments of change, and the processes involved in change. I have developed something that I call the ESR model of change.[11] Commonly there are three progressive stages involved: efficiency (E), substitution (S) and redesign (R). Redesign/design is an example of a "deep" approach, compared with the more "shallow" strategies of efficiency and substitution. Design approaches address the underlying causes of problems by changing the structure and functioning of the systems involved so that the problems—symptoms of maldesigned and mismanaged systems—no longer arise. In fact, the aim of this approach is to enable well-being and make systems as problem-proof as possible.

Efficiency and substitution approaches can be either stepping stones or stages in a progressive spiral toward redesign, or they can be barriers. Substitution, because it makes the system appear workable, at least in the short term, often acts as a barrier. This is helped by the fact that it is compatible with our market economy, which is based on the repeated purchase of products whose benefits are not long lasting.

Most modern organic farming is still dependent on substitution strategies, with synthetic chemicals being replaced by natural fertilizers and sprays, and by biological controls. Organic producers commonly purchase things like humates, seaweed sprays, botanical pesticides, microorganism inoculants and biological controls, all of which provide benefits that could be created on-site if the systems were designed and managed to provide them.

For example, optimal decomposition of organic matter in soil results in the production of growth-promoting hormones, such as cytokinins, and the release of trace minerals, which are two of the main benefits that seaweed products provide. Decomposition also results in the formation cytokinins and of humate-like materials; and the decomposers provide food for a diverse range of predators, which are, in turn, capable of controlling many of the pests.

The problem with imports is that their benefits are always temporary. At least some of the resources that they are made from are exhaustible and will eventually run out, so systems dependent on them can never be sustainable. Taking such approaches also encourages us to postpone dealing with the underlying causes of our problems. Many parallels can be recognized in the health care field and, indeed, in every area of society.

What I am describing here is a progression from taking a deceptively simple approach, in which we think that products like pesticides and fertilizers or their substitutes are the solution to a confusing and sometimes paralyzing complex approach, in which we try to understand, control and micromanage everything. It often takes considerable persistence to pass through this challenging and frustrating stage to achieve the more sustainable and rewarding profoundly simple stage. This usually involves understanding paradox and tuning in to the wisdoms of the ages and nature, including our own often untapped natural intelligence and intuition. This is one area where indigenous cultures, with their long history of having progressed through these stages to discover such core wisdoms, have much to offer our often still quite naïve cultures.

Sadly there is very little support in our society for genuine redesign (or, indeed, for wisdom-based decision making). This is particularly because of the powerful influences of the pharmaceutical and petrochemical industries on governments. They know that with appropriate redesign/design, most of their products would no longer be needed.

Also, it is relevant to realize that modern evidence-based decision making is often not based on the most important factors because evidence can be provided only for what is known, and in most situations the bulk of what is going on is unknown, focusing on the known favors (shallow) cleverness over (deep and broad) wisdom. This is why I always distinguish between "shallow" and "deep" approaches to change. André Voisin speaks about the sum total of human knowledge as being a small dot within the huge circle of what is unknown.[12] The question is: how do you engage with the whole thing, when most of it is unknown?

Carol: This too is certainly a threshold place, where one is on the edge, within liminal space. The new initiate does not really know what he or she is in for, but there is knowledge of what may need to be left behind. The uncertainty of the not-knowing is pervasive. The initiate must now step forward as there is no going back to that other place. This is the moment the human species is confronted with right now. Because we lack clear ideas about what to do in the circumstances facing our culture, there is much postponement. Many turn away, tune out and retreat from exercising any individual, let alone collective responsibility. There is much confusion about the roles we need to be taking. Climate change, for example, is not just a conversation between humans; it is a kind of *Ganma* process between humans and the Earth that has been occurring for more than 200,000 years.

Stuart: It is "guts" and "experience" that we have lost within this instrumentalized world; and the computer can't be called on to deliver the kind of holistic wisdom that is needed.

Carol: This is why I cannot understand the view that says archaic cultures are just that, a relic from the past that can offer no new ideas relevant to the present, let alone the future. We have a cultural continuity in this country that holds the memory of the last ice age and far beyond, yet where do we see partnerships being set up to share this kind of knowledge? Uncle Max is able to point out sites and teachings from these places, still important in their contemporary relevance, that are now buried under the rising oceans following the glacial melt. Peter Knudson and David Suzuki have written about such "wisdom of the elders," but for most, this remains a token gesture in our indigenous-phobic world.[13]

The officials and dignitaries in the story embody the type of ignorance and "not knowing" that I am referring to. They glance at their watches, impatient to move on, unaware of the richness, complexity and relevance of what is being offered: an extraordinary storehouse of Earth wisdom. I recall a wonderful quote by Australian writer Peter Carey in his novel *Oscar and Lucinda*:

> My great-grandfather drifted up the Bellinger River like a blind man up the central aisle of Notre Dame. He saw nothing. The country was thick with sacred stories more ancient than the ones he carried in his sweat-slippery leather Bible. He did not even imagine their presence. Some of these stories were as small as the transparent arthropods that lived in the puddles beneath the river casuarinas. These stories were like fleas, thrips, so tiny that they might inhabit a place (inside the ears of the seeds of grass) he would later walk across without even seeing. In this landscape every rock had a name, and most names had spirits, ghosts, meanings.[14]

Stuart: In our social ecology model, there is a place for engaging with the unknown, and with this kind of indigenous wisdom.[15] We need to engage with the spiritual and unconscious aspects of our lives to be able to contextualize the other circles (the personal, social and ecological) of our more conscious knowing. When we are seeking to understand the sources of wisdom, we must consider the difference between profound experience and that of the novice or neophyte. When I speak about similarity and difference, I want to stress that both are important, with neither of them having privilege over the other. This is similar to when notions of both the "known" and "unknown" are acknowledged and taken into account in every situation. We need to be in the unknown to learn and in the known (or what can be known at that moment and place) to act. Progress involves moving in an upward spiral between these two processes of engagement; and between these two stages is a less visible liminal/transitional stage, during which most creativity, development and evolution occurs.

Carol: I want to return to one of your earlier comments about edges and their horizontal and vertical relationships.

Stuart: And also the tangential!

Carol: In this regard, I like the way Deleuze and Guattari delimit an ecological model of the rhizome in *A Thousand Plateaus*. "The rhizome has no beginning or end; it is always in the middle between things, interbeing, intermezzo."[16] It seems to not only fit what we are broadly talking about, especially in reflecting in a social-ecological way, but it also captures the unique way that Aboriginal culture sits within contemporary Australia, in that liminal space.

The rhizome is both a bulb and a tuber, and has a prolific horizontal underground network. Since it is subterranean, it is unseen by most people. Traditionally, digging for tubers was women's work, with women using a digging stick with a sharp point for the task. I have an image of old women squatting together in the harsh central Australian desert, digging up their bush tucker, with the "thud, thud, thud" of the sticks penetrating the earth, the sweat of those women running like little rivulets into those holes. They trace and track those subterranean stems until the bulbs, several fleshy bush potatoes, are finally unearthed with great shrieks and hilarity. Likewise, imagine the feet of the dancers in the story, pounding their feet into the earth with a "thud, thud, thud,"—calling up the old stories, calling up the ancestors. Both of these actions constitute a conversation with the earth.

Stuart: I also like the rhizome model for thinking about Aboriginal culture, and also for its possible roles in conceptualizing progressive social change. Unlike the more common linear, hierarchical tree model, the rhizome involves a much more resilient and adaptive net of horizontal (more equitable) relationships. It also has numerous possible points of engagement, which D & G characterize as both potential entry and exit points.

The underground nature of the rhizome reminds me of the largely hidden, even secret, and sacred nature of much of Aboriginal wisdom. It is not something that can be taught simply or purchased as a commodity; it must be engaged with over an extended period in complex and comprehensive ways. And the transitions produced in such engagement, involvement and action have a liminal quality that cannot be easily seen and measured—like the influences of Uncle Max's dancers on those witnessing the performance.

The rhizome asks us to be open to other, non-hierarchical relationships, means of influence and modes of action. I think it is complementary to our social ecology model, which asks us to consider the personal, sociocultural, environmental and "spiritual" aspects operating within every situation and the complex relationships between them. Most dominant models overemphasize economic factors and control strategies, whereas we dream of the day when economics will be reframed as just one of many tools to enable us to act on our higher values. Rather than aiming to control everything, we need to enable and support the emergence of life-affirming actions. This involves a long-term, indirect, subtle, whole-system nurturing and, most often, an anonymous role, instead of the more common heavy-handed, quick, control and manipulation interventions.

By working with and nurturing the land and its processes, we can support the plants, which can in turn support the animals, including ourselves.[17] The relationships involved are complex and largely unknown. To know what to do, we must rely on our wisdom, experience, intuition and on cultural stories, such as those Uncle Max is keeping alive.

Carol: Yes. When Deleuze and Guattari discuss the rhizome as a model, they are articulating the notion of "multiplicities."[18] When breaks or ruptures occur in socio-ecological systems, as they must in both Aboriginal and non-Aboriginal

Australia, then the rhizome starts up again at one of its nodes. Surely this relates to your "whole-system nurturing role"?

So, what I have referred to earlier as the underbelly between whites and blacks in the story of the dance performance now reveals itself to be two cultural groups forming a rhizomatic relationship. One that is far more cohesive and integrative than could be imagined from the ostensibly separate reality being acted out here. This notion seems to flesh out the complexity, much more than the more common dichotomous relationship can allow. It admits ambiguity as the vital place of generative force, as the in-between. I imagine this links with your concept of the "profoundly simple stage of understanding paradox."

Stuart: Indeed it does. Profound simplicity, unlike deceptive simplicity (aspirin for a headache, when nobody suffers from this because of a deficiency of aspirin in the blood) involves the contextually appropriate thing to do in the moment. Such action takes less energy, has fewer harmful side effects and may solve a problem permanently. It often involves paradox—like creating and nurturing boundaries and borderlands, rather than trying to get rid of or control them—thereby enabling ecological and cultural development, and increasing productivity, resilience and sustainability; resulting ultimately in whole-system health and well-being.

Carol: We began our dialogue with looking at the role of story, particularly, by using a social ecology framework, keeping in mind the need to find practical solutions for a world in crisis. I would like to conclude with a remark on the ending of the Australia Day story. The emphatic statement "Biamunga lives!" reveals a profound sense of optimism and a profound simplicity all at once. I take that to be the emergence of a life-affirming action.

The Earth holds this story too.

NOTES

1 *Country* here refers to the land to which a particular Aboriginal group (and its family origins) belongs; its place of *dreaming* (this includes the group's creation story and rules for living and relating).

2 *Mob* here refers to a particular group of Aboriginal people (and its associated place or *country*).

3 *Law* here refers to the Aboriginal law that existed prior to colonization and that is transferred orally; unlike common law, it refers to all aspects of life and culture.

4 We define social ecology as the study and practice of personal, social and ecological sustainability and progressive change based on the critical application and integration of ecological, humanistic, community and "spiritual" values to enable the sustained well-being of all (See Hill, "Social Ecology: An Australian Perspective," 2011).

5 William E. H. Stanner, *White Man Got No Dreaming: Essays 1938–1973* (Canberra: Australian University Press, 1979), 24.

6 Carol L. Birrell, "Meeting Country: Deep Engagement with Place and Indigenous Culture" (PhD diss., University of Western Sydney, 2007), 115, http://arrow.uws.edu.au:8080/vital/access/manager/Repository/uws:2519?query=birrell/.

7 *Gamma* refers to a meeting place for achieving reconciliation and collaborative community action across difference; using the metaphor of a lagoon in which saltwater and freshwater

mix. See: Raymattja Marika, "The 1998 Wentworth Lecture," *Australian Aboriginal Studies* 1 (1999): 2–9.

8 David Holmgren, *Permaculture: Principles and Pathways Beyond Sustainability* (Hepburn, Vic., Australia: Holmgren Design Services, 2002).

9 David W. Orr, *Earth in Mind: On Education, Environment and the Human Prospect* (Washington, DC: Island Press, 2004), xiii.

10 Arnold van Gennep, *The Rites of Passage*, trans. Monika B. Vizedom and Gabrielle L. Caffee (Chicago: University of Chicago Press, 1960).

11 Stuart B. Hill, "Considerations for Enabling the Ecological Redesign of Organic and Conventional Agriculture: A Social Ecology and Psychological Perspective," in *Organic Farming: Prototype for Sustainable Agricultures*, ed. Stéphane Penvern and Servane Bellon (London: Springer, 2014), 401–22.

12 Andre Voisin, *Soil, Grass and Cancer* (London: Crosby Lockwood, 1959).

13 See Peter Knudtson and David Suzuki, *Wisdom of the Elders* (Vancouver: Greystone/David Suzuki Foundation, 2006).

14 Peter Carey, *Oscar and Lucinda* (St. Lucia, Qld.: University of Queensland Press, 1988), 493.

15 Stuart B. Hill, "Social Ecology: An Australian Perspective," in *Social Ecology: Applying Ecological Understanding to Our Lives and Our Planet*, ed. David Wright, Catherine Camden-Pratt and Stuart B. Hill (Stroud, UK: Hawthorn Press, 2011), 17–30; and related PowerPoint presentations on applied social ecology available at: www.stuartbhill.com and www.scribd.com/doc/55937783/
.

16 Gilles Deleuze and Felix Guattari, trans. Brian Massumi. *A Thousand Plateaus: Capitalism and Schizophrenia* (Minneapolis: University of Minnesota Press, 1987).

17 Peter Andrews, *Beyond the Brink: Peter Andrews' Radical Vision for a Sustainable Australian Landscape* (Ultimo, NSW: ABC Books, 2008).

18 Deleuze and Guattari, *A Thousand Plateaus*, 21.

BIBLIOGRAPHY

Andrews, Peter. *Beyond the Brink: Peter Andrews' Radical Vision for a Sustainable Australian Landscape.* Ultimo, NSW: ABC Books, 2008.

Birrell, Carol L. "Meeting Country: Deep Engagement with Place and Indigenous Culture." PhD diss., University of Western Sydney, 2007, http://arrow.uws.edu.au:8080/vital/access/manager/Repository/uws:2519?query=birrell.

Carey, Peter. *Oscar and Lucinda.* St Lucia, Qld: University of Queensland Press, 1988.

Deleuze, Gilles and Felix Guattari. *A Thousand Plateaus: Capitalism and Schizophrenia. Translated by B. Massumi.* Minneapolis: University of Minnesota Press, 1987.

Hill, Stuart B. "Considerations for Enabling the Ecological Redesign of Organic and Conventional Agriculture: A Social Ecology and Psychological Perspective," in *Organic Farming: Prototype for Sustainable Agricultures. Edited by* Stéphane Penvern and Servane Bellon (401–22). London: Springer, 2014.

Hill, Stuart B. "Social Ecology: An Australian Perspective," in *Social Ecology: Applying Ecological Understanding to Our Lives and Our Planet.* Edited by David Wright, Catherine Camden-Pratt and Stuart Hill (17–30). Stroud: Hawthorn Press, 2011. Related PowerPoint presentations on applied social ecology are available at: www.stuartbhill.com and www.scribd.com/doc/55937783.

Holmgren, David. *Permaculture: Principles and Pathways Beyond Sustainability.* Hepburn, Vic: Holmgren Design Services, 2002.

Knudtson, Peter and David Suzuki. *Wisdom of the Elders.* Vancouver: Greystone/David Suzuki Foundation, 2006.

Marika, Raymattja. "The 1998 Wentworth Lecture." *Australian Aboriginal Studies* 1 (1999): 3–9.

Orr, David W. *Earth in Mind: On Education, Environment and the Human Prospect.* Washington, DC: Island Press, 2004.

Stanner, William E. H. *White Man Got No Dreaming: Essays 1938–1973.* Canberra: Australian University Press, 1979.

Van Gennep, Arnold. *Les Rites de Passage.* Paris: Nourry, 1909. Translated by Monika B. Vizedom and Gabrielle L. Caffee as *The Rites of Passage.* Chicago: University of Chicago Press, 1960.

Voisin, André. *Soil, Grass and Cancer.* London: Crosby Lockwood, 1959.

Chapter Twelve

RE-LEGISLATING THE SOIL: ENCLOSURES AND EXCEPTION AT THE AMAZON FRONTIERS

Paulo Tavares

The robbery of the honey and the robbery of our safety, the robbery of communing and the taking of liberties, have gone hand in hand.

—Peter Linebaugh[1]

As the frontiers of development move deeper into Amazonia, opening up new soils to be integrated in the international market while simultaneously expanding enclosures toward common lands of local communities, the forest's geography turns into a contested terrain between dissident modes of relating to, appropriating and managing the environment. Enhancing global flows of natural resources presupposes the enforcement of new grids, barriers and borders on the ground, sectioning and reshaping the bounds between material ecologies and social networks, reconfiguring cultural and biophysical links between land and people. The lines that define these new border zones are multivalent, deep and thick, forged through a combination between legal mechanisms, scientific knowledge, cartographic techniques, spatial structures and political forces. Within and around them, at the intersection between different institutions, agents, materials and images through which the border exists and is performed, sites of conflict and dispute coagulate. They are frictious nodes in the fluid systems of global capital, points of resistance both to the geometries that power seeks to enforce, as well as to the border regime that structures categories of knowledge and representation by which we frame and relate to the nonhuman living world.

In what follows, Amazonia is described as a frontier space wherein the borders and boundaries that demarcate the distinctions and separations between society and nature, politics and ecology, are blurry and fuzzy, and ultimately irrelevant. In this border zone, the social and the ecological form an entangled milieu, since power and environment are inseparable components of a single, though highly conflictive and divided historical field of forces. Politics is interpreted as an active agent in the production of the natural environment, inasmuch as nature is read as a historical territory, which is intrinsically social and political. Amazonia, a global frontier of capitalist plunder, is also described as an epistemic frontier, a border ecology that challenges our laws,

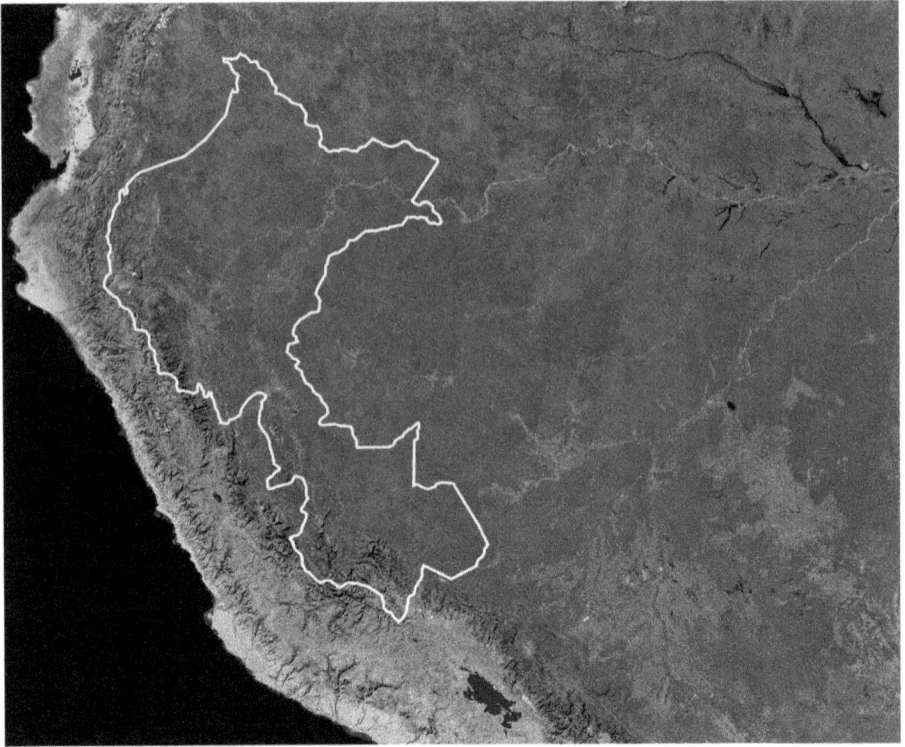

Figure 12.1 The great enclosure: Lines of the state of emergency enforced over the Peruvian Amazon in 2009. Map by Paulo Tavares.

sciences and politics, unveiling their colonial foundations and the power structures that legitimate them.

Insurgency

At the western edges of the Amazon River Basin, within the sovereign territory of Peru, conflicts over land rights came to a breaking point on June 5, 2009, when state forces violently clashed with thousands of indigenous Awajún and Wampís who were occupying a place called the Curva del Diablo—the Devil's Curve—a stretch of major national road located at the entrance of Bagua, the main gateway city to all northern Amazonian departments of the country. Thirty-three people died during the confrontation—more than half police officers—and at least 200 people were severely injured.

In the previous weeks, state repression had been escalating in response to well-orchestrated demonstrations and infrastructure disruptions that spread throughout the 60 percent of Peru's territory that is covered by the Amazon River Basin. Protests had been thus far peaceful, but not inconsequential. Marches were reported in many towns across the forest, and demonstrators held position for more than 50 days straight at various strategic points such as refineries and airports, gas valves and oil pipelines, river passages, bridges and roads. This led to the disruption of virtually all the resource-extraction channels and transport routes connecting the Amazonian forestlands to the rest of the country.[2]

Geographically distributed but politically articulated, these various demonstrations embodied a common claim against the enforcement of 99 laws that would unleash a process of massive territorial, ecological and social reorganization of the entire Peruvian Amazon in the decades to follow. In December 2007, 18 months before the confrontations at the Curva del Diablo, Peru's Congress approved a special mandate allowing the executive branch of the government to bypass parliamentary debate and rule by decree in issues related to the implementation of a free-trade agreement signed with the United States.[3] Holding extraordinary legislative powers, the cabinet of President Alan Garcia drafted a radical new legal agenda aimed at introducing land-zoning schemes and proprietary regimes that would facilitate the investment of transnational capital in large-scale extraction activities and biofuel production over the entire country, chiefly in Amazonia, where the subsoil contains large reserves of yet untapped hydrocarbon and mineral deposits, and where indigenous populations remain with relative territorial autonomy in relation to state control.

At the center of the demands formalized by the Asociación Interétnica de Desarrollo de la Selva Peruana (AIDESEP), the Peruvian coalition of Amazonian indigenous nationalities, there was the revocation of a series of articles related to use and control of land and natural resources. Most fiercely opposed by protesters was Decree 1090, otherwise known as the Forest Law, which introduced a set of modifications in the legal status of forestlands that would result in the removal of 64 percent of the Peruvian Amazon out of the national public forest heritage and thus potentially open up this vast ecology for corporate land grabs.[4]

After the legal package was made public in the middle of 2008, the public reacted immediately. Indigenous and peasants groups marched in protest, human-rights and environmental NGOs published reports that contested the legal legitimacy of the decrees, and later a special parliamentary commission was formed to probe the constitutional validity of the new laws.[5] The opposition maintained that the government was using its extraordinary mandate to push a wider neoliberal agenda on Amazonia that, in principle, had little effective connection to the legal issues related to the implementation of the free-trade contract between the United States and Peru. As the government was determined to carry on with the laws regardless of public reaction, mobilization increased and protests gradually radicalized toward direct action on the ground.

On May 10, 2009, after more than one month of sustained demonstrations and disruption by indigenous organizers, President Garcia suspended civil liberties and declared a 60-day state of emergency in several Amazonian departments, enclosing practically the entire Peruvian forest into a large zone under siege. Military police units were deployed to break peaceful blockades and regain control of strategic passages and infrastructure. Authorities conducted a nationwide campaign of political containment that was

characterized by the intimidation of entire communities, arbitrary imprisonment of protesters and legal prosecution of key activists.[6]

State violence was met with fierce resistance. The conflicts at the Curva del Diablo
in early June marked the culmination of the government's repressive campaign, as
well as a decisive turning point to the "Amazon Insurgency," as the long-standing
indigenous mobilization of 2009 became known in Peru. For a nation like Peru, still
healing from a brutal counterinsurgent war that had converted almost the entire
country into an emergency zone for almost two decades, the conflict rekindled the
historical memories of profound collective wounds. The violent mishandling of the
situation by the government generated widespread reactions locally as well as internationally, and instead of retreating, public pressure increased manifold. Solidarity
marches took place in various Andean cities and received support of tens of thousands in the capital of Lima, expanding the mobilization across different segments
of Peruvian society, including indigenous peasants of the Sierra (highlands), miners,
urban workers, teachers, students and middle-class liberal professionals. Eventually,
protesters forced President Alan Garcia to suspend the decrees and initiate debates
about forestland reforms.[7]

Re-legislating the Soil

One of the first initiatives of Alan Garcia's mandate was an attempt to modify a very specific piece of legislation, Law 28852, also known as the Law for the Promotion of Private
Investment in Reforestation and Agroforestry, which had been implemented a few days
before he assumed power on July 28, 2006.[8] Six months later, the government submitted
to Congress a proposal to alter various provisions in the second article of this law that
would change the legal framework governing state-held forestlands characterized as *terras
eriazas sin coberta boscosa*, a term that can be roughly translated as uncultivated or unpro-
ductive wastelands without forest cover. The alterations would enable forest areas that
were stripped of the vegetation cover to be transferred from the national forest heritage
to investors willing to develop activities of agroforestry, reforestation and environmental
services such as carbon sinks.

According to the Peruvian constitution, lands identified as forestlands are part
of the inalienable national patrimony of natural resources and must be managed
by state concessions, whereas regimes of private property apply exclusively to lands
identified as having greater potential for agriculture and grazing. In order to stimulate the interest of private capital, the original text of Law 28852 introduced a set
of corporate-friendly measures into the concessions regime rather than full-fledged
privatization, maintaining a form of legislation more closely associated with the
exploration of geological resources such as mineral, oil and gas. Garcia's amendments were intended to reroute that legal frame toward an agricultural model based
on global land-market rules.

The legal/ecological definition of land as "forest areas without forest cover" is of
crucial importance here. The presence of vegetation would become the index that

determines the position of land in relation to law—private property or common heritage—transforming deforestation into a mechanism by which not only the "natural nature," but also the "legal nature" of forestlands could be completely modified. By institutionalizing practices of deforestation into a mechanism of enclosure, the reforms would turn the violent practices of the lawless frontiers that advance toward the Peruvian Amazon into the very means through which an entire market-oriented environment could be enforced on the ground. Environmental destruction would then turn into an instrument of de facto legislation.

Project of Law 840/2006-PE—as the amendment proposal is registered in Congress—embodied the essence of Garcia's neoliberal-government rationale that would later be radicalized by the new Forest Law presented in Decree 1090. The public reactions it generated were responsible for triggering the first marches and protests that then escalated to the Amazon-wide conflict in 2009. The opposition criticized the amendments by arguing that they would stimulate expansion of illegal logging and land grab of indigenous territories, and tried to block the proposal by showing that it violated constitutional law.

A central element in the opposition's strategy was to demonstrate that the presence of forest cover was not a determinant factor in defining the legal/natural characterization of those lands as suitable for forest production. Since they remained as "legal forests" regardless of surface conditions, deforested zones should continue to be governed by the same constitutional provisions that establish forests as part of the national heritage and therefore prevent them from being transferred to private hands. Rights activists explained that under Peruvian legislation the concept of forest follows a biogeographic definition that "embraces a set of elements like the climate, the soil, the vegetation, water, fauna and other elements," and that the relation between land and law are not established exclusively in reference to the surface cover, but primordially in relation to "the conditions of the vulnerability of the soil that goes well beyond the presence or not of the trees."[9] The reforms Garcia's government proposed were therefore unconstitutional not only because they breached the regime of appropriation and use that governed those lands, but also because they violated the very natural concept of forests as defined by Peruvian law.

The Legal Nature of Land

The characterization of land use in Peru is determined according to a national geological index defined by Supreme Decree N0062/75-AG, which was implemented in 1975 in the context of the Forest and Wildlife Law introduced by the nationalist government of General Velasco Alvarado. This decree establishes rules and methods for land classification, distinguishing five principal groups according to an economic-driven taxonomy ordered by the "best-use/productive capacity" of the soil: (1) lands suitable for *cultivo en limpio*, which are highly fertile and suitable for intense agricultural production; (2) lands for *cultivo permanente*, less productive yet capable of accommodating sustained cultivation; (3) lands suitable for pasture, which are inappropriate for agriculture; (4) lands suitable for forest production; and (5) protected lands. At one extreme, *cultivo en limpio* can encompass every other form of use—agricultural, pasture, forest production and protection. At the other extreme, *protected lands* are defined as incapable of sustaining any of the former types, for "even if they present vegetation its use is not economic," and therefore should be designated to other purposes such as "natural conservation, aesthetic values, social recreation or scientific interest." In between, forestlands are defined as ones that do not present ecological conditions necessary for agriculture or pasture, but can be explored for wood and extraction of other natural forest products.[10]

This interpolation between ecological and legal taxonomies is reflected in variations of the position occupied by each land category in relation to constitutional law. Whereas all types of land are included as part of the national patrimony of natural resources—as defined by Article 66 of the Peruvian constitution, *Of the Environment and Natural Resources*—only lands suited for agriculture and pasture are included in provisions that define land-property rights that must be provided and protected by the state. This includes agricultural and pasture lands be they private, communal or belonging to any other form of legal persona, as defined by Article 88 of the Peruvian constitution, *Of the Agrarian Regime and Peasant and Indigenous Communities*. Since lands characterized as forests are governed under provisions of Article 66 and not Article 88, the applicable modes of use and exploration of those areas are governed by a regime of state concessions and cannot be turned into private property, agricultural or grazing lands.[11]

Supreme Decree N0062/75-AG also institutes the official method for allocating land into these five categories. It establishes that the process of identification must follow the ecological map of the Peruvian territory designed according to a model originally developed by American botanist Leslie R. Holdridge. First published in 1947 in the magazine *Science* under the title "Determination of World Plant Formations from Simple Climatic Data,"[12] Holdridge's system is based on a diagram that divides the entire climate range of the Earth into discrete ecological units, which he initially named *plant formations* and later *life zones*. Through mathematical operations, a combination between bio-climate data such as temperature, precipitation and estimated evapo-transpiration is equated with different patterns of vegetation and soil, forming a global abstract grid of *plant formations/life zones* that can be applied to the codification of complex environmental settings.

Holdridge's model contends that best capacity of land use is defined in relation to the climate factors that condition a certain life zone, and inside each life zone according to edaphic characteristics. The law that governs the land is therefore defined not in relation to the surface cover, but to its integral biogeographic consistency as part of a specific life zone, which includes but is not limited to plant formations, and which ultimately must be characterized by climatic and edaphic variables.[13] In order to oppose the government's proposal to reform Law 28852, rights activists held to the legality of the ecologically oriented framework that is intrinsic to this system of land classification, arguing that the amendments violated the "legal nature" of forestlands.

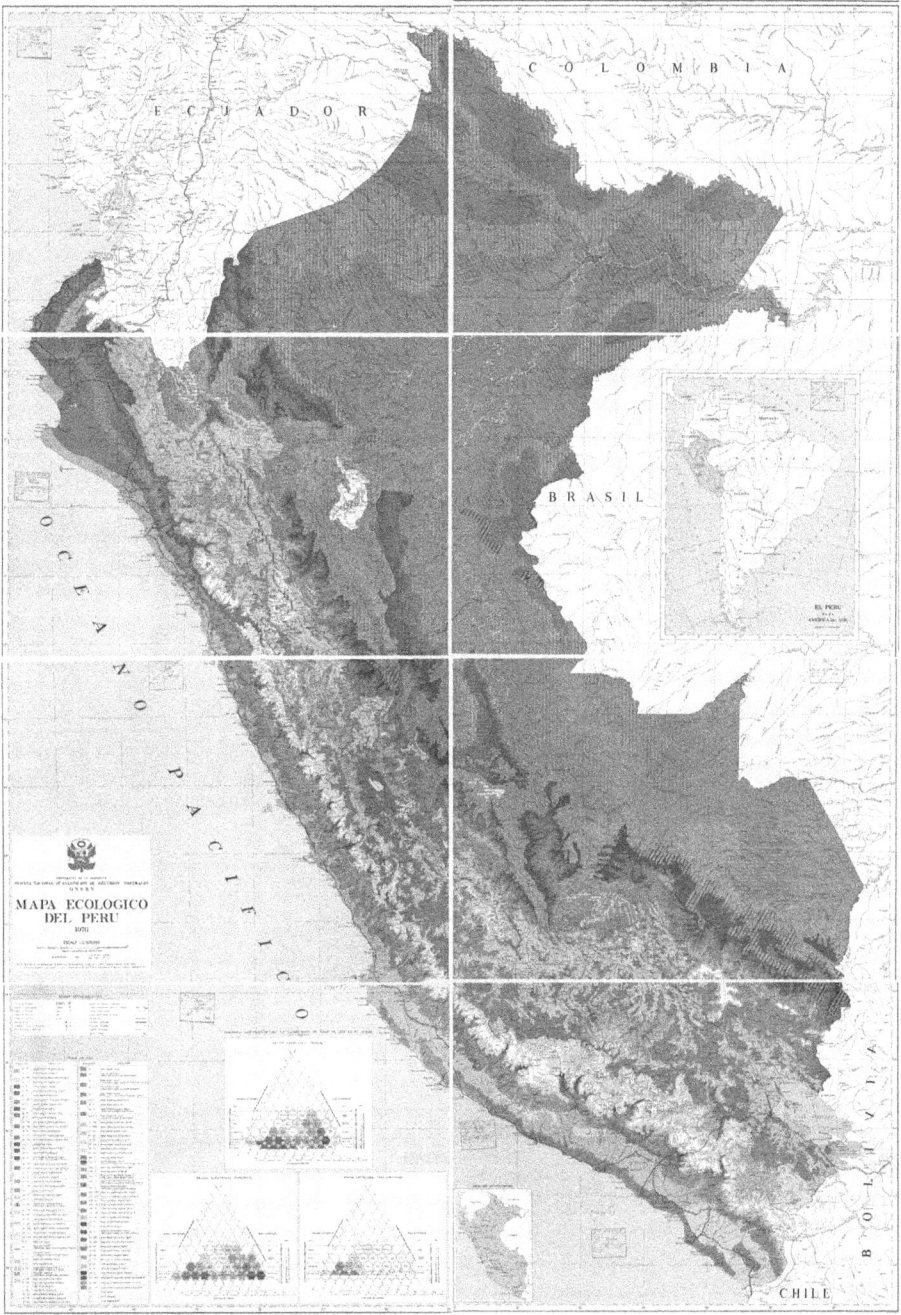

Figure 12.2 Life-zoning cartography: *Mapa Ecologico del Peru*. Public domain image, Republic of Peru, National Office for Evaluation of Natural Resources (Oficina Nacional de Evaluación de Recursos Naturales—ONERN, 1976).

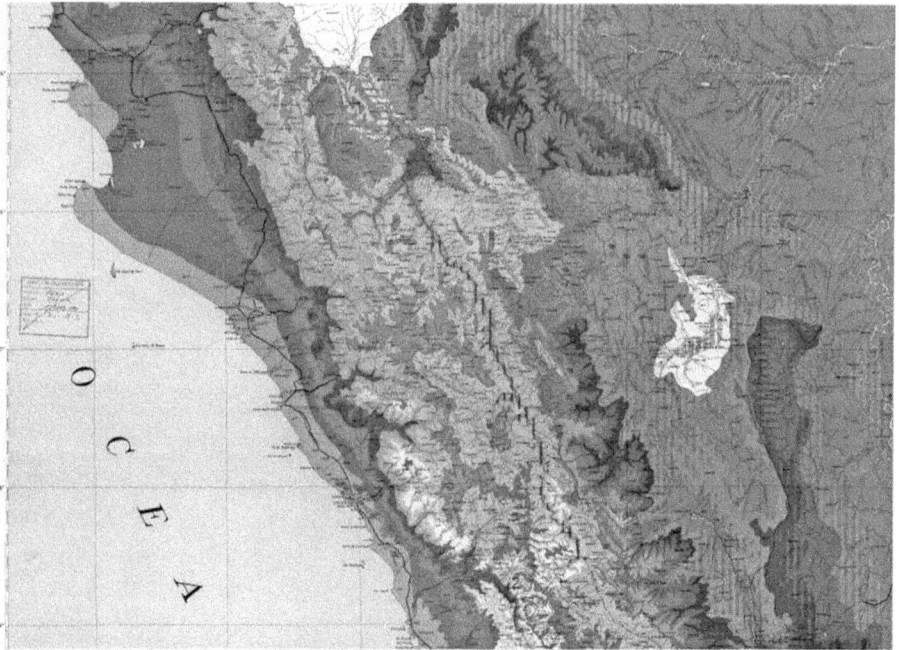

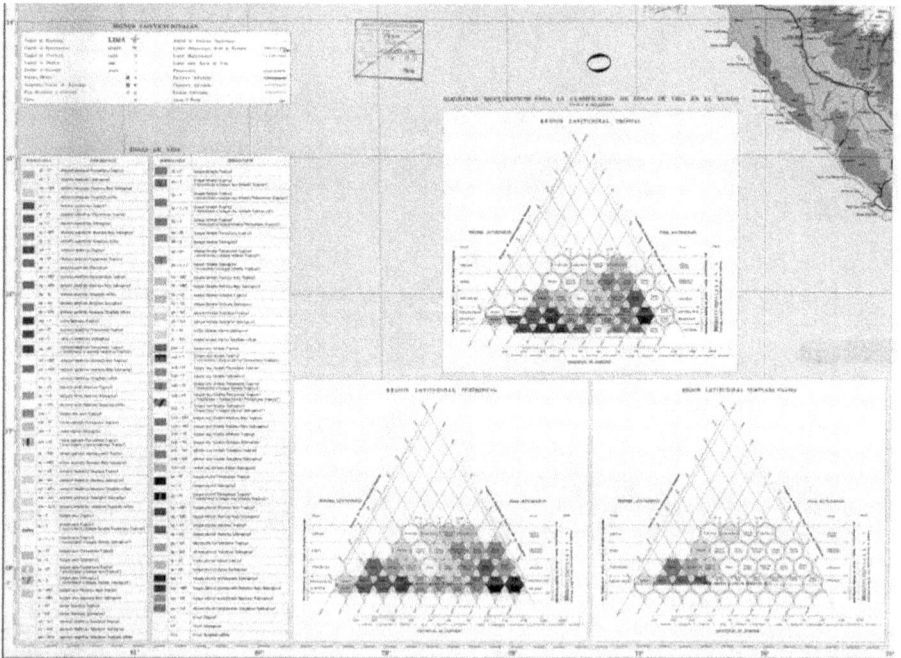

Figures 12.3 and 12.4 Life-zoning diagram. Leslie R. Holdridge's ecology of Peru's territory.

REPUBLICA DEL PERU
MINISTERIO DE AGRICULTURA

INSTITUTO NACIONAL DE RECURSOS NATURALES
INRENA

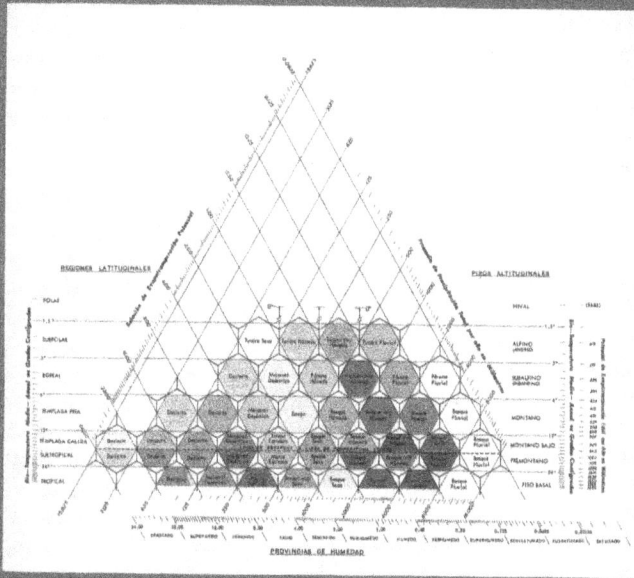

MAPA ECOLOGICO DEL PERU
Guía Explicativa

LIMA - PERU
1995

Figures 12.5 and 12.6 Land taxonomy. (a) Cover from *Mapa Ecológico del Peru: Guía Explicativa* (*Ecological Map of Peru: A Descriptive Guide*) showing Leslie Holdridge's diagram (1995) and (b) extracts from the descriptive guide accompanying the life-zoning map of Peru (1995 edition based on the original designed by Tosi). Public domain images, Republic of Peru, National Institute for Natural Resources (INRENA).

(b)

Figures 12.5 and 12.6 (*Cont*)

Figure 12.7 Resource terrain. Excerpt from the guide to the *Mapa Ecológico del Peru: Guía Explicativa* (*Ecological Map of Peru: A Descriptive Guide*), chapter 47, section E, 1995 on actual and potential land use: "The original population, consisting of tribal groups, only uses resources for subsistence without causing major changes to the ecology. […] A large portion of the tropical forest's total area is ecologically capable of producing great quantities of wood as the basis for development of industrial-scale timber production activities within the rainforest itself. This constitutes the region's real and optimal potential." Translated by P. Tavares. Public domain image, Republic of Peru, National Institute for Natural Resources (INRENA).

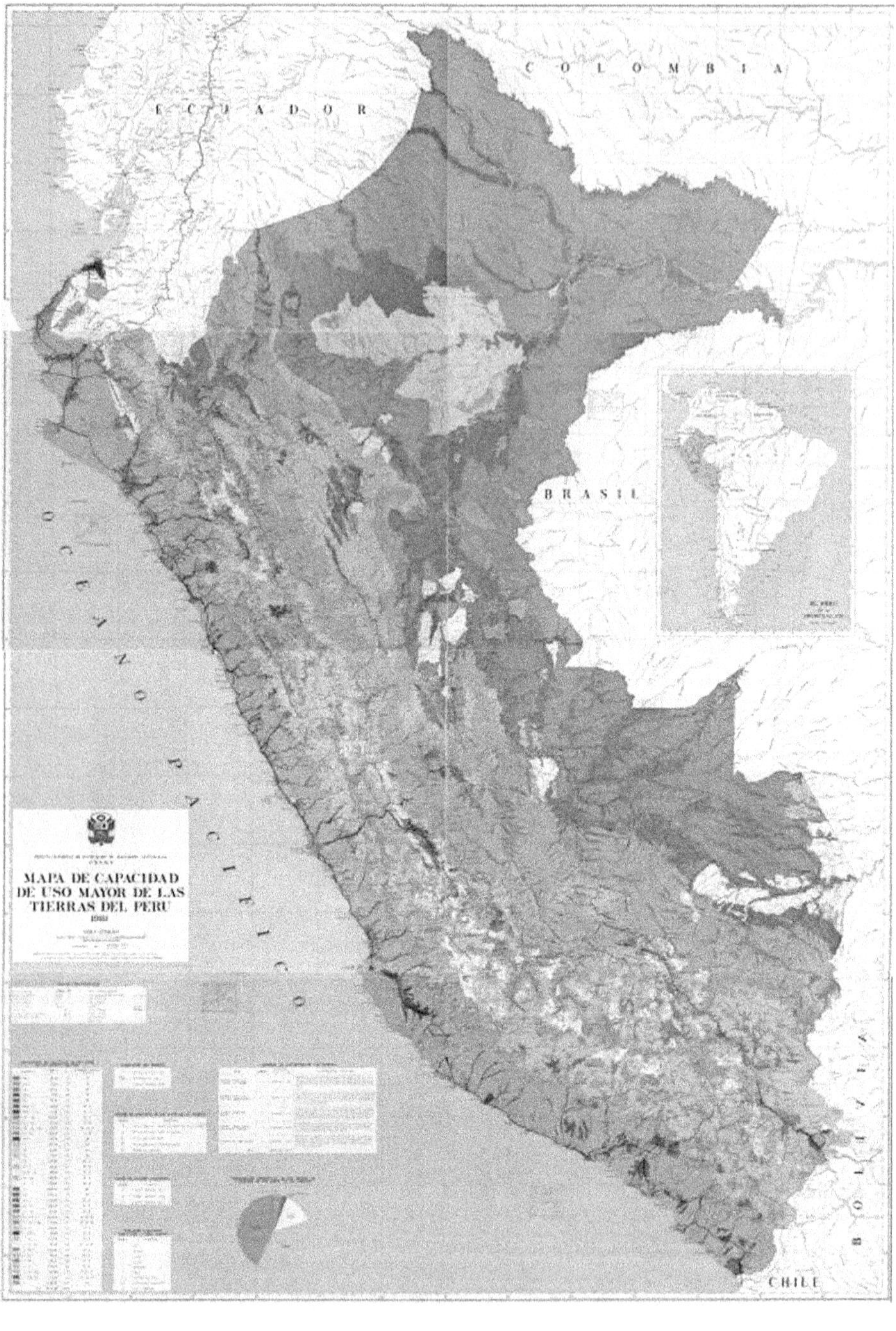

Figures 12.8 and 12.9 Ecology coded by law. Map of Peru's land use potential, ONERN 1981: 3.81 percent of lands suitable for *cultivo limpio*; 2.11 percent of lands suitable for *cultivo permanente*; 13.84 percent of pasture lands; 37.89 percent of forestlands; 42.25 percent are considered protected lands. Public domain image, Republic of Peru, ONERN 1981.

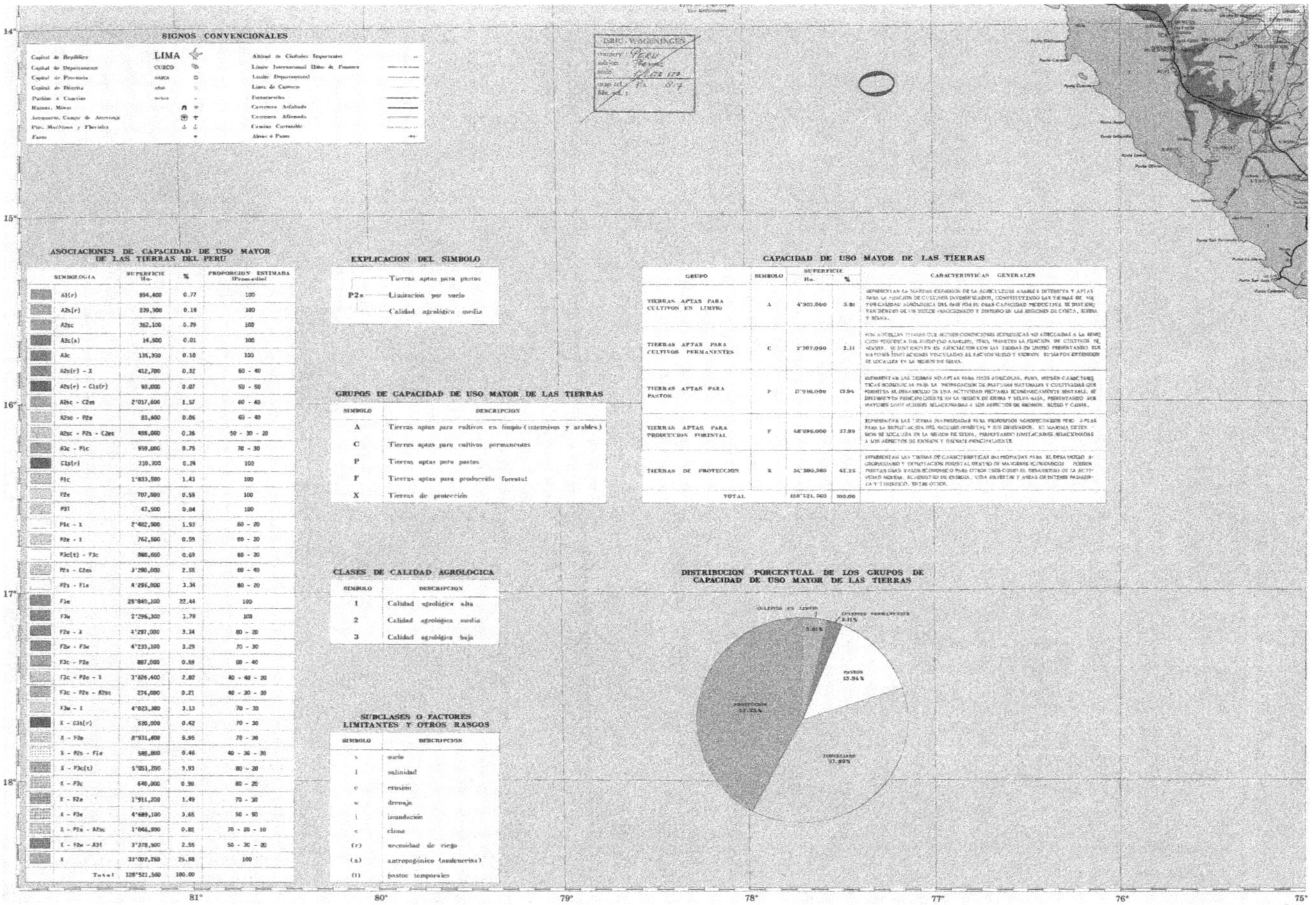

Figures 12.8 and 12.9 (*Cont*)

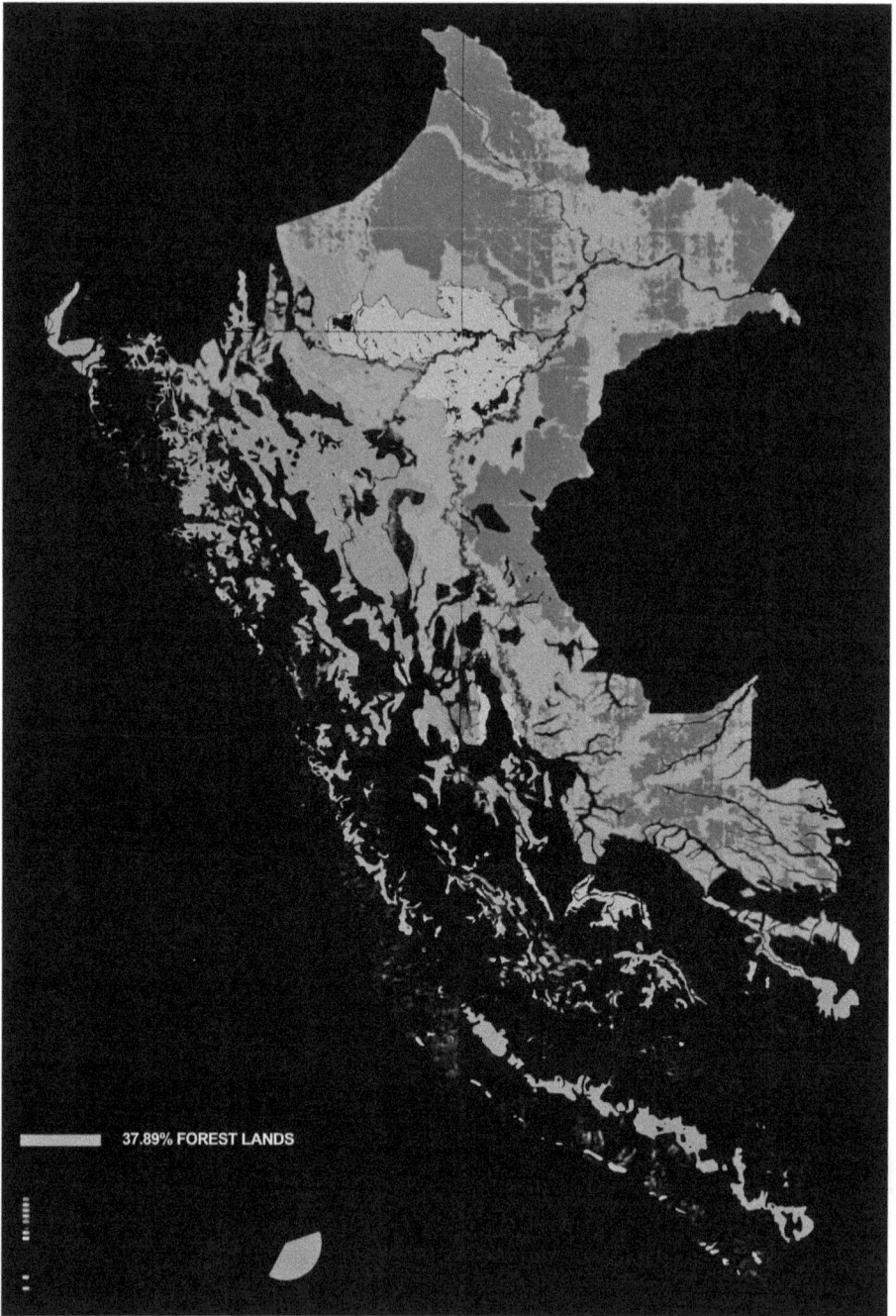

Figures 12.10, 12.11, 12.12 Political-legal enclosures. An analysis of Peru's geological-index map reveals that 37.89 percent of the territory is defined as forestland. Taking out the area legally defined as protected lands and indigenous territories, the remaining 64 percent of Peru's Amazon land would be potentially re-legislated by the new Forest Law. This area practically overlaps the lines of the siege-zone enforced during the 2009 state of emergency. Images by Paulo Tavares.

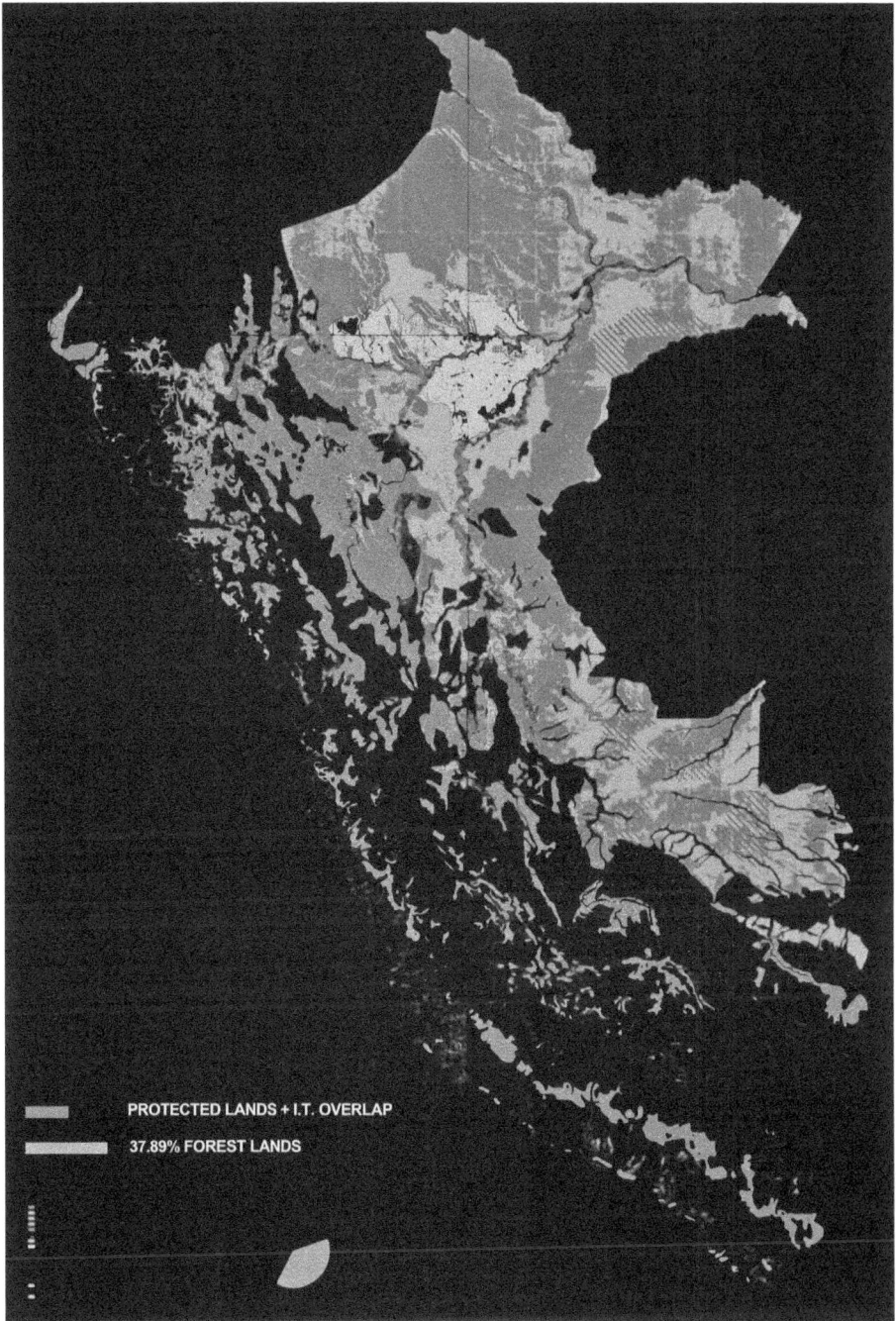

Figures 12.10, 12.11, 12.12 (*Cont*)

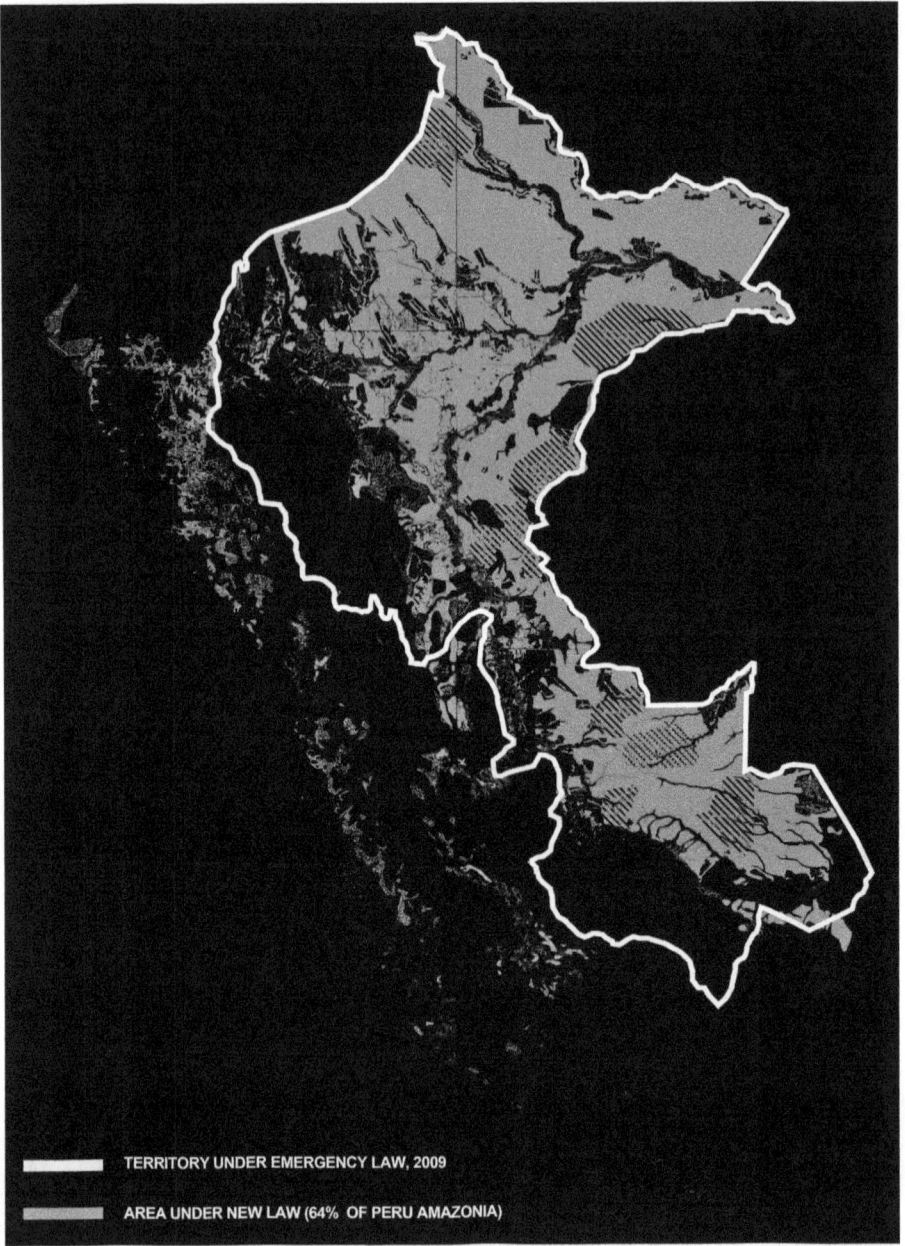

Figures 12.10, 12.11, 12.12 (*Cont*)

The Ecological Nature of the Law

Holdridge's scientific diagram expresses the paradoxical yet complementary logics of the environmentalism that was forged through the Cold War's resource race. On the one hand, maps generated by the life zone modeling system are the product of the decisive influence that the episteme of ecology had on scientific practices of that time. As such, those cartographies embody a certain environmental ethos informed by the intent of "harmonizing" anthropogenic action with the dynamics and limited capacities of the Earth's ecosystems. On the other hand, the diagram offers a relatively easy and fast methodology for charting out resources and locating economic land potential over large territorial extensions, thus reflecting the hegemonic position that the imperatives of the development doctrine occupied at that time.

Holdridge elaborated the world life zone diagram based on the vast information and knowledge he accumulated about the ecology of tropical environments while working for the US government on botanic and climatic research projects in the Caribbean and South America. During the 1950s, he encountered adequate financial and institutional conditions to develop the model further as the director of the Inter-American Institute for Cooperation on Agriculture (IICA),[14] the agricultural-development branch of the Organization of the American States (OAS) founded in 1948, an agency that throughout the Cold War served foremost as a proxy of the geopolitical interests of the United States on the continent. In collaboration with US development offices and international aid institutions, and in some cases with the direct support of the US military, the OAS founded the production of life zone maps for a series of countries in Latin America during the 1950s–1970s.[15]

The first life zone classification map of the Peruvian territory was designed in 1958 by American geographer Joseph A. Tosi, at the time an associate researcher at the IICA and a close collaborator of Holdridge.[16] Accompanying the multicolored cartographies of the *Ecologic Map of Peru*, a descriptive catalogue authored by Tosi and Holdridge was published under the title *Natural Life Zones of Peru*, replacing the original expression "vegetal formation" with "life zones," the term that later named Holdridge's updated and definitive version of the diagram presented in the 1967 book *Life Zone Ecology*.[17] As one contemporary commentator noted, this modification was conceptual, attributed to the fact that the scientists wanted to shift the emphasis from the "the presumed original plant cover, admittedly extensively modified almost everywhere, to the climatic elements on which the system is really based."[18] The 271-page catalogue provided a detailed textual characterization of climate, topography and soil for each of the 33 life zones that compose the incredible biodiversity of the Peruvian territory, and illustrated each of them with photographic representations of the respective "natural vegetation typologies." The authors also presented a series of recommendations on land use potential and limitations for every ecological unit, suggesting basic directions for territorial planning, conservation policies and future modes of occupation.

Produced in the context of the aid programs financed by Kennedy's Alliance for Progress, the *Ecological Map of Peru* was designed as a "planning guide" for the development projects that president-architect Fernando Belaunde Terry sought to diffuse throughout

Amazonia. Its publication by the ICCA/OAS came amid a process of growing "governmentalization" of Peru's forest areas, which ran in parallel with an unprecedented expansion of colonization schemes directed toward the tropical lowlands. Joseph Tosi's cartography anticipated the creation of the Office for Evaluation of Natural Resources (ONERN) in 1961, the foundation of the FAO-sponsored Institute of Forest Research in 1963, and the implementation of the first proper forest law of Peru by Belaunde Terry, also in 1963. Tosi and Holdridge were outspokenly critical of the penetration of highways into the more humid parts of the Basin, especially of schemes of agricultural colonization, yet they described tropical forests as vast resource terrains that could potentially support industrial production of lumber, paper and cellulosic products. They also suggested that those areas would be best served as part of a national reserve.

Only in 1975, with the implementation of Supreme Decree N0062/75-AG, was the life zone cartography institutionalized, thus turning the natural ecology of the Peruvian territory into law. This was followed by the publication of an updated version of the *Ecological Map of Peru* and a correspondent national map of land use potential by ONERN. Using the geotaxonomy established by the decree, this latter cartography describes the territory of Peru formed by 3.81 percent for *cultivo en limpio*; 2.11 percent for *cultivo permanente*; 13.84 percent as pasture lands; 37.89 percent as forestlands; and 42.25 percent as protected lands. Through the implementation of the 1975 Forest Law (Law 21147), which superseded the legislation of 1963, the nationalist government of General Velasco Alvarado incorporated the recommendations of Holdridge and Tozi, establishing that land defined as forest was part of Peru's inalienable national patrimony. In 2000, while attempting to reverse what is currently described as the "socialist influence"[19] of Alvarado's legislation, the neoliberal government of President Alberto Fujimori successfully passed a new code introducing a more flexible and corporate-oriented concession regime. Nevertheless, forestlands remained part of the national patrimony, which prevented its conversion to private property.

Decree 1090—President Alan Garcia's new Forest Law published on July 28, 2008—legislated precisely over these lands, removing 37.89 percent of the territory defined as "forest" from the national patrimony, most of which is located in the Amazon River Basin. Hence the claim held by the opposition that 64 percent of the Peruvian Amazon—that is, all the forestlands that are not defined as "protected lands" or within indigenous territories—could be suddenly converted into private property. Decree 1090 would trigger a rapid and extensive process of ruralization of forestlands, institutionalizing one of the vastest enclosure movements in modern history. By force of law, a complete reconfiguration of the "nature" of Amazonia could be unleashed.

Law and Land, Politics and Ecology

The conflicts that were at the center of the "Amazon Insurgency" show how law operated as a design tool through which a completely new cartography was projected over Amazonia, transforming not only the legal nature of forestlands, but potentially altering the very ecological nature of the forest itself. The articulations between land and law, nature and politics cannot be limited to superimposition or description. It is instead a productive relationship that we may look for, one in which human laws have the force of "producing nature" inasmuch as the environment is not the passive background of social conflicts, but the very medium through which politics unfold.

In order to liberate natural materials to circulate freely as commodities in the global market, the Peruvian government attempted to redraw the map of Amazonia through the legal recoding of its soils. The history of the implementation of this new legal/natural regime illuminates the dialectics between two apparently opposed yet interconnected poles—free-market policies and strategies of containment, liberalization and encircling—thus demonstrating that the ideology of freedom promoted through economic *laissez-faire* was intrinsically related to the enforcement of restrictions and boundaries and, ultimately, violent state repression. This governmental logic combines neoliberal forms of managing resources with primitive forms of expropriation, simultaneously enhancing certain forms of circulation while creating new confinements. Articulated at the same time in Congress and on the ground, a state-of-exception was employed as a legal-political mechanism through which the reorganization of an entire ecology could come into force. The curtailing of civil rights and the erosion of rights to common function as two entangled engines mutually reinforced each other.[20]

Enclosures were not only legal and territorial, but also political and epistemic. Besides expressing the continuous resistance against land dispossession and erosion of customary rights of indigenous peoples, the conflicts that culminated at the Curva Del Diablo rendered visible the disagreement over the monolithic notion of nature that was being inscribed by the new forest law. If ecology can be thought of as politics, it must be defined as theory and practice that is less concerned with the ethical imperatives of "saving" or "protecting" nature rather than with the necessity to destabilize the very hegemonic notion of nature imposed by the contemporary neoliberal enclosures. In that sense, the crucial conflict fought in Amazonia was not so much to defend land rights, but to resist the enforcement of a concept of land that would limit the socio-ecological diversity on which the customary rights that have historically shaped those territories are based.

NOTES

The author would like to thank the Coordenação de Aperfeiçoamento de Pessoal de Nível Superior (CAPES) and Brazil's Ministry of Culture for kind support of this research.

1   Peter Linebaugh, *The Magna Carta Manifesto: Liberties and Commons for All* (Los Angeles: University of California Press, 2008), 10.

2   The Asociación Interétnica de Desarrollo de la Selva Peruana (AIDESEP), one of the main organizations behind the protests, published day-to-day online reports (accessible at: www.aidesep. org.pe/) Several local and international NGOs also monitored the conflict. See AmazonWatch, "Day 50 of Indigenous protests in Peru" (2009); World Rain Forest Movement, "Peru: Amazon Peoples, Bastions of Resistance" (2009), and Amnesty International, *Peru: Baguá Six Months On* (2009). Among the corporations operating in the affected regions are the national oil company Petroperu, Spanish Repsol and Argentinean Plurispetrol. Protests were also related to

conflicts around mining sites operated by Chinese gold-mining firm Zijin, Canadian consortium Dorata, and British-owned Monterico Metal.

3 The United States–Peru Trade Promotion Agreement (PTPA) was signed by Presidents Alejandro Toledo (2001–6) and George W. Bush (2001–9) in April 2006 to supersede the "Law of Andean Commercial Promotion and Eradication of Drugs." After a long process of economic, legal and technical negotiations prior to ratification by the US Congress, Presidents Garcia and Bush approved its implementation and the PTPA entered into force in February 2009.

4 See Raul Zibechi, "Masacre en La Amazonia: la Guerra por los bienes comunes," available at: www.argenpress.info/2009/06/masacre-en-la-amazonia-la-guerra-por.html, accessed April 2013.

5 For a detailed analysis of the unconstitutionality of the decrees, see the report commissioned by Oxfam, Francisco José Eguiguren Praeli, *Análises de la conformidad constitucional del uso de las faculdades legislativas otorgadas por el congreso al pode Eecutivo mediante la Ley no. 29157* (Lima: Oxfam America, 2008).

6 The state of emergency was imposed in four districts of eastern Peru, including Loreto, Amazonas Ucayali and Cusco. In the aftermath of Bagua, the president of AIDESEP, Alberto Pizango, was charged with sedition and sought asylum in the Nicaraguan embassy, and later had to flee the country. For a journalistic account of the events. see: "Amazon Update: Peru government declares state of emergency in 9 eastern districts," *Andean Air Mail & Peruvian Times* (May 9, 2009), accessed April 11, 2014, www.peruviantimes.com/09/amazon-update-peru-government-declares-state-of-emergency-in-9-eastern-districts/2835/.

7 Luis Arce, "Peru: Massive protests against García government over Amazon massacre (June 13, 2009), accessed April 11, 2014, www.wsws.org/articles/2009/jun2009/peru-j13.shtml.

8 Ley de promoción de la inversion privada en reforestación y agroforesteria, Ley 28852, implemented in 19 July 2006 under the presidency of Alejandro Toledo.

9 DARN (Derechos, Ambiente e Recursos Naturales), Hechos y Aspectos Vulneratorios de Los Decretos Legislativos 1090 y 1064 (June 2009), p. 4.

10 Reglamento de Clasificación de Tierras, Decreto Supremo N° 0062/75-AG.

11 DARN.

12 L. R. Holdridge, "Determination of World Plant Formations from Simple Climatic Data," *Science*, 105(2727): 367–68, which later appeared in L. R. Holdridge, *Life Zone Ecology*, 1967.

13 DARN.

14 Leslie Holdridge was the general director of IICA between 1950 and 1951 and subsequently served as director of IICA's Natural Resources Department until 1960.

15 Karl S. Zimmerer, "Vertical Environment," in *Mapping Latin America: A Cartographic Reader*, ed. Jordana Dym and Karl Offen (Chicago: University of Chicago Press, 2011), 263–68.

16 Joseph A. Tosi, *Mapa Ecologico del Peru*, accompanied by Joseph A. Tosi, *Zonas de Vida Natural en el Peru*, with an appendix by L. R. Holdridge (Lima: IICA—Instituto Interamericano de Ciencias Agricolas de la OEA, 1958).

17 L. R. Holdridge, *Life Zone Ecology* (San José, Costa Rica: Tropical Science Center, 1967).

18 James J. Persons, "Review of Mapa Ecológico do Peru," *Economic Geography* 38, no. 3 (1962), 278–80. See also: Joseph A. Tosi, "Climatic Control of Terrestrial Ecosystems: A Report on the Holdridge Model," *Economic Geography* 40 (1964), 173–81.

19 This is the term that today is used in the official website of the Peruvian government to describe the 1975 Forest Law.

20 This is the crucial point of the much-needed manifesto written by Peter Linebaugh, *The Magna Carta Manifesto*. Linebaugh recalls that the elaboration of "The Great Charter of the Liberties of England" in 1215, the landmark medieval law that limited the monarchy's power over its subjects, was accompanied by the formulation of another law named "The Charter of the Forest" that guaranteed access to the common forests of the kingdom. The former provided

political rights, the latter limited material expropriation: the right to the practice of common-
ing was integral to minimizing state power over people, it was a freedom guarantee—hence
Linebaugh's conclusion that one and the other are mutually constitutive and, conversely, that
enclosures have been historically related to the erosion of civil and political liberties. Conflicts
around resource-extraction operations carried out by large corporations in indigenous territories have been escalating in recent years in many countries in Latin America, chiefly in Peru,
whose recent high index of GDP growth is heavily dependent on natural resources exports.
In turn, resource-extraction sites have become more securitized and militarized, while protes-
tors are constantly dealt with using exceptional political measures. Recently, in May 2012, the
region of Cuzco was again put under a 30-day state of emergency after violent clashes erupted
during indigenous protests against the Swiss mining corporation Xstrata plc.

BIBLIOGRAPHY

"Amazon Update: Peru Government Declares State of Emergency in 9 eastern districts" (May 9,
    2009). *Andean Air Mail & Peruvian Times*. Accessed April 11, 2014, www.peruviantimes.com/09/
    amazon-update-peru-government-declares-state-of-emergency-in-9-eastern-districts/2835/.
AmazonWatch. Press Release: "Day 50 of Indigenous protests in Peru" (May 28, 2009). Accessed April
    11, 2014. http://amazonwatch.org/news/2009/0528-day-50-of-indigenous-protests-in-peru.
Amnesty International. *Peru: Baguá Six Months On*. AMR 46/017/2009. London: Amnesty
    International Publications, 2009.
Arce, Luis. "Peru: Massive protests against García government over Amazon massacre" (June 13,
    2009). Accessed April 11, 2014. www.wsws. org/articles/2009/jun2009/peru-j13.shtml.
Eguiguren Praeli, Francisco José. Análisis de la Conformidad Constitucional del Uso de las
    Faculdades Legislativas Otorgadas por el Congreso al Poder Ejecutivo Mediante la Ley
    no. 29157. Lima: Oxfam America, 2008.
Holdridge, L. R. "Determination of World Plant Formations from Simple Climatic Data." *Science*
    105 (1947): 367–68.
Holdridge, L. R. *Life Zone Ecology*. San José, Costa Rica: Tropical Science Center, 1967.
Linebaugh, Peter. *The Magna Carta Manifesto: Liberties and Commons for All*. Los Angeles: University
    of California Press, 2008.
Persons, James. J. "Review of Mapa Ecológico del Perú." *Economic Geography* 38 (1962): 278–80.
Tosi, Joseph A. "Climatic Control of Terrestrial Ecosystems: A Report on the Holdridge Model."
    Economic Geography 40 (1964): 173–81.
Tosi, Joseph A. *Zonas de Vida Natural en el Perú*: Memoria Explicativa sobre el Mapa Ecológico
    del Perú. *Explication of the* Mapa Ecológico del Perú with an appendix by L. R. Holdridge.
    Technical Bulletin No. 5. Lima: Instituto Interamericano de Ciencias Agricolas de la OEA
    (IICA), 1960.
World Rainforest Movement. "Peru: Amazon Peoples, Bastions of Resistance." *World Rainforest
    Movement Bulletin* 142 (2009). Accessed April 11, 2014. http://wrm.org.uy/articles-from-the-
    wrm-bulletin/section1/peru-amazon-peoples-bastions-of-resistance/.
Zibechi, Raul. "Masacre en La Amazonia: la Guerra por los bienes comunes." (2009). Accessed
    April 11, 2014. www.argenpress.info/2009/06/masacreen-la-amazonia-la-guerra-por.html.
Zimmerer, Karl S. "Vertical Environment." In *Mapping Latin America: A Cartographic Reader*, edited by
    Jordana Dym and Karl Offen, 263–68. Chicago: University of Chicago Press, 2011.

Chapter Thirteen

MEDITERRANEAN EDGES: RETERRITORIALIZING NATURAL AND SOCIAL ECOLOGIES

Verena Andermatt Conley

Introduction

Be they natural or artificial, borders are what link and divide. They impede circulation but enable passage and exchange of humans, of goods and of ideas. From time immemorial, especially when drawn across arable land or narrow straits, they have been ribbon-like swaths of intense conflict. While borders striate the surface of our globe, conflict dictates that some are more visible than others, particularly those that separate North and South, between the United States and Mexico or Latin America on one side of our hemisphere and those separating Europe from Africa. In this chapter, I will focus on the Mediterranean, broadly defined, the sea whose width—on his maps drawn around 145 CE—Ptolemy extended far beyond the limits the modern world has known. At any and every point it has been a site of crossing and a barrier for a myriad of cultures and populations. For economic and increasingly ecological reasons the sea has accrued importance as a source of water and food production. At the same time, Fernand Braudel reminds us, while it is more important than ever for sustaining the large populations huddled around it, the Mediterranean is a site of global exchange of goods and people.[1] Under the impact of postcolonial as well as global migration and policies owing to fears of fundamentalism and terrorism, it has become, once again, a seemingly impermeable border.[2]

A tightening of borders is taking place at the very moment when their loosening is urgently needed for the causes of both social and natural ecologies. Thus, when seen not as a sea but as a border, the Mediterranean must be considered in equally theoretical and practical terms. In the context of a reshaping of social processes that defines national identities, the Mediterranean assures constant passage of ships and their cargoes in every cardinal direction. More delicately, where migration is at stake, the Mediterranean becomes the site of the transference of peoples of vastly different origin, language, and social process. When populations move across its waters to land and to live in different milieus, we witness how adaptation to new and different environments on the part of peoples' different origins compels us to think of ecology in both physical and human terms.

In what follows, the Mediterranean will be understood as a site of complex social exchange, a sea—to be sure—but also a crucible and a melting pot, where different modes and types of "subjectivation" take place. By subjectivation is meant the process by which individuals or members of a community moving or emigrating from one shore to another continually adapt and, according to different circumstances, relate to the physical and social conditions into which they are displaced. Compelled to negotiate and revise aspects of the *habitus*, or ways of living they have known, with that of new or unforeseen environments, they generally change the cultural and physical milieus in which they move.

Looking North

In his celebrated *Three Ecologies* (French edition 1989, English translation 2000), arguing for an "ecosophy" composed of mental, social and natural ecologies, Felix Guattari underlined a global need for understanding and enabling new processes of what he called "subjectivation." Indeed, mental ecologies or attention paid to the circulation of ideas is tantamount to addressing social ecologies intent on producing a better exchange among people and their environments. Drawing on a concept he developed with Gilles Deleuze in *A Thousand Plateaus* (French edition 1980, English translation 1987), Guattari advocates a process of *deterritorialization* and reterritorialization that would entail increase and acceleration of human movement across inherited borders.[3] The reader will note that Grichting's use of the term *intangible*, or psychological, borders in her Introduction bears similarity to the "concept" of mental space put forth in the 1980s by Guattari and Deleuze, and is now recognized by border scholars and social ecologists.

Without discrediting the utopian vision of his enterprise, we would do well to renew attention to Guattari's implementation of the mental—or in Grichting's terms, psychological—element. However, we cannot simply argue for movement "across" mental and physical spaces, for it almost goes without saying that the idea would play into what Etienne Balibar called the ideology of a media hyperspace.[4] In the geographies in which we live, borders become lines of concomitantly physical and mental demarcation. Physical and mental demarcation tend to fix into place the idea of what is "here" from what is "over there." Writing in 1989, after the fall of the Iron Curtain, Guattari tells his French and "Northern" readers that now the time has come to rethink injustices along the North–South axis. This meridian or axis that crosses the Mediterranean has been abundantly examined from the standpoint of the North, in peoples calling into question what it means for those who, facing southward, believe that they are "looking down." A first world casts its gaze upon undeveloped milieus that it had assumed to be its right to exploit for its own ends. A first goal of this chapter, then, is to invert that point of view by focusing on the southern Mediterranean edges that can be countenanced facing northward. A second goal is to see how one can productively use the concept of reterritorialization not only to facilitate passages of goods and to alter the movement of people, but also to reroute the circulation of ideas for collectively ecological ends. Drawing on Etienne Balibar and avoiding the pitfall into a media hyperspace, we can say that—in order to undo the violence of a fixed mentality upholding the status quo of today's Mediterranean borders—we need to reassess the subject in relation to the citizen and the nation-state by separating "nation" from "state," that is, by separating blood ties to the soil and linking the loose ends with others focused on a collective building of spaces in common. While this author makes no presumption that scholarly writing will transform borders, it is only by rethinking processes of subjectivation and citizenship that we can begin to implement natural ecology on the foundation of social ecologies where both mental and physical borders are indeed supple and permeable.

The edges of the Mediterranean have linked and divided continents, countries and provinces across the ages: Numidians, Carthaginians, Berbers, Phoenicians, Greeks, Romans, Arabs, Spaniards, French and others have populated the shores and moved swiftly across the sea to reach far beyond Gibraltar up and down the Atlantic coast, while trading in goods and humans. It suffices to imagine how many footprints have been left on Mediterranean shores in order to countenance how, over and again, the Mediterranean has been inhabited, conquered and colonized. The Romans were the first to populate the entire shoreline of the Mediterranean they called the *Mare Nostrum*, Our Sea. After the decline of Rome, Arabs invaded North Africa in the seventh century before crossing the sea to conquer and colonize the Iberian Peninsula where they—and after them the Berber dynasties—established their capital in Cordova. Even after their defeat and their retreat back onto African shores, the Mediterranean remained on edge. Pirates threatened commercial ships crossing the sea to and from India and beyond, and also terrorized the general population. It is in response to such "disturbances" as well as for profitable economic reasons that, in 1832, the French, in turn, began to colonize North Africa, specifically Algeria.

The Algerian Shore

From 1830 to 1962, the French transformed Algeria progressively into a French province. From the edge of the sea, the border shifted to points of divide and of crossing inside the province of Algeria. The French brought their "civilization" to the indigenous population, while in the process eradicating their very being. For much of the nineteenth and part of the twentieth century, the border passed between the French and the indigenous Arab and Berber populations. The French imposed their own social and cultural values through education, architecture and the reorganization of space, notably by virtue of the compartmentalization of cities that Frantz Fanon so vehemently denounces in *The Wretched of the Earth*.[5] In the city of Algiers, in architectural programs and urban planning, they confined the Muslim population to its own neighborhoods in the *casbah*, spaces built on the ruins of the Roman city that the Spaniards had already transformed. Under colonial rule, Europeans circulated freely while largely overlooking the indigenous population. Social ecologies, the product of a circulation of ideas based on the "superiority" of a white, Christian population with its "superior" culture, justified the control both of colonized people and of nature. Reigning ideologies furthered the belief that the country was part of a French nation in which Algerians were tolerated, but from which they were excluded as citizens.

It is only after World War II that colonial ideas were challenged as part of a worldwide contestation and a shift in sensibilities. Not only did indigenous people begin to mobilize and assert their own rights, many French, especially those living in urban centers, acutely felt the social injustices imposed by colonial rule and militated against colonial dictates. In Algeria, the conflicts culminated in the War of Independence from 1954 to 1962, during which many horrors were perpetrated on all sides, but foremost on that of the French—all in the name of national ideals. Torture and massacres of civilians, as well as gratuitous violence, were the order of an agenda motivated by beliefs in patriotism in the service of self-interest. When the war ended, 1 million French settlers, known as *pieds noirs*, left Algeria for France accompanied by several hundred thousand *harkis*, or Algerians who had fought on the side of the French. They were joined by Algerian economic refugees, leaving the new nation with its weak economy to find work in France. Their families followed around the time of the economic crisis in the early 1970s that put an end in France to the so-called *trente glorieuses*, that is, the post–World War II boom years. As many of the immigrants became unemployed, they also became increasingly unwanted. The borders crossed once again inside the country, yet this time they were in France.

On the southern shores, where patriotic fervor of a newly independent nation was contagious, and in an effort to separate from the former colonizer, Algeria closed its border with France. In France, spatial borders were erected between citizens and immigrants living in urban outposts known as the infamous *banlieues*, while the situation differed on the other side of the Mediterranean. The Algerians' efforts to call for a break between the two countries coincided with a worsening of the economy, the spread of fundamentalism and a civil war in the late 1980s and early 1990s. After 2001, when fear of terrorism spread in the North on the heels of 9/11, the borders closed their gates of passage. Clandestine migrants, or *haras*, that is, those who—dissatisfied with their own governments and having burned their papers—attempted to cross the sea. News of spectacular drownings due to the capsizing of makeshift boats piloted by ruthless individuals mobilized public opinion in Algeria and France. Attention was brought to the social and economic plight, especially of the young Algerian population.

Clearly, people affiliated with international conglomerates, such as gas and oil corporations or construction companies engaged in large public projects, travel easily— unemployed individuals do not. They are denied entry visas into France, but also passports to leave Algeria, as we can see and read in many films and novels from Merzak Allouache's *Bab el Oued* (1993) or *Salut Cousin!* (1996) to Tahar Djaout's *The Watchers* (2001). In *The Watchers*, Djaout writes, shortly before his assassination at the hands of Islamic fundamentalists in 1993, how Algerians are denied passports by incompetent and even malevolent bureaucrats in their own country. Conservative thinkers on both sides, from the Front National in France to fundamentalist Algerians, call for an increased separation of the two countries as part of a process of decolonization and national independence.

The *Jardin d'Essai*: A Common Space?

Yet what if, as Etienne Balibar asks in *Droit de cité*, it were impossible to separate the two countries?[26] What if, over and above the history sketched in the preceding paragraphs, the two are inextricably linked? What if a truly progressive way of thinking were based on the belief of the necessity of exchange and on making the borders more porous? Even if the Mediterranean may at times look less like a *Mare Nostrum* than a world border separating a wealthy North from a poorer South, private ties as well as more public ties, the result of forms of exchange that have gone on for centuries, even millennia, cannot be entirely severed. How can people from the North and the South do away with colonial ideas so that the role of the Mediterranean borders can be actively rethought? How, in this process, can we rethink social and mental ecologies while giving a nod to natural ecologies? A visit to Algeria from the French president in 2012 has perhaps begun to broach officially a remote possibility of renewing ties at a moment when it becomes clear that the latter cannot be severed not only because of economic and familial ties, but also because of increasingly important problems of natural ecologies, for example, the critical situation of water around the Mediterranean.

For a questioning of borders, we can turn to the *Jardin d'Essai*, a park in the city of Algiers, that seems symptomatic both of the intertwining of two cultures—those of France and Algeria—as well as an ongoing transformation of mental and social ecologies with, hopefully, a new focus on the construction of common spaces. A park, to be sure, but also a botanical garden, the *Jardin d'Essai* can be understood as a site where cultural exchanges take place in a space that, as its title suggests, crossing of borders and cultures is "essayed" or tried. A microcosm of the Mediterranean, the *Jardin* has been taken to emphasize the need for people living around the Mediterranean, regardless of nationality or origin of passport, to cooperate with one another. Named after the adjacent neighborhood, *Hamma*, which means marsh or fever in Arabic, the *Jardin* is an experimental garden-park of French design whose history documents the shift over time from colonial ideas and their social implications to others today based on very different mental—that is, intangible/psychological, social and natural ecologies. The large *Jardin d'Essai*—there were several in the colonies as well as in Paris—was first conceived in 1832 as one of the most important botanical gardens for experimenting in the acclimatization of plants from other regions of the world. In France, the existing *jardins* were also called colonial gardens. The *Jardin d'Essai* in Algiers was, as its name indicates, built on drained marshlands. The goal was to cultivate vegetables that could be adapted to the North African soil and climate. In 1842, with a series of further purchases, the *Jardin* became a tree farm that sold to colonizers and public organisms. It experimented with the acclimatization of trees from all over the world, beginning with a row of prototypical plane trees near the main entrance in 1845. Other rows followed, each with its own distinct trees: tropical palm trees; giant bamboos in 1847; and a grand *ficus* in 1863. The garden became active in the domains of agriculture and horticulture. From trees, it expanded to vegetables as well as ornamental and industrial plants that were also sold to the public. Those in charge introduced livestock, from ostriches to emus and lamas. Alpaca and angora sheep were introduced to improve the indigenous herds. Of importance too were technological experiments to increase the quality of silk, cotton, sugarcane and olive oil. Between 1847 and 1867, a lake was dug and an outer boulevard, similar to that in Paris, was built.

Figure 13.1 Imposing the space of the colonizer (ca. 1905). Photography reprinted with permission, Smithsonian Institution, Eliot Elisofon Photographic Archives.

After his 1865 visit, Napoleon III decided to hand the *Jardin* over to the colonial organization Société générale algérienne. Within its quadrangle were drawn lateral and longitudinal paths, or *allées*, reminding visitors of the layout of French parks. In 1900, a zoo was created. Several decades later, the movie *Tarzan* was shot on its premises. In 1914, two French architects presented a project to build the well-known perspective of the park, consisting of five successive plateaus and numerous fountains that created a strong resemblance to Versailles. The perspective still stretches today from the Musée National des Beaux Arts (National Fine Arts Museum) on the upper hillside of the garden to the bottom of the hill nearest the sea. In 1932, French architects built the museum to commemorate and celebrate the 100-year anniversary of the French occupation and its contribution to culture! During World War II, when Allied troops occupied the garden, it was bombed and damaged by the Germans. After 1962, the *Jardin* was opened to the public in independent Algeria.

Today, the *Jardin* is a center of botanical and horticultural production that is also a place for leisure and teaching. It serves as a much-needed green space in a densely populated city. The French garden, separated from the original garden by the *allée* of plane trees, still occupies the western part. The southeastern corner represents an English garden with a small lake while a Japanese garden is now defunct. Most striking is the contrast between the carefully manicured French garden, whose panoramic view looks onto the Mediterranean, and other parts of the park, where tropical vegetation, tortuous tree trunks and exuberant vines plunge visitors into an exotic world that would be otherwise unknown in these latitudes. The garden no longer favors acclimatization, though it accepts tree specimens as gifts from other countries. Recent gifts include araucaria trees from Chile as well as shrubs from Austria. These trees are seen as part of an international cooperative effort and no longer as a colonial project, a *conquête de terres*—or conquest of land.

In a paper presented in the context of a conference at the Getty Museum on "Gardens," Charles Salas comments on a well-known, seemingly exotic, yellowish photograph of colonial times that features palms and other tropical trees at the foot of which we can discern an indigenous person donned in what looks like traditional garb. "Bursting leaves of date palms," he writes, "grab the attention first and bring to mind the desert oasis. Beneath them stands a man wearing a fez, tunic and seroual [baggy Punjabi pants]. And behind, the stiff leaves of drought-resistant dragon trees. A desert garden?"[7] He shows how the trees gathered in this botanical garden come in fact from all over the world. They were used in colonial times for experimenting with adaptation of foreign plants in the region. The most successful adaptation was the eucalyptus tree from Australia that many Algerians now believe to be native. The photo taken from an anodyne travel album, Salas comments, was meant to reveal a "typical, exotic landscape" that the traveler found in the *Jardin d'Essai*, one of the sites that was a "must see" for highbrow tourists, though it was a composite of many species from France and other colonies.

In colonial times, the Garden welcomed many distinguished visitors such as George Vanderbilt who, in 1892, commissioned a painting of the palms by Auguste Renoir. The latter, like Delacroix, had produced several landscapes in and around Algiers. The photograph and paintings, Salas rightfully concludes, are both very Western representations of what was supposed to be an "exotic landscape."[8] Edith Wharton also visited the Garden and wrote in her diary:

> Nowhere in Europe could one see anything so Oriental as the little arcaded café at Mustapha, where white-robed Algerines sit crouched on the terrace, drinking their coffee under a group of plane-trees. […] [The *Vallon de la Femme sauvage*], a wild little ravine, led us to the Sahel; and here we found the *Jardin d'Essai* which I was particularly anxious to see. We walked under avenues of India-rubber trees as large as oaks and between quarters called Mustapha Inférieur, lying near the sea on the lower slope of trellises of tea-roses in bloom, and high clumps of Arundo domax.[9]

The Garden has been a favorite of painters and literati past and present, from Edith Wharton to André Gide, who praised its sensuousness in *The Fruits of the Earth* (1997)—quoted in turn by Jacques Derrida—to, more recently, Hélène Cixous, who alludes to it throughout her writings. Evoking her childhood and a blissful communion with a fragrant nature, she writes:

> To enjoy blissfully a walk from the path of the summit ridge to the ground of the *Jardin d'essai*, to make the trip faithfully, in accord with life, with the body we have to exit softly; to leave all phrases of recommendation and now live, simply live, live entirely there where we live; to begin the way it begins; to let things happen according to their mode; to let the rose be felt in a rosy way; to descend to the garden attracted, led by the appeal of its freshness; to descend trusting the body, the way my childhood descended before knowing the names of the street, but the sense know their ways before the proper noun and the common nouns, along the perfumes, walking with feet wearing sandals in the heavy perfumes. (Translated by Conley)[10]

In her lyrical passage, Cixous praises a natural way of life. She who is always keen on denouncing colonial vestiges never alludes to the *Jardin*'s origins. This may not be surprising since, on one hand, the *Jardin* is reported to have been less segregated during the colonial period than other parts of town—though old photographs show primarily French and European couples milling about—and, on the other hand, the colonial architecture in the park was less obvious and almost melded with the Mauresque style of the surrounding city. Apart from the museum's façade, its terraces and fountains carried an eerie resemblance to French classical gardens. Its origins, contrary to those of colonial gardens in Paris and elsewhere, were often overlooked.

Since independence, the *Jardin* is being steadily transformed. The Monument to the Martyrs now towers behind the National Museum of Art and the park itself was restored in the early 2000s. Its access has been modernized with a subway station and a couple of cable cars that help visitors avoid the steep climb. A Sofitel Hotel, belonging to a French-based global chain, has been placed on the park's edge. The *Jardin d'Essai*—whose name has not been changed though its Arabic name, *Jardin du Hamma*, is used more frequently—is a popular park that Algerians have re-appropriated. The ideas that underlie its creation are now part of a defunct mental and social ecology of a colonial era while those of an intense Algerian nationalism that followed have, in turn, been complicated by social unrest as well as by an entirely new and unforeseen twist—that is, problems of the environment.

However, to further awareness of the environment and transform social ecologies, each year the Garden now celebrates Arbor Day. Schoolchildren flock there to enjoy educational programs and to learn about the many tree species from all over the world. What served to promote colonial ideals has now been re-grafted to produce new sensibilities and forms of intelligence better suited to understanding and preserving the environment. The great number of species of plants once introduced under the ideal of the *conquête des terres*, or territorial conquest, are now examined through a pedagogical lens that emphasizes the contrast with indigenous vegetation from Algeria. The wealth of specimens inherited from colonial days is reoriented toward a transformation of a common future based on a greater awareness of the environment.

As ecological pressures grow in Algeria and the Mediterranean basin, those in charge of the *Jardin* have opened a new area, called the *zone humide*, or humid zone. The latter is one of the many zones in Algeria and the world that contribute to the preservation of fauna and flora and to an increased awareness of the relation between humans and their environment. In another reversal of its founding policies, those responsible for managing the park have brought in many indigenous plants and animals species in order to emphasize the importance of strengthening local ecosystems. As elsewhere in former colonial and other spaces, the excesses of a certain ideal of control are corrected by reverting to more traditional technologies. Ideas of draining marshes for the construction of the Garden have been superseded by others emphasizing their vital importance. Algeria itself has close to 50 sites or *zones humides* that are of national and international importance. The main objective of these sites is to preserve Algerian biodiversity rather than, in a mode of botanical colonization, favor the importation and adaptation of foreign species. In addition to emphasizing the importance of the local ecosystem, The

252   *ALGER. — Un Coin du Jardin d'Essai. — LL.*

Figure 13.2 Reappropriating the colonized space (ca. 1905). Photography reprinted with permission, Smithsonian Institution, Eliot Elisofon Photographic Archives.

Garden's *zone humide* also stresses the latter's interrelation with others elsewhere. Visitors, especially students, come to study the importance of biodiversity and ecosystems, the cause and prevention of pollution and how to protect the environment. Given its 150 acres and more than 1,500 vegetal species, the Garden welcomes more than a million visitors every year and thus is an excellent site for raising awareness.

The *Jardin d'Essai du Hamma* in Algiers, riddled as it is by its colonial origins, remains a particularly striking example of changing social and mental ecologies. Its present state shows how their transformations are necessary as a precondition to tackling natural ecologies. From the original plans in the 1830s to import and adapt French and international varieties of plants, trees and animals to benefit the colonies and to make it a destination for wealthy Europeans and Americans, as well as a playground for the local *pieds-noirs*, the *Jardin d'Essai* is now a site where Algerians following independence can reclaim themselves, but in a way that includes a new awareness of social and mental ecologies. Rather than destroying the monument, Algerians in charge of the *Jardin* have maintained its global heritage of plants and animals while attempting to reorient its colonial goals. In the words of Deleuze and Guattari, they have effectively deterritorialized and reterritorialized its use. Today, it is not only a park from colonial times and a green setting in a densely populated city, but also a space to which have been added newly important ecological themes. With the fading of a "control ethos," there is a return to the local that is also related to the global.

The *Jardin d'Essai du Hamma* is a symptom of transformation in social ecologies and mental ecologies that are prerequisites for changes in natural ecologies. While colonial ideals no longer hold sway, persons, like vegetation, are also no longer entirely "indigenous" or "native." Many have been imported and come from other places. The earlier goal of adaptation and control gives way to another emphasizing preservation and the building of a common space. With its utopian ecological views and its emphasis in the words of Félix Guattari on producing different sensibilities and forms of intelligence, the *Jardin* serves to show how the Mediterranean can no longer be simply considered as a border separating two countries or two continents. The sea—with its sinuous borders and rocky edges—has again to be thought of as dividing *and* uniting populations, much like a new *Mare Nostrum* that will help reassess notions of "here" and "there." Such a rethinking will have to help put in place social ecologies that go beyond the restrictions imposed by national borders. Citizens—no longer tied only by blood and soil, but also by fate—will actively contribute to the construction of common spaces. This leads to a new feeling that nothing is truly native and that humans, like plants in the *Jardin*, are products of border crossings extending over the millennia. These crossing must be facilitated so that we think less in terms of inclusion and exclusion along the lines of national borders than, as Etienne Balibar again has shown, in terms of citizens gathered by fate and engaged in the construction of common spaces toward collective ecological ends.

NOTES

1 Fernand Braudel, *Memory and the Mediterranean*, trans. Sîan Reynolds (New York: Alfred A. Knopf, 2001); see also Michel Mollat du Jourdin, "Le Front de mer," in *Les Lieux de mémoire*, ed. Pierre Nora, vol. 2 (Paris: Gallimard/Quarto, 1997), 2721–64, especially 2721–22.

2 This chapter deals with border problems specifically between Algeria and France and not the refugee problems due to several wars mainly in the eastern part of the Mediterranean.

3 See Gilles Deleuze and Félix Guattari, *Mille Plateaux* (Paris: Editions de Minuit, 1980), 143–63.

4 Étienne Balibar, *We, the People of Europe: Reflections on Transnational Citizenship*, trans. James Swenson (Princeton, NJ: Princeton University Press, 2004), 4 and passim.

5 See Frantz Fanon, *The Wretched of the Earth*, trans. Constance Farrington (New York: Grove Press, 1963).

6 Etienne Balibar, *Droit de cité* (La Tour d'Aigues, France: Editions de l'Aube, 1998).

7 Charles Salas, "Jardin d'Essai, Algiers," *Australian Humanities Review*. Eco-humanities Corner, 36 (July 2005), n.p., accessed February 10, 2013, www.australianhumanitiesreview.org/archive/Issue-July-2005/home.html.

8 Ibid., 3.

9 Ibid.

10 Hélène Cixous, *Illa* (Paris: Editions des femmes, 1980), 137.

BIBLIOGRAPHY

Balibar, Etienne. *Droit de cité*. La Tour d'Aigues, France: Editions de l'Aube, 1998.

Balibar, Etienne. *We, the People of Europe? Reflections on Transnational Citizenship*. Translated by James Swenson. Princeton, NJ: Princeton University Press, 2004.

Braudel, Fernand. *Memory and the Mediterranean*. Translated by Sîan Reynolds. New York: Alfred A. Knopf, 2001.

Carra, Paul and M. Gueit. *Le Jardin d'Essai du Hamma*. Accessed February 10, 2013. http://alger-roi.fr/Alger//jardin_essai/textes/4/crra/gueit.htm.

Cixous, Hélène. *Illa*. Paris: Editions des femmes, 1980.

Deleuze, Gilles and Félix Guattari. *A Thousand Plateaus: Capitalism and Schizophrenia*. Translated by Brian Massumi. Minneapolis: University of Minnesota Press, 1987.

Fanon, Frantz. *The Wretched of the Earth*. Translated by Constance Farrington. New York: Grove Press, 1963.

Gide, André. *Fruits of the Earth*. Translated by Dorothy Bussy. Baltimore, MD: Penguin, 1970.

"Journée mondiale des zones humides @ Jardin botanique du Hamma." Last modified February 2, 2013. Accessed February 10, 2013. www.Sortiraalger.com/event/journee-mondiale-des-zones-humides/.

Laribi, Ghanem and Sofiane Hadjadj, "Le Jardin d'essai du Hamma : histoire d'un jardin colonial," dans Abderrahmane Bouchène, Jean-Pierre Peyroulou, Ouanassa Siari Tengour et Sylvie Thénault, *Histoire de l'Algérie à la période coloniale: 1830–1962*, Éditions La Découverte et Éditions Barzakh, 2012, 120–3.

"Le jardin d'Essai du Hamma doté d'un nouvel espace dédié aux zones humides." Accessed April 1, 2013. http://elmoudjahid.com/fr/actualites/37745/.

"Les zones humides en Algérie." Accessed April 1, 2013. www.Dgf.gov.dz/zones_humides/zhu-mide/php/.

Malek, Alloula. *Alger, Photographiée au XIXe siècle*. Alger: Editions Marval, 2001.

Mollat du Jourdin, Michel. "Le Front de mer." In *Les Lieux de mémoire*, edited by Pierre Nora, vol. 2, 2721–64. Paris: Gallimard/Quarto, 1997.

Salas, Charles. "Jardin d'Essai, Algiers." *Australian Humanities Review*. Eco-humanities Corner. 36 (July 2005). Accessed February 10, 2013. http://australianhumanitiesreview.org/archive/Issue-July2005/.

Sampol, Marceline. "Louis Auguste Hardy, Directeur du Jardin d'Essai, 1842–1868." Accessed February 10, 2013. http://alger-roi.fr/Alger/jardin_essai/textes/3_auguste_hardy_directeur_aea102htm.

Site officiel du Jardin d'essai du Hamma. Accessed February 1, 2013. www.jardindessai.com.

Vidal-Bué, Marion. *L'Algérie des peintres, 1830–1960*. Paris: Editions Paris-Méditerranée, 2000.

Wharton, Edith. *The Cruise of the Vanadis*. New York: Saint Martin/Rizzoli, 2004.

Zaher. "Le Jardin d'Essai et ses zones humides." Accessed April 1, 2013. www.jardindessai.com/2013/02/03/le-jardindessai-et-ses…/.

Conclusion

MAKING SENSE OF SOCIAL ECOLOGY, BORDERS AND THE ENVIRONMENT

Michele Zebich-Knos

Borders, Culture and Equity

One lesson that this rich array of chapters conveys is that borders are not only physical divisions between nation-states (or states), but are also lines of separation between peoples, places, things and even mindsets. These lines of separation occur tangibly between *and* within states, and intangibly within one's own psyche. Put simply, borders (also referred to as *frontiers*) define the difference between *us* and *them*, whether they are physical barriers such as the Israeli-constructed wall surrounding Palestinian territory, or psychological barriers resulting from years of political turmoil between Protestants and Catholics in Belfast, Northern Ireland. Brunet-Jailly argues that, since 9/11, the notion of an increasingly securitized border is a familiar mainstay between states, yet also extends from the periphery (territorial border) to the core (state's heartland) via airports, pre-clearance areas and other security-check locations. Brunet-Jailly emphasizes the "non-territorial border" that, in turn, broadens the concept of border space and gives it a new and more fluid meaning.[1] The non-territorial border transforms into a "third space" that, according to Konrad and Nicol, is "occupied by heterogeneous and hybrid culture, with […] people who share new visions of community across borders."[2] It is a space in which culture plays a key role in explaining how a landscape emerges socially, environmentally and politically. One might even liken Konrad and Nicol's third space to that of Cunningham's edge effect resulting in the intersection of two bordering communities.

It is in that intersection that a hybrid culture can develop. The intersection of two cultures may indeed manifest "new visions of community" and apply, for example, to Belfast, Northern Ireland, where Murtagh admits to the decrease of housing segregation and the increase of "ethno-religious mixed housing." Yet, following the 1998 Belfast Peace Agreement, he also recognizes the increase of "peace lines" that separate Protestants and Catholic communities. Such lines foster a newly securitized Belfast in keeping with Brunet-Jailly's assertions in Chapter 1; and, one might question how that contributes to a new vision of community in Belfast.

Schneider and Ingram's examination of culture's impact on policy making is especially relevant to the chapters in this volume as they make a case that people's decisions result not merely from incentive-based choice, but also from "culturally-induced values, and that they need to be convinced that a policy preferred alternative fits into their value scheme."[3] Without cultural acknowledgment, policies, according to Schneider and Ingram, are likely to be less successful in achieving their goals. Uncle Max, the revered Elder, and others like him are transmitters of native Australian culture, yet, that culture, according to Birrell and Hill, is "unseen by most." (See Chapter 11.) It is also unlikely that the Aboriginal world Uncle Max represents has any impact on the Japanese loggers cutting trees on the *sacred* mountain, presumably with an Australian government permit. Perhaps the key is not in one's culture, but in the organizational effort put forth to get heard, as Tavares points out in his Peruvian Amazon example.

The concept of "equity across boundaries" developed by Whiteley, Ingram, and Perry (in their study of water use) as well as Laird-Benner and Ingram is a salient US–Mexico border concept where asymmetrical power relationships are the norm.[4] The US–Mexico border region also takes on a life of its own—that is, third space—in which people behave in a cross-cultural manner, and natural ecosystems attempt to survive as they did before fences blocked many of their migratory routes. House-Peters aptly examines another border fencing process and gives special consideration to the consequences of the shift from Mexico's communal (*ejido*) land to private ownership on the riparian zones of the San Pedro River. This case attributes many of the asymmetrical water-use problems in the zone to heavy water users from the mining sector. The author develops an in-depth critique of neoliberal policies, which emphasize "individualized, market-based solutions" over political solutions that may benefit ecosystems as a whole. House-Peters scopes out the drivers of policy and its implications for this riparian space, which allows for better-informed policy making in the future.

Often, border policy interrupts traditional life as the case of the Tohono-O'odham tribe illustrates. While not explicitly examined by other contributors to this book, the Tohono-O'odham case informs a general discussion of how long-standing border traditions and seasonal migratory behaviors can clash with governments whose rule making is based on political circumstances far removed from border communities. The tribe's members span the US–Mexico border from Arizona (United States) to Sonora (Mexico), yet, in a post-9/11 world, they no longer have freedom to cross the border as they please. Placement of a US border fence along parts of the Tohono-O'odham reservation is an example of the gated "border barrier" Cunningham describes in Chapter 3 and of how the securitized border also impedes free movement of wildlife (Sonoran pronghorn antelope and desert tortoise) and people.[5] While Cunningham conceptualizes the meaning of the word gate in the abstract, Madsen elaborates on the actual "Gate," which he explains was a traditional border crossing (literally, an opening in the fence) and means for social interaction between both sides of Tohono-O'odham land that spanned a fluid US–Mexico border. Nothing more than a gate in a fence originally intended to keep cattle from wandering, it was rebuilt as a security barrier and has now become a symbol of contemporary border securitization.[6]

Unlike their Blackfeet tribal counterparts—whose US–Canada cross-border existence was officially recognized in the Jay Treaty (1794) and provided for travel and/or residence between the two countries—the Tohono-O'odham have no mutually assured freedom of movement. By statute (8 U.S.C. 1359), "nothing in this title shall be construed to affect the right of American Indians born in Canada to pass the borders of the United States, but such right shall extend only to persons who possess at least 50 per centum of blood of the American Indian race."[7] This indigenous caveat for preferred treatment of Northern tribes is recognized by the US Citizenship and Immigration Services as it provides directions on how to obtain a green card and recognizes that "American Indians born in Canada [...] cannot be denied admission to the United States."[8] Equal application of the law is not identical for the United States' Northern versus Southern cross-border tribes.

Seeking Balance and Community

The preceding chapters also remind us constantly that, since borders are so diverse in their composition and structure, they should be studied using more than one approach, and not merely from the obvious political or policy method of analysis. Governments do not have a monopoly on border issues, but they frequently precipitate and influence the course of events. Indeed, this is the case as Conley seeks to fold political aspects of colonialism into the subtle and natural surroundings of a botanical garden, the *Jardin d'Essai*, created by French landscape designers in the former colony of Algeria. A natural border separating *Arab* Algeria from *French* Algeria, the Jardin d'Essai was intended as a leisurely respite for French colonists. Today, the Jardin d'Essai is a pleasant repose for Algerian citizens within the busy capital city of Algiers—not a *peace* park in Walters and Ali's sense of the term, but simply a *peaceful* park. Upon reading this volume, and for better or worse, we see that borders have an intrinsic value as *separator*, but the separation is not static, and while the Jardin d'Essai represented one set of beliefs in the French colonial era, its function evolved to benefit Algerians and now serves to separate the busy urban environment of Algiers from the quiet green space within its confines.

How people deal with such separations as time passes becomes evident in every chapter, but is especially evident in Grichting's coverage of the Berlin wall and communism in Chapter 7. Very much the architect and urban planner, Grichting observes that the Berlin Wall's demise did not spark the creation of a formal ecological buffer zone or peace park. However, the end of communism was instrumental in the creation of the Pan-European Green Belt stretching along the former Iron Curtain borders with its people-friendly trail and ecological corridor conducive for the propagation of endangered native species such as the wolf bear and lynx. The dissolution of one border, that is, the Iron Curtain divide, has led to a positive redefinition of what was formerly an insidious political divide between Eastern and Western Europe. The result is a pleasant and productive ecosystem for humans and nonhumans alike.

Residents affected within a politically divided border area seek balance and a sense of community that adds purpose and joy within what might otherwise become a rather drab existence—especially in highly conflicted border zones. From the chapters, we see that residents often create a border lifestyle that is capable of yielding art, social activity and a natural environment replete with plant life. As is the case of Israel and Palestine, the border is not merely a wall, or an inanimate object, but an area in which residents must adapt so that life does not remain at a standstill. And sometimes borders facilitate creation of an *accidental park*, or de facto conservation area, as is the case of the Korean Demilitarized Zone (DMZ). The rich diversity in Korean flora and fauna is the unintended consequence of the strictly controlled (and heavily mined) DMZ, which regulates traffic and keeps most people out of the area, with a few exceptions.

The DMZ is perhaps one of the world's most infamous borders, yet it is ironically acknowledged as a significant ecological wildlife zone. This strained border is the setting in which North and South Korea's migratory Red-crowned Cranes must exist. Healy and colleagues elaborate on the stately grandeur of this bird held so dear to Korean (and Asian) culture. Unlike humans, who are subject to legal/physical barriers inherent in the border-crossing experience between nation-states, Red-crowned Cranes are oblivious to the legal/physical barriers the DMZ presents. Following the rules of nature and not governments, these magnificent birds migrate freely between North and South Korea as they have done prior to the DMZ's creation. The Red-crowned Cranes thus represent a sense of freedom that Bookchin tried to capture in his writings—freedom from economic, social and political domination for, according to him, domination is at the heart of environmental degradation.[9] While some border areas like the DMZ result in significant ecological conservation, others, such as the Palestinian camps in Lebanon or East Jerusalem (Shu'fat), nurture small backyard gardens of green instead of entire nature zones. Each border area is different, thus conferring unique characteristics to each chapter within this book.

Walters and Ali's chapter on the Balkan Peace Park Project (B3P) is a fine example of the slow process involved in achieving environmental change. Slowness is the norm in environmental conservation rather than the exception—just think of climate change negotiations. This peace park is a work in progress that awaits formal legal approval. While there is no formal park at this writing, at least students from across the globe are getting a solid field experience in what is a beautiful mountainous border region. The park's future fruition could prove an excellent example of what Armitage, Plummer and colleagues call "adaptive co-management" that enables formerly conflicted nation-states to jointly conserve spectacular mountainous terrain in a cooperative manner.[10] While Walters and Ali delve into the intricacies of a *peace park in the making*, Zunckel's years of experience in transboundary conservation management and his chapter's focus on facilitation and "cooperation between nations that share common natural features" offers solid advice that B3P stakeholders would do well to consider in their ongoing efforts to realize their goal. Zunckel's coverage of basic transboundary conservation principles (trust, confidence and capacity) is a practical method in which he argues in Chapter 2 that stakeholders must "avoid creating unrealistic expectations." The reader can only conclude that many of the non-Balkan stakeholders in Walters and Ali's case study failed to heed practitioner Zunckel's simple steps for creation of a transboundary conservation area. Once it becomes a legally recognized peace park, those directly involved in its administration would do well to incorporate Zunckel's (and IUCN) principles into the park's management.

Bringing stakeholders together to discuss common environmental and social goals for the area is something that Walters and Ali's chapter examines in detail, and when plans fail, they move to important lessons learned so that the Balkans Peace Park Project will have not been for naught. Their stakeholder-focused method of analysis for lessons learned is a technique worthy of consideration where transboundary peace parks are on the drawing board. Combining Walters and Ali's lessons-learned method with that outlined by Zunckel will make useful reading for stakeholders involved in peace park projects elsewhere in the world.

Brunet-Jailly's brief mention of climate change in a tome devoted to the social ecology of borders also reminds us that border ecologies are inherently intertwined with environmental issues, many of which bear the mark of anthropogenic or human influence. Climate change is certainly one such example, and border environments have attracted the attention of economists and environmental scholars alike. One result is the development of "border carbon adjustments" (BCA) aimed at letting state borders contribute to carbon reduction efforts without causing undue burden to their economy. This is accomplished, as Helm and Schmidt assert, through a "policy instrument designed to prevent competitive disadvantages for firms located in countries that implement unilateral climate policies."[11] Helm and Schmidt's assumption is that BCA "reduces the abatement cost of signatories (due to export exemptions) and raises the costs of non-signatories (due to import tariffs)" thereby inducing a "stabilizing effect" that encourages greater climate change cooperation by non-signatories.[12]

This border model for climate cooperation could *potentially* yield better results in bringing states together to reach a climate agreement, in a post–Kyoto Protocol era, than will the traditional investment in carbon-reduction methods. This latter method, while useful for pollution abatement, may aggravate the well-known "free rider" problem.[13] In the long term, BCAs may even be better at improving climate agreement outcomes than the original Kyoto Protocol, whose strategy was largely one of greenhouse gas (GHG) reductions within signatory countries. Under that approach, non-signatories were given a GHG-reduction exemption, which some developed countries, the United States in particular, perceived as an unfair trade advantage. In short, the standard border ecology of trade has transformed into a future tool for improving the environment.

Trade and Activism: Local Developments in Bounded Spaces

This border ecology of trade is also evident, even in antithetical ways, in other chapters. Shibli's depiction of the militarized landscapes in South Lebanon's Marwaheen village and the Ein El Hilwi Palestinian refugee camp is one of harsh circumstances and poor public services, yet these locales are filled with ongoing activity as residents seek to improve their economic plight largely by farming and herding and by selling their agricultural products. When government-subsidized agriculture yields less than expected results, the young frequently migrate to jobs elsewhere in Lebanon. These South Lebanese examples are not far from the Israeli border, yet political/military tensions preclude border trade that exists normally between neighboring countries in other parts of the world. Isolation, estrangement and lack of hope tend to typify such harshscapes in which small steps to create a semblance of nature might include something as simple as planting an herb garden. The informal attempt at *greenscaping*, albeit small, is one way to alleviate the daily tension of life in a conflicted border area.

Like the Lebanese examples mentioned by Shibli, Bulle's examination of the Shu'fat refugee camp of East Jerusalem depicts a similar social ecology of strife and turmoil caused by political/military events. The most obvious manifestation is the construction of a barrier that physically "walls residents in" and creates a marked "us versus them" environment all within the greater Jerusalem area. Israel controls the legal right of passage (movement) to the "other side" in this asymmetrical power relationship. Lesser activities such as small-scale gardening and cottage industry exist among Shu'fat's residents while more dynamic advances take place on the Israeli side of the wall. To make life bearable, Bulle reminds us that residents create what she calls a "regime of the local" in which they imbue a sense of culture, greenspace and shared identity within their camp's physical surroundings. To control one's surroundings even in small ways imparts a sense of empowerment that Shibli's Lebanese example did not explicitly reveal, but surely exists. This is also a sentiment Brunet-Jailly raises in Chapter 1 when he writes about the articulation (and empowerment) of local forces and how essential it is to the well-being of local communities whether they border Israel or exist within the city limits of Belfast, Northern Ireland.

The asymmetrical power relationship Palestinians experience in their dealings along the Israeli wall, or within Lebanon's southern village and refugee camp confines, serves as natural transition to yet another disjuncture between two groups of people—that of Catholic and Protestant residents in Belfast. This time we see Murtagh's analysis of Belfast's internal borders manifested by land use patterns reflective of what he calls segregated spaces, spaces mentioned earlier in the context of Konrad and Nicols' new visions of community. It is within the poorest of these working-class spaces that we see environmental degradation, strained socioeconomic conditions, residential divides between ethno-religious groups and greater policing of these communities.

Murtagh remains hopeful as he describes the case of the Suffolk/Lenadoon area in west Belfast in which joint Catholic–Protestant cooperation emerged as a result of very basic needs such as installation of a traffic light on the Stewartstown Road and childcare for working mothers. Out of these needs, community representatives from Protestant Suffolk and Catholic Lenadoon formed the Suffolk-Lenadoon Interface Group (SLIG) and, ultimately, the Stewartstown Road Regeneration Project (SRRP). This latter creation reveals a local effort to spark economic viability within the area through creation of shops and office space, and eventually expanded, thanks to EU and US funding, to open a mixed-use commercial, retail and community center. Residents—both Catholic and Protestant—did not want their Suffolk/Lenadoon community overlooked as middle-class Belfast continued to make economic strides forward. Theirs was as locally generated a decision to expand community development as was the Ein el-Hilwi decision to create six vocational training centers in the camp. These two examples, one in Northern Ireland and the other in Lebanon, represent the ability for areas under sociopolitical and economic distress to improve their landscape and lifestyle through grassroots efforts originating within the community. We learn from Murtagh and Shibli that bordered spaces within Belfast's neighborhoods as defined by its *interfaces* and South Lebanon's villages and refugee camps near the Lebanese–Israeli buffer zone share something in common—the mundane pursuit of life in a former conflict zone with all the past baggage that such a zone brings to present-day and future life. One can only hope that these areas remain *former* conflict zones.

Implications for the Future

Governance in increasingly complex societies exacerbates the *Weberian* attempt by policy makers and administrators to create rational methods for resolving modern-day problems. Lejano and Stokols remind us that "this process of rationalization involves the artificial separating of reasoning into different systems (e.g., cultural, financial, etc.), and allowing each system to operate autonomously."[14] Through acceptance of this method of governance, we risk overlooking cultural values imbedded in certain behaviors that run against the grain of "rational" policy, laws or regulations. We also risk losing sight of whose "rationality" do governing bodies actually espouse. Surely placing a wall along the natural Sonoran Desert path of migrating antelope, a Green Line in Cyprus, or the DMZ across Korea's 38th Parallel does not represent a rational/natural ecological order.

More than anything, this book provides two important lessons for future policy making and border management. The first lesson is to take into account local needs and behaviors. This is perhaps the most overlooked and counterintuitive element, especially in conflicted borders areas. For example, why should the Jerusalem municipality go beyond the pale and address the concerns of Shu'fat's Palestinian community? The answer for Israelis should be obvious for it can foster a better-managed and safer environment for all area residents, not just those of Shu'fat. After construction of the Israeli wall in 2003 the camp found itself on the West Bank side of the barrier, but Jerusalem technically still maintains jurisdiction over the camp. Residents pay city and state taxes, but must now travel into Jerusalem through a security checkpoint even though they hold Jerusalem identity cards. We can hypothesize that the more Shu'fat camp improves in the eyes of its residents and the more harmonious its internal environment becomes, the less likely its residents will contribute to future security threats in Israel. The United Nations Relief and Works Agency (UNWRA) began such an effort in 2013 by founding the Healthy Camp Initiative to improve community problems in keys areas such as solid waste management, school dropout rates for male students and domestic violence. Attention to the social ecology and needs of a people in limbo could, in an ironic twist, enhance border securitization. For Jerusalem's own well-being, future improvements should include Israeli efforts in Shu'fat since the camp falls under the city's jurisdiction and not that of the Palestinian Authority. One place to start is the creation of more streamlined and faster checkpoint control for Shu'fat residents who work in Jerusalem. Another critical Jerusalem municipal effort would be to assist in waste management, which has grown to near-crisis proportions, according to Shu'fat residents, and whose unsanitary conditions will eventually impact the Israeli settlement of Pisgat Ze'ev in East Jerusalem.

The second lesson is to view border environments as part of a larger global community and not as an isolated ecosystem. While border ecotones may develop and possess their own unique traits, today's vital global issues like climate change are transboundary and not deterred by political frontiers. The future of border ecosystems such as the Tijuana Estuary, first mentioned in this book's Preface, represents one ongoing effort to preserve and protect the area's wildlife. It also offers value in the long-term quest to better understand climate change, for example, and track its effects within the estuary and marshland. This value for scientific research comes from the practical role played by the Tijuana Estuary's species that represent "narrow habitat tolerance" and can serve as a bellwether of forthcoming climate changes.[15]

Bookchin might say that it is the profit-seeking capitalist's rationality that governments seek, and Tavares's chapter certainly agrees with this premise. Tavares documents a classic Latin American struggle of "us versus them" that erupted in the 2009 violent clashes between local indigenous peoples and a national government bent on economic growth—this time in Peru's Amazon River Basin. The wall was not physical, but legal, and the *divide* was land-use change to facilitate extraction activities in the Amazon. Added to this nonphysical, legal divide is Peru's Amazon River Basin that came to represent a very physical line of demarcation between the contested area in question and the rest of Peru.

House-Peters's chapter also shares Tavares's view that land tenure is critical to understanding environmental issues affecting inherently disadvantaged border populations whose political and economic power cannot compete with neoliberal forces. While other chapters may allude to economic influences on social-ecological systems, these two chapters spell it out for the reader in unabashed critiques of the contemporary neoliberal world. What they do is to jar us into recognition that environmental issues, more often than not, possess underlying economic structures, which can exacerbate the balance within both nonhuman and local human communities in a given social-ecological system. Both House-Peters and Tavares's methodological frameworks tend toward the concept of environmental justice within their respective case studies, and thus guide the reader back to social ecology's core beliefs explained in the introductory pages of this book.

Perhaps, as Ingram, Lejano and other scholars urge, we should employ greater "contextual analysis" in our attempts to govern border spaces (wherever they may be located) and to integrate normative *context* into a systems approach complete with feedback loops that take into consideration social, economic and environmental variables.[16] However, in our quantifiably oriented world, there is increasing apprehension against accepting *normative* rather than measured dimensions.[17] It soon becomes obvious that the normative, social ecological path is not one that policy makers always follow. However, few behaviors and policies are 100 percent rational and devoid of any normative context. If they were, then we could not talk about French, British or Argentine sovereign, territorial claims in Antarctica—a continent without globally recognized borders—where no formal customs or immigration procedures impede visitors from entering Esperanza Base, which Argentina considers its *sovereign* territory.[18] In the name of environmental protection, such contradictions exist—but not only in Antarctica.

Figure C.1 Esperanza Base, Argentina's research station on the Antarctic Peninsula. Photograph by Michele Zebich-Knos, 2004.

NOTES

1 Emmanuel Brunet-Jailly, "Borders, Borderlands and Theory: An Introduction," *Geopolitics* 16 (2011): 4.
2 Victor Konrad and Heather N. Nicol, "Border Culture, the Boundary Between Canada and the United States of America, and the Advancement of Borderlands Theory," *Geopolitics* 16 (2011): 72.
3 Anne Schneider and Helen Ingram, "Behavioral Assumptions of Policy Tools," *Journal of Politics* 52 (1990): 520.
4 Wendy Laird-Benner and Helen Ingram, "Sonoran Desert Network Weavers: Surprising Environmental Successes on the U.S./Mexico Border," *Environmental Magazine* 53 (2011): 7–16; and John M. Whiteley, Helen Ingram and Richard Perry, eds. *Water, Place, and Equity* (Cambridge, MA: MIT Press, 2008).
5 Laird-Benner and Ingram, "Sonoran Desert Network Weavers," 14.
6 Kenneth D. Madsen, "A Basis for Bordering: Land, Migration, and Inter-Tohono O'odham Distinction along the U.S.–Mexico Line," in *Placing the Border in Everyday Life*, eds. Reece Jones and Corey Johnson (London: Ashgate Publishers, 2014), 109.
7 Aliens and Nationality: Application to American Indians Born in Canada, 8 U.S.C. 1359 § 289 (1952).
8 US Citizenship and Immigration Services, "Green Card for an American Indian Born in Canada," accessed June 6, 2014, www.uscis.gov/green-card/other-ways-get-green-card/green-card-american-indian-born-canada/.

9 Michael E. Zimmerman, *Contesting Earth's Future: Radical Ecology and Postmodernity* (Berkeley: University of California Press, 1994), 153.

10 Derek R. Armitage, Ryan Plummer, Fikret Berkes et al. "Adaptive Co-management for Social-Ecological Complexity," *Frontiers in Ecology and the Environment*, 7 (2009): 95–102.

11 Carsten Helm and Robert C. Schmidt, "Climate Cooperation with Technology Investments and Border Carbon Adjustment," Discussion Paper 2014–65 (Cambridge, MA: Harvard Project on Climate Agreement, 2014), 2.

12 Ibid., 3.

13 Ibid., 22.

14 Raul P. Lejano and Daniel Stokols, "Social Ecology, Sustainability, and Economics," *Ecological Economics* 89 (2013): 1.

15 Mathew L. James and Joy B. Zedler, "Dynamics of Wetland and Upland Subshrubs at the Salt Marsh Coastal Sage Scrub Ecotone," *American Midland Naturalist* 143 (2000): 298–311.

16 Ibid., 3; and Daniel Stokols, Raul Perez Lejano and John Hipp, "Enhancing the Resilience of Human-Environmental Systems: A Social Ecological Perspective," *Ecology and Society* 18 (2013): 7, accessed June 6, 2014, doi:10.5751/ES-05301-180107.

17 Jonathan J. Pierce, Saba Siddiki, Michael D. Jones, Kristin Schumacher, Andrew Pattison and Holly Peterson, "Social Construction and Policy Design: A Review of Past Applications," *Policy Studies Journal* 42 (2014): 1–28.

18 Michele Zebich-Knos, "Conflict Avoidance and Environmental Protection: The Antarctic Paradigm," in *Peace Parks: Conservation and Conflict Resolution*, ed. Saleem Ali (Cambridge, MA: MIT Press, 2007), 176.

BIBLIOGRAPHY

Aliens and Nationality: Application to American Indians Born in Canada, 8 U.S.C. 1359 § 289 (1952).

Armitage, Derek R., Ryan Plummer, Fikret Berkes et al. "Adaptive Co-management for Social-Ecological Complexity." *Frontiers in Ecology and the Environment*, 7 (2009): 95–102.

Brunet-Jailly, Emmanuel. "Borders, Borderlands and Theory: An Introduction." *Geopolitics* 16 (2011): 1–6.

Helm, Carsten, and Robert C. Schmidt. "Climate Cooperation with Technology Investments and Border Carbon Adjustment," Discussion Paper 2014–65. Cambridge, MA: Harvard Project on Climate Agreement, 2014.

James, Mathew L. and Joy B. Zedler. "Dynamics of Wetland and Upland Subshrubs at the Salt Marsh Coastal Sage Scrub Ecotone." *American Midland Naturalist* 143 (2000): 298–311.

Konrad, Victor and Heather N. Nicol. "Border Culture, the Boundary Between Canada and the United States of America, and the Advancement of Borderlands Theory." *Geopolitics* 16 (2011): 70–90.

Laird-Brenner, Wendy and Helen Ingram. "Sonoran Desert Network Weavers: Surprising Environmental Successes on the U.S./Mexico Border." *Environmental Magazine* 53 (2011): 7–16.

Lejano, Raul P. and Daniel Stokols. "Social Ecology, Sustainability, and Economics." *Ecological Economics* 89 (2013): 1–6.

Madsen Kenneth. D. "A Basis for Bordering: Land, Migration, and Inter-Tohono O'odham Distinction along the U.S.–Mexico Line." In *Placing the Border in Everyday Life*, edited by Reece Jones and Corey Johnson, 93–116. London: Ashgate Publishers, 2014.

Pierce, Jonathan J., Saba Siddiki, Michael D. Jones, Kristin Schumacher, Andrew Pattison and Holly Peterson. "Social Construction and Policy Design: A Review of Past Applications." *Policy Studies Journal* 42 (2014): 1–28.

Schneider, Anne and Helen Ingram. "Behavioral Assumptions of Policy Tools." *Journal of Politics* 52 (1990): 510–29.

Stokols, Daniel, Raul Perez Lejano and John Hipp. "Enhancing the Resilience of Human-Environmental Systems: A Social Ecological Perspective." *Ecology and Society* 18 (2013): 7. Accessed June 6, 2014. doi:10.5751/ES-05301-180107.

US Citizenship and Immigration Services, "Green Card for an American Indian Born in Canada," accessed June 6, 2014, www.uscis.gov/green-card/other-ways-get-green-card/green-card-american-indian-born-canada/.

Whiteley, John M., Helen Ingram and Richard Perry, eds. *Water, Place, and Equity.* Cambridge, MA: MIT Press, 2008.

Zebich-Knos, Michele. "Conflict Avoidance and Environmental Protection: The Antarctic Paradigm." In *Peace Parks: Conservation and Conflict Resolution,* edited by Saleem Ali, 163–82. Cambridge, MA: MIT Press, 2007.

Zimmerman, Michael E. *Contesting Earth's Future: Radical Ecology and Postmodernity.* Berkeley: University of California Press, 1994.

INDEX

A Thousand Plateaus 204, 232
abandoned spaces 144
Africa
    Algeria 12, 233–36, 238, 245
    colonial rule, Algeria 233–34
    decolonization 234
    Great Limpopo Transfrontier Park 27, 42
    Jardin d'essai, Algiers 12, 90, 235,
        237–39, 245
    Melilla and Ceuta 55
    Monument to the Martyrs, Algiers 238
    Morocco 22, 55
    Mozambique 27, 42
    Musée National des Beaux Arts,
        Algiers 236
    South Africa 27, 37–38, 42, 93
    Southern African Development Community
        (SADC) 44
    spatial borders, citizens and immigrants
        between 234
    Xolobeni 42
    Zimbabwe 23, 27, 42
Allouache, Merzak 234
Ancestors 198, 205
Antarctica 29, 250
Association for Historical Dialogue 132, 141
Australia
    Aborigenes 8
    Aboriginal wisdom 205
    Australia Day 197, 199, 206
    Ganma process 203
    van Gennep, Arnold 202
Austrian Development Agency (ADA) 79

Bab el Oued 234
Balibar, Etienne 29, 232, 234, 240
Balkans 8–9, 12, 23, 71–74, 76–77, 80–81, 83,
    85, 246. *See also* Europe
Beuys, Joseph 135–36
Bhabha, Homi K. 19–20, 134
bighorn sheep 62

biodiversity x, 9–10, 23–24, 37–38, 41, 45,
    48, 54, 83, 96, 102, 113, 131, 134, 136,
    139–40, 144–45, 225, 238
biophilia 89
Biosphere Reserve 92
Bohai and Yellow Seas region 27
Bookchin, Murray ix, 2, 20, 30, 54,
    89–90, 92–93, 132–33, 153–54,
    165, 246, 250
border carbon adjustments 247
border environments 2–3, 8, 11, 53,
    247, 250
border studies 3, 22, 53–54, 74
border traditions 244
border villages 156–57
border walls 22, 54, 56–58, 60–61
bordering 5, 9, 20, 22–24, 28, 30, 53, 58, 62,
    173, 243
borderlands 6–7, 9, 11, 20–28, 30, 56,
    89, 91–92, 100, 109–12, 116–17,
    121, 123, 125, 132, 134, 206
Borders in Globalization (BIG) project 53
borderscapes 59, 132, 181, 188, 192
boundary-making 53
Braudel, Fernand 231
Brexit 58
Buffer Zone 10, 131–32, 140–44.
    See also Cyprus

California red-legged frog 62
Carey, Peter 204
Carson, Rachel 1
Chinese State Forestry
    Administration 96
civil rights 177, 227
Cixous, Hélène 237
Clément, Gilles 134, 138, 145
climate change
    borders 247
    greenhouse gas (GHG) reductions 247
    Kyoto Protocol 247

cognitive borders 4, 6
Cold War 57, 225
communism 72, 81, 245
conflict resolution x, 8, 92, 188
containment 211, 227
cross-border pollution x
cross-border trek. *See also* Balkans
Cyprus
    Cypriot communities 10, 131–32, 141
    Cyprus Buffer Zone 131
    Cyprus GreenLine Scapes Laboratory 1
    Greek Cypriots 141–42
    Green Line 132, 138, 140–41,
        144–45, 249
    Nicosia, Cyprus 132, 138, 142–44
    Turkish Cypriots 141
    United Nations Buffer Zone (UNBZ)
        131–32, 142

de facto conservation area 246. *See also*
    Korean Demilitarized Zone (DMZ)
Deleuze, G., French eco-philosopher 133,
    204–5, 232, 239
deterritorialization 232
Djaout, Tahar 234

ecological corridor 139, 245
EcoPeace Middle East 41
ecosystems 131
ecotone x, 5
ecotourism 74–76, 81, 92, 140
edge effect 5, 54, 58, 170, 243
egrets 100
environmental degradation 7, 54, 59, 121,
    246, 248
environmental diversity 135
environmental management and
    cooperation 246
Environmentally Responsible Action (ERA)
    Group 76. *See also* Balkans
ethno-religious groups 248
Europe
    Albania 23, 73–78, 81, 83–84
    Belfast, Northern Ireland 10–11, 165, 243,
        248
    Berlin 2, 5, 12, 55, 57–58, 131–32, 136–40,
        245
    Berlin Wall 5, 12, 55, 57–58, 136–40
    Bialowieza Forest 23
    Bjeshket e Nemuna National Park, Kosovo
        76, 84

Germany 9, 90, 93, 132, 134, 139
    Green Belt 1, 41, 74, 132, 139–40, 245
    Iron Curtain 1, 41, 139, 232, 245
    Kosovo 28, 59, 73–77, 81–84. *See also*
        Balkans
    Lohmuehle Wagendorf, Germany 136
    Macedonia 23, 59, 83
    Mauer Park 131, 136
    Montenegro 73–77, 81–84
    Prespa Park 23
    Prokletije National Park 76
    Serbia 57, 73, 82
    Shala Valley, Albania 73, 75, 81
    Suffolk/Lenadoon community, Belfast 248
    Yugoslav conflict 73
European Union 21, 58, 78, 132, 190, 248
expropriation, land 10, 109, 111, 117,
    121, 227

Fanon, Frantz 233
forestlands 211–14, 226
fortified fencing 56–57, 60, 62
Fortress Europe 58
free-market policies 227
Friends of the Earth, Germany 49, 139
Front National, France 234
Fugitive Landscapes 125

Galtung's positive peace theory 81
gated ecologies 5, 9, 153
German Green Party 135
Golan Heights 7
great wall of globalization 57
Greenfield-Gilat, Yehuda 7, 15
Grey Herons 100
groundwater 109, 111–14, 119–21, 123
Grus japonensis. *See also* Red-crowned Crane
Guattari, F., French eco-philosopher 133,
    204–5, 232, 239–40

Hadiqat As-Samah garden, Beirut 143
hamma, marsh, Arabic for 235
Healthy Camp Initiative, UNWRA creation
    249
human, non-human displacement 62
human–nature interaction 3

incentive-based choice 243
indigenous cultures 203
indigenous peoples 12, 37, 227, 250
informal human corridors 62

intangible rifts 3
International Boundary Commission x
International Crane Foundation 6, 90, 95, 99.
    See also Red-crowned Crane
International Peace Park Expeditions 76
International Union for the Conservation of
    Nature (IUCN) 29, 37, 74, 83. *See also*
    IUCN
Ioannidou, Colette 141
isolation 247
Israel 7, 10–12, 55, 169, 177, 245, 248–49
IUCN 23, 29, 37, 43–44, 47–49, 74, 83,
    89, 246

jaguars 62

Konrad, Victor 3–4, 6, 243, 248
Korea, North and South
    Anbyon 9, 90, 94–97, 99–102
    as National Natural Treasure #202 94
    Cheorwon Plain 96, 100
    Crane Pavilion 94
    Democratic People's Republic of Korea
        (DPRK) 89
    Dorasan Peace Park 40
    flora and fauna 5, 9, 12, 54, 137, 246
    Korea Otter Research Center 92
    Korean DMZ 1, 5, 13, 48
    Koryo Dynasty 94
    Mount Keumgang 92
    Park Geun Hye, president South Korea 91
    Pisan Cooperative 90, 96–97, 102
    re-unification 40, 90, 100, 182
    World Peace Park 41
Korean Demilitarized Zone (DMZ) 9, 246.
    See also Korea

laissez-faire, economic and environment 227
land-use change 250
Latin America
    Amazon Basin 210, 226, 250
    Amazon River Basin 210
    Amazonia 209, 211, 226–27
    Asociación Interetnica de Desarollo de la
        Selva Peruana, indigenous nationalities
        coalition Peruvian 211
    best-use/productive capacity, soil Amazon
        213
    blockades, land conflict Amazon 211
    Constitution, Peru, Article 66, *Of the
        Environment and Natural Resources* 214

Constitution, Peru, Article 88, *Of the
    Agrarian Regime and Peasant and Indigenous
    Communities* 214
Cordillera del Condor Transboundary
    Protected Area 48, 92
Decree 1090, Peru 211, 213, 226
Devil's Curve, curva del Diablo, Peru 210
Forest and Wildlife Law, Peru 213
Garcia, A., president Peru 211–13, 226
Law 28852, land concessions, Amazon
    Peruvian 212
Law for the Promotion of Private
    Investment in Reforestation and
    Agroforestry, Peru 212
Peru 8, 12, 48, 92, 102, 210–13, 225–26,
    250
Peruvian Amazon 211, 213, 226, 244
Supreme Decree N0062/75-AG, national
    geological index, Peru 213–14, 226
Velasco Alvarado general, Peru 213, 226
Lebanese–Israeli border 11
Lebanon
    Army of 155, 161
    Birki, communal pond 158
    blue-line, demarcation of border 157
    customary codes ('*urf*) 158
    Ein El Hilwi, refugee camp 153, 247
    El-Kifah El-Mosallah (Armed Defiance),
        checkpoint 162
    Jabal-Amel 155
    Litani River 155
    Marwaheen 11, 153–54, 157–58, 160, 247
    mashaa, communal land 160
    Palestine Liberation Organization, PLO 161
    South Lebanon 153–55, 157, 160, 165
    Sykes-Picot treaty (1916) 155
    Women's Vocational Training Center
        (WVTC) 162–63
    Zaari't, Israeli settlement, border 11, 157
Lefebvre, Henri 124
liminal space 11, 19, 200, 203–4
liminality 19–20, 182

Maastricht Treaty 57
Maja Shkurt peak 76
marginal spaces 3, 20, 136
marginalization 1, 7, 54, 58, 117, 124,
    131, 165
marshland, border x, 250
Mediterranean Sea 7, 12, 131, 139, 231–36,
    238, 240

Melitpolous, Angela 138
mental and physical borders 233
mental demarcation 232
mental space 232
mental territories 6
militarization, border 155
Millennium Ecosystem Assessment 46
Milosevic, Slobodan 72

natural reserves 20–21, 23, 25–27, 30, 137.
    See also peace parks
natural spaces 12
naturally evolving landscapes 138
nature and politics 226
negotiations 3, 10, 13, 42, 91, 134, 246
neoliberalism 25, 124, 182–83
Nicol, Heather N. 248
no-man's-land 40
North–South axis 232

Oscar and Lucinda 204

Palestinian refugees 1, 153, 160, 170
Palestinian–Israeli issues
    Israeli wall 1–2, 5–6, 248–49
    Jerusalem 7, 11, 22, 169–70, 172, 175–77,
        246, 248–49
    Palestinian Authority 249
    Pisgat Ze'ev 249
    refugee camps 161
    SAYA/Design for Change 7
    Shu'fat 1, 6–7, 11, 165, 169–70, 171f.9.1,
        171–73, 175–77, 246, 248–49. See also
        Shu'fat Refugee Camp
participatory design 165
peace lines 182–83, 185, 188, 243
peace parks
    5th International Union for the
        Conservation of Nature (IUCN) World
        Parks Congress 37
    Ali, Saleem H. 9, 23, 245–47
    Balkans Peace Park 1, 9, 71, 73–74, 76–78,
        81, 84, 246. See also Balkans
    Peace Parks Foundation 42
    Peace Parks–Conservation and Conflict
        Resolution ix
    Waterton-Glacier International Peace Park
        48, 81
Perera, Suvendrini 4
permaculture 135, 201
political ecology 7–8
post-Westphalian formation 56

Property 115, 172
protected area management 37
psychological barriers ix, 243
psychological woundedness 3
psycho-social barriers 3
Ptolemy 231
pygmy owl 62

Ramsar Convention 96
reconciliation 23, 26, 71–72, 132, 135, 145
Red-crowned Crane 6–7, 89, 94, 100–101,
    246. See also Korea, North and South
Redesign/design 202
regime of the local 172, 248
regulations 3, 24, 82, 161, 191, 249
religious faiths
    Catholics and Protestants, Belfast 11, 184
    Muslim, Orthodox Christian, Catholic,
        Armenian, Maronite 143
Remodeling Harshscapes 153
resilience 2, 9–11, 23, 44–45, 47, 56, 110,
    114–15, 132, 135, 206
reterritorialization 11–13, 182, 185, 232
rhizomatic relationship 133, 206
rhizome 133, 204–5
riparian corridor 109, 111–14, 119, 121–22
riparian space 10, 109–10, 122, 244

Salut Cousin! 234
Schengen Agreement 57
seasonal migratory behaviors 244
security 4, 53–57, 91, 125, 156–58, 169–70,
    173, 175, 177, 181–82, 184, 190, 198,
    244, 249
    and energy 9
    and food 9
    and obligations 91
    and the environment 91
    and the state 22
    barriers 5
    border 123
    fencing 9, 54, 57–63
    food 98, 101
    installations 61
    pre-clearance areas 243
    primacy 4, 6
    securitized borders 1, 243–44
    Security Belt 155
sewage, border ix, x, 175
shorebirds 100
Shu'fat Refugee Camp 1, 6–7. See also
    Palestinian–Israeli issues

social ecology
  and security 9
  definition 2
  social-ecological system 2, 23, 250
solid waste disposal x
spatial ecology 6–7
spatial environment 6
stakeholders 6, 10, 46–47, 75, 79–80, 132, 144, 188, 246
  empowerment of 6
Stockholm Resilience Center (SRC) 53
Syrian refugee crisis 56

tangible rifts 3, 6–8, 10, 28, 41, 173
Terray, Emmanuel 136
territorialization 137
terrorism 1, 57, 231, 234
  9/11 49, 62, 234, 243–44
  World Trade Center, attacks on 55
The Kingdom of Women 161
The Location of Culture 19–20
The Terminal 19
The Watchers 234
The Wretched of the Earth 233
thirdscape 131
Three Ecologies 232
Tohono O'odham, tribe 244
trade, border ecology of 247
transboundary conservation 39t.2.1, 37–44, 61, 72, 246
  land and/or seascapes 39
  Transboundary Conservation—A Systematic and Integrated Approach 37
  transboundary migration conservation areas 39
  transboundary protected areas 29, 38, 85

US Fish and Wildlife Service x
US–Canada border
  American Indians, statute on 245
  Blackfeet, tribe 244
  Jay Treaty, 1794 244
US–Mexico border
  Arizona 8, 10, 67, 107, 109–10, 112, 117, 121–22, 244

Buenavista del Cobre 107, 111
Bureau of Land Management 122
colonias x
communally managed lands 116, 118
ejidos 108–9, 111, 118
latifundio 108–9, 111, 121, 123
Mexican mining interests 10
Salinas de Gotari, Carlos, Mexican president 118
San Diego ix, x, 62
San Pedro Riparian National Conservation Area (SPRNCA) 10, 117, 122
San Pedro River 5, 10, 107–10, 112, 114, 116–17, 120–21, 123–24, 244
San Ysidro port of entry x
Sonoran Desert 4, 249
South Bay International Wastewater Treatment Plant (SBIWTP) x
Tijuana Estuary National Wildlife Refuge ix
Tohono O'odham, border interaction 8
United Nations Development Programme (UNDP) 91
United Nations Environment Programme (UNEP) 91
United Nations Relief and Works Agency (UNRWA) 162, 249
urban interface x, 7, 24, 27, 56, 113, 123, 132, 136–38, 144, 159, 161, 163, 165, 175, 181–84, 187, 189, 212, 233–34, 245

Vanderbilt, George 237
Vasilijević, Maja 49

walls 11, 20, 22–23, 30, 54–56, 59–60, 62, 136, 138–39, 141, 156, 158, 163f.8.7, 160–64, 169, 173, 177, 188, 194, 201, 248
waste management, border 81, 249
Westphalia 21, 29
White-naped Crane 94, 100. *See also* Korea, North and South
world life-zone diagram, Holdridge, L. R. 225
world systems approach 2

Young, Antonia 72–75